# House Most High
# The Temples of Ancient Mesopotamia

# Mesopotamian Civilizations



1. *The Lamentation over the Destruction of Sumer and Ur*
   Piotr Michalowski
2. *Schlaf, Kindchen, Schlaf! Mesopotamische Baby-Beschwörungen und -Rituale*
   Walter Farber
3. *Adoption in Old Babylonian Nippur and the Archive of Mannum-mešu-liṣṣur*
   Elizabeth C. Stone and David I. Owen
4. *Third-Millennium Legal and Administrative Texts in the Iraq Museum, Baghdad*
   Piotr Steinkeller and J. N. Postgate
5. *House Most High: The Temples of Ancient Mesopotamia*
   A. R. George

# House Most High

## The Temples of Ancient Mesopotamia

A. R. George



Eisenbrauns
Winona Lake, Indiana
1993

Printed in the United States of America.

**Library of Congress Cataloging-in-Publication Data**

House most high : the temples of ancient Mesopotamia / [compiled and edited by]
A. R. George.
p. cm. — (Mesopotamian civilizations ; 5)
Commentary in English; Sumerian texts in cuneiform and romanization.
Includes bibliographical references and index.
ISBN 0-931464-80-3
I. George, A. R. II. Series.
PJ4031.H68 1993
499′.95—dc20 93-15336

The paper used in this publication meets the minimum requirements of the American National Standard for Information Sciences—Permanence of Paper for Printed Library Materials, ANSI Z39.48-1984. ♾™

*To Professor William L. Moran*

List, list, O, list!
*Hamlet* I. v. 22

# Contents

# Preface

This work grew from what was originally envisaged as a collaboration with Professor William L. Moran. The material for many of the texts presented in the first part of the book was collected, studied and edited in first draft many years ago by Prof. Moran. A few other temple lists were discovered more recently in the British Museum's Sippar collections by the author while working on a previous volume, *Babylonian Topographical Texts*. After the completion of that book it seemed desirable to put these out along with the remaining temple lists. Prof. Moran, when approached with this proposal, with great generosity put at my disposal an early draft of the Canonical Temple list and other lists, but commitments elsewhere regrettably prevented him from taking an active part in the preparation of the editions as they appear in the present book, and in the compilation of the gazetteer of temple names which forms the second part of the book. Nevertheless I must acknowledge with pleasure the huge debt the book owes to the initial groundwork done by Prof. Moran. I also record with gratitude how his constant encouragement so eased the burden of writing it, and thank him for his patient reading of my results, and for the warmth of the hospitality extended to me during a few days' stay at his house in Belmont, Mass., in the summer of 1989. It must be hoped that the loss of the full benefit of Prof. Moran's long immersion in the lists has not left us too much the poorer, and the book is dedicated to him in the hope that he will find it worthy.

Thanks are also due to Prof. W. G. Lambert and Dr I. L. Finkel, who identified K 19475 and K 20537 respectively as belonging to the Canonical Temple List., and also to Prof. R. Borger, whose own interest in the Canonical Temple List produced the joining of K 12023, and who put his personal transliteration at my disposal. New material from the British Museum is published by permission of the Trustees. Prof. C. Wilcke generously sent his copy of a fragment from Isin, IM 96881, and kindly allows its edition here in advance of its publication in a forthcoming volume of copies. A tablet from Khorsabad, DŠ 32-14, is published in Prof. Moran's provisional transliteration by permission of Prof. J. A. Brinkman of the Oriental Institute, University of Chicago.

A word must also be said about the transliteration of Sumerian in this book. In Part One I have conformed to conservative Assyriological practice in ignoring the distinction between the voiced consonant [g] and the nasal consonant [ng]. However in Part Two and its indexes, where there is both a wider intrusion of material from periods when Sumerian was still a spoken language and a greater interest in the lexical aspect of the temple names themselves, the nasal consonant is distinguished, according to convention, as [g̃].

London, 24th October 1992
A. R. G.

# Abbreviations

Bibliographical and other abbreviations are those conventionally used in the English language dictionaries, the *Chicago Assyrian Dictionary* and the *Pennsylvania Sumerian Dictionary*, with the following exceptions and additions:

| | |
|---|---|
| *Bar-Ilan Studies Artzi* | Jacob Klein and Aaron Skaist (eds.), *Bar-Ilan Studies in Assyriology dedicated to Pinḥas Artzi.* Ramat Gan, 1990 |
| Cavigneaux, *Textes scolaires* | Antoine Cavigneaux, *Textes scolaires du temple de Nabû ša ḫarê*, I. Baghdad, 1981 |
| Cohen, *Lamentations* | Mark E. Cohen, *The Canonical Lamentations of Mesopotamia.* Potomac, Md., 1988 |
| CTL | Canonical Temple List |
| *Études Garelli* | D. Charpin and F. Joannès (eds.), *Marchands, diplomates et empereurs. Études . . . offertes à Paul Garelli.* Paris, 1991 |
| Götteradreßbuch | Divine Directory of Aššur, ll. 1-198 ed. Menzel, *Tempel* II, no. 64; ll. 120-98 ed. *Topog. Texts* no. 20 |
| Livingstone, *Mystical Works* | Alasdair Livingstone, *Mystical and Mythological Explanatory Works of Assyrian and Babylonian Scholars.* Oxford, 1986 |
| Maul, *Eršaḫunga* | Stefan M. Maul, *'Herzberuhigungsklagen'. Die sumerisch-akkadischen Eršaḫunga-Gebete.* Wiesbaden, 1988 |
| Michalowski, *Lamentation* | Piotr Michalowski, *The Lamentation over the Destruction of Sumer and Ur.* Mesopotamian Civilizations 1. Winona Lake, 1989 |
| *Oberhuber AV* | Wolfgang Meid and Helga Trenkwalder (eds.), *Im Bannkreis des Alten Orients. Studien . . . Karl Oberhuber zum 70. Geburtstag gewidmet.* Innsbrucker Beiträge zur Kulturwissenschaft, 24. Innsbruck, 1986 |
| Pinches, *Wedge-Writing* | T. G. Pinches, *Texts in the Babylonian Wedge-Writing, autographed from the original documents.* London, 1882 |

| | |
|---|---|
| *RIMA* | Royal Inscriptions of Mesopotamia, Assyrian Periods |
| *RIME* | Royal Inscriptions of Mesopotamia, Early Periods |
| *RIM Suppl.* | Royal Inscriptions of Mesopotamia, Supplements |
| *Studies Moran* | Tzvi Abusch, John Huehnergard, Piotr Steinkeller (eds.), *Lingering over Words: Studies ... in Honor of William L. Moran.* Harvard Semitic Studies, 37. Atlanta, 1990 |
| *Studies Sachs* | Erle Leichty, Maria deJ. Ellis, and Pamela Gerardi (eds.), *A Scientific Humanist: Studies in Memory of Abraham Sachs.* Occasional Publications of the Samuel Noah Kramer Fund, 9. Philadelphia, 1988 |
| *Studies Sjöberg* | Hermann Behrens, Darlene Loding, and Martha T. Roth (eds.), *dumu-e$_2$-dub-ba-a: Studies in Honor of Åke W. Sjöberg.* Occasional Publications of the Samuel Noah Kramer Fund, 11. Philadelphia, 1989 |
| Thompson, *Prisms* | R. Campbell Thompson, *The Prisms of Esarhaddon and of Ashurbanipal.* London, 1931 |
| *Tintir* | tin.tir$^{ki}$ = *Bābilu*, topographical series, ed. *Topog. Texts* no. 1 |
| TL | temple list |
| *Topog. Texts* | A. R. George, *Babylonian Topographical Texts.* Orientalia Lovaniensia Analecta, 40. Louvain, 1992 |
| Walker, *CBI* | C. B. F. Walker, *Cuneiform Brick Inscriptions.* London, 1981 |

# Part One

# The Temple Lists of Ancient Mesopotamia

## *Introduction*

An attempt to collect and edit in one place all the extant cuneiform tablets inscribed with lists of temples was last made by T. G. Pinches in 1900.[1] The first part of this book aims to bring the subject up to date. A number of lexical and topographical temple lists have recently appeared in modern editions,[2] and these will not be repeated here, but all other lists known to me are included. The lists are given here without detailed historical and geographical commentary on each entry, since such information is incorporated in the gazetteer presented in the second part of the book. Accordingly the textual notes are usually confined to discussion of problems of decipherment, restoration, and philology.

The known temple lists exhibit several different principles of organization. There are those that are closely associated with lexical lists, and they are at least partly organized on thematic and acrographic principles. Other lists are organized on theological lines, grouping temples according to the deity or deities to whom they were dedicated. One list appears to be hierarchical, presenting its temples according to importance. Still others list temples according to their geographical location, and are thus topographical in outlook. The earliest temple lists recovered are of the first kind, which for want of a better phrase are here called lexical temple lists.

[1] "The Temples of Ancient Babylonia, I," *PSBA* 22 (1900), pp. 358–71, in which were presented three sources of the Canonical Temple List and two of *Tintir* = Babylon. A sequel, which one supposes would have edited those lists already published by E. Norris (in II *R*) but not included in the article, was never published.

[2] For lexical lists see below, nn. 4–6, and, for topographical lists, n. 41 on p. 40.

## *Lexical Temple Lists*

One may presume that lexical temple lists came into being when Sumerian compounds beginning with the element é, "house," were collected for their own sake, eventually to be incorporated into the great lexical lists. Naturally many buildings and parts of buildings denoted by such compounds were not sacred but secular, so to speak of any lexical list of words beginning with é as a temple list would be misleading. However, such lists of buildings, for which we may coin the term "é-lists," are plentiful sources of Sumerian temple names. These names I have dubbed elsewhere "ceremonial temple names," in recognition of their continued life in Babylonian usage long after the extinction of Sumerian as a vernacular language.[3] The principal é-lists that include ceremonial temple names are embedded in two unilingual Old Babylonian lexical texts: the big forerunner to *Hh* XXI-XXII now in Oxford,[4] and the list known as Proto-*Kagal*.[5] Fragments of a bilingual lexical list dealing with names of buildings and found at Boğazköy are now also considered to belong to *Kagal*.[6] Since modern transliterations of these lists are available in *MSL* there seems no need to repeat them here, but I can offer these few comments.

The Oxford tablet presents ceremonial temple names in columns vii and viii. This section of the list is partly acrographic in Civil's terminology,[7] but there are signs of theological organization also, with temples of Ištar predominant in vii 15–24.

In Proto-*Kagal* the é-list runs from line 49 to line 233, but there are almost no certain ceremonial temple names until line 168, which lists é.abzu, the temple of Ea at Eridu and one of the most venerable cult-centers of ancient Mesopotamia. Following this highly significant item the list contains only a few entries which are not ceremonial names, and even those are, apart from a single temple name of the everyday variety (é.$^{d}$en.líl.lá, which may in fact be sim-

[3] See *Topog. Texts*, the opening remarks to Chapter Two. A temple's Sumerian or ceremonial name (é.TN) is that used in most royal inscriptions, in hymns and liturgical texts, and in sacred and erudite literature generally. By contrast we find the usage é // *bīt* DN, "Temple of the god So-and-so," which appears in many rituals and most secular texts, and which I consider the temple's everyday or "popular" name.

[4] *OECT* IV 161, edited in *MSL* XI, pp. 140–43. The compiler of SB *Hh* followed the Nippur forerunners in omitting this forerunner's é-list. Thus the only é-componds to be found in *Hh* XXI are geographical names, and as the text now stands only one of these, é.sa.bad$^{ki}$ = *bi-it* $^{d}$*gu-la* (XXI/4 10), is by origin a ceremonial temple name.

[5] *MSL* XIII, pp. 63–88. Another OB text, the geographical list K 4248 + 11985, presents what may be a few isolated temple names interspersed in its é-list (e.g., é.gal.maḫ, é.sag.dil), but as now extant the list is almost entirely given over to secular compounds of é (*MSL* XI, p. 61, iv).

[6] *MSL* XIII, pp. 148–53, *Kagal* Boğazköy I. The late OB tablet which is the main source for canonical *Kagal* I is very poorly preserved at the point where one expects the é-list, and it is only represented by lines 56–63 in col. ii (*MSL* XIII, p. 229).

[7] See *MSL* XIII, pp. 3ff., and by way of example note the sequence é.mes, é.mes.lam, é.mes.lam.me.lám.íl.la in vii 34–36 (*MSL* XI, p. 142; on the organization of this list see further Moran, *JCS* 26 [1974], p. 58[9]).

ply a summary of the preceding section), nouns particular to sacred buildings (e.g., ama$_5$, itima, ki.dagal). In contrast with lines 49–167 there is in this second part of the list little sign of thematic or acrographic organization. Instead there are clear signs of theological and apparently also geographical organization. The section devoted, partly at least, to Ea closes with two more of his temples in lines 174–75. Then comes a big section on the great temple complex of Nippur, which includes the sanctuaries of Enlil, Ninlil, and Nuska, and runs from é.kur in line 176 to é.$^{d}$en.líl.lá in line 192. It is followed by the temple of his son Ninurta[8] and then a sequence of little-known sanctuaries which concludes with a temple of, probably, Ninimma, also of the court of Enlil at Nippur.[9] Temples of the Ninurta figure Ningirsu and his family at Girsu and nearby occupy lines 202–5, and are followed by at least one sanctuary of Šara at Umma, a geographical association.[10] After a damaged section we have the cult-centers of Marad and Kazallu paired, as in the Collection of Sumerian Temple Hymns, another association that is geographical rather than theological (212–13). The next lines (214–17) are given over to temples of Nergal,[11] another son of Enlil, while the remainder of the list is mainly, if not entirely, devoted to temples of Šamaš,[12] Nissaba (221–23), Marduk (224–25) and Ištar (226–33). It is interesting that sanctuaries of Sîn, whose theological place is customarily immediately before Šamaš and Ištar, are conspicuously absent.

The organization of those parts of *Kagal* Boğazköy I that are extant and deal with ceremonial temple names is more theological, with temples of Enlil, Ninurta, Anu, and Sîn grouped in Sections E and F, and temples of, among others, Ḫaya, Nissaba, Lugalirra and Meslamtaea, Ištar and Šulpae in Section G.[13]

IM 96881, a fragmentary tablet from Old Babylonian Isin, previously unpublished, preserves part of a unilingual lexical text which, like the Oxford tablet and Proto-*Kagal*, included an é-list. While there are entries in common with the two big Old Babylonian é-lists, the Isin list is different again, but may

[8] The traces copied by Civil for é.⸢x x x⸣ (line 193) already suggested to him é.[š]u.me.ša$_4$ (*MSL* XIII, p. 72, apparatus), but note that in the following line the obvious reading of é.⸢(x).x⸣.galam is é.[i]gi.⸢šu⸣.galam, well known in association with Ninurta and probably his cella in E-šumeša (see the gazetteer).

[9] Assuming that é.nam.me.gar.ra in Proto-*Kagal* 201 is the same temple as é.nam.en.gar.ra in CTL 110.

[10] After é.bur.sa$_7$.sa$_7$ in line 206, instead of Civil's é.edin$^?$ read perhaps é.maḫ$^!$, observing the pairing of these two temples of Šara in CTL 451–52.

[11] In line 215 é.⸢x⸣.ki.a is no doubt Nergal's temple é.ḫuš.ki.a.

[12] In line 219 instead of Civil's é.u$_4$.⸢x⸣ we read é.bábbar(UD.U[D]), noting é.di.ku$_5$.kalam.[ma] in the following line: cf. CTL 281–83.

[13] The presence of only one temple of Ištar in this section acts as a caveat against assuming that theology has become the sole criterion for the organization of the list: clearly there would have been a separate section for Ištar, and the single entry here instead represents an unwillingness to place it with the others that must be put down to acrography, as already noted by Moran, *JCS* 26 (1974), p. 58[9]: *é.dim.kalam.ma ([e]-dim-ga-lam-ma) of Ištar follows *é.dim.gal.an.na (⸢e⸣-dim-kal-la-a-na) at Uzarpara (*MSL* XIII, p. 153, 11–12). On *Kagal* Boğazköy Section G, 5–10, see further Moran, *JCS* 26 (1974), pp. 55–58.

nevertheless be Proto-*Kagal*.[14] It includes temples of Enlil and Ninurta at Nippur (ii′ 3′–12′), and sanctuaries in Lagaš-Girsu, Umma, and Kiš (iii′ 2′–6′), but as the text now stands it is difficult to determine whether the underlying order is theological or geographical.

IM 96881 (IB 1559), obv. ii′ - iii′

| col. ii′ | | col. iii′ | |
|---|---|---|---|
| 1′ | é.[x] | 1′ | ⸢é⸣.[(x).x] |
| 2′ | é.ki$^{?}$.šà$^{?}$.ḫúl$^{?}$ | 2′ | é.tar.s[ír.sír] |
| 3′ | é.⸢kur⸣ | 3′ | ⸢é⸣.ninnu |
| 4′ | é.x[ x] | 4′ | é.⸢x⸣.maḫ |
| 5′ | é.gi.kù.ga | 5′ | é.maḫ |
| 6′ | é.⸢x x x⸣ | 6′ | é.{AŠ}.me.te.ur.sag |
| 7′ | é.⸢kur⸣.igi.⸢gál⸣ | 7′ | ⸢é⸣.bal.bal.x. |
| 8′ | é.gu.la$^{?}$ | 8′ | {ras.}.ní.su$^{!}$(ŠU).zi$^{!}$(NAM).ra |
| 9′ | é.šu.me.ša$_4$ | 9′ | é.zálag$^{?}$.⸢x⸣.gal |
| 10′ | é.šà.maḫ | 10′ | é.kù.x |
| 11′ | é.ŠU.IGI.galam | 11′ | é.giš.bàn.⸢da$^{!?}$⸣ |
| 12′ | ⸢é⸣.me.ur$_4$.an.na$^{!}$ (tablet: dingir.ra) | 12′ | é.⸢nu$_{11}$$^{?}$.gal⸣.an.na |
| 13′ | ⸢é.sag.x x x⸣ | 13′ | é.⸢x⸣.[x ]x |

The list continues with other sacred items, some if not all associated with Nippur (iv′ 2′–5′: bur.za.gìn, ub.šu.kin$_x$(LAGAB).na, ub.saḫar.ra, uzu.mú.a$^{!}$), before going on to géštu and anše (or gìr?).

The separation of the big Old Babylonian é-lists, exhibited by both but seen most clearly in the better-preserved Proto-*Kagal*, into two sections given over respectively to ordinary buildings and to sacred, is a natural one and need not have significance for the history of the lists' development. However, the presence in these lists of small groups of temples from distinct geographical locations or dedicated to individual deities points more strongly to the use in their compilation of geographically and theologically organized lists that were already in existence. Though these are now lost, the principles of organization that they employed, theology and geography, survived and were used by all the later lists.

## *Theological Temple Lists*

The best example of a temple list which groups temples according to divine owner is the Canonical Temple List.[15]

[14] Prof. C. Wilcke, by whose generous leave the relevant section of IM 96881 is transliterated here, draws our attention to the fact that there was an Isin version of Proto-*Kagal*, represented at least by IB 813, that differed from the Nippur version. IB 1559 is catalogued in Wilcke, *Isin* III, p. 104.

[15] Another such list is perhaps van Dijk and Meyer, *Bagh. Mitt.* Beiheft 2, no. 97 = *Topog. Texts* no. 31, in which the names of temples of a single deity, probably Ištar, are collected and explained.

## *1. The Canonical Temple List*

The Canonical Temple List (CTL) is a name that was first coined by Moran when writing about the great temple list in 1976, with the qualification: "by [canonical] we mean only that it was standardized and was in its comprehensiveness *the* temple list."[16] The canonicity of the text is, even by this definition, restricted, for the text is so far known only from copies found in Aššurbanipal's libraries. By contrast other temple lists, such as those incorporated into the Divine Directory of Aššur (i.e., the Assyrian Temple List) and *Tintir* = Babylon (Tablet IV), are known from many more individual exemplars, which, coming from two or more sites, bear witness to their established positions within the literary canon. No external evidence, such as a colophon or a catalogue entry, survives to yield evidence for the history of the text of the Canonical Temple List, of where it was compiled and by whom. But the text itself holds clues which can lead to a better understanding. As preserved, the list deals mostly with Babylonian cult-centers, showing little interest in Assyrian temples, and this would suggest that, despite the lack of Babylonian exemplars, it was compiled in the south.[17] The lack of Assyrian material in particular suggests that the compiler was not familiar with the Assyrian Temple List, well known at Nineveh as well as at Aššur, but not, one imagines, circulated in Babylonia. So an Assyrian origin of the text, at least in Sargonid times when the Assyrian Temple List had wide currency, is again ruled out. In fact there are obvious hints of a much older date of compilation, for example the absence of the late name of the cult-center at Ḫursag-kalamma, E-kur-ni-zu, from the appropriate place in the section of the list devoted to temples of Ištar.[18] A comparison with the temple list of Babylon (*Tintir* IV) is more revealing still. This comparison is made difficult by the fragmentary state of the Canonical Temple List, since there are few gods listed in it for whom complete entries of temple names survive. Thus we are not in a position to check the presence in the Canonical Temple List of such temples of Babylon as E-kar-zaginna of Ea, E-maḫ of Bēlet-ilī, E-gišnugal of Sîn, E-namtila of Enlil and E-namḫe of Adad, to mention only the most obviously famous foundations. But where the big list is well preserved some significant omissions can be observed. Most striking of these is the ziqqurrat of Babylon, E-temen-anki (*Tintir* IV 2), missing from the section on Marduk. Only one of the three sanctuaries of Nabû known to *Tintir* IV is to be found in the Canonical Temple List, namely E-niggidar-kalamma-summa. And E-ka-dimma, the temple of Belili at Babylon (*Tintir* IV 36), finds no place there either. *Tintir* was such a popular and much-copied text, both in

[16] *Kramer AV*, p. 336[7].

[17] Note in the extant text the northern excursion to Subartu, Nineveh and, as we restore it, Mari in lines 392–96. Other localities beyond the bounds of Babylonia proper are Susa (lines 391 and, implicitly, 475) and Tilmun (359). It is significant that such a famous cult-center as é.gašan.kalam.ma at Arbil finds no place among the Assyrian temples of Ištar, where, noting its absence also from the rather brief and Nippur-oriented section on Ninlil (lines 57–62), one would certainly have expected it.

[18] See the note on lines 366–67.

Babylonia and in Assyria, that it is inconceivable that the compiler of the Canonical Temple List could have failed to use it. The obvious conclusion is that *Tintir* IV was not yet to hand, and thus that the big list was drawn up before it was. I have dated the compilation of *Tintir* elsewhere to the twelfth century, the reign of Nebuchadnezzar I (1124–03) or shortly after,[19] a time which, incidentally, is also seen by some as the likely date for the original founding of the ziqqurrat of Babylon.[20] So on both these counts this reign would form a terminus ante quem for the compilation of the Canonical Temple List. The terminus post quem is the reign of the Kassite monarch Kurigalzu, two hundred years earlier, for his foundations at the new capital of Dūr-Kurigalzu are included (lines 55, 62, 95, 106?). This evidence places the list squarely in the second half of the rule of the Kassite dynasty, and it can then best be viewed as a product of the lexical and literary scholarship that is the hallmark of scribal activity in this period.

The organization of the text is a topic demanding less speculation. Landsberger's suggestion, passed on to Moran, that the Canonical Temple List was modeled on the Great God List, An = *Anum*—a text also compiled in the Kassite period—holds good: as Moran noted, the order of the two lists is, with only slight deviation, the same.[21] The very beginning of the temple list is lost, but it is presumed to begin with Anu. The extant text starts with Enlil and the court of Nippur, including Ninurta, before moving on to the Mother Goddess and her entourage, and then Ea and his family, including Marduk and Nabû. Sîn, Šamaš, Adad, and Ištar follow with their respective entourages, and then comes a collection of junior gods, most of whom were seen by the ancient syncretists as local manifestations of Ninurta, the warrior son: Lugal-Maradda, Lugalbanda, Amurru, Tišpak, Inšušinak, Ištarān, Zababa, Uraš, and Ningirsu and his family. The list is continued with Gula and the court of Isin and ends with Nergal and other chthonic deities.

Like the Great God List, the Canonical Temple List is a text arranged like a lexical list in two sub-columns. On the left appears each temple's Sumerian ceremonial name. Opposite this, in the right-hand sub-column, is given by way of explanation the comment *bīt* DN, "temple of the god So-and-so," the temple's popular name.[22] Thus the text explains the erudite and sacred in terms of the familiar. Appended to the popular name is often, but not always, a geographical comment, *šá* GN, "in the city Such-and-such," or more rarely some other reference. It should be stressed that while we refer to the text as a temple list probably the majority of sanctuaries listed were not buildings in their own right. Some were certainly only small shrines within larger sacred buildings. The clearest examples of these are cellas (*papāḫu*) such as é.umuš.a and é.dàra.an.na in é.sag.íl, which are listed under Marduk and Zarpanītum respectively, or the

[19] *Topog. Texts*, pp. 6ff.
[20] Ibid., pp. 299ff.
[21] *Kramer AV*, p. 336 and nn. 8–9.
[22] On the distinction between ceremonial and popular name see above, n. 3.

many parts of é.kur at Nippur listed in the Enlil section. Separate lists were devoted to the ceremonial names of the large numbers of small shrines that were housed in the big temples (see below, n. 41), but there is no doubt that many structures represented by an entry in CTL were also quite small. Accordingly one should think of CTL as not so much a list of temples as an encyclopedia of the various ceremonial temple names associated with each particular deity. The reason for its organization according to a theological framework, and not a topographical or geographical one, then becomes clear.

The method of compilation can only be guessed at. It is unlikely that the text is to be understood as a gazetteer of all the sanctuaries of Babylonia standing at a particular given moment, as it were a directory of churches. Not only is it inconceivable that every one of the temples and shrines listed here was standing at any one moment in history, but the paucity of the topographical information which the compiler has managed to collect reveals an ignorance of the whereabouts of many of them.[23] If it is right to propose that the list is to be seen as an encyclopedia of temple names, then it is easier to imagine that it was produced not by cataloguing actual buildings, but by a scholarly search of all available literary and historical sources, particularly existing temple lists.[24] That it was organized according to an existing framework, and one which was in arrangement theological rather than topographical, would again tally with such an hypothesis.

A word of caution must be offered with regard to the data presented by the list. There are several places where we have reason to be doubtful of the accuracy of the material. Some of the temple names look hopelessly garbled, and when, on occasion, evidence permits, a few can be proved to be markedly corrupt.[25] A number of the toponyms also come under suspicion.[26] Accordingly the list must be used with reservation, if not in fact mistrust, particularly where it presents data for which there is no corroboration from other sources. Thus I have felt justified to bring to the text a much greater skepticism than is usually employed in editing a cuneiform text from Kuyunjik, and the discussion of possible emendations occupies a significant proportion of the appended notes.

It seems likely that all extant fragments of the Canonical Temple List from Aššurbanipal's libraries can be seen to belong to one of only three tablets,

[23] But note Moran's tentative thesis on the list's system of geographical notation: see *Kramer AV*, p. 338.

[24] Symptomatic of such a search would be the presence of false TNs such as might arise from misreadings or other misunderstandings. One such may be é.di.ku$_5$.dá of Šamaš (line 284), which incorporates an archaic orthography, significantly also found in an OB votive inscription, which is not expected in a ceremonial TN of the period of the list.

[25] Two examples from the section on temples of Ningublag (lines 276–79) serve as illustrations: as proposed in the notes, the meaningless TN é.pa$_4$.ul.ḫé is a corruption of older é.gu$_4$.du$_7$(UL).šár(ḪE), while the—at first sight—equally opaque é.ga.ra.ni derives from é.ì.gara$_{10}$.

[26] For example, Ištar's temple é.igi.du$_8$ (line 388) is placed in Kullab by an éš.dam hymn, but the list apparently contaminates the toponym with the temple name, and so places é.igi.du$_8$ in Kutha (gú.du$_8$.a$^{ki}$).

which share a common format of three double-columns on each side. These manuscripts are here given the sigla A, B and C. Ms A is the largest of the three, especially well preserved on the reverse, and comprises four separate fragments which present parts of columns i, ii, iv, v, and vi. Ms B is known from six smaller fragments, which cover parts of columns i, ii, iii, and vi. Ms C, which is set apart from Mss AB by the presence of firing holes, is similar to B in respect of the quantity of text extant, and retains parts of columns ii, iii, iv, and v.[27] Wherever in the text Mss AC are both preserved they present identical text, as demonstrated by their mutual lack of variant readings and their joint omission of signs (lines 446–48) and, on one occasion, a whole line (384). Quite probably both manuscripts derive from the same original, or the one was copied directly from the other.

Regarding the line numbering, a rough consecutive numeration can be given, especially now that six sources of Ms B are available and the lines missing to the bottom edge of the obverse can be calculated by physical comparison of the three columns. The first extant line of col. i, which lists the 41st temple of Enlil, is obviously no lower than line 41 of the composition, and if temples of Anu preceded those of Enlil—which will be the case if the Canonical Temple List follows the system of the god list An = *Anum* in this particular as in others—it will be line $x + 41$, where $x$ represents the unknown number of temples listed for Anu and family. The neighboring line of col. ii, listing the temple é.utul of Panigingarra ($B_4$ ii 8′ + $B_5$ ii 2′), will then be ii ($x$) + 41. The temple of Lisi, four lines later, will be ii ($x$) + 45, and its counterpart in column iii, the é.me.te.è of Šamaš, will be iii ($x$) + 45. The rest of col. iii of Ms B is preserved but for two lacunae, that between Sm 522 ($B_5$) and K 12024 + ($B_2$), which on physical grounds must be at least three lines, but is probably not much greater, and that between K 12024 + ($B_2$) and K 20537 ($B_3$) (+) Rm II 417 ($B_6$), which thanks to the numbering of the temples in the list is a known quantity, i.e., seven lines. Between the line iii ($x$) + 45 and the bottom of the column there will then be at least 55 lines. Consequently, in Ms B, an average column would be at least 100 lines long if the list began with Enlil's temples, and rather longer if it began, as is supposed, with Anu's. I have opted to presume twelve lines missing for Anu at the beginning[28] and suggest a lacuna of not three but six lines between Sm 522 ($B_5$) and K 12024 + ($B_2$). This gives a provisional column length in Ms B of about 115 lines, and so provides fixed points at about lines 115, 230, and 345, the last lines in Ms B of columns i, ii, and iii respectively, with which to anchor the extant portions of text. It must be emphasized that these figures are provisional only, since exact calculations of the length of the lacunae will be scuppered by

[27] The small fragment K 19495, which duplicates Ms A, lacks firing holes, but on other physical grounds is nevertheless more probably part of C than B.

[28] Temples names associated with Anu, ten in number, are collected in the liturgical hymn *BRM* IV 8, 9–18 = Cohen, *Lamentations*, p. 729, 7–11. Some of these, if not all, will have been entered in the Canonical Temple List, together with a smaller number of temples attributed to Anu's consort, Ninzalle or Antu, and entourage. Thus in our view the number of lines preceding Enlil is not likely to be less than about twelve.

several unpredictable factors, such as the writing of long temple names on two lines (which is more prevalent in Ms A than in B), or the squeezing of lines on the tablet (cf. the bottom of col. ii in Ms B).

The application of this numeration to the obverse of the other two tablets, Mss A and C, is largely straightforward. Ms A has columns on average about three lines shorter than those of Ms B, since the last line of col. iii on B is the ninth of col. iv on A, and, later still, B begins col. vi seventeen lines after A. The first line of col. iii on Ms C is the fifth from last on Ms B, col. ii, which suggests C's columns are at first still shorter than A's, but by the end of col. iv Ms C is ahead of A. There is a problem, however, in col. ii of A. If we assume columns of 115 lines in B, those of A will be about 112 lines long. The end of col. ii in A, which can be estimated at no more than six lines below the point where the surface is lost, should thus be line 224 or thereabouts. The first extant line of A, col. ii, can be seen, by working back from the point where the numbers of the right-hand sub-column are preserved, to list the fourth temple of Ea. Thus it duplicates $B_5$ ii 16′. $B_5$ ii 16′, according to the calculations put forward in the previous paragraph, is B ii $x + 55$, which in a tablet of 115 lines per column (where $x = 12$) will be line 182. By this calculation col. ii of Ms A will end at line 212, some twelve lines before it should. No solution to this problem presents itself to me.

On the reverse, one starts with a fixed point at A iv 9 // B iii end = 345. Given the estimate of 112 lines per column in A we then have a further fixed point at A v 1 = 449. Column vi of A would then be expected to begin at line 561, but A vi [1] is assigned to 560, instead, to take account of two particulars: A vi 18 // B vi 1 is line 576 not 577, if calculated from the column lengths of Ms B; and at the end of col. v Ms A is out of step with Ms C by at least one line (here occupying two lines of tablet), as it was in col. iv. So provisionally one may draw up the following chart of column divisions in the three extant manuscripts of the Canonical Temple List:

| | | | | | | | |
|---|---|---|---|---|---|---|---|
| A | obv. | i | [1–112] | ii | [113–212?] | iii | [213?–336] |
| | rev. | iv | [337]–448 | v | 449–559 | vi | [560–end] |
| B | obv. | i | [1]–115 | ii | [116]–230 | iii | [231]–345 |
| | rev. | iv | [346–460] | v | [461–575] | vi | 576–[end] |
| C | obv. | i | [1–113] | ii | 114–[225] | iii | 226–[337] |
| | rev. | iv | [338]–449 | v | [450]–560 | vi | [561–end] |

Sources of the great temple list first appeared in 1866 from the hand of Norris.[29] Some of these were edited by Pinches in 1900, and further pieces were published by Craig in 1897 and Meek in 1920. Since that time many joins have been made, especially by Moran, and a number of further manuscripts identified.[30] To accompany this edition autograph copies have been prepared of all extant manuscripts.

[29] For bibliographical details see the table, p. 10.
[30] Cf. above, the preface.

## List of Manuscripts and Bibliography of Previous Publication

| Ms | *Museum Number* | *Plate* | *Previous Publication* | *Treatment* |
|---|---|---|---|---|
| $A_1$ | K 3012 + 14325 | 2, 5 | 1866: Norris, II *R* 61, no. 7 (K 3012 only) | C |
| $A_2$ | K 3436 + 4186 + 4218B + 4414 + 4772 + 12023 + 13377 | 2–6 | 1866: Norris, II *R* 61, nos. 1 (K 4772 only) and 2 (K 4414 only) | C |
| $A_3$ | K 4224 + 10092 + 11188 | 4 | — | |
| $B_1$ | K 4374 + 8377 | 8 | 1866: Norris, II *R* 61, no. 6 (K 4374 only) | C |
| | | | 1900: Pinches, *PSBA* 22, pp. 362–4 | CTTr |
| $A_4$ | K 4413 + 8376 | 1 | 1866: Norris, II *R* 61, no. 3 (K 4413 only) | C |
| | | | 1900: Pinches, *PSBA* 22, pp. 365–6 | CT |
| $B_2$ | K 12024 + 12025 | 9 | — | |
| $C_1$ | K 15262 + Sm 289 | 11–12 | 1896/1897: Craig, *AJSL* 13, p. 220 (Sm 289 only) | C |
| | | | 1976: Moran, *Kramer AV*, pl. 11 | P |
| $C_2$ | K 19495 | 10 | — | |
| $B_3$ | K 20537 | 9 | — | |
| $C_3$ | Sm 277 | 10 | — | |
| $B_4$ | Sm 278 | 7 | 1900: Pinches, *PSBA* 22, pp. 370–71 | CTTr |
| | | | 1976: Moran, *Kramer AV*, pl. 11 | P |
| $B_5$ | Sm 522 | 7 | 1976: Moran, *Kramer AV*, pl. 11 | P |
| $B_6$ | Rm II 417 | 9 | 1920: Meek, *RA* 17, p. 186 | C |

## Preservation of Manuscripts

| Ms | | *Lines on obverse* | | *Lines on reverse* |
|---|---|---|---|---|
| A | i | 18–47 ($A_4$), 56–70 ($A_1$), 89–96 ($A_2$) | iv | 340–90 ($A_2$), 434–**448** ($A_3$) |
| | ii | 182–206 ($A_2$) | v | **449**–501 ($A_2$), **559** ($A_3$) |
| | iii | - | vi | 562–80, 591–94 ($A_2$), 599–603 ($A_1$) |
| B | i | 53–63 ($B_4$), 103–**115** ($B_1$) | iv | - |
| | ii | 161–88 ($B_4$(+)$B_5$), 222–**230** ($B_1$) | v | - |
| | iii | 283–302 ($B_5$), 309–27 ($B_2$), 335–**345** ($B_3$(+)$B_6$) | vi | **576**–580 ($B_1$) |
| C | i | - | iv | 379–402 ($C_1$), 433–**449** ($C_3$) |
| | ii | **114**–19 ($C_3$), 152–73 ($C_1$) | v | 463–70 ($C_2$), 488–511 ($C_1$), 551–**560** ($C_3$) |
| | iii | **226**–46 ($C_3$), 270–85 ($C_1$) | vi | - |

1ff. [*Temples of Anu, Antu, and their entourage.*]

| | | | |
|---|---|---|---|
| | 13 | [é.kur] | [*bīt* $^{d}$*en-líl* (*šá nippur*$^{ki}$)] |
| | 14 | [é . . . ] | [*bīt* 2] |
| | 15 | [é . . . ] | [*bīt* 3] |
| | 16 | [é . . . ] | [*bīt* 4] |
| | 17 | [é . . . ] | [*bīt* 5] |
| $A_4$ | 18 | [é . . . ] | [*bīt*] 6 |
| $A_4$ | 19 | [é . . . ] | ⸢*bīt*⸣ 7 |
| $A_4$ | 20 | [é . . . ] | *bīt* 8 |
| $A_4$ | 21 | [é . . . ] | *bīt* 9 |
| $A_4$ | 22 | [é.šár.r]a | *bīt* 10 |
| $A_4$ | 23 | [é x g]i.na | *bīt* 11 |
| $A_4$ | 24 | [é.sa]g.dil | *bīt* 12 |
| $A_4$ | 25 | [é.me$^{?}$.b]i.šè.dù.a | *bīt* 13 |
| $A_4$ | 26 | [é.m]e$^{?}$.bi.šè.dagal.la | *bīt* 14 |
| $A_4$ | 27 | [é.š]à$^{?}$.zu.gal.kalam.ma | *bīt* 15 |
| $A_4$ | 28 | [é.ḫ]ur.sag.kalam.ma | *bīt* 16 |
| $A_4$ | 29 | ⸢é⸣.KAL.dù.a | *bīt* 17 |
| $A_4$ | 30 | ⸢é⸣.èš.maḫ | *bīt* 18 |
| $A_4$ | 31 | ⸢é⸣.tílla.maḫ | *bīt* 19 |
| $A_4$ | 32 | ⸢é⸣.maḫ | *bīt* 20 |
| $A_4$ | 33 | ⸢é⸣.nisag$^{!}$(DÉ)$^{ni\text{-}sag}$.maḫ | ⸢*bīt*⸣ [21 ( . . . )] |
| $A_4$ | 34 | ⸢é⸣.ÚS.GÍD.DA | *bīt* 2[2 ( . . . )] |
| $A_4$ | 35 | ⸢é⸣.ÚS.GÍD.DA.gíd.da | *bīt* 23 |
| $A_4$ | 36 | ⸢é⸣.dur.an.ki | *bīt* 24 |
| $A_4$ | 37 | [é].kur.igi.gál | *bīt* 25 |
| $A_4$ | 38 | [é].bára.dúr.gar.ra | *bīt* 26 |
| $A_4$ | 39 | [é].⸢bára⸣.a.ri.a | *bīt* 27 |
| $A_4$ | 40 | [é].bur.šu$^{!}$(NA).šú.a | *bīt* 28 |
| $A_4$ | 41 | ⸢é⸣.uru.na.nam | *bīt* 29 |
| $A_4$ | 42 | [é].ní.te.ḫur.sag | *bīt* 30 |
| $A_4$ | 43 | [é].šà.zukum$^{kum}$ | *bīt* 31 |
| $A_4$ | 44 | [é.itim]a.kù | *bīt* 32 |
| $A_4$ | 45 | [é.me/igi$^{?}$].kár.kár | *bīt* 33 *šá ú*[*ri*$^{ki}$] |
| $A_4$ | 46 | [é.g]i.[di]m.dim | *bīt* 34 ⸢*šá* KI⸣.[ . . . ] |
| $A_4$ | 47 | [é . . . ] | ⸢*bīt*⸣ 35 *š*[*á* . . . ] |
| | 48 | [é . . . ] | [*bīt* 36 (*šá* . . . )] |
| | 49 | [é . . . ] | [*bīt* 37 (*šá* . . . )] |
| | 50 | [é . . . ] | [*bīt* 38 (*šá* . . . )] |
| | 51 | [é . . . ] | [*bīt* 39 (*šá* . . . )] |
| | 52 | [é . . . ] | [*bīt* 40 (*šá* . . . )] |
| $B_4$ | 53 | [é . . . ] | [*bīt* 41] ⸢*šá gír-su*⸣$^{ki}$ |
| $B_4$ | 54 | [é . . . ] | [*bīt*] ⸢42 *šá*⸣ *é-uru-kù* |
| $B_4$ | 55 | [é.u.gal] / [(vacat)] | [*bīt*] 43 / [*šá d*]*ūr*(bàd)-*ku-ri-gal-zi* |

| | | | |
|---|---|---|---|
| A$_1$B$_4$ | 56 | [é . . . ] | ⸢*bīt*⸣ 44 *šá dūr*(bàd)-$^{d}$*suen-na*$^{ki}$ [31] |
| A$_1$B$_4$ | 57 | [é.ki.ùr] | *bīt* $^{d}$*nin-líl šá nippur*$^{ki}$ |
| A$_1$B$_4$ | 58 | [é.mi.tum].⸢ma.al⸣ | *bīt* 2 |
| A$_1$B$_4$ | 59 | [é.kur].igi.gál | *bīt* 3 |
| A$_1$B$_4$ | 60 | [é.me$^?$.b]i.šè.dù.a | *bīt* 4 |
| A$_1$B$_4$ | 61 | [é.gá].giš.šú.a | *bīt* 5 |
| A$_1$B$_4$ | 62 | [é].gašan./[an.t]a.gál | *bīt* 6 / *šá dūr*(bàd)-*ku-ri-*g[*al-z*]*i* |
| A$_1$B$_4$ | 63 | [é.síg$^?$.ù]z | *bīt* $^{d}$*s*[*ù*]*d* |
| A$_1$ | 64 | é.dim.gal.a]n.na | *bīt* 2 |
| A$_1$ | 65 | [é.ki.ág.gá.šu].⸢du$_7$⸣ | *bīt* $^{d}$[*šu*]-⸢*zi*⸣-[*an-na*] |
| A$_1$ | 66 | [é.du$_6$.sag].dil | ⸢*bīt* 2⸣ [(*šá* . . . )] |
| A$_1$ | 67 | [é.gá.gi].maḫ | *bīt* [3 (*šá* . . . )] |
| A$_1$ | 68 | [é x (x)].ra | *bīt* $^{d}$[ . . . ] |
| A$_1$ | 69 | [é x (x)].ku$_4$ | ⸢*bīt*⸣ [ . . . ] |
| A$_1$ | 70 | [é x (x) x ]x | [*bīt* . . . ] |

*Lacuna of uncertain length, in which we expect the list of temples of Ninurta to begin, no doubt with:*

| | | | |
|---|---|---|---|
| | | [é.šu.me.ša$_4$] | [*bīt* $^{d}$*nin-urta šá nippur*$^{ki}$] |

*The text resumes:*

| | | | | |
|---|---|---|---|---|
| A$_2$ | 89 | [é . . . ] | [*bīt x* + 1] | (vacat) |
| A$_2$ | 90 | [é . . . ] | [*bīt x* + 2] | (vacat) |
| A$_2$ | 91 | [é . . . ] | [*bīt x* + 3] | (vacat) |
| A$_2$ | 92 | [é . . . ] | [*bīt x* + 4] | (vacat) |
| A$_2$ | 93 | [é . . . ] | [*bīt x* + 5] | (vacat) |
| A$_2$ | 94 | [é . . . ] | [*bīt* $^{d}$*nissaba šá m*]*aš-re-e* | |
| A$_2$ | 95 | [é . . . ] / [ . . . ] | [*bīt* 2] / [*šá dūr*(bàd)-*ku-ri-ga*]*l-zu* | |
| A$_2$ | 96 | [é . . . ] | *bīt* 3 *šá nip*]*pur*$^{k[i]}$ | |

*Lacuna of a few lines*

| | | | |
|---|---|---|---|
| B$_1$ | 103 | ⸢é.me.lám.an⸣.[na] | [*bīt* $^{d}$*nuska*] |
| B$_1$ | 104 | é.me.lám.ḫ[uš] | [*bīt* 2 (*šá* . . . )] |
| B$_1$ | 105 | é.šu.$^{d}$en.líl.le | ⸢*bīt*⸣ [$^{d}$ . . . ] |
| B$_1$ | 106 | é.su.lim.ḫuš.ri.a | *bīt* 2 *šá d*[*ūr*(bàd)-*ku-ri-gal-zu*?] |
| B$_1$ | 107 | é.pàd.da.nu.nus | *bīt* $^{d}$*sa-dà*[*r-nun-na*] |
| B$_1$ | 108 | é.me.lám.ḫuš | *bīt* $^{d}$*gìr*[*a*] |
| B$_1$ | 109 | é.me.kìlib.šu.du$_7$ | *bīt* $^{d}$*nin-ìmm*[*a*] |
| B$_1$ | 110 | é.nam.en.gar.ra | *bīt* 2 |
| B$_1$ | 111 | é.rab.ri.ri | *bīt* $^{d}$*en-nu-gi* |
| B$_1$ | 112 | é.rab.ša$_5$.ša$_5$ | *bīt* 2 |
| B$_1$ | 113 | é.sánga.maḫ | *bīt* $^{d}$*kù-sù* |
| B$_1$C$_3$ | 114 | é.šùd.dè.giš.tuku | *bīt* 2 [32] |

[31] So A$_1$, B$_4$ om. bàd
[32] So B$_1$, C$_3$: *bīt* $^{d}$*kù*]-*sù*

| | | | |
|---|---|---|---|
| $B_1C_3$ | 115 | é.šu.luḫ.ḫa.túm.ma | *bīt* $^{d}$*nin-šar* |
| $C_3$ | 116 | [é . . . ] | [*bīt* $^{d}$*nin-ka*$^{ka}$]$^{s}$*-si* |
| $C_3$ | 117 | [é . . . ] | [*bīt* $^{d}$*nin-ka*$^{ka}$]$^{s}$*-si* |
| $C_3$ | 118 | [é . . . ] | [*bīt* $^{d}$*nin-ma*]*-da* |
| $C_3$ | 119 | [é . . . ] | [*bīt* $^{d}$*ug-elam*]*-ma* |

*Lacuna, in which we expect temples of the Mother Goddess to begin, no doubt with:*

| | | | |
|---|---|---|---|
| | | [é.maḫ] | [*bīt* $^{d}$*bēlet-ilī* (*šá kèš*$^{ki}$)] |

*The text resumes:*

| | | | |
|---|---|---|---|
| | 148 | [é . . . ] | [*bīt x šá . . .* ] |
| | 149 | [é . . . ] | [*bīt x* + 1 *šá* 2] |
| | 150 | [é . . . ] | [*bīt x* + 2 *šá* 3] |
| | 151 | [é . . . ] | [*bīt x* + 3 *šá* 4] |
| $C_1$ | 152 | [é . . . ] | [*bīt x* + 4 *šá*] 5 |
| $C_1$ | 153 | [é . . . ] | [*bīt x* + 5 *šá*] 6 |
| $C_1$ | 154 | [é . . . ] | [*bīt* $^{d}$*šu*]*l-pa-è* |
| $C_1$ | 155 | [é . . . ] | [*bīt*] ⸢2⸣ |
| $C_1$ | 156 | [é . . . ] | [*bīt*] 3 |
| $C_1$ | 157 | [é . . . ] | ⸢*bīt*⸣ 4 |
| $C_1$ | 158 | [é . . . ] | ⸢*bīt*⸣ 5 |
| $C_1$ | 159 | [é . . . ] | *bīt* 6 |
| $C_1$ | 160 | [é . . . ] | *bīt* 7 |
| $B_4C_1$ | 161 | ⸢é⸣.[ . . . ] | *bīt* 8 |
| $B_4C_1$ | 162 | é.[ . . . ] | *bīt* 9 |
| $B_4C_1$ | 163 | é.x[ . . . n]a$^{?}$ | *bīt* 10 |
| $B_4C_1$ | 164 | é.ur.s[a]g./[ . . . ]x | *bīt* $^{d}$*pa*$_4$*-nìgin-gar-ra* / *šá adab*$^{ki}$ |
| $B_4C_1$ | 165 | é.me.te.[ur.sag?] | *bīt* 2 |
| $B_4C_1$ | 166 | é.ḫi.li.x[ x] | *bīt* 3 |
| $B_4B_5C_1$ | 167 | é.ní.gù[r.ru] | *bīt* 4 |
| $B_4B_5C_1$ | 168 | é.ut[ul] | *bīt* 5 |
| $B_4B_5C_1$ | 169 | é.$^{mi\text{-}is}$[mes] | ⸢*bīt*⸣ $^{d}$lil |
| $B_4B_5C_1$ | 170 | é.usu$^{uš\text{-}}$[$^{šu}$.x] | ⸢*bīt* $^{d}$⸣*uta-u*$_{18}$$^{(33)}$*-lu* |
| $B_4B_5C_1$ | 171 | é.u$_4$.gim.x[.x] | [*bīt* $^{d}$].$^{aš}$*aš*$_7$*-gi* |
| $B_4B_5C_1$ | 172 | é.$^{ur}$ur$_5$.[šà.ba] | [*bīt*] ⸢$^{d}$⸣*li*$_9$*-si*$_4$ |
| $B_4B_5C_1$ | 173 | é.lú.[maḫ] | [*bīt*] *lumaḫḫi* (lú.maḫ) |
| $B_4B_5$ | 174 | é.išib.[ba?] | [*bīt*] ⸢2⸣ |
| $B_4B_5$ | 175 | é.gi$_6$.[pàr] | [*bīt ē*]*ni*(en) |
| $B_4B_5$ | 176 | é.gi$_6$.[pàr.kù?] | [*bīt*] *a-te-e* |
| $B_4B_5$ | 177 | é.x[ . . . ] | ⸢*bīt*⸣ $^{d}$TU |
| $B_4B_5$ | 178 | é.x[ . . . ] | *bīt* $^{d}$*làl-a-šà-ga* |
| $B_5$ | 179 | [é.abzu] | *bīt* $^{d}$*é-a šá eridu*$^{ki}$ |

33 So $B_5$, $C_1$: URU

| | | | | |
|---|---|---|---|---|
| B$_5$ | 180 | [é.engur.ra] | *bīt* 2 | |
| B$_5$ | 181 | [é . . . ] | *bīt* 3 | |
| A$_2$B$_5$ | 182 | [é].x[ . . . ] | *bīt* 4 | |
| A$_2$B$_5$ | 183 | ⸢é⸣.úr[u.zé.eb?] | ⸢*bīt*⸣ 5 | |
| A$_2$B$_5$ | 184 | é.u$_6$.[nir] | [*bīt*] ⸢6⸣ | |
| A$_2$B$_5$ | 185 | é.èš.[maḫ] | [*bīt* 7] | (vacat) |
| A$_2$B$_5$ | 186 | é.igi.[kù?] | [*bīt* 8] | (vacat) |
| A$_2$B$_5$ | 187 | é.làl.g[ar] | [*bīt* 9] | (vacat) |
| A$_2$B$_5$ | 188 | é.šèš.$^{\text{ga-⸢ra!}}$gar⸣ | [*bīt* 10] | (vacat) |
| A$_2$ | 189 | é.šeg$_9$.[bar] | [*bīt* 11 (*šá* . . . )] | |
| A$_2$ | 190 | é.á.nun.[na] | [*bīt* 12 (*šá* . . . )] | |
| A$_2$ | 191 | é.gal.an.[zu] | [*bīt* 13] | (vacat?) |
| A$_2$ | 192 | é.gán.nun.[na] | [*bīt* 14] | (vacat?) |
| A$_2$ | 193 | é.ḫal.an.[kù] | [*bīt* 15] | (vacat?) |
| A$_2$ | 194 | é.géšt[u] | [*bīt* 16] | (vacat?) |
| A$_2$ | 195 | é.géštu.tukur.ra.sum.⸢mu⸣ | [*bīt* 17] | (vacat?) |
| A$_2$ | 196 | [é].⸢géštu⸣.kalam.ma.sum.mu | [*bīt* 18] | (vacat?) |
| A$_2$ | 197 | [é.géštu.m]aḫ.šu.du$_7$ | ⸢*bīt*⸣ [19 *šá ú*]*r*[*i* (Š]E[Š.UNUG)$^{ki}$?] | |
| A$_2$ | 198 | [é.ad.g]i$_4$.gi$_4$ | ⸢*bīt*⸣ [20 *šá*] x[ x x] | |
| A$_2$ | 199 | [é.géštu?].maḫ./[ . . . su]m.mu | ⸢*bīt*⸣ [21] / *šá* ⸢*uruk*(MÚRU)⸣[$^{ki}$] | |
| A$_2$ | 200 | [é.me.zi?].da | *bīt* 22 *šá* UD.[NUN?$^{ki}$] | |
| A$_2$ | 201 | [é.(x).mul.m]ul | *bīt* 23 *šá* ŠÁR×GAL$^?$.MIN [x] | |
| A$_2$ | 202 | [é . . . m]a$^?$./[ . . . ]x | *bīt* 24 / *šá nēmed*(UŠ)-$^{d}$⸢*la*⸣-[*gu-da*] | |
| A$_2$ | 203 | [é . . . NI]M×X$^?$ | *bīt* 25 *šá* x[ . . . ] | |
| A$_2$ | 204 | [é . . . ]x | ⸢*bīt*⸣ 26 *š*[*á* . . . ] | |
| A$_2$ | 205 | [é . . . ] | ⸢*bīt*⸣ 27 [(*šá* . . . )] | |
| A$_2$ | 206 | [é . . . ] | ⸢*bīt*⸣ [ . . . ] | |

*Short lacuna*

| | | | |
|---|---|---|---|
| B$_1$ | 222 | [é].⸢abzu⸣.[ . . . ] | [*bīt* . . . ] |
| B$_1$ | 223 | é.abzu.[x] | [*bīt* . . . ] |
| B$_1$ | 224 | é.abzu.[x] | [*bīt* . . . ] |
| B$_1$ | 225 | é.ud.⸢x⸣ | [*bīt* . . . ] |
| B$_1$C$_3$ | 226 | é.umuš.a | [*bīt* $^{d}$*marduk* (*šá bābili* $^{ki}$)] |
| B$_1$C$_3$ | 227 | é.a.ra.⟨zu⟩.giš.tu[ku] (34) | [*bīt* 2 (*šá* 2)] |
| B$_1$C$_3$ | 228 | é.sag.íl | ⸢*bīt*⸣ [3 (*šá* 3)] |
| B$_1$C$_3$ | 229 | é.pirig.babbar | ⸢*bīt*⸣ [4 (*šá* . . . )] |
| B$_1$C$_3$ | 230 | é.mes | ⸢*bīt*⸣ [5 (*šá* . . . )] |
| C$_3$ | 231 | é.zi.da | ⸢*bīt*⸣ [6 (*šá bár-sipa*$^{ki}$)] |
| C$_3$ | 232 | é.zi.sù.ud.gal | ⸢*bīt*⸣ [7 (*šá* . . . )] |
| C$_3$ | 233 | é.nam.⸢ti.la⸣ | ⸢*bīt*⸣ [8 (*šá* . . . )] |
| C$_3$ | 234 | é.KAS$_4$.gi.⸢na⸣ / (vacat) | ⸢*bīt*⸣ [9] / *šá* x[ . . . ] |
| C$_3$ | 235 | ⸢é⸣.dàra.an.na | *bīt* ⸢$^{d}$⸣*z*[*ar-pa-ni-tum*] |

[34] So B$_1$, C$_3$: é.⟨ . . . ⟩.giš.tuku

| | | | |
|---|---|---|---|
| $C_3$ | 236 | ⸢é⸣.zi.da | *bīt* $^{d}$*nabû*(nà) *š*[*á bár-sipa*$^{ki}$] |
| $C_3$ | 237 | ⸢é⸣.nam.bi.zi.da | *bīt* 2 |
| $C_3$ | 238 | é.gidru.kalam.ma.sum.mu | *bīt* 3 *šá ḫa-r*[*e-e*] |
| $C_3$ | 239 | ⸢é.níg⸣.[(x).d]a$^{?}$.ús.sa | *bīt* 4 *šá* [2] |
| $C_3$ | 240 | ⸢é⸣.[giš.l]á.an.ki | *bīt* 5 *šá* [*nikkassi* (níg.ka$_9$)] |
| $C_3$ | 241 | ⸢é⸣.[x (x) ḫ]é.du$_7$ | *bīt* 6 ⸢*šá*⸣ [ . . . ] |
| $C_3$ | 242 | ⸢é⸣.[0].mul | ⸢*bīt*⸣ [ . . . ] |
| $C_3$ | 243 | é.⸢íd⸣.[lú].ru.⸢gú⸣ | [*bīt* $^{d}$íd (*šá* . . . )] |
| $C_3$ | 244 | é.íd.l[ú.r]u.[gú.kalam.ma?] | [*bīt* 2 (*šá* . . . )] |
| $C_3$ | 245 | é.ku[r$^{?}$ . . . ] | [*bīt* . . . ] |
| $C_3$ | 246 | ⸢é⸣.[ . . . ] | [*bīt* . . . ] |

*Lacuna, in which are expected temples of Sîn*

| | | | |
|---|---|---|---|
| $C_1$ | 270 | ⸢é⸣.[ . . . ] | [*bīt* . . . ] |
| $C_1$ | 271 | ⸢é.gissu$^{?}$.bi$^{?}$.du$_{10}$.ga$^{?}$⸣ | ⸢*bīt*⸣ [ . . . ] |
| $C_1$ | 272 | é.šà.ga.bi.du$_{10}$.ga | *bīt* 10 + [(*x* . . . )] |
| $C_1$ | 273 | é.an.gim | *bīt* ⸢$^{d}$⸣[*nin-gal*] |
| $C_1$ | 274 | é.an.gim.kù.ga | *bīt* [2 (*šá* . . . )] |
| $C_1$ | 275 | é.gán.nun.kù | *bīt* [3 (*šá* . . . )] |
| $C_1$ | 276 | é.pa$_4$.ul.ḫé | ⸢*bīt*⸣ [$^{d}$*nin-gublag*] |
| $C_1$ | 277 | é.NUN.ud.da | *bīt* ⸢2⸣ [(*šá* . . . )] |
| $C_1$ | 278 | é.ga.ra.ni | *bīt* ⸢3⸣ [(*šá* . . . )] |
| $C_1$ | 279 | é.báḫar | *bīt* [4 (*šá* . . . )] |
| $C_1$ | 280 | é.bur.sa$_7$.sa$_7$ | *bīt* [ . . . ] |
| $C_1$ | 281 | é.babbar.ra | ⸢*bīt*⸣ [$^{d}$*šamaš* (utu) (*šá sippar*$^{ki}$)] |
| $C_1$ | 282 | é.babbar.ra | ⸢*bīt*⸣ [2 (*šá larsa*$^{ki}$)] |
| $B_5C_1$ | 283 | é.di.ku$_5$.kalam.ma | ⸢*bīt*⸣ [3 (*šá bābili*$^{ki}$)] |
| $B_5C_1$ | 284 | é.di.ku$_5$.dá | [*bīt* 4 (*šá* . . . )] |
| $B_5C_1$ | 285 | é.nam.tar.kalam.m[a] | [*bīt* 5 (*šá* . . . )] |
| $B_5$ | 286 | é.giš.túl$^{giš-ṭu-lá}$lá | ⸢*bīt*⸣ [6 (*šá* . . . )] |
| $B_5$ | 287 | é.me.te.è | *bīt* [7 (*šá* . . . )] |
| $B_5$ | 288 | é.an.ta.sur.ra | *bīt* [8 (*šá* . . . )] |
| $B_5$ | 289 | é.pa$_4$.gál.an.na | ⸢*bīt*⸣ [9 (*šá* . . . )] |
| $B_5$ | 290 | é.kù.ki$^{ki-na-a}$ná | *bīt* [10 (*šá* . . . )] |
| $B_5$ | 291 | é.kù.mul.mul | *bīt* [11 (*šá* . . . )] |
| $B_5$ | 292 | é.tukur$^{tu-kur}$.ra | *bīt* ⸢$^{d}$⸣[*bu-ne-ne*] |
| $B_5$ | 293 | é.dim.gal.an.na | *bīt* $^{d}$⸢*a*⸣-[*a* (*šá* . . . )] |
| $B_5$ | 294 | é.ka.aš.bar.sum.mu | *bīt* $^{d}$*pa*$_4$-*n*[*un-na* ( . . . )] |
| $B_5$ | 295 | é.u$_4$.gal.gal.la | *bīt* $^{d}$*ada*[*d* (iškur) *šá karkara*(IM)$^{ki}$] |
| $B_5$ | 296 | é.u$_4$.gal | *bīt* 2 |
| $B_5$ | 297 | é.u$_4$.⸢gal⸣.gim | *bīt* 3 |
| $B_5$ | 298 | é.x[ (x) g]im | *bīt* 4 |
| $B_5$ | 299 | é.u[$_4$ . . . ] | *bīt* 5 *š*[*á* . . . ] |
| $B_5$ | 300 | é.u[$_4$ . . . ] | ⸢*bīt* 6⸣ [(*šá* . . . )] |
| $B_5$ | 301 | é.[ . . . ] | [*bīt* . . . ] |

| | | | |
|---|---|---|---|
| B$_5$ | 302 | ⸢é⸣.[ . . . ] | [*bīt* . . . ] |
| | | *Short lacuna* | |
| B$_2$ | 309 | ⸢é⸣.n[am.ḫé? ( . . . )] | [*bīt* . . . ] |
| B$_2$ | 310 | é.na[m.ḫé? ( . . . )] | [*bīt* . . . ] |
| B$_2$ | 311 | é.nam.ḫ[é x x] | [*bīt* . . . ] |
| B$_2$ | 312 | é.me.bi.za[lag.ga?]/ .ní.su.zi.b[ar.ra] | [*bīt* . . . ] / [( . . . )] |
| B$_2$ | 313 | é.an.n[a] | [*bīt* $^{d}$*bēlet*(nin)-*é-an-na*?] |
| B$_2$ | 314 | é.an.na | [*bīt* $^{d}$*uruk*$^{ki}$-*a-a-i-tum*?] |
| B$_2$ | 315 | é.èš.gal | [*bīt* 2 (*šá* . . . )] |
| B$_2$ | 316 | ⸢é⸣.ub.imin | [*bīt* 3 (*šá* . . . )] |
| B$_2$ | 317 | [é].da.imin | [*bīt* 4 (*šá* . . . )] |
| B$_2$ | 318 | [é.g]i$_6$.pàr.imin | [*bīt* 5 (*šá* . . . )] |
| B$_2$ | 319 | [é.temen?].ní.gùr.ru | [*bīt* $^{d}$]⸢*su-pa*$^{?}$⸣-*l*[*i-tum*?] |
| B$_2$ | 320 | [é.s]ù.sù.gar.ra | ⸢*bīt* 2⸣ |
| B$_2$ | 321 | [é.A]N$^{?}$.kum | *bīt* 3 |
| B$_2$ | 322 | [é.g]i.gun$_4$.na | *bīt* 4 *šá mùru*$^{mu\text{-}rù.[ki]}$ |
| B$_2$ | 323 | [é.g]i$^{?}$.⸢gun$_4$$^{?}$.kù$^{?}$.⸣/[ . . . ] | *bīt* $^{d}$*iš*$_8$-*tár ummā*[*ni* (ki.$^{kuš}$lu.úb.gar)] / (vacat) |
| B$_2$ | 324 | [é.galga.sù] | *bīt* $^{d}$*ištar*(inanna) *malka*[*ti* (galga.sù)] |
| B$_2$ | 325 | [é . . . ] | *bīt* 2 |
| B$_2$ | 326 | [é . . . ] | *bīt* 3 |
| B$_2$ | 327 | [é . . . ] | ⸢*bīt* 4⸣ [*šá*] ⸢x x⸣ [ . . . ] |
| | 328 | [é . . . ] | [*bīt* 5 (*šá* . . . )] |
| | 329 | [é . . . ] | [*bīt* 6 (*šá* . . . )] |
| | 330 | [é . . . ] | [*bīt* 7 (*šá* . . . )] |
| | 331 | [é . . . ] | [*bīt* 8 (*šá* . . . )] |
| | 332 | [é . . . ] | [*bīt* 9 (*šá* . . . )] |
| | 333 | [é . . . ] | [*bīt* 10 (*šá* . . . )] |
| | 334 | [é . . . ] | [*bīt* 11 (*šá* . . . )] |
| B$_3$ | 335 | [é . . . ].⸢na⸣ | ⸢*bīt* 12⸣ [(*šá* . . . )] |
| B$_3$ | 336 | [é . . . k]u$_4$$^{?}$ | *bīt* 1[3 (*šá* . . . )] |
| B$_3$ | 337 | [é . . . s]a$^{?}$ | *bīt* 14 [(*šá* . . . )] |
| B$_3$ | 338 | [é . . . ]x | *bīt* 15 [(*šá* . . . )] |
| B$_3$B$_6$ | 339 | [é.dur.an.k]i$^{?}$ | ⸢*bīt*⸣ [16 *šá nippu*]*r* $^{ki}$ |
| A$_2$B$_6$ | 340 | ⸢é⸣.[bára.dúr.gar.ra] | [*bīt* 17 *šá*] 2 |
| A$_2$B$_6$ | 341 | ⸢é⸣.[kù.nun.na] | [*bīt* 18 *š*]*á eridu*$^{ki}$ |
| A$_2$B$_6$ | 342 | é.[sar.ra] | [*bīt* 19] *šá adab*$^{ki}$ |
| A$_2$B$_6$ | 343 | é.[tilmun.na] | [*bīt*] 20 *šá úri* $^{ki}$ |
| A$_2$B$_6$ | 344 | é.si[g$_4$$^{!}$.me.šè.du$_7$/túm] | ⸢*bīt*⸣ 21 *šá isin*(PA.ŠE)$^{ki}$ |
| A$_2$B$_6$ | 345 | é.bú[r.x] | [*bīt* 2]2 *šá* ⟨ . . . ⟩ |
| A$_2$ | 346 | é.šà.ḫ[úl.la] | [*bīt* 2]3 [*šá ka-zal-lu*$^{ki}$] |
| A$_2$ | 347 | é.šà.d[u$_{10}$.ga] | [*bīt*] 24 [(*šá* . . . )] |
| A$_2$ | 348 | é.me.u[r$_4$.ur$_4$] | ⸢*bīt*⸣ 25 [(*šá larsa*$^{ki}$)] |

| | | | |
|---|---|---|---|
| $A_2$ | 349 | é.me.[ur$_4$] | ⸢*bīt*⸣ 26 *šá* ⸢KA⸣.[ . . . ] |
| $A_2$ | 350 | é.$^{maš-na?}$[x] | ⸢*bīt*⸣ 27 *šá dūr*(bàd)-[ . . . ] |
| $A_2$ | 351 | é.IM.x[ x] | *bīt* 28 *šá dūr*(bàd)-[ . . . ] |
| $A_2$ | 352 | é.sig$_4$.x[ x] | *bīt* 29 *šá* [2] |
| $A_2$ | 353 | é.⸢šu⸣.bil.⸢lá⸣ | *bīt* 30 *šá* [3] |
| $A_2$ | 354 | é.AN.za.gàr | *bīt* 31 *šá akša*[*k*$^{ki}$] |
| $A_2$ | 355 | é.gi.gun$_4$.na | [*bīt*] ⸢32 *šá*⸣ *már-d*[*a*$^{ki}$] |
| $A_2$ | 356 | é.nìgin.gar.ra | [*bīt* 33 *šá šúr*]*up*[*pak*$^{ki}$] |
| $A_2$ | 357 | é.šúruppak$^{ki}$ | [*bīt* 34 *šá* 2] |
| $A_2$ | 358 | é.kur.me.sikil | ⸢*bīt* 35⸣ [*šá* . . . ] |
| $A_2$ | 359 | é.sag.íl.la | *bīt* 36 ⸢*šá*⸣ *tilm*[*un*$^{ki}$] |
| $A_2$ | 360 | é.su$_{11}$.lum.ma / (vacat) | *bīt* 37 *šá nap-sa-n*[*u*$^{ki}$] / su$_{11}$.lum.[ma] |
| $A_2$ | 361 | é.dun$_x$(ÍL)$^{du}$.na | *bīt* 38 *šá maš-kán*$^!$-d[ingir$^{ki}$?] |
| $A_2$ | 362 | é.ul.maš | ⸢*bīt*⸣ 39 *šá a-kà-*[*dè*$^{ki}$] |
| $A_2$ | 363 | é.tùn.gal | ⸢*bīt*⸣ 40 *šá šuba*[*t*(ki.tuš)-x$^{ki}$] |
| $A_2$ | 364 | é.sù.sù.gar.ra | *bīt* 41 $^{ḫe-[pí]}$ |
| $A_2$ | 365 | é.edin.na | *bīt* 42 *šá sippa*[*r*$^{ki}$] |
| $A_2$ | 366 | é.ḫur.sag.kalam.ma | *bīt* 43 *šá kiš*[$^{ki}$] |
| $A_2$ | 367 | é.su.lim.an.na | *bīt* 44 *šá* [2] |
| $A_2$ | 368 | é.tùr.kalam.ma | *bīt* ⸢45 *šá bābili*⸣[$^{ki}$] |
| $A_2$ | 369 | é.amaš.kalam.ma | *bīt* 4[6 *šá* . . . ] |
| $A_2$ | 370 | é.ur$_5$.šà.ba / (vacat) | *bīt* [47] / *šá b*[*ár-sipa*$^{ki}$] |
| $A_2$ | 371 | é $^{ḫe-pí}$ | *bīt* [48 *šá* . . . ] |
| $A_2$ | 372 | é.⟨ . . . ⟩ / (vacat) | ⸢*bīt*⸣ [49] / *š*[*á* . . . ] |
| $A_2$ | 373 | ⸢é.ki x x x⸣ | [*bīt* 50 *šá* . . . ] |
| $A_2$ | 374 | é.du$_6$.⸢kù⸣ | [*bīt* 51 *šá* . . . ] |
| $A_2$ | 375 | é.du$_6$.⟨kalam?⟩.ma | [*bīt* 52 *šá* . . . ] |
| $A_2$ | 376 | é.gaba.ri.nu.tuku | [*bīt* 53 *šá* . . . ] |
| $A_2$ | 377 | é.sukud.da | ⸢*bīt* 54 *šá*⸣ [$^{uru}$*kar-*$^{d}$*bēl-mātāti*?] |
| $A_2$ | 378 | é.an.ki | *bīt* 55 *šá* [2] |
| $A_2C_1$ | 379 | é.dúbur$^?$.ní.gùr.ru [35] | *bīt* 56 *šá* ZA-*a*-x[ (x)] |
| $A_2C_1$ | 380 | é.nu.úr.ma | *bīt* 57 *šá maš-kán-a-ti*[$^{ki}$] |
| $A_2C_1$ | 381 | é.šaga.ra | *bīt* 58 *šá da-ad-muš*$^{k}$[$^{i}$] |
| $A_2C_1$ | 382 | é.ninda.dù.a | *bīt* 59 *šá* LIBIR.RA$^{k}$[$^{i}$] |
| $A_2C_1$ | 383 | é.éš.dam$^!$(NIN).kù | *bīt* 60 *šá gír-su*$^{k}$[$^{i}$] |
| | 384 | ⟨é . . . ⟩ | ⟨*bīt* 61 (*šá* . . . )⟩ |
| $A_2C_1$ | 385 | é.ki.sikil.bi.kar.za.gìn.na | *bīt* 62 |
| $A_2C_1$ | 386 | é.amaš.kù | *bīt* 63 *šá* BÀD.AN$^{k}$[$^{i}$] |
| $A_2C_1$ | 387 | é.nu$_{11}$.gal.an.na | *bīt* 64 ⟨*šá*⟩ *lagaš*$^{k}$[$^{i}$] |
| $A_2C_1$ | 388 | é.igi.du$_8$.a | *bīt* 65 *šá kutê*(gú.du$_8$.⟨a⟩)$^{k}$[$^{i}$] |
| $A_2C_1$ | 389 | é.síg.ùz | *bīt* 66 *šá* gú.a.ab.⸢ba⸣$^{ki}$ |
| $A_2C_1$ | 390 | é.ki.tuš.gir$_{17}$.zal | *bīt* 67 *š*[*á*] ⸢ki⸣.bal.maš.dà$^{ki}$ |
| $C_1$ | 391 | é.za.gìn.na | ⸢*bīt*⸣ 68 *š*[*á š*]*ušina*(MÙŠ.⸢ŠÉŠ⸣)$^{ki}$ |

35 So $A_2$, $C_1$: é.⸢ḪI⸣.[ . . .

| | | | | |
|---|---|---|---|---|
| $C_1$ | 392 | é.ùn.na | [*bīt* 6]9 *šá* ⸢su.bir$_4$$^{ki}$⸣ | |
| $C_1$ | 393 | é.mes.mes | [*bīt* 70 *šá n*]*i-n*[*ú-a*$^{ki}$] | |
| $C_1$ | 394 | é.nun.na | [*bīt* 71 *šá* $^{u}$]$^{ru?}$T[A$^?$ x (x)$^{ki}$] | |
| $C_1$ | 395 | é.šà.ba.na | [*bīt* 72 *šá ma-rí*$^{ki}$] | |
| $C_1$ | 396 | é.me.ur$_4$ | [*bīt* 73 *šá* 2?] | |
| $C_1$ | 397 | é.ní.gal./su.lim.gùr.r[u] | [*bīt* 74] / [(*šá* . . . )] | |
| $C_1$ | 398 | é.gir$_{17}$.zal.z[i$^?$] | [*bīt* 75 (*šá* . . . )] | |
| $C_1$ | 399 | é.še.er.⟨zi⟩.⸢gùr⸣.r[u] | [*bīt* 76 *šá zabalam*$^{ki}$] | |
| $C_1$ | 400 | é.kalam.ta.⟨ní⟩.⸢gùr⸣.[(ru)] | [*bīt* 77 *šá* 2] | |
| $C_1$ | 401 | é.zi.ka[lam.ma] | [*bīt* 78 *šá* 3] | |
| $C_1$ | 402 | ⸢é⸣.[ . . . ] | [*bīt* 79 (*šá* . . . )] | |
| | | *Lacuna* | | |
| $C_3$ | 433 | ⸢é⸣.[x] | [*bīt* . . . ] | |
| $A_3C_3$ | 434 | ⸢é⸣.an.da.sá.a | *bīt* ⸢d⸣[*iš*$_8$*-tár-kakkabi* (mul)$^{meš}$] | |
| $A_3C_3$ | 435 | é.me.ur$_4$.ur$_4$ | *bīt* ⸢d⸣[*na-na-a*?] | |
| $A_3C_3$ | 436 | é.igi.kalam.ma | *bīt* ⸢2⸣ [(*šá* . . . )] | |
| $A_3C_3$ | 437 | é.sud | *bīt* ⸢3⸣ [(*šá* . . . )] | |
| $A_3C_3$ | 438 | é.sag.sur | *bīt* ⸢d⸣[ . . . ] | |
| $A_3C_3$ | 439 | é.i.lu.zi./ù.li | *bīt* $^{d}$⸢*iš*$_8$$^?$⸣*-t*[*ár*$^?$] / *ta-ma-*[*ti*] | |
| $A_3C_3$ | 440 | é.$^{muš}$múš | *bīt* $^{d}$*dumu-z*[*i*] | |
| $A_3C_3$ | 441 | é.múš.kalam.ma | *bīt* 2 | |
| $A_3C_3$ | 442 | é.múš.za.gìn.na | ⸢*bīt*⸣ 3 | |
| $A_3C_3$ | 443 | é.za.gìn.na | ⸢*bīt*⸣ 4 | |
| $A_3C_3$ | 444 | é.ér.ra | *bīt* 5 | |
| $A_3C_3$ | 445 | é.a.ra.li | *bīt* 6 | |
| $A_3C_3$ | 446 | é.⟨ . . . ⟩ | *bīt* 7 | |
| $A_3C_3$ | 447 | é.⟨ . . . ⟩ | *bīt* 8 | |
| $A_3C_3$ | 448 | é.⟨ . . . ⟩ | *bīt* ⸢9⸣ | |
| $A_2C_3$ | 449 | ⸢é⸣.[zi.da.(giš).nu$_{11}$.gal] | [*bīt* 10 *šá ki-mi-t*]*i* | |
| $A_2$ | 450 | [é.níg.lu].⸢lu⸣ | [*bīt* 11 *šá b*]*i-*⸢*ki*⸣*-ti* | |
| $A_2$ | 451 | ⸢é⸣.maḫ | [*bīt*] ⸢d⸣*šara* | |
| $A_2$ | 452 | é.bur.⸢sa$_7$.sa$_7$⸣ | [*bīt* 2] | (vacat) |
| $A_2$ | 453 | é.bur.dù.dù | [*bīt* 3] | (vacat) |
| $A_2$ | 454 | é.šà.ge.pàd.da | [*bīt* 4] | (vacat) |
| $A_2$ | 455 | é.u$_4$.⸢sakar⸣.ra | [*bīt* 5] | (vacat) |
| $A_2$ | 456 | é.akkil | ⸢*bīt* d⸣[*nin-š*]*ubur šá kiš*$^{ki}$ | |
| $A_2$ | 457 | é.akkil.du$_6$.kù | *bīt* 2 [*š*]*á nippur*$^{ki}$ | |
| $A_2$ | 458 | é.tilmun.na | *bīt* 3 | |
| $A_2$ | 459 | é.tilmun.na.ŠA | *bīt* 4 | |
| $A_2$ | 460 | é.igi.zu.uru$_{16}$ | *bīt* 5 | |
| $A_2$ | 461 | é.gada.a.ri.a | *bīt* 6 | |
| $A_2$ | 462 | é.eš.bar.me.luḫ.ḫa | *bīt* 7 *šá gír-su*$^{ki}$ | |
| $A_2C_2$ | 463 | é.níg.lu.lu | *bīt* $^{d}$*nin-geštin-an-na* (36) | |

[36] So $A_2$, $C_2$: $^{d}$*nin*-TI[N$^?$-

| | | | |
|---|---|---|---|
| $A_2C_2$ | 464 | é.sag.DUL | *bīt* 2 |
| $A_2C_2$ | 465 | é.úru.kù | *bīt* $^{d}$*be-li-li* |
| $A_2C_2$ | 466 | é.ér.ra | *bīt* 2 |
| $A_2C_2$ | 467 | é.a.ra.li | *bīt* 3 |
| $A_2C_2$ | 468 | é.TIN(kúrun?).na | *bīt* 4 |
| $A_2C_2$ | 469 | é.igi.kalam.ma / (vacat) | *bīt* $^{d}$*lugal-már-da* / *šá már-da*$^{ki}$ |
| $A_2C_2$ | 470 | é.ki.kal / (vacat) | *bīt* $^{d}$*lugal-bàn-da* / *šá kul-*[*a*]*ba*$_4$(MÚRU)$^{ki}$ |
| $A_2$ | 471 | é.sag | *bīt* 2 |
| $A_2$ | 472 | é.me.sikil | *bīt* ⸢$^{d}$⸣*amurru*(AN.mar.dú) |
| $A_2$ | 473 | ⸢é⸣.nam.tag.ga.duḫ.ù | *bīt* 2 |
| $A_2$ | 474 | [é.sikil].la | *bīt* $^{d}$*t*[*i*]*špak šá èš-nun-na*$^{ki}$ |
| $A_2$ | 475 | [é x d]é.a | *bīt* $^{d}$AN-*šušinak* |
| $A_2$ | 476 | [é (x) k]a./[x (x) ]x | *bīt* $^{d}$*ištarān*(KA.DI) / *šá dēr*(BÀD.AN)$^{ki}$ |
| $A_2$ | 477 | [é.dim.gal.kalam.ma] | ⸢*bīt* 2⸣ |
| $A_2$ | 478 | ⸢é.ḪI⸣.[ . . . ] | [*bīt*] ⸢$^{d}$⸣KU$_7$ *šá a-ḫu-ud*$^{ki}$ |
| $A_2$ | 479 | é.me.[te]/.ur.[sag] | [*bīt*] ⸢$^{d}$⸣*za-ba*$_4$-*ba*$_4$ / [*šá k*]*iš*$^{ki}$ |
| $A_2$ | 480 | é.dub.[ba] | [*bīt*] ⸢2⸣ |
| $A_2$ | 481 | é.*i*-[*bí*]-/$^{d}$⸢*a*⸣-[*nu-um*] | [*bīt*] ⸢$^{d}$⸣*uraš* / [*šá dil-ba*]*t*$^{ki}$ |
| $A_2$ | 482 | [é . . . ] | [*bīt* 2 *šá dil-ba*]*t*-GÁN$^{ki}$ |
| $A_2$ | 483 | [é.sa.pàr] | [*bīt* $^{d}$*bēlet*(nin)]-*ekalli*(⸢é?⸣.gal) |
| $A_2$ | 484 | [é.ninnu]./[(anzu$^{mušen}$.babbar)] | [*bīt* $^{d}$*nin-gír-su*] / [*šá gír-su*$^{k}$]$^{i}$ |
| $A_2$ | 485 | [é . . . ] | [*bīt* ( . . . )] 2 |
| $A_2$ | 486 | [é . . . ] | [*bīt* 3 *šá*] 2 |
| $A_2$ | 487 | [é . . . ] | [*bīt* 4] ⸢*šá*⸣ 3 |
| $A_2C_1$ | 488 | [é . . . ] | [*bīt* 5] *šá* 4 |
| $A_2C_1$ | 489 | [é . . . ] | [*bīt* 6] *šá* 5 |
| $A_2C_1$ | 490 | [é . . . ] | [*bīt* 7] *šá* 6 |
| $A_2C_1$ | 491 | [é.tar]./[sír.sír] | [*bīt* $^{d}$]*ba-ba*$_6$ / [*šá gí*]*r-su*$^{ki}$ |
| $A_2C_1$ | 492 | [é.galga.sù] | [*bīt*] 2 *šá kiš*$^{ki}$ |
| $A_2C_1$ | 493 | [é . . . ] | [*bī*]*t* 3 *šá* 2 |
| $A_2C_1$ | 494 | [é . . . ] | [*bī*]*t* 4 *šá* 3 |
| $A_2C_1$ | 495 | [é . . . ] | [*bī*]*t* 5 *šá* 4 |
| $A_2C_1$ | 496 | [é . . . ] | [*b*]*īt* 6 *šá* 5 |
| $A_2C_1$ | 497 | [é . . . ] | *bīt* 7 *šá* 6$^{!}$ [37] |
| $A_2C_1$ | 498 | [é.me.ḫuš.gal.an.ki] | *bīt* $^{d}$*ig-alim-ma* |
| $A_2C_1$ | 499 | [é.ki.tuš.akkil.lé] | *bīt* $^{d}$*šul-šà-ga-na* |
| $A_2C_1$ | 500 | [é . . . ] | *bīt* 2 |
| $A_2C_1$ | 501 | [é . . . ] | *bīt* $^{d}$*si-ra-ra* |
| $C_1$ | 502 | [é.ab.šà.ga.lá] | *bīt* $^{d}$*nin-mar-kù-ga* |
| $C_1$ | 503 | [é . . . ] | *bīt* 2 |
| $C_1$ | 504 | [é.gal.maḫ] | *bīt* $^{d}$*gu-la šá isin*(PA.ŠE)$^{ki}$ |
| $C_1$ | 505 | [é . . . ] | *bīt* 2 |

[37] Both MSS: 7

| | | | | |
|---|---|---|---|---|
| $C_1$ | 506 | [é . . . ] | *bīt* 3 | |
| $C_1$ | 507 | [é . . . ] | *bīt* 4 | |
| $C_1$ | 508 | [é . . . ] | *bīt* 5 | |
| $C_1$ | 509 | [é . . . ] | [*b*]*īt* 6 | |
| $C_1$ | 510 | [é . . . ] | [*bīt*] ⸢7⸣ | |
| $C_1$ | 511 | [é . . . ] | [*bīt* 8] | (vacat) |
| | | *Lacuna, continuing with temples of Gula and her court* | | |
| $C_3$ | 551 | [é . . . ] | [*bīt x*] | (vacat) |
| $C_3$ | 552 | [é . . . ] | [*bīt x* + 1] | (vacat) |
| $C_3$ | 553 | [é . . . ] | [*bīt x* + 2] | (vacat) |
| $C_3$ | 554 | [é.gíd.da] | [*bīt* $^{d}$*nin*]-*a-zu* | |
| $C_3$ | 555 | [é.sikil.la] | [*bīt* 2] | (vacat) |
| $C_3$ | 556 | [é . . . ] | [*bīt* 3] | (vacat) |
| $C_3$ | 557 | [é . . . ] | [*bīt* 4] | (vacat) |
| $C_3$ | 558 | [é . . . ] | [*bīt*] $^{d}$*nin-gìri-da* | |
| $A_3C_3$ | 559 | [é . . . ] | [*bī*]*t* 2 | |
| $C_3$ | 560 | [é . . . ] / [( . . . )] | [*bī*]*t* $^{d}$*la-ku-up-pi-ti* / [*šá*] *i-si-in*$^{ki}$ | |
| | | *Short lacuna* | | |
| $A_2$ | 562 | [é . . . ] | [*bīt* $^{d}$*gú-bar*]-*ra* | |
| $A_2$ | 563 | [é . . . ] | [*bīt* $^{d}$*bēlet-ṣe*]-*ri* | |
| $A_2$ | 564 | [é.mes.lam] | [*bīt* $^{d}$*nergal šá k*]*utê*(gú.du$_8$.a)$^{ki}$ | |
| $A_2$ | 565 | [é.ḫuš.ki.a] | [*bīt* $^{d}$*ḫuš*]-*ki-a* | |
| $A_2$ | 566 | [é . . . ] | [*bīt* 2] | (vacat) |
| $A_2$ | 567 | [é . . . ] | [*bīt* 3] | (vacat) |
| $A_2$ | 568 | [é . . . ] | [*bīt* 4] | (vacat) |
| $A_2$ | 569 | [é . . . ] | [*bīt* 5] | (vacat) |
| $A_2$ | 570 | [é . . . ] | [*bīt* 6] | (vacat) |
| $A_2$ | 571 | [é . . . ] | *bīt* 7 *ša a-pa-ak*$^{ki}$ | |
| $A_2$ | 572 | [é . . . ] | *bīt* $^{d}$*šu-bu-lá* | |
| $A_2$ | 573 | [é . . . ] | *bīt* $^{d}$*u*$_4$-*mi* | |
| $A_2$ | 574 | [é . . . ] | *bīt* $^{d}$*u-qur šá isin*(PA.ŠE)$^{ki}$ | |
| $A_2$ | 575 | [é . . . ] | *bīt* 2 | |
| $A_2B_1$ | 576 | é.mes.lam.ní.gùr.ru | *bīt* 3 [(38)] *šá gír-su*$^{ki}$ | |
| $A_2B_1$ | 577 | é.su.lim.$^{d}$en.líl.le | *bīt* $^{d}$*u-qur* / *šá gír-su*$^{ki}$ [(39)] | |
| $A_2B_1$ | 578 | é.me.lám.su.lim.gùr.ru | *bīt* $^{d}$*mes-lam-ta-è* | |
| $A_2B_1$ | 579 | é.su.lim./gùr.ru.e.dè / (vacat) | *bīt* ⸢$^{d}$⸣*lugal-ir*$_9$-*ra* / *u* ⸢$^{d}$⸣[*mes-lam-t*]*a-è* / ⸢*šá*⸣ [ . . . ]x$^{ki}$ | |
| $A_2B_1$ | 580 | ⸢é x x x x x⸣ | [*bīt* . . . -*n*]*a* | |
| | | *Lacuna of ten lines* | | |
| $A_2$ | 591 | [é . . . ] | [*bīt* . . . ]x | |

[38] So $A_2$, $B_1$: $^{d}$*u-qur*
[39] So $A_2$, $B_1$: *bīt* 2

| | | | | |
|---|---|---|---|---|
| A$_2$ | 592 | [é . . . ] | [*bīt* . . . ]-⸢*na*⸣ | |
| A$_2$ | 593 | [é . . . ] | [*bīt* 2] | (vacat) |
| A$_2$ | 594 | [é . . . ] | [*bīt* 3] | (vacat) |
| | | *Short lacuna* | | |
| A$_1$ | 599 | [é].an.ki.šár.⸢ra⸣ | [*bīt* . . . ] | |
| A$_1$ | 600 | [é].an.ki | [*bīt* . . . ] | |
| A$_1$ | 601 | [é.l]a$^{?}$.la | [*bīt* . . . ] | |
| A$_1$ | 602 | [é x (x) n]í.te.na | [*bīt* . . . ] | |
| A$_1$ | 603 | [é x x].an.šu./[ . . . t]i$^{?}$.⸢la$^{?}$⸣ | [*bīt* . . . ] / [*šá* . . . ] | |
| | | *Remainder, perhaps another fifty lines, lost* | | |

## *Commentary*[40]

22 The restoration of this TN is justified on the grounds that it is a well-known by-name of é.kur or a shrine within it.

24 For this, a by-name of the ziqqurrat of Nippur, in other lists see below, text nos. 4, 6; 5, 6′.

25–26 There is space for only a very short sign between [é] and bi, so me looks a good candidate, especially in view of the trace preserved in line 26.

28 Presumably this is a variant of, or a mistake for, (é).ḫur.sag.galam.ma, a name for the ziqqurrat temple of Enlil that dates back at least to Ur III times.

33 Compare ne.sag.maḫ in Proto-*Kagal* 186. Here I assume that, as elsewhere in the list, what was once a gloss (ni-sag) has been treated as if it were part of the name and written full-size. In view also of the slight miswriting of nisag, with DÉ instead of MURUB$_4$, quite possibly the name has been reinterpreted or misunderstood as é.úmun.ni.sag.maḫ.

40 The error, corrected from Proto-*Kagal* 180 and elsewhere, is excusable: in some Neo-Assyrian scripts NA and ŠU are easily confused.

42 Presumably this is a variant of é.IM.ḫur.sag, a name of the ziqqurrat of Nippur (see below, list nos. 4, 5; 5, 5′). In a late commentary, IM.ḫur.sag as a name of Enlil is glossed tu$_{15}$$^{tu}$.ḫur.sag, “mountain wind” (= $^{d}$*en-líl* = *šá-a-ri*, “wind”: Biggs, *RA* 62 [1968], p. 54, 18), and it may be that ní.te in the TN given here is owed to the misinterpretation of just such a gloss, IM$^{tu}$ or IM$^{tú}$.

43 Note that what is taken as a gloss is in fact written full-size. The suspicion is that this ceremonial name may represent a corruption of (é).du$_6$.númun.búr, a well-known sanctuary of Enlil’s temple complex.

[40] For general information on individual TNs see the gazetteer. The documentation given there is not usually repeated in the following notes.

44 The name is restored from liturgical texts, in which itima.kù is the bedchamber of Ninlil, often paired with é.gi.dim.dim (cf. line 46).

45 To judge from the space available, the sign missing between [é] and kár.kár can only have been a very short one.

46 In liturgical texts this is part of é.kur, but here the TN is evidently borne by a temple elsewhere than Nippur.

54 In Sumerian sources (é).uru.kù$^{ki}$ is well known as the location of é.tar.sír.sír of Baba, and also of é.ninnu of Ningirsu and other sanctuaries, and so there is good reason to think that it can refer to the sacred quarter of Girsu, the toponym of the preceding line. However, other early evidence associates the place Uru-ku just as much with neighboring Lagaš (see the summary of V. Crawford, *Iraq* 36 [1974], pp. 29ff.). As é.uru.kù.ga it later became the traditional home of the First Sealand Dynasty (Lambert, *JCS* 26 [1974], pp. 208ff.; but note the doubts cast by Biggs, *BiMes* 3, p. 2).

55 I read é.u.gal rather than é.umun.gal in the light of list no. 3, 42′, and Erra IV 63, where its name is é.u$_4$.gal and the city in which it is located is called Parsâ: the sign umun(U) = *bēlu, šarru*, etc., is glossed ú as well as u-mun and ú-mu-un (*MSL* XIV, p. 253, *Ea* II 153; p. 280, *A* II/4 17; p. 282, *A* II/4 74). Current opinion assumes Parsâ to be the name of the older settlement rebuilt as Dūr-Kurigalzu (see the references cited below in the note on list no. 3, 42′). If so, then é.u$_4$.gal is probably also an older coinage and the orthography é.u(mun).gal used by Kurigalzu can be viewed as a secondary interpretation (so already Moran, *OrNS* 29 [1960], p. 104, who also wondered whether the deity of é.u$_4$.gal was thus originally Adad, whom the TN suits especially well, and not Enlil).

57 This is the well-known sanctuary of Ninlil in é.kur. In lists it appears in Proto-*Kagal* 188–88a and the Nippur Temple List 2′–10′.

58 é.mi.tum.ma.al is restored after the standard litany of temples of the gods of Nippur, where it falls between é.nam.ti.la and (šà).é.dìm.ma. The spacing of the signs in the line militates against reading simply [é.tum].⌜ma.al⌝, as is found, for example, in the Sumerian Temple Hymns 46. I understand é.mi in this TN as representing ama$_5$/áme (GÁ×SAL) = *maštaku*, following Krecher, *Kultlyrik*, p. 111 (who notes Falkenstein's interpretation of another phonetic writing, á.mi, in the cylinders of Gudea as standing for ᵓà(É).mí).

59–60 These are the shrines already listed for Enlil in lines 25 and 37.

61 The cella of é.ki.ùr is restored here. In lists it also appears in Proto-*Kagal* 183.

62 The restoration is certain from inscriptions of Kurigalzu.

63 Cf. line 389, where a temple of this name is listed for Ištar in Guabba. Elsewhere Sud becomes simply a name of Ninlil (e.g., *An* I: *CT* 24 5, 9 // 22, 109), but here she is evidently treated as an independent figure.

64 The ceremonial name is restored from the lament to Sud and an inscription of Enlil-bāni (see the gazetteer).

65 The temple's name is restored from a late cultic text which lists the divine residents of this temple and two temples of Gula, é.ùru.sag.gá and é.gal.maḫ (Nougayrol, *RA* 41 [1947], pp. 33–38, AO 17662). There the first two residents of é.ki.ág.gá.šu.$du_7$ are Enlil and Šuzianna, and these will be the principal occupants of the sanctuary. As Nougayrol observed, "la présence d'un lit (l. 2) indique plutôt que l'Ekiaggašudu était une chambre nuptiale d'Enlil" (p. 33[3]), but evidently it was Enlil's junior wife, not Ninlil, who welcomed him within. According to the Sumerian Temple Hymns 77, the name of Šuzianna's temple was é.gá.$du_7$.da, of which it appears that é.ki.ág.gá.šu.$du_7$ is a later expansion. In the light of this an alternative restoration in the present line might be [é.gá.$du_7$].⌜$du_7$⌝, which would be closer to the older name. This suggestion relies on a comparison with the name of the ziqqurrat of Marad (text no. 4, 17; cf. no. 5, 20′), which demonstrates that in at least one ceremonial name gá.$du_7$.$du_7$, though obscure of meaning, is a known combination of elements.

66–67 The restorations in these lines are taken from the hymn to Šuzianna's cult-center in the Sumerian Temple Hymns, where $du_6$.sag.dil (lines 81, 85) is an epithet of é.gá.$du_7$.da, and gá.gi.maḫ (line 86) is its location.

70–88 This lacuna is likely to have dealt with temples of Dagān and Išḫara, who in *An* I are the major deities falling between Šuzianna and Enlil's son Ninurta. The deity with at least six temples, listed in lines 88–93, will then be Ninurta himself. No temples are listed at this point for his wife, Gula as Ungal-Nibru, no doubt because she is treated to her own section later in the text (lines 504ff.).

94 Nissaba's presence is expected somewhere in this section of the list. The position given her in *An* I, between Sadarnunna and Ninimma (*CT* 24 9, 31 // 23, 15), is denied her here (line 108 is occupied by Girra), so plainly the temple list differed from the Great God List in her placement. Her restoration at this point is encouraged by another god list, An = *Anu ša amēli*, which, in equating her with her lesser-known consort Ḫaya, gives her the very epithet found in this line (*CT* 24 41, 87: $^{d}$*ḫa-a-a* = $^{d}$*nissaba šá maš-re-e*, "N. of riches").

103–4 The restoration here of Enlil's vizier Nuska relies on his well-known association with these two temple names (but only é.me.lám.ḫuš is listed in Proto-*Kagal*, line 191; é.me.lám.an.na in line 218b of that text is unlikely to be his). Both are used of his sanctuary at Nippur, while é.me.lám.an.na is also the name given to Nuska's temple at Ḫarrān, as rebuilt by Aššurbanipal (see the gazetteer).

105 The TN calls to mind a problematical ceremonial name in a šu.íl.lá prayer to Nuska, in which his inner sanctum (*kummu*) appears to be entitled [é?].$ša_6$.$^{d}$en.líl.lá in one manuscript (*KAR* 58, rev. 26) but 'x + ŠU'.$^{d}$en.líl in

another (von Weiher, *Uruk* II 9, obv. 23). The sign ʻx + ŠUʼ in the latter was read as $u_5$ by Mayer (*Gebetsbeschwörungen*, p. 487, apparatus 26), as *ti*[?]*-šu* by von Weiher (*Uruk* II, p. 56, with the comment "das erste Zeichen wie AN + U geschrieben"); one could also read AN.KISAL. It does not seem possible to decipher this satisfactorily, nor to reconcile the two sources. If é.šu.-$^{d}$en.líl.le, which is not attested outside CTL, does derive from the TN of the šu.íl.lá, it gives us the reassurance that at least one ancient scholar found the name passed down in the tradition equally impenetrable. Whatever the truth of this, the list attributes this and the following temple not to Nuska, nor even to his consort Sadarnunna, who follows in line 107, but to some other deity, whose name is unfortunately lost. A deity intruding in this way on Nuska and Sadarnunna is quite unexpected. The only solution that occurs to me is that the list's compiler has followed a god list so assiduously that he has inadvertently interpreted a secondary name of Nuska, or even Sadarnunna, as an independent figure.

107 Compare the name of Sadarnunna's processional barge, [$^{giš}$má.pàd.da].nu.nus = *eleppi* $^{d}$*sa-dàr-nun-na* (*MSL* V, p. 178, *Hh* IV 319c).

108 No doubt this is the same temple as that listed for Nuska in line 104: as fire, Girra is an agent of Nuska (cf. the boundary stone of Nazi-Maruttaš, *MDP* 2, p. 90, iv 18–19: $^{d}$*gìra ez-zu šip-ru ša* $^{d}$*nuska*), and follows him and Sadarnunna in the Weidner god list (see now Cavigneaux, *Textes scolaires*, p. 82, 7).

109 Note $^{d}$me.kìlib.šu.$du_7$ as a name of Ninimma, who is Enlil's scribe, in *An* I (*CT* 24 10, 4).

111 é.rab.ri.ri is here the temple of Enlil's chamberlain (gu.za.lá), just as at Babylon it is the temple of Madānu, who acted in the same capacity for Marduk (see *Topog. Texts*, commentary on *Tintir* IV 4).

113 The temple name, as often, incorporates the function of its occupant: for Kusu as the sánga.maḫ of Enlil see the references collected in *CAD* Š/1, s.v. *šangammāḫu*.

116–19 The restoration of these deities of Enlil's court relies on the last column of *An* I (*CT* 24 10f., K 4333 iv and dupls.). Ninimma, Ennugi, Kusu, and Enlil's butcher Ninšar having already appeared here in the order observed in the god list, it is fair to restore the traces of further divine names from the same source. Ninkasi is the brewer of E-kur, her daughter Ninmada is Enlil's snake-charmer as well as Anu's (*MSL* IV, p. 5, Emesal Voc. I 29), and Ugelamma appears as one of three attendants of the lock (*ša šigari*). The repetition of Ninkasi's name in full when MIN would normally be expected indicates that at some time in the tradition of copying col. ii began at line 117.

152–78 On this section, which begins with the last few entries for Bēlet-ilī and continues with her consort Šulpae, their children and their servants, see the discussion of Moran, *Kramer AV*, pp. 336ff.

163 The trace of the name of Šulpae's tenth temple could also be of UD. Of the known temple names associated with this god only two are compatible with this trace, namely èš.nam.UD and é.zi.ba.na. They are attested together in a liturgical text (Cohen, *Lamentations*, p. 733, 59–60).

165 The restoration is a guess: ur.sag is an attribute of Panigingarra in the preceding line. The resulting TN is of course also famously borne by Zababa's temple at Kiš (line 479).

167 Possibly the ceremonial name represents a corruption of é.nìgin.gar.ra, the eponymous temple of Panigingarra. In support of this derivation is the OB forerunner of *Hh* XXI, where é.nìgin.gar.ra and é.mes appear together (*MSL* XI, p. 142, vii 33–34): in our list é.mes follows in the line after next. The phrases ní.gùr.ru and nìgin.gar.ra are easier to confuse than they look, for syllabic writings show that the latter, as a temple name also used of Ištar's temple at Šuruppak (CTL 356), can be contracted to ni$_{9}$(nig$_{6}$).gar.ra (see Sjöberg, *TCS* III, pp. 92f.). The divine name Panigingarra can contract in the same way of course, as witnessed by the OB orthography $^{d}$*pa-an-ni-gá-ra* (*TCL* XVIII 89, 17; PN).

170 The gloss uš-šu on usu(Á.KAL) is also found in *MSL* XII, p. 110, *Lu* Excerpt II 213. As noted by Moran, *Kramer AV*, p. 337, the placement of Utaulu, a name of Ninurta, among the four children of the Mother Goddess disagrees with *An* II and presumably represents an intrusion.

173–75 Cf. the shrine list of E-sagil, *Tintir* II 6′–7′: [é].gi$_{6}$.pàr = *šubat* $^{d}$⌜*e*⌝-[*ni* . . . ], [é].lú.maḫ = *šubat* $^{d}$*l*[*ú-maḫ-ḫi* . . . ].

177 $^{d}$TU is possibly a relic of third millennium practice, a short form of the birth goddess Nintu (cf. Lambert in L. Cagni [ed.], *Il bilinguismo a Ebla*, p. 398).

178 For the divine midwife Lalašaga, see Moran, loc. cit., and also Lambert, *JAOS* 103 (1983), p. 65.

179–80 The restoration of the twin names of Ea's venerable cult-center needs no justification, but their order is not necessarily fixed. The name é.abzu is placed first on the grounds that it appears alone in list no. 2 (at least as I read the trace in line 4) and so evidently took precedence in the later period.

183 The temple name is restored tentatively in Emesal after the traditional etymology Eridu > uru.du$_{10}$(g).

184 é.u$_{6}$.nir is the ziqqurrat of Eridu (e.g., as listed below, nos. 4, 21; 5, 19′).

185 For this as a by-name of Apsû and as a temple at Eridu and Babylon see George, *Iraq* 48 (1986), p. 136, and the gazetteer.

186 The restoration supposes that this temple name is parallel to what might be seen as a learned secondary interpretation of the well-known name of Ea, $^{d}$nin.ši.kù < *niššīku*, i.e., $^{d}$nin.igi.kù (cf. Moran, *JCS* 31 [1979], p. 94).

187 làl.gar is another name for Ea's cosmic domain (= *apsû*): many references are collected in *CAD* L, p. 47; see also Lambert, *AfO* 17 (1954–56), p. 319. For the variant làl.ḫar see Civil, *Studies Oppenheim*, pp. 69, 5.7; 74f.; *RA* 60 (1966), p. 92, corrected by Lambert; also Enki and Eridu 38, quoted by Sjöberg, *AfO* 24 (1973), p. 45.

188 Temples of this name are elsewhere attributed to Ninšešegarra at Badtibira and Nanše at Girsu (see the gazetteer).

189 šeg$_9$.bar is yet another name of Apsû: see *MSL* XIV, p. 195, *Ea* I 368: $^{\text{še-en-bar}}$šeg$_9$ *ša* šeg$_9$.bar = *ap-su-u*, and the bilingual citations collected in *CAD* A/2, p. 194).

191 With the temple name as restored cf. gal.an.zu = *eršu*, "sagacious," as epithets typical of Ea (e.g., in the Sum. hymn *CT* 36 31, 3; Akk. references collected in *CAD* E, p. 314).

193 The restoration is again based on a synonym for Ea's cosmic abode: see *MSL* XIV, p. 142, 18: $^{\text{ḫal-an-kù}}$HAL = *ap-su-ú-um*, and ḫal.an.kù (var. ḫal.la.kù) = *ḫa-(al)-la-an-ku* as a by-name of Apsû in Nissaba and Enki 42 (Hallo, *CRRA* 17, p. 125; cf. p. 132). Note also $^{\text{d}}$ḫal.la.an.kù as a name of Ea, and also of Damkina, in *An* II: Edzard, *RlA* IV, p. 60. A shrine of Ea in E-sagil at Babylon, é.ḫal.an.ki (*Tintir* II 20), is presumably a corruption of this TN.

197 The traces of the toponym are as copied, but given the state of the surface of Ms A$_2$ at this point, which is smooth but abraded, ŠEŠ looks a good candidate for restoration. Such a reading is supported by evidence from the reign of Rīm-Sîn I of Larsa: an inscription of his records the building of an é.géštu.šu.du$_7$ for Enki, while the name of his eighth year commemorates a temple of Enki at Ur (for documentation see the gazetteer).

198 The name is an obvious restoration, but for confirmation note its presence concluding the section on Ea's temples in Proto-*Kagal* 175 and among sanctuaries of Ea in a litany (gazetteer).

199 An unnamed temple of Enki at Uruk was built by Sîn-kāšid, whose inscription refers to this work in the following phrases: u$_4$ é.an.na mu.dù.a géštu nì.maḫ.a mu.na.ni.in.sum.ma ki.tuš kù ki.ág.gá.ni mu.na.dù, "when he had built E-anna and (Enki) had given him wisdom of great power, he built for him his beloved sacred abode" (Frayne, *RIME* 4, p. 456, 8–12). The fragmentary ceremonial name given here strikes me as suspiciously reminiscent of Sîn-kāšid's words, and on this account the possibility arises that it was indeed ultimately derived from that very passage (or that Sîn-kāšid's phrasing alluded to an already existing name which was for some reason not quoted itself). Hence one might prefer to restore our entry as [é.géštu.ní].maḫ.[ . . . su]m.mu. The sole element then missing cannot be extracted from Sîn-kāšid's words, however, and would have to have been invented freely (e.g., kalam.ma or the like: cf. the parallel name in line 196).

200 According to the remains of the toponym this will be Ea's sanctuary at Larsa, at Adab, or at Sippar. A temple of Ea known to end in the sign DA is

é.me.zi.da, which is listed in Proto-*Kagal* 174 alongside é.ad.$gi_4$.$gi_4$ (cf. line 198) and was rebuilt by Enlil-bāni of Isin (year i). This king cannot have operated in Larsa, and Sippar was also rather outside his dominion, but it is conceivable that Adab may have lain within Enlil-bāni's authority, and so tentatively é.me.zi.da is restored here.

201 The sign-group ŠÁR×GAL.MIN is attested as a very high number ($60^3$ or $60^4 \times 2$: *ŠL* no. 408). The only comparable toponym known to me is pre-Sargonic ŠÁR×DIŠ($^{ki}$), a part of Umma or town in its vicinity (Steible, *FAOS* 5/ II, pp. 265f.; Lambert, *JNES* 49 [1990], p. 78). Of course, there is no certainty that ŠÁR×GAL.MIN has to be a toponym, and its significance remains highly obscure.

202 Nēmed-Laguda is also known as a cult-center of Ea from a NB royal letter in which concern is expressed as to whether a seal belongs to Ea of Eridu or of Nēmed-Laguda (Sidney Smith, *JRAS* 1926, p. 443, 14–15). Like Ea's principal cult-center Eridu, Nēmed-Laguda is a town given freedom by Sargon II (Weissbach, *ZDMG* 72 [1918], p. 176, 4; cf. Winckler, *Sargon* I, p. 96, 9; p. 174, 16) and situated in the territory of Bīt-Yakīn (Luckenbill, *OIP* 2, p. 53, 48; for further references to the place see Zadok, *Rép. géogr.* VIII, p. 237). The god Laguda is associated with Tilmun and the Gulf (see Lambert, *RlA* VI, pp. 430f.), and this would substantiate the location in the deep south of Sumer of the town named as his seat.

225 The traces do not permit a restoration é.$u_4$.u[l], and so the section on Marduk is presumed not to start until line 226. This and the preceding lines should then list sanctuaries of Ea's consort, Damkina.

227 The emendation is based on *Tintir* II 19, which lists a shrine by the name of é.a.ra.zu.giš.tuku.$^{d}$asal.lú.ḫi in E-sagil.

232 The temple is also listed in text no. 3, 19′. Cf. zi.sù.ud.gál as an epithet of Asaralimnunna-Marduk in a bilingual hymn (*STC* I, p. 180, 4′–5′, = *na-din na-p*[*iš-ti ruq-ti*]).

233 Cf. $^{d}$nam.ti.la as the second name of Marduk in the aspect of Asalluḫi in the Creation Epic (*Enūma eliš* VI 151) and *An* II (*CT* 24 15, 65 // 27, 24).

234 The TN is obscure and may be an orthographic mistake for an otherwise unknown *é.suḫuš.gi.na.

235 The occupant of é.dàra.an.na is now confirmed as Marduk's consort—who is, of course, the very deity expected between Marduk and Nabû—by other lists: see *Topog. Texts* nos. 6, 7; 39, rev. 1.

239 While this is most probably the same temple as the é.KÉŠDA.sag.ús.sa of Nabû which appears in the standard litanies of temples in liturgical texts (where it always follows the ziqqurrat é.$ur_4$.me.imin.an.ki), the traces here suggest a variant form of the name. Read é.k[éš$^{!?}$.d]a.ús.sa?

240 Restored from *Tintir* IV 12 where it is a sanctuary in Babylon, though one cannot discount the alternative reading é.[$ur_4$.m]e.⟨imin⟩.an.ki = *bīt* 5 *šá* [3], i.e., the ziqqurrat of Borsippa.

241 Perhaps é.[šu.nigin.ḫ]é.du$_7$, which would be a variant of é.šu.nigin.šu.du$_7$, a temple name associated with Nabû at Aššur and probably elsewhere (see the gazetteer).

242 The position of the firing hole makes it unlikely that any sign is missing between É and MUL.

243 Given the temple's name, "House of the River Ordeal," the restoration of the river god Id as its occupant is obvious (compare his position, immediately following the section on Marduk's court, in *An* II, where $^{d}$íd.lú.ru.gú is the last of his four names: *CT* 24 16, 23–26 // 28, 77–78). Note also the name of his processional barge, $^{giš}$má.íd.lú.ru.gú = *eleppi* $^{d}$íd (*MSL* V, p. 176, *Hh* IV 305).

245–69 After the river god we might expect one or two minor figures from the divine court of Eridu and Babylon. However, two of the more important deities listed hereabouts in *An* II, Amurru and Girra, occupy different positions in our list, at lines 108 and 472–73 and cannot be considered candidates for restoration in this lacuna. Quite possibly the list moved on directly to Sîn. If it is right to restore Ningal and Ningublag in lines 273–79, then his temples, which would certainly have been many in number, are still being enumerated when the text resumes.

271 If the reading is correct, it confirms my suspicion that the entries in lines 270–72 are temples of Sîn, for é.gissu.bi.du$_{10}$.ga is the name of his cult-center at Damru, a town near Babylon (see the gazetteer).

273–75 The attribution of all three temples to Sîn's wife Ningal assumes that é.gán.nun.kù is a variant of ʻGÁʼ.NUN.kù, her well-known sanctuary at Ur (see the gazetteer sub é.gar$_6$.kù).

276–79 As the son of Sîn and Ningal, Ningublag occupies a position immediately after them in *An* III (von Weiher, *Uruk* III 107, 27) and so is expected here. This placement is confirmed by the TNs: the first of the four temples is evidently a corruption of é.gu$_4$.du$_7$(UL).šár(ḪE), Ningublag's cult-center in Kiabrig (Sumerian Temple Hymns 147). Since Ningublag's wife is $^{d}$nin.é.ì.gára/gara$_{10}$ (see Lambert, *Mélanges Birot*, p. 183, 97–98, and note on p. 188), the third TN, é.ga.ra.ni, is certainly to be seen as deriving from é.ì.gára/gara$_{10}$, presumably through a carelessly read gloss GA$^{ga\text{-}ra}$NI (or similar). One can safely assume that the temples of Ningublag continue at least as far as é.báḫar, noting $^{d}$lugal.báḫar as a name of his in *An* III 31. Whether é.bur.sa$_7$.sa$_7$ also belonged to Ningublag, to Nin-Eigara or to another god of Sîn's court, such as his vizier Alammuš, cannot be determined at present.

281–82 It is proposed that as a cult-center of Šamaš the more ancient city of Sippar takes precedence over Larsa, a tradition attested in temple list no. 2.

284 The orthography é.di.ku$_5$.dá(TA) is also known from an inscription of Ammī-ṣaduqa, where it varies with é.di.ku$_5$.da as the rendering of the temple name in the phrases lugal/$^{d}$utu é-dikud-a(k) (Frayne, *RIME* 4, pp. 428f., 4.25). There the genitive is not part of the ceremonial name, and the orthog-

raphy of the present text, and of a lament which uses the same spelling, is thus seen to derive from a misunderstanding of the sign TA in the inscription of Ammī-ṣaduqa—or in some other source which utilized the same writing. The implication of this is that the compiler of the temple list utilized documentary sources in putting together his text, and that among these sources would have been copies of royal inscriptions of bygone ages.

289 Given the character of Šamaš the ceremonial name listed here may well be a corruption of the much more suitable *é.nu.gál.an.na, "House of the Light of Heaven" (where nu.gál would be a variation of $nu_{11}$.gal = *nūru*, as in the TNs of Sîn, é.giš.$nu_{11}$.gal and é.kiš.nu.gál; cf. also é.$nu_{11}$.gal.an.na of Ištar in line 387).

292 The deity sandwiched between Šamaš and his consort Aya can hardly be other than his vizier Bunene, who shared with them the great tripartite cult-center of Sippar, and in fact he appears in a *lipšur*-litany as [$^{d}$*bu*]-*n*[*e-ne*] . . . *a-šib* é.tukur.re (Nougayrol, *JCS* 1 [1947], p. 330, 3′ = Wiseman, *Iraq* 31 [1969], p. 176, 14). The sanctuary of Bunene at Sippar was known to Nabonidus as é.kur.ra (see the gazetteer, ad loc.), which in the light of the present entry might thus have to be emended to é.⟨tu⟩.kur.ra. Note also $^{d}$tu.$^{kur}$$kur_4$ as a name of Šamaš (*An* III: von Weiher, *Uruk* III 107, 100 // *CT* 25 25, 16).

294 Panunna is another vizier of Šamaš, paired with Bunene in god lists (*An* III: *CT* 24 31, 77–78 // von Weiher, *Uruk* III 107, 129–30; Cavigneaux, *Textes scolaires*, p. 84, 32–33).

295 The restoration of IM$^{ki}$ in the reading *karkara* relies on the syncretistic hymn to Nanāy (Reiner, *JNES* 33 [1974], p. 227, 37: *ina bīt kar-ka-ra ina* é.$u_4$.gal.gal . . . ). On Karkara see Renger, *AfO* 23 (1970), pp. 73–78; Edzard, *RlA* V, p. 64.

297 The temple name is probably a variant of é.úg.gal.gim, a name or epithet of Iškur's temple at Karkara in the Sumerian Temple Hymns (line 328; var. é.$u_6$.gal.gim).

309–12 Temples of Adad and his entourage are concluded in these lines, continuing a theme which must have begun in the break with é.nam.ḫé, his temple at Babylon (*Tintir* IV 40, etc.). For references in Sumerian literature to the idiom ní su.zi bar, as restored in the temple name of line 312, see *PSD* B, p. 111, 4.3; a reading ní su.zi r[i.a] looks less convincing on the tablet.

313–14 é.an.na is the name given to shrines of Ištar at Lagaš and Girsu, as well as to the great cult-center of Uruk, but since the other five temples of lines 313–18 are all certainly sanctuaries of Uruk, we are not expecting the intrusion of another toponym at line 314. Accordingly the two entries of lines 313–14 will probably refer to the same temple. It is significant that the list does not begin to count in sequence the temples of the great goddess in her name Ištar until line 324, which implies that one cannot restore $^{d}$*ištar*(inanna) as early as line 313. Thus I have turned to her local names instead (noting the example of line 319), and since there are two of these that are appropriate to Ištar of Uruk, the presence of the twin entries for é.an.na becomes more easily explained. Other temples are listed twice in our list, e.g., é.kur.igi.gál and é.sikil.la, but this is the only occasion on which two such entries are paired. For another example of a deity listed under different names in consecutive lines, see my partial restoration of lines 564–65.

316–18 With these temples compare three of the names of Uruk, as given in the geographical list II *R* 50 (*MSL* XI, p. 54, 17–19): [ub].imin$^{ki}$, [d]a.imin$^{ki}$, [gi$_6$].pàr.imin$^{ki}$ = *ú-ru-uk* (cf. also *MSL* XI, p. 63, 10′–12′; Kilmer, *JAOS* 83 [1963], p. 428, *Malku* I 213–15). The last-named is the ziqqurrat of E-anna (see below, texts nos. 4, 20; 5, 18′).

319 Only a short sign is missing, so disallowing a reading [é.kalam.ta].ní.gùr.ru, although this is the name given to a temple of Ištar of Zabalam by Warad-Sîn and is in fact listed as such later on (line 400). Nevertheless, if the right-hand column is correctly restored as Supalītum, Ištar's title at Zabalam—and though by way of caution it must be remarked that the trace of *pa* is not quite as expected, the restoration is supported by the presence in line 322 of é.gi.gun$_4$.na, the name given to the temple of Ištar at Zabalam in Inanna's Descent and the éš.dam hymns (Wilcke, *RlA* V, p. 78), and also elsewhere—then presumably the present entry preserves a variant form or corruption of é.kalam.ta.ní.gùr.ru. With the proposed restoration compare the use, by Ur-Nammu and later builders, of the same temple name for the ziqqurrat of Ur, but note also the alternative offered in line 379.

320–27 In the sole source for this part of the list (B$_2$) the second sub-column is distinctly out of step with the first: my edition assumes that the lines step down rather than up as they cross the central margin. The TNs é.sù.sù.gar.ra and é.gi.gun$_4$.na are also found together in the Uruk Shrine List, where they are probably parts of the é.an.na temple complex (*Topog. Texts* no. 25, obv. 2′–3′). Another é.sù.sù.gar.ra is listed for Ištar in line 364.

322 With Ištar as Supalītum of Muru compare perhaps $^{d}$inanna-mu.ur$_5^{ki}$ (Frayne, *RIME* 4, p. 59, 1–2: Lipit-Ištar), though at that time her temple was known as é.mar.uru$_5$ (line 13). Otherwise Muru, near Bad-tibira, is known as a cult-center of the archaic divine exorcist, Ningirim (Sumerian Temple Hymn no. 19) and later of Ninkilim and his wife $^{d}$nin.mùru(IM)$^{mu\text{-}ru.ki}$ (*An* V: *CT* 25 1, 2–7; note also that in II *R* 60, no. 1 = *TuL* no. 2, i 22–3, a text whose organization is suspect, Ninkilim and IM$^{ki}$ appear at one line's remove: $^{d}$*ma-ga-ri-da* = *šarru ša* IM$^{ki}$, $^{d}$*nin-kilim* = *šarru ša di-nik-ti*$^{ki}$).

324 é.galga.sù is well known as the name of sanctuaries of Baba, in é.tar.sír.sír at Girsu (Proto-*Kagal* 204, etc.), and at Kiš (cf. below, lines 491–92), but, as the consort of Zababa, Baba is usually seen as an aspect of Gula rather than as an Ištar figure. The restoration of the temple name in this line assumes that the ancient compiler would have found the use in the second column of the same phrase galga.sù to express *malkatu*, "queen," the title of Ištar, ample justification for the attribution of Baba's temple to Ištar.

339–40 The two names of Ištar's sanctuary at Nippur are also paired in the Old Babylonian lists (Proto-*Kagal* 232–33; *MSL* XI, p. 142, vii 15–16). é.bára.dúr. gar.ra also appears in the Enlil section of the present list (line 38).

341 The restoration of this TN is the proposal of M. W. Green, *Eridu in Sumerian Literature* (unpub. Ph.D., Chicago, 1975), p. 210, quoting Inanna D 63f.: é.kù.nun.na úru.zé.eb$^{ki}$.ba.za . . . dúr.zu bí.in.gar, "you took up residence in your é.TN of Eridu." kù.nun.na is an epithet of Inanna used by Ur-Baba of Lagaš with reference to her temple at URU×KÁR$^{ki}$ (Steible, *FAOS* 9/I, UrB 1, iv 8; 8, iii 1), and also by Ur-Nammu in inscriptions found at Ur (Steible, *FAOS* 9/II, UrN 6, 2; 17, 2 var.; unidentified ruler: Ur 24, 1). The latter usage, at least, is probably the result of the removal to Ur of cults of Eridu (on this see Charpin, *Le clergé d'Ur*, pp. 415 ff.).

342 The name of Ištar's temple at Adab is restored from Inanna's Descent and the éš.dam hymns (see Sjöberg, *TCS* III, p. 120). In the OB list *MSL* XI, p. 142, vii 17, é.sar.ra follows é.dur.an.ki and é.bára.dúr.gar.ra. The temple in Eridu in line 341 of our list thus represents an intrusion into an established sequence. The silence of Inanna's Descent and the éš.dam hymns with respect to a temple of Ištar at Eridu suggests that this intrusion is late, even though the temple would be old.

343 The name of Ištar's sanctuary in Ur is given thus in Inanna's Descent and the éš.dam hymns and in an inscription of Warad-Sîn (see the gazetteer).

344 Ištar's temple at Isin is known thus in Inanna's Descent and the éš.dam hymns.

346 The restoration follows Inanna's Descent and an éš.dam hymn. To Sîn-kāšid and Rīm-Sîn the goddess of the temple was known as Nanāy.

348 The name is borne in éš.dam hymns by Ištar's temple at Larsa, but as with é.šà.ḫúl.la the goddess is manifested there as Nanāy (cf. below, line 435).

354 This temple, well known from Inanna's Descent and the éš.dam hymns, also finds a place in list no. 3, 38′.

356 The restoration of the geographical name is assured: not only does é.šúruppak appear in the following line, but é.nìgin.gar.(kù) is in any case well attested as Ištar's temple in the city (Inanna's Descent and the éš.dam hymns).

360 This cult-center of Ištar is also known from an OB document, Grant, *Smith College* 271, 15: $^{d}$inanna nin su$_{11}$.lum.ma $^{uru}$*na-ap-sa-nu*$^{ki}$, "Ištar, Lady of (E)-sulumma at Napsanu." Though it may be just possible that [nin] should be squeezed in after the toponym in the present text, I prefer to presume that the place name is followed simply by su$_{11}$.lum.ma, which qualifies it by means of its temple: "Napsanu of (E)-sulumma."

362 For Ištar's famous cult-center at Akkade in other lists see text no. 3, 31′; Proto-*Kagal* 231; and the OB forerunner to *Hh* XXI, *MSL* XI, p. 142, vii 30.

366–67 The section on Kiš omits é.kur.ní.zu, the name of the temple at Ḫursag-kalamma in the first millennium. Though $^{d}$nin.líl (i.e., Mulliltu) is given as the name of the goddess of this temple in Merodach-baladan's brick and elsewhere (cf. list no. 6, 12), even so it seems unlikely, given the age-old association of the cult-center at Ḫursag-kalamma with Ištar, that it could have been ignored as a temple of Ištar, especially since it has no place in the section on Ninlil (57–62). The silence of CTL in this regard can thus be taken as a clue to the age of the text, which, as argued above, is likely to have been late Kassite.

370 é.ur$_5$.šà.ba is another temple where Ištar is better known as Nanāy. See also the é.ur$_5$.šà.ba of Lisi (line 172).

374 This is not a TN usually associated with Ištar, but note the mention of a du$_6$.kù at Raqnana in the Syncretistic Ištar Hymn (*KAR* 109, rev. 5).

377 The restoration of the toponym as the location of é.sukud.da and, in the next line, é.an.ki relies on the cultic calendar *BRM* IV 25, where the goddess of é.an.ki resides in Kār-Bēl-mātāti (line 24): see the note on text no. 3, 23′, which also lists a temple of Ištar in this town, though the TN is there somewhat expanded. The cultic association of the great goddess with Kār-Bēl-mātāti is confirmed by the Divine Love Lyrics, in which Marduk reports a journey of his lover, Ištar of E-tur-kalamma, to that town (Lambert, *Love Lyrics*, p. 120, 10.13; on Kār-Bēl-mātāti, a satellite of Babylon, see further Röllig, *RlA* V, pp. 422f.).

381 One might propose emendation of the TN to é.šaga.ér.ra, a name also borne by the chapel of Iqbi-damiq in the temple of Bēlet-ekalli at Aššur (Götteradreßbuch 167), but compare text no. 3, 25′.

383 The emendation follows the listing of Ištar's sanctuary in Girsu under this name in the éš.dam hymns.

385 After the number 62 the tablet has traces of an erased *šá*.

386 BÀD.AN$^{ki}$ is here certainly not Dēr but either Dūrum or Kissig. Falkenstein's proposal, that Dūrum(BÀD.(AN)$^{ki}$) and Kissig(EZEN×KÙ$^{ki}$) were one and the same place, is seen as less likely nowadays: Dūrum is to be sought near Uruk, Kissig in the Sealand, in the deep south (see the discussions of Michalowski, *Mesopotamia* 12 [1977], pp. 84ff., and Röllig, *RlA* V, pp. 620f.; some of their points are repeated here). With regard to the TN, in Inanna's Descent and three éš.dam hymns amaš.kù.(ga) is Ištar's sanctuary at Kissig (written respectively EZEN[×x?]$^{ki}$ // EZEN×KÙ$^{ki}$ (2 Mss) // [ki-s]i-ka), while an é.amaš.kù.ga of Ningal was rebuilt by Nabonidus at a place EZEN×X$^{ki}$ according to a foundation cylinder excavated in the later of the two mounds at Tell al-Lahm (Saggs, *Sumer* 13 [1957], p. 191, i 36–39; on the site, some miles southeast of Eridu and Ur, which comprised an older mound exhibiting traces of settlement from the ED to Kassite periods and a later mound occupied in NA, NB, and Persian times, see now P. P. Vértesalji, *RlA* VI, pp. 431f.). This toponym was read BÀD$^{ki}$ by Saggs and all since, with the result that Tell al-Lahm has often been identified with Dūrum (e.g., Edzard and Farber, *Rép. géogr.* II, p. 36). However, as copied (Saggs, loc. cit., pl. 2, 39) the sign inscribed inside EZEN is certainly not BAD, but more like BAR, comprising a

vertical wedge with a slightly oblique horizontal wedge at its foot. These wedges are very probably vestiges of KÙ (right shape, some vertical wedges lacking or not seen). Even though Kissig had earlier been a cult-center of Dumuzi (as in the Lamentation over Sumer and Ur 263ff., 279) as well as of Ištar, Sîn and Ningal are confirmed as patron deities of the town in the late period by their place in the greetings formulas of letters of the citizens of Kissig to Aššurbanipal (*ABL* 210, 3.5; 736, 3.5; note also a man of Kissig as *šatammu* of Ningal: 1000, 19). It is therefore likely that EZEN×X$^{ki}$ in Nabonidus's inscription is Kissig whatever the inscribed sign, and this is another reason for identifying Kissig with modern Tell al-Lahm, as first proposed by Jacobsen (*Iraq* 22 [1960], p. 183).

Though the temple is here listed as belonging to Ištar, repeating the claims of Inanna's Descent and the éš.dam hymns, this entry in CTL is probably based on knowledge of that very tradition. Not all the cult-centers claimed by Inanna in that tradition are exclusively hers (e.g., é.babbar.ra of Šamaš at Sippar, and é.sìrara of Nanše at "Nina"), and thus the attribution of the temple to Ištar is not seen as fatal to its identification with the one dedicated to her mother Ningal by Nabonidus (though its site must have been moved from the older mound to the later in the course of the town's revival in the early first millennium). Accordingly it would seem that BÀD.AN$^{ki}$ is on this occasion Kissig rather than Dūrum. This might simply be an isolated corruption, resulting from the similarity of BÀD and EZEN×KÙ, in which a rare toponym is supplanted by a better-known one, but note that the opposite confusion also occurs, with EZEN×KÙ$^{ki}$ clearly written when Dūrum is required (in a hymn of Ibbi-Suen: Michalowski, loc. cit., p. 86). I am inclined to suspect with Michalowski that there was a history of ancient confusion of the two toponyms.

387 The missing *šá*, omitted by haplography in Ms $A_2$, was also left out by the poorly preserved Ms $C_1$, to judge from the space available.

388 While the entry of é.igi.du$_8$.a under Kutha may be legitimate one is struck by the similarity between the temple name and the toponym. The defective writing of the toponym is also suspicious. According to the éš.dam hymns this is the name of Ištar's temple in Kullab.

390 The temple shares its name with one of Bēlet-Eanna's temples at Babylon. The place ki.bal.maš.dà$^{ki}$ = *nēber ṣabî* (*MSL* XI, p. 14, *Hh* XXI/4, 33) is a by-name of Ilip, earlier Urum (see now Charpin, *RA* 72 [1978], pp. 17f.).

392–93 The first of Ištar's Assyrian temples is otherwise unknown. It ought to be her cult-center at Aššur, but none of the names collected for that sanctuary in the Assyrian Temple List (Götteradreßbuch 164ff.) is even similar to our é.ùn.na. The second is better known as one of her most venerable cult-centers, é.maš.maš of Nineveh.

395 The toponym is restored on the assumption that this temple is the same as Ištar's é.šà.ba.an.na known from a votive inscription of Yasmaḫ-Addu found at Mari (see the gazetteer).

396 I presume that this is the sanctuary known to Šamšī-Adad I as é.me.ur$_4$.ur$_4$, apparently also at Mari (see the gazetteer sub é.TN 4).

399 The first name of Ištar's temple at Zabalam is emended after the Sumerian Temple Hymns 315 and an OB forerunner to *Hh* XXI (*MSL* XI, p. 142, vii 23).

400 The reading follows a date of Warad-Sîn, which knows the sanctuary of Ištar of Zabalam as é.kalam.ta.ní.gùr.(ru) (year 6). Cf. above, on line 319.

401 The third name of the temple of Ištar at Zabalam is restored from an inscription of Ḫammurapi (see the gazetteer).

434 This manifestation of Ištar, the planet Venus, is restored opposite é.an.da.sá.a after *Tintir* IV 23, but note also that the temple name is used of her ziqqurrat at Akkade (list no. 4, 9). Possibly the DN here should be the Sumerian name of Venus, $^{d}$nin.si$_4$.an.na.

435 é.me.ur$_4$.ur$_4$ is given a double entry in the Ištar section of one of the OB lists (*MSL* XI, p. 142, vii 27–28), which I assume to vouch for the existence at that time of two major sanctuaries of this name. One of these was certainly at Larsa (Gungunum year 16, etc.), the other probably at Uruk, though another was to be found, at least in the later periods, at Babylon (*Tintir* IV 30). In the present list the two entries are distributed between this line and line 348 (cf. also 349, 396). While in *An* IV, the OB god list *TCL* XV 10 262–66, and elsewhere, Ninsianna is regularly partnered by Kabta, there is no evidence to connect this deity with é.me.ur$_4$.ur$_4$, and so it seems unwise to restore his name in the right-hand sub-column. The occupant of é.me.ur$_4$.ur$_4$, wherever situated, seems always to have been Ištar as Queen of Larsa or Nanāy, and I choose the latter name. The order of deities is thus in agreement with the Emesal Vocabulary where, at the very end of the Ištar section, Ninzilzil = Nanāy follows Ninsianna = Ištar-kakkabi (*MSL* IV, p. 9, 89–90).

438 After Nanāy we might expect Kanisurra, who is most probably her daughter, or Gazbaba, who certainly is. The TN could be seen as exhibiting contamination with the name of the former.

439 For Ištar of the Seas see the god list *KAV* 145, rev. 3 + 73, 4: [$^{d}$]⌜inanna⌝ a.ab.ba$^{ki}$ = *ia-bi-i-*[*tu*], and the mention in an omen text of $^{d!}$*iš*$_8$-*tár* a.ab.ba-*ta* (*CT* 28 38, K 4079a, 11: *Šumma ālu*).

444–45 These sanctuaries reappear in the section on Dumuzi's sister, the goddess Belili (466–67).

449 The restoration follows the temple list of Babylon (*Tintir* IV 11). For Dumuzi "of captivity" see the commentary, *Topog. Texts*, p. 309; also Kutscher in *Bar-Ilan Studies Artzi*, p. 42.

450 This sanctuary is also listed for Dumuzi's sister Geštinanna in line 463. The TN suits his pastoral role, for níg.lu.lu, "things that proliferate," traditionally describes the teeming flocks of Dumuzi's sheepfold (see *SBH* 68, rev. 12; Alster, *Acta Sum* 14 [1992], p. 15, 147–52; *CAD* D, p. 199b). Dumuzi *ša*

*bikīti*, "of wailing," is of course the dead god famously mourned by Geštinanna and others.

459 The appended ŠA probably derives from an Akkadian context, i.e., "her é.TN": by chance this very phrase survives in an OB compendium of royal inscriptions, though with reference to the temple of Ištar of the same name (Wilcke, *Isin* III, p. 109, iv′ 7′: é.tilmun-*ša ú-ru*; cf. p. 110).

460 Elsewhere the temple name is written with $u_{18}$.ru (see the gazetteer).

464 This may be a garbling of é.sag.$ug_5$(BÀD), the name given by Enannatum I and Uruinimgina to a sanctuary of the goddess Ama-Geštin(anna) at or near Girsu (BÀD reinterpreted as *dūr* = $dur_8$?). Otherwise it will represent an orthographic corruption of *é.sag.ùb($^{ki}$), a name one may posit for her cult-center at the eponymous town near Lagaš (and of which é.sag.$ug_5$ is presumed to be a variant: see the gazetteer).

474 The name of the temple of Tišpak in Ešnunna, as restored here, is well known from, e.g., the Sumerian Temple Hymns and inscriptions of Šulgi and Bilalama (see the gazetteer).

477 Since the extant traces rule out the well-known name of Ištarān's cult-center at Dēr in the previous line, it must be restored here.

478 The god $^{d}$$KU_7$ is known from *An* VI 203–4, *Ea* IV 188–90, and *A* IV/3 173′–75′, but which of the several glosses given in these lists is to be preferred is unclear: see Lambert, *RlA* V, p. 288, s.v. Kakkala. The placing of $^{d}$$KU_7$ in this section, among gods listed in *An* V, may be the result of confusion with the orthographically similar $^{d.ni\text{-}ta}$nita = ŠU, who appears there with his wife, Kigula, between the sections on Uraš and Zababa (*CT* 25 1, 16). A place *a-ḫu-ud*$^{ki}$ occurs in an Old Babylonian letter (*CT* 2 11, 13–14), and in *Hh* XXI/7 12, among other geographical lists (*MSL* XI, p. 16, etc.), and may be the same locality as the later *a-ḫu-du*, a stronghold of Bīt-Amukkāni conquered by Sennacherib (Luckenbill, *OIP* 2, p. 53, 42).

483 The temple name is restored from a *lipšur*-litany which, immediately after Uraš, invokes $^{d}$*bēlet-ekalli . . . ina* é.sa.pàr (Nougayrol, *JCS* 1 [1947], p. 330, 19′ // Wiseman, *Iraq* 31 [1969], p. 177, 31′). At first sight it struck both Borger and myself, independently, that the traces of the divine name on the tablet appear to yield ⸢èš⸣.gal rather than ⸢é⸣.gal, but there is so little remaining of the sign in question that the transliteration refrains from introducing on such slight evidence a new spelling of the name of Uraš's consort.

484 Ningirsu and his famous cult-center at Girsu must be restored here in view of the following sections, which treat temples of his consort Baba and of other deities of the court of Lagaš and its satellites.

485 The obvious reading of the second sub-column is [*bīt* 2 *šá*] 2. Simple *bīt* 2 is always written at the left of the column, with the figure following É immediately, and if that were all the sub-column held for this line a blank space would be all that was left as the tablet now stands. But both restorations

create difficulty with the numerical notation in lines 486–90, and it must be assumed something is amiss in the tradition. Probably one should emend line 486 to [*bīt* 3 *šá*] 3, and the following lines in sequence.

491–92 The two temples of Baba restored here are paired in Proto-*Kagal* 203–4. Since they occur there between é.ninnu and é.ab.šà.ga.lá, there they are probably both the well-known sanctuaries of Girsu. For é.galga.sù of Kiš in lists see below, list no. 6, 2, and parallel, *Topog. Texts* no. 22, 4′.

498–99 The names of the sanctuaries of Ningirsu's two sons at Girsu are restored from inscriptions of Uruinimgina, where they are also paired (see the gazetteer).

501 Sirara is the name of a place rather than a deity, though it can appear with the divine determinative (e.g., Gudea Cyl. A ii 2; iii 27; *ITT* 2844, rev. 3). In view of the general context, and especially the next entry, one expects Ninmar's mother Nanše in this line. Sirara was her cult-center at the city written AB×ḪA$^{ki}$ ("Nina"), where she was considered Ningirsu's sister (on Sirara and AB×ḪA$^{ki}$ see recently Heimpel, *JCS* 33 [1981], pp. 98ff.). Here, either Sirara has become a name of Nanše herself or the text has become corrupted and we should emend the right-hand column to read *bīt* $^{d}$⟨*nanše šá*⟩ *si-ra-ra*. The temple name would then be restored as é.sìrara$^{ki}$ or similar.

502 The temple of Ninmar at Guabba is known thus in the Sumerian Temple Hymns, where it also follows Sirara (line 283); see also Proto-*Kagal* 205, following é.galga.sù. The addition of kù.ga to the divine name is curious. Possibly it is misplaced from the following line, which may once have read *bīt* 2 ⟨*šá é-uru*⟩*-kù-ga*. If so, this refers to the sacred quarter of Girsu (cf. above, on line 54), and the entry in line 503 can then be restored as é.munus.gi$_{16}$.sa, Ninmar's temple at Girsu (see the gazetteer).

504 The famous cult-center of Gula at Isin is well known in this name from royal inscriptions (e.g., CḪ ii 54), liturgical and other texts, including *An* V.

512–53 In the lacuna between Gula and Ninazu one would expect temples of Gula's entourage: her consort Pabilsag, their children Gunura and Damu, and her vizier Urmašum, at least.

554 The temple is provisionally restored from the Sumerian Temple Hymns, where é.gíd.da of Ninazu at Enegi is the subject of the fourteenth hymn. Ninazu is the first of the chthonic deities in the big god lists *TCL* XV 10 and *An* V, where, as here, he follows Gula and her court presumably because his name, "Lord Medicine-Man," connects him with her field of expertise (though he and his spouse Ningirida are on occasion seen as aspects of Ninurta and Gula: *CT* 25 8, 13–14). Otherwise he is seen as son of Ereškigal, Nanna or Enlil (Sjöberg, *TCS* III, p. 88; Behrens, *Enlil und Ninlil*, p. 195f.; on the god generally see further Lambert's discussion in B. Alster (ed.), *Death in Mesopotamia* = *CRRA* 26, pp. 61–63). The identification of Ninazu as a son of Gula herself, tentatively proposed by Tallqvist, *Götterepitheta*, p. 317, and reiterated most recently by Black and Green, *Gods*,

*Demons and Symbols of Ancient Mesopotamia* (London, 1992), p. 101, seems to be based on no firm evidence.

555 This is the temple of Ešnunna, already listed for Tišpak (line 474). On the relationship between the two deities and their sharing of é.sikil.la, see Sjöberg, *TCS* III, pp. 133f.

558 Following this goddess, who is the wife of Ninazu (see above, on line 554; also *TCL* XV 10, 401: ${}^{d}$*nin-giri*$_{16}$*-da*; *MSL* IV, p. 9, Emesal Voc. I 104; etc.), one is surprised not to find their son Ningišzida, the god of Gišbanda (on whom see recently Lambert, *Studies Moran*, pp. 295ff.). Probably his temple é.giš.bàn.da appeared somewhere in the short lacuna which follows line 560. See further below, on 562–63.

560 The goddess Lakuppîtu ought to be a child of the preceding pair and so a chthonic deity. The fact that she had a cult in Isin reminds us of Ninazu's apparent association with Gula and of the presence at Isin of other gods of the netherworld (for Ningišzida and Nergal in OB Isin see Kraus, *JCS* 3 [1949], pp. 86f., and note the god list fragment Wilcke, *Isin* III, p. 93, IB 1616, 3′–4′: ${}^{d}$nè.er[i$_{11}$.gal] lugal ì.si.[in${}^{ki}$]; cf. also Uqur at Isin in line 574 below). She is not otherwise known to me in this spelling. However, it is possible that she is the deity of Lagaba, a place near Kutha which is well known from an Old Babylonian archive (on the town see Leemans, *RlA* VI, pp. 417f.). There the city goddess is known as "Ištar of Lagaba" (${}^{d}$nín(MÙŠ)-*la-ga-ba*${}^{ki}$, probably better Bēlet-Lagaba), but also Lagabîtum (Leemans, *Ishtar of Lagaba*, pp. 35f.), which might be the antecedent of our Lakuppîtu. What makes this identification likely is the circumstance that the local cults of Lagaba involved at least two well-known if minor deities of the netherworld. The apparel of Lagabîtum was kept in the temple of an aspect of Nergal, Išar-kīdiššu (ibid., p. 2, 42), while Nergal's son Šubula appears in an offering list as one of the lesser gods of the city (Leemans, *TLB* I 76 = *SLB* I/3, p. 19, 17; on Šubula see recently Maul, *Eršaḫunga*, p. 199). If Lagabîtum had connections with the netherworld, then she fits very well the place of Lakuppîtu among chthonic gods in the present text. (A link with ${}^{d}$*la-qu-pu*, one of three names of Nergal *šá di-i-ʾi*, "N. of pestilence," listed in An = *Anu ša amēli* [*CT* 24 41, 73] is uncertain.)

562–63 If Ningišzida is placed in the lacuna after Lakuppîtu (i.e., in line 561), his family will be expected next, and the traces seem to confirm this. Ningišzida's wives are discussed by Lambert, *Studies Moran*, pp. 298f. In *An* V he has two, Azidamua and Ekurrītum, neither of whom is compatible with the traces preserved. In another tradition Ningišzida's consort is Geštinanna, the scribe of the netherworld. There is no room in the present section for this name either, but then it has already appeared in our list among the entourage of Ištar and Dumuzi (lines 463–64), a position also suspected for her in the broken *An* IV. Regarding the restorations proposed instead, Bēlet-ṣēri is the common Akkadian name of Geštinanna (Lambert, loc. cit., p. 299) and so fits well; Gubarra is the Sumerian name of Ašratu, the wife of

Amurru, who also bears the epithet *bēlet ṣēri* (// gašan gú.edin.na: see now Cohen, *Lamentations*, pp. 241, 348 = 309, 222; 390, 150). The evidence for a syncretism of Amurru and Ningišzida noted by Lambert includes the pairing with Amurru of Ningišzida's wives Geštinanna and Ekurrītum (*Studies Moran*, p. 300). My restorations, if correct, are an additional witness to the equation of the two gods and their various consorts.

564–65 For the god whose name is half preserved in line 565 see Lambert, *RlA* IV, pp. 522f. Ḫuškia can be a subsidiary of Nergal, but here, with no less than seven temples, he is likely to be Nergal himself. This is supported by the appearance of Nergal's son Šubula and vizier Uqur in the immediately following lines, and by the lack of room for him in the preceding text (the length of the lacuna following line 560 is not likely to be great—though possibly more than the single line allowed in this reconstruction—for Mss A and C will not be out of step by more than a few lines in their place of transfer from col. v to vi). However it seems most unlikely that his best-known name was omitted entirely, and accordingly I have restored it and his famous cult-center é.mes.lam in line 564; indeed the presence of Kutha at the end of that line seems a compelling invitation to do so. Since a by-name of é.mes.lam is é.ḫuš.ki.a (see the gazetteer) the temptation to restore the latter as a second entry for Nergal's sanctuary, opposite the eponymous deity, has proved irresistible. The position of Nergal in the list marks another deviation from the order of gods in An = *Anum*, in which Lugalirra and Meslamtaea conclude Tablet V and Nergal opens Tablet VI (see *CT* 25 6).

571 Apak is well-known as a cult-center of Nergal: see below, list no. 6, 28 and commentary.

571–72 The copy is restored after Norris's (II *R* 61, no. 1), since whose time a small flake has evidently been lost from K 4772.

573 This god appears among the demonic deities of Nergal's entourage in *An* VI (*CT* 24 47, ii 14 // 25 22, 35: $^{d}$(u$_4$).ug = $^{d}$*u$_4$-mu*).

577 The reiteration of the divine name in Ms A$_2$ (cf. MIN in B$_1$) is a legacy of the start here of a new column in a former copy. Note that Ms B$_1$ has just started col. vi at line 576. Uqur cannot here be Nergal himself, but his vizier: four temples are hardly enough for Nergal, and his principal cult-center is of course neither Isin nor Girsu, but Kutha. As I understand it, the lord of the netherworld has in any case already appeared in his own name and as Ḫuškia. On Uqur as an independent agent of Nergal see Lambert, *BiOr* 30 (1973), p. 356.

## A Hierarchical Temple List

*(no. 2)*

*2. The Babylonian Temple List*

This fragment was first published alongside many pieces of the Canonical Temple List as II *R* 61, no. 5. Since Norris made his copy the piece has deteriorated, with some of the surface flaking off. One such flake had become separated and been given a new number, and after its discovery and rejoining the piece is now registered as K 4407+21429. The new copy given here restores from Norris's original publication the small area of surface that remains missing. The fragment is from the top left corner of a tablet whose single column is subdivided into three. The text presents in the first sub-column the ceremonial names of well-known temples of Sumer and Akkad, then gives their popular names (*bīt* DN), and finally their location (*šá* GN). The second and third columns remain largely intact up to the point where the text breaks off completely, and the facts presented in them make the recovery of the more fragmentary first sub-column straightforward. When restored in this manner the order of the temples in the list is seen to be neither theological, like the Canonical Temple List, nor even geographical. Two pieces of evidence make this plain at once: the temples of Šamaš in Sippar and Larsa appear separately, so disallowing a theological arrangement, and the temples of Enlil and Ninurta at Nippur are also listed at a distance, discounting geographical ordering. Probably the list is ordered according to the fame, cosmological importance, or presumed antiquity of the temples themselves. Certainly the first four entries in the list were considered by scholars of the late period to be the leaders in all three departments. While the temple of Enlil at Nippur appears first, ahead of E-sagil of Marduk, the elevation of E-zida of Borsippa to stand foremost among the temples of the second rank, well ahead of E-šumeša of Ninurta at Nippur, implies that this list is a compilation of the first millennium. The most remarkable feature in the list is the absence of Anu and Ištar of Uruk, but then the deep south is not well represented in the preserved text: apart from one temple each in Eridu, Ur, and Larsa, the list has a strong northern bias, and for this reason I call it the Babylonian Temple List.

K 4407 + 21429 Copy: plate 13

| | | | |
|---|---|---|---|
| 1 | é.kur | [*bīt* $^{d}$*en-líl*] | [*šá nippur*$^{ki}$] |
| 2 | é.babbar.⸢ra⸣ | ⸢*bīt*⸣ $^{d}$*šamaš* | [*šá sippar*$^{ki}$] |
| 3 | ⸢é.sag.íl⸣ | *bīt* $^{d}$*marduk* | [*šá bābili*$^{ki}$] |
| 4 | [é.abz]u | *bīt* $^{d}$*é-a* | *šá eridu*[$^{ki}$] |
| 5 | [é.zi.da] | [*b*]*īt* $^{d}$*nabû*(nà) | *šá bár-s*[*ipa*$^{ki}$] |
| 6 | [é.kiš.nu.gál] | [*bī*]*t* $^{d}$*sîn*(30) | *šá úri*[$^{ki}$] |
| 7 | [é.babbar.ra] | [*bī*]*t* $^{d}$*šamaš* | *šá lars*[*a*$^{ki}$] |
| 8 | [é.šu.me.š]a$_4$ | [*b*]*īt* $^{d}$*nin-urta* | *šá nippur*[$^{ki}$] |
| 9 | [é.*i-bí-*$^{d}$*a*]*-nu-um* | *bīt* $^{d}$*uraš* | *šá dil-b*[*at*$^{ki}$] |
| 10 | [é.dub.b]a | *bīt* $^{d}$*za-ba*$_4$*-ba*$_4$ | *šá kiš*[$^{ki}$] |
| 11 | [é.mes.lam] | *bīt* $^{d}$*nergal*(u.gur) | *šá ku*[*tê*(gú.du$_8$.a)$^{ki}$] |
| 12 | [é.igi.kalam.ma] | *bīt* $^{d}$*lugal-már-da* | *šá már-*[*da*$^{ki}$] |
| 13 | [é.dim.gal.kalam.ma] | *bīt ištarān*(an.gal) | *šá d*[*ēr*(BÀD.AN)$^{ki}$] |
| 14 | [é . . . ] | [*bīt* $^{d}$ . . . ] | *šá* x[ . . . $^{ki}$] |

*remainder lost*

A tiny fragment which may perhaps belong to K 4407+21429 (on grounds of its clay and general physical appearance, so far as one can judge) is K 19309 (plate 13). It yields just a few signs on three lines, followed by a ruling and then blank clay, and may thus preserve the very end of the list (| = column ruling):

. . . ] x [ . . .
. . . ] | *bīt* $^{d}$[ . . .
. . . ] | *bīt* $^{d}$x[ . . .

## Geographical Temple Lists

Lists of temples organized according to location are the commonest sort of temple list extant. The group can be subdivided into two sets: lists which deal with a region, and thus include temples of a number of different towns and cities, and lists which deal with the sanctuaries of a single location. The latter type of list is that commonly found included in texts of the topographical genre, such as *Tintir* = Babylon, the Nippur Compendium, and the Divine Directory (Götteradreßbuch) of Aššur. These have been collected already in *Babylonian Topographical Texts*[41] and are not edited again here.

### 3. The Khorsabad Temple List

A temple list found by the American expedition to Khorsabad, DŠ 32-14, is known to me only in a preliminary transliteration of Moran, since more recently it could not be found for collation. As noted previously by Moran the tablet contains the temple list on the obverse and an unparalleled geographical list on the reverse.[42] Only the obverse is presented here. The text appears to be very poorly preserved in places, and the edition given below is highly provisional. In format the list is identical with the preceding text, with ceremonial name, popular name (*bīt* DN), and location (*šá* GN) entered in three sub-columns. It is clear that the Khorsabad list, also like the preceding text, has a strong northern orientation. There are almost no temples at all from Sumer proper—the only locations which can be considered at all southern are Marad and

[41] The temple list of Babylon, *Tintir* IV, is given in *Topog. Texts* as part of text no. 1, and is accompanied by editions of associated expository lists (nos. 2–4). Two lists treat the temples of Nippur, one incorporated into the Nippur Compendium (nibru$^{ki}$-ní. bi.ta-dù.a) and one found in a single exemplar, the Nippur Temple List. They are edited there as texts no. 18, §§ 5–6, and no. 19. The Assyrian Temple List, which appends temples of Assyria and Babylon to those of Aššur itself, also appears there as part of text no. 20, the Divine Directory of Aššur (§§ 4–5). Lists of Kiš are extant as well (nos. 22–24): see below, on text no. 6. Other such lists of ceremonial names are not temple lists but shrine lists. The extant shrine lists collect the names of shrines and other cultic locations in big cult-centers such as E-sagil at Babylon (*Tintir* II), E-rab-riri, E-šarra at Aššur (*CT* 46 51), the temple of Ištar at Uruk and, probably, the complex of Sîn at Ur. These are all also collected in *Topog. Texts* (texts nos. 1, 12, 21, 25, and 26).

[42] *OrNS* 29 (1960), p. 103, where line 42′ of the obverse is quoted (as line 36′).

maybe Adab[43]—and the extant text appears to be confined to temples of northern Babylonia, including the Diyala and trans-Tigridian regions. The cult-centers of the latter areas are not well documented in the available literature, and many of the entries in the list are otherwise unknown, a circumstance which adds to our difficulties of decipherment. The organization of the list is certainly geographical, since temples are often grouped according to city, and it may be that the list represents a conscious effort to collect the names of the temples of a region that roughly corresponds to ancient Akkad.

DŠ 32–14, obverse

| | | | |
|---|---|---|---|
| 1′-12′ | *lost or illegible* | | |
| 13′ | [é x (x)] x | ⸢*bīt*⸣ [$^{d}$ . . . ] | [*šá* . . . ] |
| 14′ | [é].x.⸢kalam⸣.ma | ⸢*bīt*⸣ [$^{d}$ . . . ] | [*šá* . . . ] |
| 15′ | ⸢é⸣.x.kalam | *bīt* [$^{d}$ . . . ] | [*šá* . . . ] |
| 16′ | ⸢é⸣ x(ḫal$^{?}$) x(an$^{?}$) x x | *bīt* $^{d}$[x] | [*šá* . . . ] |
| 17′ | é.sa.[bad] | *bīt* $^{d}$*nin-kar*$^{?!}$*-rak*$^{?!}$ | *šá* [ . . . ] |
| 18′ | é.galam.ma.lugal | *bīt* $^{d}$x | *šá* [ . . . ] |
| 19′ | é.zi.sù.ud.gal | *bīt* $^{d}$*mar*[*duk*] | *šá* [ . . . ] |
| 20′ | é.⸢di⸣.ku$_{5}$.maḫ | *bīt ìl-a-b*[*a*$_{4}$] | *šá* [ . . . ] |
| 21′ | é.igi.kalam.ma | *bīt* $^{d}$*lugal-már-*⸢*da*⸣ | [*šá*] *már-da*$^{ki}$ |
| 22′ | é.⸢gi⸣.GUN$_{4}^{?}$.un.nu | *bīt* $^{d}$*ištar*(inanna) | [*šá*] KIMIN |
| 23′ | é.x x.[a]n.ki | *bīt* $^{d}$*ištar*(inanna) | [*šá* $^{u}$]$^{ru}$*ka*[*r*]-⸢$^{d}$*bēl*⸣-*mātāti*(kur.kur) |
| 24′ | é.še.ri.⸢ga⸣ | *bīt* $^{d}$*ši-da-da* | [*šá dūr*(bàd)]-*šarru-kīn* |
| 25′ | é.⸢šaga⸣.r[a] | *bīt* $^{d}$*ištar*(inanna) | ⸢*šá*⸣ [$^{uru}$*d*]*a-ad-uš* |
| 26′ | é.nam.zu | *bīt bēlet-ilī*(dingir.maḫ) | *šá* [*ada*]*b*$^{ki}$ |
| 27′ | ⸢é⸣.gu.la | *bīt* $^{d}$x x | *šá di-*⸢*nik*⸣*-ti*$^{ki}$ |
| 28′ | ⸢é⸣.nun.maḫ | *bīt* ⸢$^{d}$*ištar*(inanna)⸣ | *šá* $^{uru}$⸢*ḫu*⸣*-da-da* |
| 29′ | ⸢é⸣.x x UD.SIG$_{7}$ x ⸢ra⸣ | *bīt* $^{d}$*ištar*(inanna) | *šá* $^{uru}$*raq-na-na* |
| 30′ | [é].maḫ | *bīt* $^{d}$*ištar*(inanna) | *šá* $^{uru}$x BAL |
| 31′ | [é.u]l.maš | *bīt* $^{d}$*ištar*(inanna) | *šá a-kà-dè*$^{ki}$ |
| 32′ | [é].x.maḫ.di | *bīt* ⸢$^{d}$⸣*a-nun-ni-tum* | *šá* [KIMIN] |
| 33′ | [é.dim.gal.kal]am.ma | *bīt ištarān*(an.gal) | *šá dēr*[$^{k}$]$^{i}$ |
| 34′ | [é.n]í.gal.kur.kur.ra.du[l.l]a | *bīt* $^{d}$*adad* | *šá* $^{uru}$⸢*dun*⸣*-n*[*u*] |
| 35′ | ⸢é⸣.šà.ḫúl.la | *bīt* $^{d}$*nergal*(u.gur) | *šá* $^{uru}$í[D.SUMUN.D]AR |
| 36′ | ⸢é⸣.sikil.la | *bīt* $^{d}$*tišpak*!(ŠUŠINAK) | *šá* $^{uru}$*èš-nu*[*n-n*]*a*$^{ki}$ |
| 37′ | ⸢é⸣.galam.ma!(LA).dím.ma | *bīt* $^{d}$i[gi].du | *šá akšak*[$^{k}$]$^{i}$ |
| 38′ | é.za.an.gàr$^{gar}$ | *bīt* $^{d}$*ištar*(inanna) | *šá* [K]IMIN |
| 39′ | é.maḫ | *bīt* $^{d}$*ištar*(inanna) | *šá* $^{uru}$x |
| 40′ | é.sikil.la | *bī*[*t* $^{d}$]*nin-a-*⸢*zu*⸣ | *šá* $^{uru}$x x x |
| 41′ | é.maḫ.maḫ | *bīt* $^{d}$*ištar*(inanna) | *šá* $^{uru}$x [x] |
| 42′ | é.u$_{4}$.gal | *bīt* $^{d}$*en-líl* | *šá* ⸢*pàr*⸣-[*sa-a*] |

[43] We have reservations about Adab: see the note on line 26′.

| | | | |
|---|---|---|---|
| 43′ | é.máš.da.ri | *bīt* $^{d}$*ištar*(inanna) | *šá* [. . . ] |
| 44′ | é.dúr.gi.na | *bīt* $^{d}$*bēl-ṣar-bi* | [*šá* $^{uru}$*ba-aṣ*] |
| 45′ | é.$^{d}$*é-a-ba-a-ni* | *bīt* x | [*šá* . . . ] |
| 46′ | [é].x.ra | *bīt* $^{d}$[x (x)] | [*šá* . . . ] |
| 47′ | [é.sís]kur | *bīt* [. . . ] | [*šá* . . . ] |
| 48′ | [é.x ]x.ra | [*bīt* . . . ] | [*šá* . . . ] |
| 49′ | [é.x (x) x ]x | [*bīt* . . . ] | [*šá* . . . ] |
| | *remainder lost* | | |

*Notes*

17′ I suppose that this is a temple of Gula, at Babylon or elsewhere, but her name Ninkarrak can apparently be so read only with some difficulty.

22′ Evidently this is a phonetic writing of é.gi.gun$_4$.na: see CTL 355.

23′ In the cultic calendar *BRM* IV 25, 24, the goddess of Kār-Bēl-mātāti is known as $^{d}$*bēlet*(gašan)-é.an.ki, "Lady of E-anki," which may be the same temple as that listed here, but in abbreviated form (cf. also CTL 378). The longer form of the name given here, é.x.x.an.ki, might be é.è(UD.DU).an.ki, which is already known as the name given to a temple (of Ištar?) at Malgium in the Syncretistic Ištar Hymn (see the gazetteer); é.an.ki and é.è.an.ki would then form a pair of variant names exactly parallel with é.umuš.a and é.è.umuš.a, in which the interpolation of è is certainly secondary.

24′–29′ Some of the cities listed in these lines form a distinct group of north Babylonian toponyms that also appear in close association in two geographical lists, the one embedded in II *R* 50, the other in *Antagal*:

| | | |
|---|---|---|
| [bàd.z]imbir.$^{d}$a.ru.ru$^{ki}$ | = | *dūr*(bàd)-*šarru*(lugal)-*kīn*(gi.na) |
| [da].ad$^{!}$.muš$^{ki}$ | = | *da-tu-na* |
| [KI.I]B$^{eš\text{-}še\text{-}eb.ki}$ | = | *ḫu-da-du* |
| [uru.k]i.ág.$^{d}$inanna$^{ki}$ | = | *ra-aq-na-na* |
| [uru.ki.á]g.$^{d}$ME.ME$^{ki}$ | = | *ra-ki-ma* |
| | | *MSL* XI, p. 54, 26–30 (between Kullab and Karkara) |

| | | |
|---|---|---|
| da.ad.uš | = | *da-tu-nu* |
| uru.ki.ág.$^{d}$inanna | = | *raq-na-na* |
| uru.ki.ág.ME.ME | = | *ra-ki-mu* |
| ⌜uru⌝.sag.an.na | = | *dun-nu* |
| $^{⌜uru⌝}$*dun-nu-sà-i-du* | = | NÍG.DIRI.IM |
| KI$^{⌜eš⌝\text{-}še\text{-}eb}$IB | = | *ḫu-da-du* |
| KUR.TI$^{ki}$ | = | *dūr*(bàd)-⟨*ku-ri*⟩-*gal-zi* |
| | | *MSL* XVII, p. 226, *Antagal* G 185–91 |

The Syncretistic Hymn to Ištar presents a similar group: uru.ki.ág.$^{⌜d⌝}$[inanna], eššeb(KI.IB), *di-nik-ti*$^{ki}$ and *adab*(UD.NUN)$^{ki}$, whose chief temples are given respectively as é.dadag.lál and du$_6$.kù, é.nun.maḫ, é.gu.la, and é.nam.zu (*KAR* 109, rev. 4–12), the last three in agreement with the present text. The hymn goes on to Dēr and then, in the unpublished continuation, to Karkara.

24′ This temple is also found in the exercise tablet K 8382, among temples of Babylon (*Topog. Texts* no. 39, obv. 3). In view of the topographical context here my former proposal in *AfO* 32 (1985), p. 90, that it lay in Assyrian Dūr-Šarru-kēn must be rejected. The occupant of the temple, the rarely attested deity Šidada, has now appeared in the unilingual Weidner god list, following aspects of Ištar (Cavigneaux, *Textes scolaires*, p. 93, 164).

25′ See CTL 381 and note.

26′ The toponym is restored after the Syncretistic Hymn to Ištar, as cited above. The striking thing about both that hymn and the present list is the apparent intrusion of the southern city Adab into a set of towns that seem all to belong to a restricted area of north Babylonia, near the convergence of the Tigris and Euphrates. The temple of the Mother Goddess at Adab, as elsewhere, is the well-known é.maḫ. It is legitimate to enquire as to whether the temple é.nam.zu listed for her here and in the hymn really is the same temple and not another, and as to whether the toponym written UD.NUN$^{ki}$ must always be Adab and not on occasion some other location more suited to its place here.

27′ See also the syncretistic hymn to Nanāy (Reiner, *JNES* 33 [1974], p. 228, 42: *i-na di-ni-ik-ti ina* é.gu.la *be-l*[*et* . . . ), where the goddess proclaims her identity as the wife of Ḫaya, i.e., Nissaba. Otherwise the patron deities of Diniktu are Ninkilim and, especially, the Mother Goddess as Bēlet-ilī or Ninmaḫ (see Reiner, *JNES* 33 [1974], p. 235; Nashef, *Rép. géogr.* V, p. 82); at the original collation the traces did not favour Ninkilim.

29′ Raqnana is a particular cult-center of Ištar according to the lexical entries quoted above in the note on lines 24′–29′. However, the temple of Raqnana known to the Syncretistic Ištar Hymn is called é.dadag.lál (*KAR* 109, rev. 4). Obscurely, the similar hymn to Nanāy has é.gal.*ta-bi-ri* in *Ra-qa-na-an* (Reiner, *JNES* 33 [1974], p. 230, 19). Neither TN seems easily compatible with the traces observed on our tablet.

30′ One might suggest that the toponym is GIŠ.ÙḪ$^{!}$, and the temple therefore that dedicated to Šara, a son of Ištar and one of her lovers, but for geographical reasons one would not expect the intrusion of the southern town of Umma at this point in the list.

31′ The presence of Akkade here in the list, in association with such towns as Diniktu, Ḫudādu, and Dēr, is further evidence for a Tigridian location of Ištar's venerable cult-center, as proposed recently by McEwan (*AfO* Beiheft 19 = *CRRA* 28, pp. 11f.) and, at length, by C. Wall-Romana, "An Areal Location of Agade" (*JNES* 49 [1990], pp. 205–45).

34′ Note a temple of the same name at Zabban, somewhere on the border of Assyria and Babylonia, as given in the Assyrian Temple List (*Topog. Texts* no. 20, 184). Could this Dunnu be an alternative name for Zabban? Or might the traces allow a reading $^{uru⌜}$*zab-ba*⌝*-a*[*n*]?

35′ The temple shares its name with a temple of Ištar as Nanāy at Kazallu (see CTL 346). Despite his chthonic connection Nergal can be a god of joy (cf. Nergal *ša ḫadê* and *ša rīšāti*, documented in *Topog. Texts*, p. 362), and so is not out of place in the "House of the Joyful Heart." The restoration of the toponym relies on Nergal's association with Sumundar as found in the cultic calendar *SBH* no. VII, rev. 3–4 // *BRM* IV 25, 53: *a-na kinūni šá* $^{d}$*ner-gal*(U.GUR) $^{d}$*šib-bu u* $^{d}$*nam-tar šá bāb* $^{íd}$*sumun-dar išāti i-na-du-ú.* A river Sumundar is attested near Uruk and Borsippa (see Nashef, *Rép. géogr.* V, p. 316), but neither location really suits the context of our list or the cultic calendar. More promising is an identification with the place Sumundar in the Diyala region, Ur III Simudar, which also gave its name to a waterway (see Edzard and Farber, *Rép. géogr.* II, p. 167; Lieberman, *JCS* 22 [1969], p. 59ff.). However, since the tablet was seen, fresh evidence has appeared which leads one to question the original reading. Duplicate inscriptions of Aššurbanipal from a NA temple at Tell Haddad on the middle Diyala report restoration work done for "Nergal who dwells in é.šà.ḫúl.la, lord of *si-ra-ra*$^{ki}$" (Fawzi Rashid, *Sumer* 37 [1981], p. 80 [Arabic section], figs. 1 and 2, line 2; for a brief report of the excavated temple see *Iraq* 43 [1981], p. 177). At first sight the mention of a place Sirara is odd, for plentiful evidence now identifies Tell Haddad with Mê-Turna (*Iraq* 47 [1985], p. 220; Nashef, *Bagh. Mitt.* 13 [1982], p. 128[52]). This toponym also appears as Mê-Turan and, in the NA period, Mê-Turnat (the various orthographies attested for this town are listed by Borger, *AfO* 23 [1970], p. 1). Indeed, the syncretistic hymn to Nanāy places é.šà.ḫúl.la in $^{uru}$*me-túr-na* (Reiner, *JNES* 33 [1974], p. 228, 48). Bearing in mind that Tell Haddad is not an isolated site but one of a group of settlements, probably we are looking at a situation in which a smaller (and so lesser-known) place, i.e., Sirara, is a part of a larger (and so better-known) urban entity, i.e., Mê-Turna. In such a view Sirara might be Tell Haddad proper, one of a group of neighboring sites (including Tulul al-Sib and Tell Baradan) which became known collectively as Mê-Turna.

In the light of this new evidence one would certainly wish to have the opportunity to collate the traces on the tablet. As originally read, these certainly seem to be incompatible with Aššurbanipal's Sirara, but Mê-Turna looks a distinct possibility: instead of $^{uru}$A.[ENGUR.SUMUN.D]AR one might have $^{uru}$A[$^{meš}$-*tú*]*r-na* or similar. But if when the tablet is found such should turn out not to be the case we would then be driven simply to equate this $^{uru}$ÍD. SUMUN.DAR with Sirara or Mê-Turna, and by implication in the latter case, the Sumundar river with the Turna (modern Diyala).

36′ See also CTL 474. šušinak(MÙŠ + EREN) is presumed to be a simple error for tišpak(MÚŠ), but note that they appear together in CTL 474–75.

37′ The cult of $^{d}$igi.du at Akšak is also known from the cultic calendar *BRM* IV 25, 50.

38′ This is the temple of CTL 354.

40′ Traces rule out Ešnunna in the third sub-column, and the é.sikil.la of that place has, in any case, already appeared in the list, four lines earlier. Presumably this is some other temple of Ninazu.

42′ This is the temple more often written é.u(mun).gal: see the note on CTL 55 and the gazetteer. On Parsâ, the older name of the settlement rebuilt as Dūr-Kurigalzu and sometimes written KUR.TI$^{ki}$, see Lambert, *AfO* 18 (1957–58), pp. 396f., and Moran, *OrNS* 29 (1960), pp. 103f. British Museum tablet 82-3-23, 24, the geographical list cited in an addendum by Moran, loc. cit., to clinch the equation KUR.TI$^{ki}$ = *Parsâ*, is now edited in *MSL* XI, p. 63, and a copy is published in *Topog. Texts* as no. 49. My reading of *Antagal* G 191 (quoted above, note on lines 24′–29′), if correct, demonstrates that KUR.TI$^{ki}$ can stand for Dūr-Kurigalzu as well as Parsâ.

43′ This is the name of a temple of Ištar as Bēlet-Akkade at Babylon (*Tintir* IV 16), but Babylon is not probable at this point in the list, nor in a single entry, so we expect this to be some other cult-center of the Akkadian goddess.

44′ The toponym is restored in this form from inscriptions of Nebuchadnezzar II (V *R* 34, ii 30; etc.), but $^{uru}$*šá-pa-zu* is also a candidate: see George, *SAA Bulletin* 1/I (1987), p. 35, on line 8.

45′ Ceremonial temple names in Akkadian are very rare. Possibly this is a corruption of the best-known example, é.*ibbi-Anu*, the cult-center of Uraš at Dilbat.

47′ é.sískur is of course the name of Marduk's Akītu temple outside Babylon (as rebuilt by Nebuchadnezzar II: I *R* 55, iv 7; etc.), but while it is conceivable that a section on the temples of Babylon began here, equally this might be another sanctuary of the same name.

### *4. The Kuyunjik Ziqqurrat List*

The geographical text K 4337, a tablet in four columns from Kuyunjik, was published in the cuneiform copy of Norris as II *R* 50, before it was joined to K 2035A. The tablet as a whole was edited by Weissbach in 1899,[44] and parts of it have since been included in *MSL* XI.[45] The text, which takes the form of a list in two sub-columns, opens with the names of cities and goes on to mountains and rivers. Then the compiler collects a whole series of bilingual lexical entries for *šamû*, "heaven."[46] Only the end of the text, as preserved in the tablet's fourth column, is of interest here, for it gives a list of the ceremonial names of ziqqurrats and city walls, collected according to location. In both parts of the list the order of the cities is the same, beginning with Babylon, Borsippa, Nippur and KUR.TI$^{ki}$ (Parsâ or Dūr-Kurigalzu), and going on to Sippar, Akkade, Kiš and Ḫursag-kalamma, Kutha, Dilbat, Marad, Ur, Larsa, Uruk, Eridu, and IM$^{ki}$ (presumably Karkara). The prominent position of the town which became the capital of Kurigalzu points to the Kassite period as the likely date of the list's composition. The precedence given to the northern cities and the inferior position of the

44 "Die geographische Liste II R 50," *ZDMG* 53, pp. 653–67, with Norris's obverse and reverse exchanged.
45 Cols. i, ii and iii 1–16, on pp. 54ff.
46 Col. iii 17–33.

old southern centers is noteworthy and also a mark of the post-Old Babylonian status quo. Only Nippur is out of place in this geographical division, presumably as a mark of Enlil's importance. It is interesting to note that no wall is listed for Akkade, which is skipped in the second part of the list. The revival in fortune which is documented for this city in the Kassite period apparently did not provide a new city wall, and the name of the original wall was evidently lost.[47] A new copy of this list has not been prepared, but the text has been collated against the original tablet.

K 2053A + 4337, col. iv

| | | |
|---|---|---|
| 1 | [u$_6$].nir | *ziq-qur-ra-tum* |
| 2 | [é.temen.an].ki | MIN *šu-an-na*$^{ki}$ |
| 3 | [é.ur$_4$].⸢me.imin.an⸣.ki | MIN *bár-sipa*$^{ki}$ |
| 4 | ⸢é⸣.[$^{giš?}$]gigir | MIN *nippur*$^{ki}$ |
| 5 | é.IM.ḫur.sag | MIN *nippur*$^{ki}$ |
| 6 | é.sag.dil | MIN *nippur*$^{ki}$ |
| 7 | é.gi.rin | MIN KUR.TI$^{ki}$ |
| 8 | é.kun$_4$.an.kù.ga | MIN *sippar*$^{ki}$ |
| 9 | é.an.da.sá.a | MIN *a-kà-dè*$^{ki}$ |
| 10 | é.su.gal | MIN $^{d}$*dumu-zi* MIN |
| 11 | é.bára.u$_6$.de | MIN $^{d}$*dumu-zi* MIN |
| 12 | é.u$_6$.nir.ki.tuš.maḫ | MIN *kiš*$^{ki}$ |
| 13 | é.kur.maḫ | MIN é.ḫur.sag.kalam.ma |
| 14 | é.me.lám.maḫ | MIN $^{d}$*en-líl* ⟨MIN⟩ |
| 15 | é.AN.ÙRU.ki | MIN *kutê*(gú.du$_8$.a)$^{ki}$ |
| 16 | é.gub.ba.an.ki | MIN *dil-bat*$^{ki}$ |
| 17 | é.gán.gá.du$_7$.du$_7$ | MIN *már-da*$^{ki}$ |
| 18 | é.šu.gán.du$_7$.du$_7$ | MIN *úri*$^{ki}$ |
| 19 | é.dur.an.ki | MIN *larsa*$^{ki}$ |
| 20 | ⸢é⸣.gi$_6$.pàr.imin | ⸢MIN⸣ *uruk*$^{ki}$ |
| 21 | ⸢é⸣.u$_6$.⸢nir⸣ | ⸢MIN⸣ *eridu*$^{ki}$ |
| 22 | ⸢é⸣.u$_6$.de.gal.⸢an.na⸣ | MIN IM$^{ki}$ |
| 23 | é.aratta$^{ki}$.ki.šár.ra | MIN IM$^{ki}$ |
| 24 | bàd | *du-ú-ru* |
| 25 | [bà]d.*im-gur-*$^{d}$*en-líl* | MIN *šu-an-na*$^{ki}$ |
| 26 | [bà]d.*ni-mit-*$^{d}$*en-líl* | *šal-ḫu-ú-šu* |
| 27 | [bà]d.*ṭāb*(dùg)$^{ab}$*-su-pur-šu* | *dūr*(bàd) *bár-sipa*$^{ki}$ |
| 28 | [bà]d.*im-gur-*$^{d}$*marduk* | *dūr*(bàd) *nippur*$^{ki}$ |
| 29 | [bà]d.*ni-mit-*$^{d}$*marduk* | *šal-ḫu-ú-*⟨*šu*⟩ |
| 30 | [bàd?] AN ⸢x x⸣ *din-di* | *šal-ḫu-ú* |
| 31 | [bà]d? SU$^{?}$ MU LUD | *šal-ḫu-ú* |
| 32 | [bàd].úr$^{?}$.me.an.ki | *dūr*(bàd) KUR.TI$^{ki}$ |

[47] On Akkade in the Kassite period see McEwan, *AfO Beiheft* 19 = *CRRA* 28, p. 8.

| | | |
|---|---|---|
| 33 | [bàd].$u_4$.ul.dù.a | *dūr*(bàd) *sippar*$^{ki}$ |
| 34 | [bàd].me.lám.kur.kur.ra.dul.la | *dūr*(bàd) *kiš*$^{ki}$ |
| 35 | [bàd.$^{d}$u.gur].lugal.mè.dù | [*dū*]*r*(bàd) *kutê*(gú.$du_8$.a)$^{ki}$ |
| 36 | [bàd. . . . ]x.$^{d}$en.líl | [*dūr*(bàd)] *dil-bat*[$^{ki}$] |
| 37 | [bàd. . . . . . ].gi | [*dūr*(bàd) *má*]*r-d*[*a*$^{ki}$] |

*remainder lost*

*Notes*

1 This lexical entry is also found in *MSL* XII, p. 108, *Lu* Excerpt II 120; XVII, p. 91, *Erimḫuš* c 20′; and Landsberger and Gurney, *AfO* 18 (1957–58), p. 82, 133 (*Igituḫ*).

7 KUR.TI$^{ki}$ stands for the town known as Parsâ or Dūr-Kurigalzu: see the note on list no. 3, 42′.

9–11 The existence of more than one ziqqurrat at Akkade is confirmed by Nabonidus, who reports the discovery and rebuilding of Narām-Sîn's E-ulmaš "together with its two ziqqurrats" (*CT* 34 33, iii 1: *a-di šitta*$^{ta}$ *ziq-qur-re-e-ti-šú*). If one of these was certainly é.an.da.sá.a, the other may well have belonged to a sanctuary of Dumuzi within the same temple. The two names offered in this list suggest variant traditions rather than the existence of a third ziqqurrat not found by Nabonidus. The cult of Inanna-Ištar and Dumuzi is best known from Sumer, and Uruk especially, but if we accept this late evidence as authentic there was also a similar cult at Akkade, presumably in Ištar's cult-center E-ulmaš. By analogy with later southern practice one can assume that Narām-Sîn and other Sargonic kings of Akkade personified Dumuzi in the rites of sacred marriage. Just as this cultic function was a factor in the divination of the kings of Isin and Larsa, and probably also in the divination of the legendary Early Dynastic kings of Uruk, so too it may have been with Narām-Sîn.

14 ⟨MIN⟩ is restored, after the pattern of lines 10–11, to express the toponym E-ḫursag-kalamma, where there is known to have been a ziqqurrat of Enlil, as well as of Ištar-Ninlil: see below, text no. 6, 17.

15 Miswritten for é.ùru.an.ki: see below, nos. 5, 9′, and 6, 24.

18 Most probably ŠU.GÁN is a corruption of AGA: for é.aga.$du_7$.$du_7$ as a sanctuary of Sîn, see the gazetteer, and cf. list no. 5, 15′.

24 The lexical equation bàd = *dūru* is too well known to need documentation.

25–29 This passage is discussed by me already in the commentary on *Tintir* V 57–58, which list the twin walls of Babylon (*Topog. Texts*, pp. 349f.).

33 The wall's name is appropriate, for in late tradition Sippar was the uru ul.dù.a = *āl ṣâti* par excellence (see *Topog. Texts*, p. 246). Šamaš-šuma-ukīn, who repaired the wall of Sippar, knew a slightly expanded name, bàd.$u_4$.ul.dù.$sa_4$.a (V *R* 62, no. 2, 53).

34–35 For the walls of Kiš and Kutha see below, no. 6, 10.23, and notes.

### 5. *The Neo-Babylonian Ziqqurrat List*

The joining of two fragments from the obverse of a Neo-Babylonian tablet now in the British Museum provides the text of a list of ziqqurrats in two sub-columns which is very similar to list no. 4. As part of the 82-3-23 collection, the provenance of this tablet would have been Sippar, Babylon, or Borsippa. There are points of disagreement with the list from Kuyunjik, principally in the order of the lines, for the sequence of cities as restored here is Akkade, KUR.TI$^{ki}$, Nippur, Sippar, Babylon, Kutha, Kiš and Ḫursag-kalamma, IM$^{ki}$, Ur, Larsa, Uruk, Eridu, Marad, Dilbat, and Borsippa.[48] This is exactly the same set, which suggests that line 1′ is in fact the first line of the list (though not necessarily of the tablet). There is also disagreement in some temple names, for which the Babylonian list exhibits a number of variants, and in the orthography of the geographical names, where the conventional logographic writings are usually avoided. One of the temple names is certainly corrupt: the second ziqqurrat listed for Ur in line 16′ is assuredly a miswriting of the well-known é.lugal. galga.si.sá. This error means that variant names in this list can only be preferred to names in the Kuyunjik list with caution.[49] The phonetic orthography of most geographical names in the second sub-column (in the text as preserved only IM$^{ki}$ is logographic) compares with that found in col. i of the Kuyunjik list, where literary and archaic geographical names and epithets are explained by equation with well-known cities.

In this list, as in the other, the ziqqurrats are followed by city walls, but most of the continuation on this tablet is now missing, and no comparison can be made beyond the observation that the Neo-Babylonian list omits the lexical equation bàd = *dūru* which prefaced the list of walls in the Kuyunjik tablet. Presumably it also lacked the initial equation $u_6$.nir = *ziqqurratu*.

BM 51124 + 52640 (82–3–23, 2120 + 3674) Copy: plate 14

| | | |
|---|---|---|
| 1′ | [é.an.d]a.s[á.a] | [MIN *a-kà-dè*$^{ki}$] |
| 2′ | [é.su].[gal] | [MIN $^{d}$*dumu-zi* MIN] |
| 3′ | [é.bár]a.$u_6$.d[e$^{!?}$] | [MIN $^{d}$*dumu-zi* MIN] |
| 4′ | [é.g]i.⸢x⸣ | [MIN KUR.TI$^{ki}$?] |
| 5′ | [é.I]M.ḫur.sa[g] | [MIN *ni-ip-pu-ru*$^{ki}$] |
| 6′ | [é.s]ag.di[l] | [MIN *ni-ip-pu-ru*$^{ki}$] |

48 Of these only the restoration of KUR.TI$^{ki}$ in line 4′ is open to doubt: the TN is evidently not [é.g]i.r[in], as given in list no. 4. Instead the traces might be read [é.g]i.S[I], which would presuppose an ancient confusion of the rather similar signs LAGAB and SI. But if KUR.TI$^{ki}$ is placed here in the list, there is only room for two ziqqurrats at Nippur, while list no. 4 has three (lines 7–9). Accordingly it is possible that a variant or corruption of the first of those three ziqqurrats should be placed here instead, in which case KUR.TI$^{ki}$, if it was present at all, would have to have preceded Akkade in line 1′.

49 But note that the name of the first ziqqurrat of Ur as given here (line 15′) may be confirmed by an independent source, while the variant in the Kuyunjik list looks corrupt (line 18 and note).

| | | |
|---|---|---|
| 7′ | [é.ku]n$_4$.an.kù.g[a] | [MIN *si-ip-par*$^{ki}$] |
| 8′ | [é.t]e.me.en.an.k[i] | [MIN *šu-an-na*$^{ki}$] |
| 9′ | [é.ùr]u.an.ki | [MIN *ku-te-e*$^{ki}$] |
| 10′ | [é].⸢u$_6$⸣.nir.ki.tuš.ma[ḫ] | [MIN *kiš*$^{ki}$] |
| 11′ | [é].kur.m[aḫ] | [MIN é.ḫur.sag.kalam.ma] |
| 12′ | [é].me.lám.ma[ḫ] | [MIN $^{d}$*en-líl* MIN] |
| 13′ | [é].⸢u$_6$.de⸣.gal.an.ga[l$^?$] | [MIN IM$^{ki}$] |
| 14′ | [é.aratt]a$^{ki}$.⸢ki.šár$^?$⸣.r[a$^?$] | ⸢MIN⸣ IM[$^{ki}$] |
| 15′ | [é.ag]a$^?$.du$_7$.du$_7$ | MIN *ú-ri*[$^{ki}$] |
| 16′ | [é.luga]l.gá.gá.si.sá | MIN *ú-ri*[$^{ki}$] |
| 17′ | [é.du]r.an.na | MIN *la-ár-sa*[$^{ki}$] |
| 18′ | [é.gi$_6$].pàr.imin.na | MIN *ú-ru-uk*[$^{ki}$] |
| 19′ | [é].⸢u$_6$⸣.nir | MIN *eri-du*$_{10}$[$^{ki}$] |
| 20′ | [é.gán.g]á.du.du | MIN *ma-rad*[$^{ki}$] |
| 21′ | [é.te?.me?.e]n.an.ki | MIN *dil-bat*[$^{ki}$] |
| 22′ | [é.ur$_4$.me.imin].⸢an.ki⸣ | MIN *bár-sip*[*a*$^{ki}$] |
| 23′ | [bàd . . . ] | ⸢*du-úr*⸣ [ . . . ] |
| 24′ | [bàd . . . ] | ⸢MIN⸣ [ . . . ] |
| | *remainder lost* | |

*6. An Explanatory Temple List, From Kiš to Apak*

Another Neo-Babylonian tablet newly discovered in the Sippar collections of the British Museum is an expository temple list of the kind already known for various individual cities of ancient Mesopotamia.[50] In these lists the Sumerian ceremonial names of a temple or temples are subject to translation into Akkadian. This can be a straightforward mechanical operation in which each Sumerian element is rendered by the appropriate Akkadian word, but often the ancient translator will feel free to speculate on the meaning of the name by manipulating its Sumerian elements with homophones and by playing with the orthography. In this way hidden significance can be extracted from a temple's name.[51] The present text is divided into four sections, each of which is effectively an individual list devoted to a particular town, namely, Kiš, Ḫursagkalamma, Kutha, and Apak. In addition to temples, the ceremonial names of city walls are also listed, as also is a river name. The text is concluded with the tantalizing rubric "26 lines: names of cities and temples, up to Apak," which

[50] See *Topog. Texts* nos. 2–5 (Babylon), 18 §§ 5–6, 19 (both Nippur), 20 §§ 4–5 (Aššur), 22–24 (Kiš), 28 and 31.

[51] The "hermeneutic" methods of the Babylonian commentators have been the subject of much recent interest: see the studies of Bottéro, *Finkelstein Mem. Vol.*, pp. 5–28; Durand, *RA* 73 (1979), pp. 168ff.; Livingstone, *Mystical Works*, pp. 49ff.; and Cavigneaux, *Aula Or* 5 (1987), pp. 246ff. On the application of such methods to temple names see *Topog. Texts*, pp. 73f.

implies that there was an established geographical sequence of these short explanatory lists, with other towns treated after Apak. Since the fact that the sequence began with Kiš is taken for granted by the rubric we may also presume that the four sections given here begin the sequence. Kiš and Ḫursag-kalamma are neighbors, of course, and Kutha is only a few miles distant, so to find them in close association is expected.[52] But this topographical connection does not continue to the next section, for Apak is believed to be located well to the south of Kiš and Kutha, west of Marad near Dilbat. Instead there seems to be a theological reason for this sequence, for Apak was, like Kutha, a cult-center of Nergal—though this circumstance is not documented in the list itself.

Material which duplicates part of the opening section, on Kiš, is known from a Neo-Assyrian tablet from Aššur, the compendium VAT 13817, and some lines have been restored from that source.[53] Curiously the best-known names of Zababa's cult-center, é.dub.ba and é.me.te.ur.sag, are omitted in the present text, though they appear as expected in VAT 13817. The sections on the other three towns are all new. In format the text is essentially that of texts in three sub-columns, such as the Assyrian Temple List, in which a ceremonial temple name is listed in one column, a translation (either straightforward or speculative) is listed in a second, and the popular name (*bīt* DN) or function of the building appears in a third. But as with the compendium VAT 13817, the lay-out of this text represents a modification of the arrangement in three sub-columns, for the translation is placed on an indented line below the main entry, and the list thus takes on the format of a list in two columns with interlinear Akkadian explanation.

The tablet is complete save for its lower left corner, but its surface is badly abraded in places and compacted with salts in others, so that not every sign is legible. As part of a collection bought from the dealer Spartali, the provenance of BM 55476 is likely to have been Babylon.

BM 55476 (82-7-4, 49) Copy: pl. 15–16

Text

1 é.abzu.kù.[ga] [*pa-paḫ* ᵈ]⌜*za*⌝-*ba*$_4$-*ba*$_4$

*bīt ap-si-*⌜*i*⌝ [*el-li u aps*]*û*(abzu) *šap-lu-ú*

2 é.galga.sù [*pa-paḫ*] ⌜ᵈ⌝*ba-ba*$_6$ *šá kiš*ᵏⁱ

*bītu šá mi-l*[*ik-šú ru-qu šá mil-k*]*a ma-lu-ú*

3 é.rab.ri.[ri] [*pa-paḫ*] ᵈ*madānu*(di.ku$_5$)

*bītu šá rab-ba* [*i-me-es-su*] ⌜*ú*⌝-*qal-la-lu*

[52] Compare the sequence Kiš—E-ḫursag-kalamma—Kutha in the ziqqurrat list no. 4, 12–15 (inverted in the parallel list, no. 5, 9′–12′). The same sequence is also used in the Syncretistic Ištar Hymn (unpublished section, courtesy Lambert). In liturgical texts Kutha and E-meslam follow Kiš and its temples in the most common of the standard litanies of Babylonian cult-centers.

[53] The compendium is edited in *Topog. Texts* as no. 22: lines 1–4, 6–9 of the present text // VAT 13817 ii 3′–4′, 10′–15′; line 5, omitted from the compendium probably by accident, is also found in another explanatory list of Kiš, *KAV* 82 = *Topog. Texts* no. 23, 2′.

4 ⸢é⸣.temen.bi.nu.[kúr] [*pa-paḫ*] $^{d}$*šarrat*(gašan)-*kiš*$^{ki}$

*bītu šá tem-mìn-*⸢*šú*⸣ [*la u*]*t-tak-*⸢*ka*⸣*-ru*

5 é.an.úr.ki.⸢tuš⸣.[ma]ḫ [*zi*]*q-qur-rat* ⸢*kiš*⸣$^{ki}$

*bītu šá i-šid šamê*(an)⸢$^{e}$⸣ [*šub*]*-ti* ⸢*ṣir-ti*⸣

6 é.su.lim.an.na *b*[*īt*] $^{d}$*bēlet*(nin)*-é-*⸢*an*⸣*-na*

*bītu šá šá-lum-mat-su* ⸢*šá*⸣*-qa-tu*

7 é.⸢ki⸣.ág.gá.a.ni *pa-pa-ḫu*

*bīt na-ram-*⸢*i*⸣*-šú*

8 é.⸢šu⸣.luḫ.⸢bi⸣.kù.ga *ki-sal-lu*

⸢*bītu šá šu*⸣*-l*[*uḫ*]*-ḫu-*⸢*šú*⸣ *el-lu*

9 ⸢é.giš.ḫur.bi⸣.[GALA]M.⸢GALAM⸣ *a-ki-ti*

*bītu šá ú-*[*ṣu-ra*]*-t*[*i*]*-šú nak-lu*

10 ⸢bàd⸣.me.lám.kur.kur.⸢ra⸣.dul.la *dūr*(bàd) *kiš*$^{ki}$

[*dū*]*ru šá me-*⸢*lam*⸣*-mu-šú mātāti*(kur)$^{meš}$ *kát-mu*

---

11 10 [*šumū*(mu)$^{m}$]$^{eš}$ *ekurrātu*(⸢é⸣.kur)$^{mes}$ *šá qé-reb kiš*$^{ki}$

---

12 [é.kur.ní.zu] [*bī*]*t* ⸢$^{d}$⸣nin.⸢líl *ḫur*⸣*-sag-kalam-ma*$^{ki}$

13 [é.x x x ]x *pa-paḫ* ⸢$^{d}$⸣nin.líl *ḫur-sag-*⸢*kalam-ma*$^{ki}$⸣

14 [é.kur.maḫ] [*ziq-q*]*ur-*⸢*rat*⸣*-ti*

15 [é.x x x x] *bīt* $^{d}$*bí-zil-lá*

16 [ . . . ] ⸢x x x *nam*$^{?}$⸣ *ḫur-*⸢*sag-kalam-ma*⸣$^{k[i]}$

17 [é.me.lám.maḫ] [*z*]*iq-qur-rat* ⟨$^{d}$⟩50 ⸢*ḫur-sag*⸣*-kalam-ma*$^{ki}$

---

18 [6?] ⸢*šumū*(mu)$^{meš}$ *ekurrāt*(é.kur)$^{meš}$⸣ *ḫur-sag-*[*ka*]*lam-ma*$^{ki}$

---

19 gú.du$_{8}$.a$^{ki}$ ⸢*ku-te*⸣*-e*

*bīt ḫé-*g[*ál*] ⸢x x x⸣

20 é.mes.lam ⸢*bīt* $^{d}$*nergal*(u.gur)⸣ [*šá* g]ú.du$_{8}$.a⸢$^{ki}$⸣

*bīt* $^{d}$*marduk šá erṣetim*(ki)⸢$^{tim}$⸣

21 é.⸢dug$_{4}$⸣.ga *pa-paḫ* $^{d}$*nergal*(u.gur) *šá* gú.du$_{8}$.⸢a$^{ki}$⸣

22 bàd.u$_{4}$.gal.⟨a⟩.má.uru$_{5}$ ⸢*dūr*(bàd) gú⸣.du$_{8}$.a$^{ki}$

*a-bu-ub* ⸢*an-zi-i*⸣

23 ⸢bàd⸣.$^{d}$u.gur.lugal.mè.dù *nēme*[*t*?(ús.bàd) g]ú.⸢du$_{8}$.a$^{ki}$⸣

24 é.ùru.⸢an⸣.ki *ziq-qur-rat* g[ú.du$_{8}$.a$^{ki}$]

[*bītu na-ṣ*]*ir šamê*(an)$^{e}$ *u erṣetim*(ki)$^{tim}$

25 x[ x x ].ma *dūr*(bàd) $^{d}$BA x[ (x)]

26 í[$^{d}$x x ]x $^{d}$⸢*ìr-ra-gal*?⸣

---

27 8 *šu*[*mū*(mu)$^{meš}$ *ekurrā*]*tu*(é.kur)⸢$^{meš}$⸣ *a-di nār*(íd) gú.d[u$_{8}$.a$^{k}$]$^{i}$

---

28 $^{uru}$⸢*a*⸣-[*pak*] ⸢x x⸣ TU TU x[ (x)]

29 [é].še.n[umun] ⟨*bīt*⟩ ⸢$^{d}$⸣*lú-là*[*l*]

*bi-it ze-er*

---

30 ⸢26$^{?}$⸣ *šumū*(mu)$^{meš}$ *šu-mi āli*(uru) *u bīti*(é) *adi*(en) $^{uru}$*a-pak*

Translation

| | | |
|---|---|---|
| 1 | E-abzu-kuga | [the cella of] Zababa: |
| | House of [pure] Apsû and lower Apsû; | |
| 2 | E-galga-su | [the cella] of Baba of Kiš: |
| | House whose counsel [is profound, which] is filled with [advice;] | |
| 3 | E-rab-riri | [the cella] of Madānu: |
| | House which [crushes,] smashes(?) the shackle; | |
| 4 | E-temenbi-nukur | [the cella] of the Queen of Kiš: |
| | House whose foundation platform [may not] be moved; | |
| 5 | E-anur-kituš-maḫ | the ziqqurrat of Kiš: |
| | House of the base of heaven, lofty abode; | |
| 6 | E-sulim-anna | the temple of Bēlet-Eanna: |
| | House whose radiance is exalted; | |
| 7 | E-kiaggani | the cella: |
| | House of his beloved; | |
| 8 | E-šuluḫbi-kuga | the courtyard: |
| | House whose purification rites are pure; | |
| 9 | E-gišḫurbi-gagalam | the Akītu (house): |
| | House whose rituals are skilful; | |
| 10 | Bad-melam-kurkurra-dulla | the wall of Kiš: |
| | Wall whose awesome splendour covers the lands. | |

---

11 10 [lines:] sacred buildings which are in Kiš.

---

| | | |
|---|---|---|
| 12 | [E-kur-nizu] | the temple of Ninlil of Ḫursag-kalamma; |
| 13 | [E- . . . ] . . . | the cella of Ninlil of Ḫursag-kalamma; |
| 14 | [E-kur-maḫ] | the ziqqurrat; |
| 15 | [E- . . . . . . ] | the temple of Bizilla; |
| 16 | [ . . . . . . ] . . . . . . Ḫursag-kalamma; | |
| 17 | [E-melam-maḫ] | the ziqqurrat of Enlil of Ḫursag-kalamma. |

---

18 [6] lines: sacred buildings of Ḫursag-kalamma.

---

| | | |
|---|---|---|
| 19 | Gudua | Kutha: |
| | House of abundance . . . . . . ; | |
| 20 | E-meslam | the temple of Nergal [at] Kutha: |
| | House of the Marduk of the Netherworld; | |
| 21 | E-dugga | the cella of Nergal at Kutha; |
| 22 | Bad-ugal-amaru | the wall of Kutha: |
| | Deluge of Anzû; | |
| 23 | Bad-Ugur-lugal-me-du | the rampart(?) of Kutha; |
| 24 | E-uru-anki | the ziqqurrat of [Kutha:] |
| | [House which] guards heaven and underworld; | |
| 25 | . . . . . . -ma | the wall of . . . [ . . . ;] |

| | | |
|---|---|---|
| 26 | River [ . . . ] . . . | Irragal(?). |
| 27 | 8 lines: [sacred buildings,] including the river, of Kutha. | |
| 28 | Apak . . . [ . . . ;] | |
| 29 | [E]-šenumun<br>House of seed. | ⟨the temple of⟩ Lulal: |
| 30 | 26 lines: names of cities and temples, up to Apak. | |

*Notes*

3 My translation of *uqallalu* relies on the equation ⸢*qul*⸣-*lu-lu* = *na-qa-r*[*u*], "to demolish," in the synonym list *Malku* VIII 81 (as cited in *CAD* Q, p. 55). The parallel text, VAT 13817, has ⸢*šu-qal*?⸣-*lu*!?-*lu* (*Topog. Texts* no. 22, 10′).

5 The temple name is a variation on é.u$_{6}$.nir.ki.tuš.maḫ, by which the ziqqurrat of Kiš is better known (see e.g., above, nos. 4, 12; 5, 10′).

8 Given the lack of any qualification of *papāḫu*, this is presumably the cella of é.su.lim.an.na. Since it will then belong to a goddess not a god, the ancient translation *bīt narāmīšu* is unintelligent and presumably mechanical.

9 The restoration of this temple name is assured by its use for a quarter of Kiš in a deed from the reign of Šamaš-šuma-ukīn (see the gazetteer). The rendering in the translation of the TN's GALAM.GALAM as gagalam relies on two lines of the bilingual Exaltation of Ištar, where the reduplicated root is glossed ga-ga-la!(ŠU)-ma and ga-ga-la-am (Hruška, *ArOr* 37 [1969], pp. 483f. = *TCL* VI 51, obv. 19.37; cf. Falkenstein, *ZA* 53 [1959], p. 100). There, however, it corresponds not to *nakālu* plural stative, as here, but to parts of a different verb, *utlellû*, "to exalt oneself."

10 The ceremonial name of the wall of Kiš is also known from list no. 4, 34, and an inscription of Nabonidus, who repaired it (*CT* 36 22, 2: bàd. me.lam.kur.kur.dul.la *dūr kiš*$^{ki}$).

11 Note *ekurru* as a term used in reference not only to temples but also to a city wall. The sacred aspect of a city's walls, gates, streets and rivers is emphasized by the bestowal on them of ceremonial names of the same sort as those given to temples, and accounts for their listing in this kind of text (see further *Topog. Texts*, pp. 12f.).

12 There is not enough room to restore é.ḫur.sag.kalam.ma here, nor do the traces permit it in the following line. But then the preceding section omitted the obvious temple names é.dub.ba and é.me.te.ur.sag. é.kur.ní.zu is the name given to the sanctuary of $^{d}$nin.líl (Mulliltu) at Ḫursag-kalamma by Merodach-baladan, and it also appears in the Syncretistic Ištar Hymn (see the gazetteer).

Ištar of Ḫursag-kalamma is often known as Mulliltu in the late periods: e.g., in a *lipšur*-litany and a cultic calendar, as well as in Merodach-baladan's inscription (see the gazetteer sub é.ḫur.sag.kalam.ma).

14 Restored from the ziqqurrat lists, nos. 4, 13 and 5, 11′.

15 The only ceremonial name of a temple known to me in connection with Bizilla appears in a tiny unpublished NB fragment, BM 99743 (1: $^{d}$*b*]*í-zil-lá šá* é.dur.šu.a[n.na?). Possibly this TN should be restored here. Bizilla is a goddess associated with Nanāy at Mari in an offering list of the time of the *šakkanakku*'s (Lambert, *MARI* 4 [1985], p. 530, 22: $^{\text{d.nin}}$*bi-ṣíl-lá*, an orthography which incidentally confirms the reading $^{d}$*bí-zil-lá*), and with Nanāy and Kanisurra in the single-column Weidner god list (see now Cavigneaux, *Textes scolaires*, pp. 82f., 20–22). This would suggest some family connection with Nanāy of Uruk or Borsippa. However, she is not excluded from the company of other deities, for in the Nungal Hymn she appears in the entourage of the eponymous goddess of penal retribution (Sjöberg, *AfO* 24 [1973], p. 34, 94: $^{d}$bí.zi.il.la, coll. courtesy M. Civil).

The connection of Bizilla with Ḫursag-kalamma, witnessed by her appearance in the present list, is in fact confirmed by two unpublished documents. The one is a cultic text which lists the two groups of seven stars equated with manifestations of Enlil and Anu and adds to the table their respective wives. The entry for the Wolf star runs as follows: $^{\text{mul}}$ur.bar.ra = $^{d}$*en-líl šá* ḫur.sag.kalam.ma$^{\text{ki}}$, $^{d}$*bí-zil-l*[*á aššat*(dam)-*su*] (*VAS* 24 119, 4′, restored from BM 68593, rev. 6′; without the last sub-column cf. the Archive of Mystic Heptads, *KAR* 142, iii 6 // Pinches, *PSBA* 33 [1911], pp. 94f., pl. 11, 5–6). The evidence of other astronomical texts suggests that Bizilla is not actually Enlil's wife, i.e., an aspect of Ninlil, but in fact Ninlil's agent: in one star list Bizilla is equated with the Star of Abundance (V *R* 46, no. 1, 9: $^{\text{mul}}$ḫé.gál-*a-a* = $^{d}$*bí-zil-lá*), while in the compendium $^{\text{mul}}$Apin I the same star is entitled the vizier of Ninlil-Mulliltu (Hunger and Pingree, *AfO* Beiheft 24, p. 22, 13: $^{\text{mul}}$ḫé.gál-*a-a-ú* sukkal $^{d}$nin.líl). The second unpublished document is a NB temple ritual, where she is mentioned in connection with the arrival of a procession of deities of Borsippa and Babylon at Ḫursag-kalamma (BM 78076, 32, to appear in a forthcoming article on "Temple Rituals from Babylon"). The place of Bizilla in the present list, between the great goddess of Ḫursag-kalamma and the god Enlil, who was evidently Mulliltu's consort in Ḫursag-kalamma as in Nippur, would appear to confirm her status as vizier of Mulliltu.

17 The name of Enlil's ziqqurrat at Ḫursag-kalamma is restored from the lists given above, nos. 4, 14; 5, 12′, where it follows é.kur.maḫ. The numeral 50, a cipher for Enlil, is not well written, but must be so read if we accept the evidence of the ziqqurrat lists.

19 The translation of the toponym uses speculative etymology: du$_8$ certainly provides *ḫengallu* (cf. du$_8$.du$_8$ = *ḫ*. in bilinguals: IV *R*$^2$ 18*, no. 5, 11–12;

20, no. 1, 21–22). gú ought to give *mātu*, *erṣetu*, or *napḫaru* (cf. e.g., *MSL* XIII, p. 196, *Izi* F 42–45), but the traces do not allow confident restoration.

20 The translation relies on $^{d}$mes as a name of Marduk, of course, and on the lexical equation lam = *erṣetu* (documented in *CAD* L, s.v. *lammu* B). The implication of such a speculative interpretation is that the original meaning of the temple's name was forgotten, and the translation given below in the gazetteer, "House, Warrior of the Netherworld," takes the ancient tradition into account. But bearing in mind the intimate association in lexical texts of $^{giš}$mes (= *mēsu*, *lammu* in *Hh* III 200–201) and $^{giš}$lam (= *lammu* and *šiqdu*, "almond," in *Diri* II Boğ. 223a-b), it is tempting to see the original derivation of the TN as a compound of the two trees.

22 The ceremonial name of this wall, too, is also known from an inscription of Nabonidus, who repaired it (*CT* 36 22, 1: bàd.$u_4$.gal.a.má.$uru_5$ *dūr* gú.$du_8$.a$^{ki}$). a.má.$uru_5$ = *abūbu* is well known, but the equation of $u_4$.gal and Anzû looks like mythological speculation: both appear as defeated enemies of divine warriors.

23 In list no. 4, 35, this is the only wall of Kutha listed, but its subordinate position here, as well as the common lexical equation ús = *emēdu*, suggest that the otherwise unattested ús.bàd stands for *nēmettu*, which in this usage is a synonym of *šalḫû*, the secondary wall that ran adjacent to a main city wall on the outside (the word *nēmettu* is used as a common noun in this meaning by Nabonidus, *PBS* XV 80 // Al-Rawi, *RIM Annual Review* 9 [1991], p. 5, no. 5, i 19–20, where it refers to the *šalḫû* of Babylon, itself of course named Nīmit-Enlil: above, no. 4, 26; also *Tintir* V 58).

26 On the rivers of Kutha see Edzard and Gallery, *RlA* VI, pp. 386f.

28 Apak (or Apâk < Apiʾak?) is a cult-center of Nergal as Lugal-Apiak or Nergal of Apiak from at least Sargonic times (see the documentation of Stol, *RlA* VII, p. 115; Frayne, *RIME* 4, p. 106, 1–2: DN *a-pi*$_5$*-ak*$^{ki}$, Damiq-ilīšu; god list fragment Wilcke, *Isin* III, p. 93, IB 1616, 0′–1′: [$^{d}$nè.$eri_{11}$.gal] *a-p*[*i-ak*$^{ki}$]; note also the temple of Nergal as Ḫuškia in *a-pa-ak*$^{ki}$ listed in CTL 571). The spelling *a-pak* is late, being also found in a litany of Nergal (Cohen, *Lamentations*, p. 502, 18, OB variant: *a-pi-ak*[$^{ki}$]; p. 507, 107), and in the Archive of Mystic Heptads (*KAR* 142, iii 32: $^{d}$*kaš-kaš* = $^{d}$*nergal*(u.gur) ⌜*šá*⌝ *a-pak*$^{ki}$). Writings *a-pi-ik* are also attested (*An* VI 60; *MSL* XI, p. 15, *Hh* XXI/5 12), and also probably $^{uru}$*ap-pa-ak*$^{ki}$ (Strassmaier, *Darius* 533, 15). The town is presumed to be west of Marad, across the Apkallatu canal, where it gave its name to a province of the Ur III empire (see Kraus, ZA 51 [1955], pp. 56, 68).

29 In view of Apak's well-documented association with Nergal, it is rather odd that the single temple listed for the town here is dedicated not to the lord of the netherworld but to the divine cowherd Lulal. The cult-centers of this god known hitherto are é.mùš.kalam.ma at Bad-tibira (Inanna's

Descent), a place Pulukku (? cf. $^{d}$lú.làl BULUG$^{ki}$ in a year name: Kienast, *Kisurra* I, p. 26 e), and possibly Isin or du$_{6}$.edin.na (see Wilcke, *OrNS* 54 [1985], pp. 312f.). With these can be compared the towns appended to his name in the Isin version of the monolingual Weidner god list: unug$^{?ki}$, x.edin$^{ki}$, Maškan-šāpir, x.a$^{ki}$ and abzu.eridu$^{ki}$ (Wilcke, *Isin* III, p. 96, A vi 13–17; two other lists are useless: *OrNS* 54, pp. 312f.). Lātarāk, the alter ego of Lulal, is equated with Nergal, to be sure, but only when Lulal himself is identified with Sîn (in the list of stars V *R* 46, no. 1, 22; see Lambert, *RlA* VII, pp. 163f.). Nergal and Lulal do share a common epithet, Lugaledinna, but for different reasons (see Lambert, *RlA* VII, p. 137), so this is not useful evidence either, and the problem remains without solution.

## *Other Temple Lists*

### *7. A Fragmentary List*

Four pieces survive of a fragmentary temple list which was catalogued in *Topog. Texts* as text no. 55 but not edited there. The fragments are VAT 10755 A (+) B, from Aššur and copied by Schroeder as *KAV* 84, and BM 123383 (+) 128602, from Kuyunjik and copied by Campbell Thompson as *CT* 51 178 and 179 (new copies in *Topog. Texts*, pl. 53). It is unlike any other temple list in format. The text is written in narrow columns subdived into short sections by horizontal rulings. Most of these sections, as the text now stands, are concerned with the temples of a given city, such as Kiš (the only section preserved on two sources), Eridu, Nippur, and Tilmun. Within each section temples are listed either by ceremonial name, by popular name (*bīt* DN), or both. At least one ceremonial name, é.ḫur.sag.kalam.ma$^{ki}$, is subject to speculative interpretation in Akkadian. One section (c) seems to have no immediate connection with this material.

a  Eridu and Tilmun: VAT 10755 A

1′ *bīt* $^{d}$*é-a* [x x]
2′ *bīt* $^{d}$*nin-ki* [x x]
3′ é.u$_{6}$.ni[r x x]
4′ é.kas.kas.$^{d}$lamma.[x x]
5′ $^{d}$*dam-ki-*[*na*]

---

6′ (vacat)

---

7′ *til-mun*$^{ki}$ : *iš-ḫa-a-*[(x) x]
8′ é.kar.ra *bīt* $^{d}$*e*[*n-zak*]
9′ [*šá*$^{?}$] *til-mun*$^{ki}$ $^{d}$*m*[*es-ki-lak*?]

b  Kiš and Nippur: VAT 10755 B // BM 123383, ii′

1 *kiš*$^{ki}$
2 é.ḫur.sag.kalam.ma$^{ki}$
3 *bīt* $^{d}$*za-ba*$_{4}$*-ba*$_{4}$

4 *bīt* $^{d}$*nin-líl* (so VAT, BM: *bīt* $^{d}$*nin-urt*[*a*])
5 *bītu šá-ad mātāti* (kur.kur.kur)
6 *bīt* $^{d}$*be-let mātāti* (kur.kur.kur) (VAT omits this line)
7 *bīt* $^{d}$*enlil* (idim) *bīt* $^{d}$*a-nim*
8 *bīt* $^{d}$*é-a*

---

9 (vacat)

---

10 $^{d}$*enlil*(idim) $^{d}$*nin-líl*
11 *ni-ip-pú-ru*
12 *bīt* $^{d}$*enlil*(idim)
13 *bīt* $^{d}$*nin-líl*
14 ⸢é⸣.kur *bīt* $^{d}$*enlil* (idim)
15 [*bī*]*t* $^{d}$*en-líl-ú-ti*
16 [*bīt šar*]*ru-ú-ti*
17 [*bīt bēlu-ú-t*]*i*?

c BM 123383, iii′

---

1′ *šu*-[ . . . ]

---

2′ en : [ . . . ]
3′ me.er.me.e[r . . . ]
4′ (vacat)
5′ (vacat)
6′ *šá-qu-t*[*u*?]
7′ *ra-bu-t*[*u*?]
8′ (vacat)
9′ *e*-[x]

d BM 128602, obverse
1′ [x] ⸢x *lum*⸣
2′ ⸢d⸣*marduk pa-ri-*ʾ
3′ *na-piš-ti a-a-bi*
4′ $^{d}$*zēr* (numun)-*bāni* (dù)-*tu*
5′ (vacat)
6′ (vacat)
7′ (vacat)

---

8′ *i-ni-ru*

---

e BM 128602, reverse
1 (vacat)

---

2 *bīt* $^{d}$*nabû*(muati) *šá* $^{u}$[$^{ru}$x x]

3 *bīt* $^{d}$60 *šá* $^{uru}$*b*[*āb*(ká)-*ili*?]
4 *bīt* $^{d}$*nabû*(muati) *šá bar-si-pa*[$^{ki}$]
5 *bīt* $^{d}$*marduk šá* $^{uru}$[x x]
6 $^{d}$*na*-⸢*bi*⸣-[*um*]
7 (vacat)

*8. K 14950*

This piece, copied for *Topog. Texts* (pl. 53) and catalogued there as text no. 54, is a fragment from the left edge of a large tablet from Kuyunjik. The extant text preserves the beginning of ten lines of what is most probably a temple list. The physical characteristics of the tablet make it unlikely that it is from the opening of the Canonical Temple List, and line 8′, if correctly read, also militates against such an identification.

1′ ⸢é⸣.[. . .
2′ ⸢é⸣.[. . .
3′ é.[. . .
4′ é.[. . .
5′ é.a[n. . . . (or: *bīt* ⸢$^{d}$⸣[. . . )
6′ é.a[n. . . . (or: *bīt* ⸢$^{d}$⸣[. . . )
7′ é.an.[. . . (or: *bīt* $^{d}$[. . . )
8′ é.⸢u$_{6}$⸣.[nir . . .
*ziq*-[*qur-rat* . . .
9′ é.x[. . .

The reverse, of which much more surface is preserved, is not inscribed.

*9. Excerpts on an Exercise Tablet*

One of the few exercise tablets from Aššurbanipal's libraries at Kuyunjik is K 8382, which contains, among other material, an excerpt of four lines from a temple list and another of four lines from, probably, a geographical list. The text of these excerpts is given in *Topog. Texts* as no. 39.

# Part Two

# The Temples of Ancient Mesopotamia: a Gazetteer

## *Introduction*

The intention of this part of the book is to furnish an up-to-date gazetteer of the ceremonial names of the temples of Sumer and Akkad, and of Babylonia and Assyria. The great majority of temples of ancient Mesopotamia bore ceremonial names (é.TN) in Sumerian; a very few had Akkadian ceremonial names. As such one may observe that these names were characteristic of Sumerian civilization, and this accounts for their distribution. Common in the southern heartland of Sumer and Akkad in all periods, Sumerian temple names are also found in those peripheral areas where the influence of Sumero-Babylonian scribal culture was strongest: Assyria, where Sumerian ceremonial names begin with Šamšī-Adad I and become increasingly the norm under the empire, culminating in their collection in the Assyrian Temple List by the eighth century; the towns of the Diyala basin; the area now known as Syrian Mesopotamia, including Mari in the Old Babylonian period, and Harran; and occasionally, Elam.

These names most often express ideas about the cosmological place and function of the ancient Mesopotamian temple, for example é.an.da.sá.a, "House which Rivals the Heavens," and é.me.ur$_4$.ur$_4$, "House which Gathers the *Me*'s." They are commonly found in building inscriptions, liturgical texts, hymns and prayers and other religious texts, but much less often in letters and in administrative, legal and commercial documents. There the convention is usually to qualify a temple by its divine owner: é // *bīt* DN. The implication is that most ceremonial temple names were not in everyday usage. The distinction between ceremonial and everyday or popular names is neatly expressed in those lists which draw up equations between items from the two sets, after the pattern é.TN = *bīt* DN. Such lists belong to the lexical tradition, explaining the uncommon or obscure in terms of the common or familiar. They have been treated in the first part of the book.

The names of the temples of ancient Mesopotamia have been collected before, first by Luckenbill in an article published in the *American Journal of Semitic Languages and Literatures* in 1908,[1] and then by Ebeling, in the form of contributions to the second volume of the *Reallexikon der Assyriologie*, which went to press in 1938.[2] Given the passage of years and the growth of the discipline, it is not surprising that as works of reference these old gazetteers have long been obsolete, and the time has come to replace them.

A truly comprehensive treatment of the temples of ancient Mesopotamia and their names would need to cover all genres of text from all periods. It would also have to collect not only ceremonial names (é.TN) but also the popular names of temples (é // *bīt* DN), since the fullest understanding would need to rely on evidence culled from sources which use the latter as well as those which use the former.[3] Such a project, if eventually brought to a conclusion, would be a lifetime's labour. However, the publication in the preceding pages and in *Babylonian Topographical Texts* of all the known temple lists really demands that some sort of an index of ceremonial temple names be made available at once. The gazetteer presented below has been put together to fill this need, but obviously the constraints of time as well as space have obliged me to limit it in terms of the sources used. Every effort has been made to enter in the list all ceremonial temple names known to me, and to include—in addition to geographical location and divine owner, where known—other relevant information, particularly anything relating to the temple's history and cult. However, there is no place for long articles on, for example, é.sag̃.íl, é.kur and é.an.na, and references to these and many other famous and well-known temples, especially, are of necessity selective.[4]

In addition to topographical texts and other lists I have scanned as many royal inscriptions and year names as I could find; a selection of the more fertile literary and religious compositions; a large number of liturgical texts; and temple rituals.[5] Having reached the point of much diminished returns I have

[1] "The Temples of Babylonia and Assyria," *AJSL* 24, pp. 291–322.

[2] *RlA* II, pp. 258–491.

[3] A brief synthesis of information on divine cults extracted from a wide selection of non-literary sources exists for the Old Babylonian period: J. Renger, "Götternamen in der altbabylonischen Zeit," *Studien Falkenstein*, pp. 137–71.

[4] Many temples and shrines listed here have been treated at greater length in *Babylonian Topographical Texts*. Whenever texts edited in Part One of that book are cited in the gazetteer the user is advised implicitly to refer also to the appropriate passage of commentary in Part Two.

[5] In this I have been greatly aided by the appearance in recent years of modern editions of many texts of the most fertile genres. For royal inscriptions up to the end of the OB period—and later in Assyria—one has the Toronto volumes of Grayson (*RIMA* 1–2) and Frayne (*RIME* 4), as well as the books of Steible (*FAOS* 5 and 9) and Gelb and Kienast (*FAOS* 7). For liturgical texts there are now Cohen's *Eršemma* and *Lamentations* (which for all their limitations do at least make the material more accessible than previously), Maul's *Eršaḫunga* and Volk's *FAOS* 18. I was privileged to be able to consult Marcel Sigrist's corpus of year names in advance of publication. During a stay in Philadelphia in 1989 Prof. Åke W. Sjöberg allowed me the run of his Sumerian Dictionary files, from which

brought the search for ceremonial names to a halt, and present the results below. Undoubtedly there will be temple names hidden away in obscure texts and rare publications which have escaped notice, but it is hoped that these are few and that the present list, though provisional, is complete enough to serve as a handy reference guide.

At this point I must add a word of caution by stressing again the limitations advertised above. Because of the confinement of its scope essentially to ceremonial temple names and the concomitant exclusion of an exhaustive listing of temples known only as "temple of DN," the present list cannot be a comprehensive statement of the known religious buildings of ancient Mesopotamia. It is evident to anyone reading even royal inscriptions only, that there are in all periods a few religious buildings whose ceremonial names, if they had them, seem never to be used (the temples of Dimgalabzu in pre-Sargonic Lagaš and of Mār-bīti in inscriptions of Nebuchadnezzar II are typical examples). Despite this, many such buildings—most, I hope, whose popular names I came across in the sources utilized in the compilation of the gazetteer—are represented in the list, and where possible the information so won has been synthesized with the gazetteer. Those popular names that could not be entered in the main list are listed as an appendix to it, alphabetically by divine name. A second appendix collects the Sumerian ceremonial names that a few rulers conferred on their palaces. But the labour of collecting and synthesizing the popular names of temples exhaustively must, as already stated, await a future work. On the other hand, though they have nothing to say about the cosmological function of the temple, and are strictly to be seen as a second variety of popular name, temple names which are composites of toponyms—i.e., "temple of GN"—are included in the gazetteer where it is supposed that they are being used as ceremonial names rather than popular names. Thus entries are admitted for é.ul.maš at Akkade and Sippar, and for é.ti.ra.áš and é.sìrara at Lagaš. However, a term such as é.g̃irsu.(k), which is in any case usually found in apposition to a ceremonial or popular temple name, is not accepted as a true name, and finds no place. Naturally it is not always easy to distinguish between such usages, and some temple names omitted from the gazetteer on the grounds that they are composites of toponyms may be proved by future discoveries to be ceremonial. Comparable difficulties occur in Sumerian literary texts, where one cannot always be sure whether a given phrase is a true temple name or a general epithet. I have tried to err on the side of generosity in these matters, and so the list may also contain items that in due course will turn out to have been included wrongly. In Sumerian anthroponymy the word é, "house, temple," is frequently used as the divine

---

I was able to reap a rich harvest of temple names in Sumerian literature. Prof. William L. Moran kindly supplied me with some invaluable references from his files. Finally I would add that Prof. W. G. Lambert has himself, over the years, shown me unpublished material, particularly temple rituals and literary texts, which by his generous leave I have been able to mine for temple names. It is a pleasurable duty to record my debt to all these scholars and to caution that they are of course not responsible for the gazetteer's failings.

element in theophoric personal names, with the result that what at first sight looks like a ceremonial temple name or epithet in fact turns out to refer to a person.[6] These compounds have not been collected.

A further note of caution must be sounded with regard to terminology. First, Sumerian ceremonial names were given to all religious structures, from a tiny symbol-pedestal (*šubtu*, "seat") to a great temple complex. In such names the word é, "house," is thus seen to be imbued with a very broad meaning. In ordinary language é // *bītu* is used to describe any religious structure from the smallest chapel to the grandest temple, and often any epithets and descriptions appended to a ceremonial name are not much help in determining the exact nature of the structure in question. Where there is decisive information I have followed it, and so many entries in the list are explained as "seat," "shrine," "cella," "chapel" or "temple." In these cases the words have precise meaning. However, many more are described as "temple" or "sanctuary" for lack of evidence, and may turn out not to have been the large structures that these terms suggest. A further difficulty here is that many temples appear to have had a number of different ceremonial names, sometimes depending on period, but not always. The temple lists, in particular, are prone to the collection of multiple names, and there is often a suspicion that not only are different names placed side by side in such texts, but also lesser shrines are included alongside the great sanctuaries. In this area I may be laying myself open to criticism for not utilizing the results of archaeological information, but again, the scope of the work does not permit the fundamental examination of the evidence that would, in any case, eventually yield positive results for a few sanctuaries only.

Second, a similar ambiguity attends the Sumerian and Akkadian terms for building. In royal inscriptions, where writers are prone to the aggrandizement of the royal deeds, it is suspected that the verb "to build" (usually dù // *epēšu*) conveys a wide range of meaning. So when King So-and-so declares that he built the Temple Such-and-such, his lofty words may suggest that he constructed a completely new building, but in reality they may refer to a little light repair work. Unless more specific details are given one is usually unable to determine the truth. Consequently the use in the gazetteer of the terms "build," "rebuild," "restore" and "repair" is often arbitrary, and such words cannot always be taken as precise indications of the scope of the work in question.

All but the most obscure ceremonial names are translated into English. Some names were already obscure in antiquity, and in these cases I have usually followed, where it is extant, the guidance of the ancient scholars who on occasion translated such names into Akkadian. Such is the nature of Sumerian, of course, that even apparently straightforward names are open to multiple interpretations. This was true even in antiquity, as the explanatory temple lists

[6] The most instructive example of this pitfall is Charpin's discovery that the bilingual text once known as the Hymn to the Temple of Ninšubur, *UET* VI 117, is in fact a scholarly list of names borne by priestly personnel (*Le clergé d'Ur*, p. 398). Many Sumerian personal names comprising compounds with é have been collected by Limet, *L'anthroponymie*, pp. 402ff.; cf. also the discussion pp. 203ff.

of Babylon and Nippur demonstrate so well. However, the gazetteer is not the place for detailed philological commentary, and most translations are offered without documentation of the lexical evidence or other justifications that might be enlisted in their support. That this will inevitably provoke others to offer alternative translations is only to be expected—and indeed welcomed—but it is hoped that the renderings given here will allow some appreciation of the enormous range of meaning and expression found in the names given to the temples of ancient Mesopotamia.

## *Gazetteer of Ceremonial Names*

1 **é.a.akkil**, see é.akkil

2 **a.ar.ke$_4$.éš**, temple of Inšušinak at Susa, rebuilt by Šulgi (Steible, *FAOS* 9/II, Š 12; cf. 6).

3 **a.edin**, see é.edin

4 **a.ga.balag̃**, "Hall(?) of the Harp," part of é.ninnu at G̃irsu (Falkenstein, *AnOr* 30, p. 122).

5 **a.ga.eren**, "Hall(?) of Cedar," part of é.ninnu at G̃irsu (Falkenstein, *AnOr* 30, p. 123).

6 **é.a.ga.su.lim**, "House, Hall(?) of Radiance," shrine of Nanše in Lagaš-G̃irsu (Falkenstein, *AnOr* 30, p. 166).

7 **a.ga.tukul.lá**, "Hall where the Weapon is Hung," part of é.ninnu at G̃irsu (Falkenstein, *AnOr* 30, p. 123).

8 **é.a.girin.na**, "House of Pure Water," a chamber of the é.kur complex at Nippur (Cohen, *Lamentations*, p. 351, 57, with the epithet é.ad.gi$_4$.gi$_4$), also written é.g̃ar.rin.na (ibid., p. 98, 57).

9 **a.ḫuš**, see é.ḫuš

10 **é.a.mir.bábbar**, "Shining House of Stormy Water," part of é.ninnu at G̃irsu (Falkenstein, *AnOr* 30, p. 124).

11 **é.a.mir.kù**, "Pure House of Stormy Water," sanctuary of Nintinugga in é.NI.gu.la of Enlil at Nippur, known from a school copy of a building inscription (Legrain, *PBS* XIII 26, 5; of Ur-Nammu? see Poebel, *OLZ* 27 [1924], 265).

12 **é.a.nir.ra**, "House of Sighs," by-name or epithet of the netherworld (Sjöberg, *AfO* 24 [1973], p. 30: Nungal 44; cf. é.a.nir.gal.gal.la, Ninmešarra 25).

13 **(é).a.ra.li**, "House, Netherworld" 1, a shrine of Dumuzi (in é.mùš at Bad-tibira?: Temple Hymns 215) commonly found in Dumuzi texts and liturgical laments, often alongside é.du$_6$.šuba (Inanna and Bilulu 3.180; Langdon, *BL* no. 8, obv. 10; *BE* XXX/1 1, ii 10; *VAS* II 1, iii 11; Cohen, *Eršemma*, p. 90, 7: e.a.ra.li; *Lamentations*, index p. 741; etc.), but also

among sanctuaries of Gula (ibid., p. 256, 47, qualified as gu$_4$.bur.nun.na). The TN occurs in Proto-*Kagal* (*MSL* XIII, p. 72, 197), and is listed for both Dumuzi and Belili in the Canonical Temple List (lines 445, 467).

14 **é.a.ra.li** 2, a temple of Dumuzi known from OB legal documents from Isin (Kraus, *JCS* 3 (1949), pp. 60, 86).

15 **é.a.ra.zu.g̃iš.tuku.($^{d}$asal.lú.ḫi)**, "House of Asalluḫi which Hears Prayers," a shrine in é.sag̃.íl at Babylon (*Topog. Texts* no. 1 = *Tintir* II 19; CTL 227, var. é.g̃iš.tuku).

16 **é.a.sikil.la**, "House of Pure Water," seat of Nādin-mê-qātī and Mukīl-mê-balāṭi in é.sag̃.íl at Babylon (*Topog. Texts* no. 1 = *Tintir* II 37).

17 **é.a.zu.ḫur.sag̃**, "House, Doctor of the Mountains," a TN or epithet known from the big OB forerunner to *Hh* XXI (*MSL* XI, p. 142, viii 46).

18 **é.á.ág̃.g̃á.kìlib.ur$_4$.ur$_4$**, "House which Gathers All Decrees," temple of Ninegal at Larsa, rebuilt for Rīm-Sîn I by his wife Simat-Ištar (Frayne, *RIME* 4, pp. 294, 19; 296, 37).

19 **é.á.ág̃.g̃á.sum.mu**, "House which Gives Decrees," a temple of Nin-šubur (at Ur?), rebuilt by Rīm-Sîn I (Frayne, *RIME* 4, p. 288, 21). See also é.nin.bi.túm.

20 **é.á.an.da**, a sanctuary known from an Ur III document (*UET* III 913, 13; cf. 270, rev. i 16′: é.an.da); presumably of Ningal (note $^{d}$nin.gal.á.an.da in OB disbursements of offerings from Ur: Figulla, *Iraq* 15 [1953], pp. 104ff.).

21 **á.gil.dab.dab**, "Seizer of the Arm of the Wicked," seat of Kūbu in é.šár.ra at Aššur (*Topog. Texts* no. 21, obv. 8′).

22 **á.lá.gù.dé**, "Booming Drum," seat of Šulšagana(?) in é.šár.ra at Aššur (*Topog. Texts* no. 21, obv. 25′).

23 **é.á.nun.[na]**, "House of the Princely Arm," a temple of Ea (CTL 190).

24 **á.sud.a-ki.dúr.g̃ar.pàd.da**, "Long Side, Place of the Chosen Throne," a chamber in é.sag̃.íl at Babylon (*Topog. Texts* no. 1 = *Tintir* II 8′.33′–34′).

25 **é.á.zág**, "House of Taboo," seat of the Asakku demon in é.sag̃.íl at Babylon (*Topog. Texts* no. 1 = *Tintir* II 5′).

26 **é.AB**, sanctuary of Enlil at G̃irsu according to Ur III documents (Lau, *OB Temple Records* 162, rev. 1; Legrain, *TRU* 289, 7; *MVN* VI 98, rev. 1; 395, obv. 7; etc.).

27 **é.AB.KI.TE**, see é.èš.ki.te(n)

28 **é.ab.šà.ga.lá**, "House which Stretches over the Midst of the Sea," temple of Ninmar at Guabba (Proto-*Kagal* 205; CTL [502]; Temple Hymns 283; Gelb, *StOr* 46 [1975], p. 49, 21–24: no TN), built by Ur-Nanše (no TN: Steible, *FAOS* 5/I, UrN 26, iii 2; 29, iv 2; etc.). See also èš.kù.šilam.

29 **é.áb.lu.a**, "House of Teeming Cattle," name or epithet of the temple of Sîn at Urum (Temple Hymns 469).

30 **(é).abzu**, "*Apsû*-House" 1, temple of Enki/Ea in Eridu (CTL [179]; TL no. 2, 4), built by Elili of Ur (Steible, *FAOS* 5/II, p. 278, 6), then Ur-Nammu, (no TN: 9/II, UrN 4; 12; 46), Šulgi, probably, and Amar-Suen (ibid., Š 10; AS 5), and later Nūr-Adad (Frayne, *RIME* 4, pp. 145, 12: ki.tuš kù ki.áğ.ğá.ni, "his beloved pure abode," no TN; 146, 23: abzu é.me.kù.kù. ga.a.ni, "TN, his house of pure *me*'s"; cf. year G), patronized by Ḫammurapi (CḪ ii 1). Also found in a liturgical text among other temples of Ea (Maul, *Eršaḫunga* no. 10, 8). See also é.engur.(ra), èš.abzu.

31 **(é).abzu** 2, sanctuary of Enki at Pasirra, built by Enmetena (Steible, *FAOS* 5/I, Ent 1, ii 11; 8, iv 7; etc.).

32 **é.abzu.$^{d}$asal.lú.ḫi**, "*Apsû*-House of Asalluḫi," seat of the Anunnaki in the chapel of Ninurta(?) in é.sağ.íl at Babylon (*Topog. Texts* no. 1 = *Tintir* II 18).

33 **é.abzu?.bàn.da**, "Little *Apsû*-House" 1, see é.èš.bàn.da

34 **abzu.bàn.da** 2, a shrine built by Ur-Nanše of Lagaš (Steible, *FAOS* 5/I, UrN 20a; 22–23), desecrated by Lugalzaggesi (Ukg. 16, i 10).

35 **abzu.e**, or abzu.ég, "*Apsû* Dike," a shrine(?) built by Ur-Nanše (Steible, *FAOS* 5/I, UrN 25, v 6; 27, iv 1: abzu; 28, iv 3; etc.), desecrated by Lugalzaggesi (ibid., Ukg 16, iii 11).

36 **abzu.$^{d}$en.líl**, "*Apsû* of Enlil," a shrine listed among gods and other parts of Enlil's cult-center at Nippur in an Ur III offering list (*TCL* II 5501, ii 5).

37 **é.abzu.kù.ga**, "Pure *Apsû*-House," cella of Zababa at Kiš (*Topog. Texts* nos. 22, 3′; 24, 2′?; TL no. 6, 1).

38 **abzu.$^{d}$nin.líl**, "*Apsû* of Ninlil," a shrine listed among gods and other parts of Enlil's cult-center at Nippur in an Ur III offering list (*TCL* II 5501, ii 11).

39 **é.abzu.[x]**, sanctuaries, of Damkina? (CTL 222–24).

40 **é.ad.da**, "House of the Father," sanctuary of Enlil of Imsağğa, rebuilt by Enmetena (Steible, *FAOS* 5/I, Ent 1, i 2; iii 6; iv 3; vi 6; 8, vi 5; etc.) and Uruinimgina (ibid., Ukg 1, iii 2′; 10, iii 8).

41 **é.ad.gi$_4$.gi$_4$**, "House of the Counsellor" 1, seat of Ennundağalla and Ğanunḫedu, the counsellors of Marduk, in é.sağ.íl at Babylon (*Topog. Texts* no. 1 = *Tintir* II 36: DN conflated as Ennunğaḫedu; Jeremias, *MVAG* 21 [1916], p. 86, 20: Kedor-laomer text).

42 **é.ad.gi$_4$.gi$_4$** 2, seat of Nuska represented by a brick found in the sanctuary of Ningal at Ur, é.ği$_6$.pàr.kù 1, made by Sîn-balāssu-iqbi (*UET* I 180).

43 **é.ad.gi$_4$.gi$_4$** 3, seat of Damu in é.rab.ri.ri (at Babylon? *Topog. Texts* no. 12, 14′).

44 **é.ad.gi$_4$.gi$_4$** 4, a shrine in the temple complex of é.kur at Nippur (Cohen, *Lamentations*, p. 351, 57, where it may only be an epithet of é.a. girin.na).

45 **é.ad.gi$_4$.gi$_4$** 5, a sanctuary of Ea (Proto-*Kagal* 175; CTL 198), which follows Eridu and é.engur.ra in a liturgical fragment (Langdon, *BL* no. 123, 6′).

46 **é.addir.kalam.ma**, "House of the Prosperity of the Land," a temple of Nabû (*Topog. Texts* no. 28, 2′).

47 **[é].aga.du$_7$.du$_7$**, "House of the Butting Crown," a temple found among TNs of Nanna-Suen in a liturgical text (*BL* no. 27, 8′), and probably in the NB ziqqurrat list (TL no. 5, 15′, = Kuyunjik é.šu.g̃án.du$_7$.du$_7$).

48 **agrun.kù**, see é.gar$_6$.kù

49 **é.(a).akkil**, "House of Lamentation" 1, temple of Ninšubur-Papsukkal at Akkil (Temple Hymns 228). Also *Diri* I 233.

50 **é.akkil** 2, temple of Ninšubur-Papsukkal at Kiš (*Topog. Texts* no. 23, 17′; CTL 456), also known from a *lipšur*-litany (Craig, *ABRT* I 58, 10: *é.ak-ki-il*).

51 **é.akkil** 3, a temple of Manungal (*Diri* I 234).

52 **é.akkil** 4, seat of Manungal in é.sag̃.íl at Babylon (*Topog. Texts* no. 1 = *Tintir* II 4′).

53 **é.akkil.du$_6$.kù**, "House of Lamentation, Pure Mound," temple of Ninšubur at Nippur (CTL 457). Ninšubur's sanctuary at Nippur is also known from a MB metrological text (Bernhardt and Kramer, *OrNS* 44 [1975], p. 98, 29; no TN).

54 **é.al.ti.la**, "House of the Life-Giving Mattock," temple of Adad in east Babylon (*Topog. Texts* no. 1 = *Tintir* IV 7). Possibly to be read é.máḫ.ti.la, despite variant é.ḪAL.ti.lu$^?$.

55 **é.alim**, "House of the Bison," a sanctuary of Lagaš known from offering lists and the personal name Ur-E-alim (*ITT* 695, rev. 10; 833, 13′; Falkenstein, *Gerichtsurkunden* II, p. 169[3]; also Hussey, *HSS* 4 54, rev. 8?).

56 **é.am.kur.kur.ra**, "House, Wild Bull of the Lands," temple of Enlil at Aššur, rebuilt by Šamšī-Adad I (Grayson, *RIMA* 1, p. 49, 52, = *bītum rīm mātātim*). An unnamed temple of Enlil may be the subject of a fragmentary inscription of Aššur-rabi I (ibid., p. 98). See also *bētum rīmum.*

57 **é.ama$_5$.du$_6$.dam**, "House, Harem . . . ," TN or epithet known from the big OB forerunner to *Hh* XXI (*MSL* XI, p. 142, viii 12). Most probably = é.g̃á.du$_6$.da.

58 **é.ama$_5$.kalam.ma**, "House, Harem of the Land," see é.gán.kalam.ma

59 **é.amaš.kalam.ma**, "House, Sheepfold of the Land," a temple of Ištar (CTL 369).

60 **é.amaš.kù**, "House, Pure Sheepfold" 1, temple of Inanna at Kissig (EZEN×KÙ$^{ki}$) according to Inanna's Descent and the éš.dam hymns (Wilcke, *RlA* V, p. 78, written amaš.é.kù), but at BÀD.AN$^{ki}$ in the Canonical Temple List (l. 386). Probably = é.amaš.kù.ga of Ningal.

61 **é.amaš.kù.ga** 2, temple of Ningal at EZEN×X$^{ki}$, rebuilt by Nabonidus (Saggs, *Sumer* 13 [1957], p. 191, 36, = *su-pu-ru e-el-li*). Probably = é.amaš.kù 1.

62 **é.an.da**, see é.á.an.da

63 **é.an.da.sá.a**, "House which Rivals Heaven" 1, ziqqurrat at Akkade (TL no. 4, 9; no. 5, 1′), no doubt of Ištar.

64 **é.an.da.sá.a** 2, temple of Ištar as Venus (Ištar of the Star) at Babylon (*Topog. Texts* nos. 1 = *Tintir* IV 23; 3, rev. 4′; 4, 23; cf. 30, 7′; CTL 434). See *Topog. Texts*, pp. 318f.

65 **é.an.gim**, "House like Heaven," a sanctuary of Ningal (CTL 273).

66 **é.an.gim.kù.ga**, "House Pure like Heaven," a sanctuary of Ningal (CTL 274).

67 **é.an.gur$_4$.ra**, see é.engur.ra

68 **é.an.ki**, "House of Heaven and Underworld" 1, temple of Ištar (CTL 378), probably in Kār-Bēl-mātāti near Babylon (cf. the cultic calendar *BRM* IV 25, 24, where offerings are made to $^{d}$gašan-é.an.ki of this town), though TL no. 3 expands the name of her temple there to é.x.x.[a]n.ki (l. 23′, read é.è.an.ki?). Gašan-é.TN is also a name of Ištar in the cultic lament a.še.er ĝi$_6$.ta (Cohen, *Lamentations*, pp. 711, 135; 714, 190).

69 **é.an.ki** 2, a sanctuary of Anu, probably at Uruk, paired with é.ĝiš.ḫur.an.ki.a 3 in a liturgical hymn to Anu (Cohen, *Lamentations*, p. 729, 11).

70 [é]**.an.ki** 3, a temple listed in CTL 600.

71 **é.an.ki.kù.ga**, "House of Pure Heaven and Underworld," socle of Kusu represented by a brick found in the sanctuary of Ningal at Ur, é.ĝi$_6$.pàr.kù 1, made by Sîn-balāssu-iqbi (*UET* I 176).

72 [é]**.an.ki.šár.ra**, "House of All Heaven and Underworld," a temple listed in CTL 599.

73 **é.an.kù.ga**, "House of Pure Heaven," seat of Gunura in é.rab.ri.ri (at Babylon? *Topog. Texts* no. 12, 16′).

74 [**é.**A]N$^{?}$**.kum**, a sanctuary of Ištar of Zabalam, Supalītu (CTL 321).

75 **é.an.na**, "House of Heaven" 1, temple of Anu and Inanna/Ištar in Uruk (Proto-*Kagal* 228; *MSL* XI, p. 142, vii 19; CTL 313–14; Temple Hymns 201.208; Inanna's Descent and the éš.dam hymns: Wilcke, *RlA* V, p. 78; *CT* 58 13, 14; cf. Falkenstein, *Topographie*, pp. 40f.). Mentioned by Narām-Sîn of Akkade (Gelb and Kienast, *FAOS* 7, p. 82, 27: *in* é.an.na$^{ki}$-*im*). Rebuilt by Ur-Nammu and Šulgi (Steible, *FAOS* 9/II, UrN 13: for DN nin é.an.na; Š 11), and by Sîn-kāšid (Frayne, *RIME* 4, p. 441, 5; p. 450, 6; p. 451, 6; p. 453, 10: é.pa.paḫ, "cella"; etc.). Restored by Anam (no TN: ibid., p. 472, 2:10; p. 474, 9; p. 475, 7; year c), patronized by Rīm-Sîn I (ibid., p. 289, 20). Rebuilt by Kara-indaš (Brinkman, *MSKH*, p. 378; Schott, *UVB* 1, pl. 26f., nos. 12–13), Kurigalzu (ibid., pl. 27, nos. 14–15; cf. *CT* 36 6: endowment to Ištar of Uruk), and Merodach-baladan (*UVB* 1, pl. 27, nos. 16–18; cf. Gadd, *Iraq* 15 [1953], pp. 123f.), repaired by Sargon II (*UVB* 1,

pl. 28, no. 19, 13; *YOS* I 38). Rebuilt by Esarhaddon (Borger, *Esarh.*, § 47, 30, = *bīt Anūti*; etc.) and Nebuchadnezzar II (V *R* 34, ii 33; etc.). Provisioned by Ḫammurapi (CH ii 43). Grant to priest of TN by Marduk-zākir-šumi (Thureau-Dangin, *RA* 16 [1919], pp. 125–26). Statue and cult of Nanāy restored by Aššurbanipal (see é.ḫi.li.an.na; cf. Bauer, *Asb.*, p. 110). Cult changes during the time of Erība-Marduk were corrected by Nabonidus (cf. Brinkman, *PKB*, p. 222). Phonetic spelling: é-ia-na (*VAS* II 48, 6: éš. dam hymn). Passim in Sumerian literature. Commonly found in liturgical texts, often alongside é.ub.imin (Cohen, *Eršemma*, pp. 66, 2–9, etc.; 88, 5; 139, 4; *Lamentations* passim, index p. 750; Maul, *Eršaḫunga* nos. 57, obv. 14′; 70–71, 8′; Krecher, *Kultlyrik*, p. 60, [39]). Also in a *lipšur*-litany (Wiseman, *Iraq* 31 [1969], p. 177, 41′).

76 **é.an.na** 2, shrine of Inanna of (é).ib.gal at Lagaš, commemorated in the full version of Eannatum's name, Eanna-Inanna-Ibgalakaka-tum (Steible, *FAOS* 5/I, Ean 1, obv. iv 20–22), and enlarged by Enannatum I (ibid., En I 9, iii 6; 10–16; etc.). See also ib.é.an.na, é.an.na 3.

77 **é.an.na** 3, temple of Inanna at G̃irsu, rebuilt by Gudea (Steible, *FAOS* 9/I, Gud. Stat. C, iii 12; Gud. 23–26; 91?; cf. Falkenstein, *AnOr* 30, p. 149). Either this or the preceding temple is listed among other cult-centers of the Lagaš district in an Ur III offering list (Hussey, *HSS* 4 54, rev. 3).

78 **é.an.na** 4, a sanctuary mentioned in a year name of Nāqimum of the Mananā dynasty (Charpin, *RA* 72 [1978], p. 30, f).

79 **é.an.na**$^{\mathbf{ki}}$ 5, a temple which gave its name to a settlement (*MSL* XI, p. 131, iii 38).

80 [**é.an.na** 6 = *RlA* Eanna 3: in inscriptions of Tukultī-Ninurta I describing the rebuilding of sanctuaries of Ištar and Šulmānītu at Aššur é.an.na is to be read as the common noun *ayakku*.]

81 **é.an.šár**, "House of All Heaven," shrine represented by a brick found in the sanctuary of Ningal at Ur, é.g̃i$_6$.pàr.kù 1, made by Sîn-balāssu-iqbi (*UET* I 177, described as ki.tuš nam.lugal.la.ni, "his (i.e., Sîn's?) seat of kingship").

82 **é.AN.ŠEŠ.ki**, see é.ùru.an.ki.

83 **(é).an.ta.sur.ra**, "House which Twinkles from Heaven" 1, temple of Nin̄girsu near G̃irsu (Falkenstein, *AnOr* 30, p. 164, transl. "vom Himmel herabgetropft"), built by Akurgal (Steible, *FAOS* 5/I, Akg 1), which gave its name to the surrounding district disputed by Umma (ibid., Ean passsim; En I 29; viii 5, etc.). Rebuilt by Enmetena (ibid., Ent 1, ii 18; 8, vi 2; 16, i 9: é.gal.TN; etc.), who also calls it é.me.lám.bi.kur.kur.ra.a.dul$_5$, and by Uruinimgina (ibid., Ukg 1, i 6; 4, i 8; etc.), for whom it is é.ḫé.g̃ál.kalam.ma. Desecrated by Lugalzaggesi (ibid., Ukg 16, i 4). Also known from the big OB forerunner to *Hh* XXI (*MSL* XI, p. 142, viii 26), and Ur III administrative documents and offering lists (e.g., *ITT* 695, rev. 9; Hussey, *HSS* 4 54, rev. 7; *MVN* VI 301, rev. ii 4).

84 **é.an.ta.sur.ra** 2, a sanctuary of Šamaš (CTL 288).

85 **é.an.ur.sağ**, "House of Heaven, the Hero," a temple near Nippur (Grayson, *Chronicles*, p. 133, 14). Possibly *bīt* $^{d}$ur.sağ, however.

86 **é.an.úr.ki.tuš.maḫ**, "House of the Horizon, Exalted Abode," ziqqurrat at Kiš (TL no. 6, 5; *Topog. Texts* no. 23, 2′). Variant of é.$u_6$.nir.ki.tuš.maḫ.

87 **é.AN.za.gàr**, "House of the Tower," temple of Inanna/Ištar at Akšak (CTL 354; TL no. 3, 38′: é.za.an.gàr$^{gar}$), also in Inanna's Descent and the éš.dam hymns (Wilcke, *RlA* V, p. 78; McEwan, *RA* 76 [1982], p. 188).

88 **é.ár$^{?}$.nu.di/sá**, "House whose Praise is Unspoken/Unrivalled," a TN or epithet known from the big OB forerunner to *Hh* XXI (*MSL* XI, p. 142, viii 22).

89 **é.aratta$^{ki}$.ki.šár.ra**, "House, Mountain/Noblest of the Universe" 1, ziqqurrat at IM$^{ki}$ (i.e., Karkara? TL no. 4, 23; no. 5, 14′!).

90 **é.aratta.ki.šár.ra** 2, ziqqurrat of Aššur-Enlil at Aššur (*Topog. Texts* no. 20 = Götteradreßbuch 186: Assyrian TL). It was rebuilt by Shalmaneser I (Grayson, *RIMA* 1, p. 204, 13′–14′: *sequrrata rabīta*, no TN).

91 **é.AŠ.AN.AMAR**, seat of Enlil represented by a brick found in the sanctuary of Ningal at Ur, é.ği$_6$.pàr.kù 1, made by Sîn-balāssu-iqbi (*UET* I 179). Read é.tilla$_x$.maḫ$^{!}$?

92 **(é).aš.te**, "House of the Throne," temple of Gula at Larak, as found in liturgical texts (Cohen, *Lamentations*, pp. 224, 8; 255ff., 10.37.56; 621, 320; Krecher, *Kultlyrik*, pp. 56, [37]; 167). Also in Sîn-iddinam's letter to Ninisinna (Hallo, *Kramer AV*, p. 214; var. aš.ti).

93 **aš.te.ki.sikil** "Throne, Pure Place" 1, a shrine in the complex of é.kur at Nippur (Kramer, *RSO* 32 [1957], p. 97, 25: Hymn to E-kur; also Cohen, *Lamentations*, pp. 98, 50; 350, 47–48, qualified as é $u_4$.de kalam.ma, $u_6$.de ka.na.áğ.ğá, "house of the wonder of the land").

94 **aš.te.ki.sikil** 2, seat of the deity $^{d}$ĞIŠ.ŠA[R.( . . . )], probably in é.dàra.an.na of é.sağ.íl at Babylon (*Topog. Texts* no. 1 = *Tintir* II 8).

95 **aš.te.kù.ga**, "Pure Throne," a name of Larsa (*MSL* XI, pp. 11, *Hh* XXI 19; 54, 11; Kilmer, *JAOS* 83 [1963], p. 428, *Malku* I 205), possibly originally a TN.

96 **(é).ba.gára**, temple of Ninğirsu at Lagaš (Falkenstein, *AnOr* 30, pp. 157f.; Gelb, *StOr* 46 [1975], p. 48, ii 9–12; Sauren, *OrNS* 38 [1969], p. 217), built by Ur-Nanše (Steible, *FAOS* 5/I, UrN 25, v 2; 28, v 1; etc; cf. Ean 66; AnLag 14–16), desecrated by Lugalzaggesi (ibid., Ukg 16, iii 3), rebuilt by Gudea (9/I, Gud. 58–59; 61; year 15, cf. 16–17). Restored by Šulgi (Steible, *FAOS* 9/II, Š 68). Administrative documents and offering lists: Ebeling, *RlA* II, p. 264, s.v. Ebaga; also *ITT* 833, 10′; Limet, *CRRA* 20, p. 93, 35; *MVN* VI, p. 411: index; VII 335, obv. 5; etc. Note kù.ba.gára$^{!}$(GA) as a shrine of Baba in the Ur Lament (Kramer, *AS* 12, p. 18, 23).

97 **é.babbar.(ra)** "Shining House" 1, temple of Šamaš and Aya in Sippar (Proto-*Kagal* 219: é.bább[ar]!; CTL 281; TL no. 2, 2; Temple Hymns 491): rebuilt by Narām-Sîn, Sābium (year 8), Samsu-iluna (along with its ziqqurrat: Frayne, *RIME* 4, p. 377, 67 // 82; year 18), Kurigalzu (Scheil, *RT* 16 [1894], pp. 90f.; Walker, *CBI* no. 61), Aššurbanipal and Šamaš-šuma-ukīn (Streck, *Asb.*, p. 230, 16; Bauer, *Asb.*, p. 76, iii 22; Scheil, *RT* 16 [1894], pp. 91f.), Nebuchadnezzar II (V *R* 34, ii 28; etc.) and Nabonidus (V *R* 64, iii 4; etc.). Patronized by Maništūšu (supposedly: Sollberger, *JEOL* 20 [1968], pp. 55, 69; Cruciform Monument), and by Apil-Sîn (year 9: bára.maḫ, no TN), Ḫammurapi (CḪ ii 30; Frayne, *RIME* 4, p. 358, obv. 6′?; cf. year 15), Samsu-iluna (year 6), Abī-ešuḫ (years t.x), Ammī-ditāna (years 6.8.13.23), Ammī-ṣaduqa (years 6–7.9.18?) and Samsu-ditāna (years 7.11). Home to a cult of Adad as well as Šamaš and Aya, according to Samsu-iluna (Frayne, *RIME* 4, p. 378, 70 // 88). Cult restored by Simbar-šipak, interrupted by the Sutians (time of Kaššu-nādin-aḫḫē) and re-instated by Nabû-apla-iddina (*BBSt* 36). In liturgical texts it is often paired with zimbir[ki] (Cohen, *Eršemma*, pp. 113, 20; 118, 35.2:7; 127, 11; *Lamentations* passim, index p. 750; Maul, *Eršaḫunga* nos. 14–15, 3; 63, 4′; 74, 31; etc.); in such texts sometimes written é.babbar.AŠ, i.e., é-babbar-*rù*? Claimed by Inanna in an éš.dam hymn (*PBS* V 157, i 4). Mentioned in the Syncretistic Ištar Hymn (*KAR* 109, obv. 10). Also in the syncretistic hymn to Nanāy (Reiner, *JNES* 33 [1974], p. 227, 32; mysteriously // Sum. é.kar.ra). Metrological text: *Topog. Texts* no. 36 (no TN). NB prebends: *CT* 44 75, 7; *VAS* IV 200, 2; V 109, 2.

98 **é.babbar.(ra)** 2, temple of Šamaš and Aya in Larsa (CTL 282; TL no. 2, [7]; Temple Hymns 170): mentioned by Eannatum of Lagaš (Steible, *FAOS* 5/I, Ean 1, rev. i 39). Rebuilt by Ur-Nammu (9/II, UrN 11; no TN), and Zabāya (Frayne, *RIME* 4, p. 112, 1:4). Enlarged by Sîn-iddinam (ibid., pp. 159, 6; 161, 8; etc.; year 3, no TN), who also erected in its main court (kisal.maḫ) a statue to his father Nūr-Adad (ibid., p. 158, 36). Patronized by Gungunum (years 2.8, no TN), Abī-sarē (year 8, no TN), Sūmû-El (year 2, no TN; cf. *RIME* 4, p. 226, 8:3–4)), Nūr-Adad (ibid., pp. 139, 6; 142, 14; etc.; cf. years B.D.J, no TN), and Sîn-iqīšam (years 3.4). Damaged in the time of Kudur-mabuk (ibid., p. 216, 16), who was its avenger (ibid., pp. 206, 10; 220, 17; 246, 14; etc.), repaired by Warad-Sîn (ibid., p. 242, 50). Patronized by him (ibid., pp. 223, 15; 246, 6; etc.; cf. years 3.5) and by Rīm-Sîn I (ibid., pp. 279, 19; 280, 5′; etc.; cf. years 11.19). Built again by Ḫammurapi (ibid, pp. 350, 7; 351, 28; CḪ ii 34), Kadašman-Enlil I/II (Arnaud, *RA* 66 [1972], p. 38, no. 7), Burnaburiaš (ibid., pp. 36f., nos. 5: é.bábbar; 6; Arnaud, *Sumer* 32 [1976], p. 101, 18), Nebuchadnezzar II (V *R* 34, ii 34; etc.) and Nabonidus (*CT* 34 29, 10; etc.). Cf. Huot, *Akkadica* 44 (Sept.-Oct. 1985), pp. 14–20.

99 **é.bábbar** 3, shrine of Šamaš at G̃irsu (Falkenstein, *AnOr* 30, p. 166; Bauer, *AWL*, p. 570; Gelb, *StOr* 46 [1975], pp. 47, 15; 52; Ur III offering

lists, etc.: *AnOr* 30, p. 166[6]; Limet, *CRRA* 20, p. 93, 15; *MVN* VI 301, rev. ii 10; 302, ii 6′; etc.), looted by Lugalzaggesi (Steible, *FAOS* 5/I, Ukg 16, ii 6; cf. 17, 2). According to Selz, dedicated to Niñg̃irsu (*FAOS* 15/I, p. 194).

100 **é.babbar.ra** 4, temple of Šamaš at Aššur (*Topog. Texts* no. 20 = Götteradreßbuch 157: Assyrian TL). An unnamed temple of Šamaš at Aššur was refounded by Arik-dīn-ili (Grayson, *RIMA* 1, pp. 121, 52; 122, 3). For the building history of the double temple of Sîn and Šamaš see é.ḫúl.ḫúl.dir.dir.ra.

101 **é.bad.rá**, "Remote House," a shrine of Dumuzi known from the big OB forerunner to *Hh* XXI (*MSL* XI, p. 142, viii 24, following é.mùš.kalam.ma).

102 **é.bàd.bar.ra**, "House, Outer Wall," temple of Nin̄g̃išzida at Lagaš-G̃irsu in Ur III times (*MVN* VI 301, obv. ii 20: offering list).

103 **é.báḫar**, "House of the Potter," a sanctuary of Ningublag (CTL 279).

104 **é.bal.bal.x.ní.su$^{!}$.zi$^{!}$.ra**, "House . . . , Clad in Terror and Radiance," a temple listed in the OB lexical list from Isin (p. 4, IM 96881, iii′ 7′–8′). The emendation and translation assume the presence of the stock phrase ní su.zi ri.a (in late bilinguals = *puluḫta šalummata ramû*, see *CAD* Š/1, p. 283; ní.su.zi.⟨bar⟩.ra is also a possible emendation).

105 [**é.balag̃.ga**, see é.dúb.dúb.bu]

106 **é.bàn.da.nu**, a sanctuary attested in a liturgical fragment (*SBH* 34, rev. 13). Its position in the litany makes it the equivalent of OB bàd$^{!?}$.ta.sal.a (Cohen, *Lamentations*, p. 98, 64) // bàd.x.a (ibid., p. 351, 62).

107 **é.bar$_6$.bar$_6$**, see é.babbar

108 **é.bára.a.ri.a**, "House where the Dais is Set down," a shrine of Enlil (CTL 39) at Nippur, listed as bára.ri.a among parts of é.kur in an OB liturgical hymn to Enlil (Cohen, *Lamentations*, p. 350, 53: qualified as bára.maḫ ki.g̃ar.ra). Note also bára.ri.a among gods and other parts of Enlil's cult-center in an Ur III offering list (*TCL* II 5501, i 27).

109 **bára.dumu.nun.na**, "Dais of the Son of the Prince," a shrine in é.šár.ra at Aššur (*Topog. Texts* no. 21, obv. 3′).

110 **é.bára.dúr.g̃ar.ra**, "House, Dais of the Throne," temple of Ištar at Nippur (Proto-*Kagal* 232; *MSL* XI, p. 142, vii 16; [CTL 340]; *Topog. Texts* no. 19 = Nippur TL 20′–21′; cf. Biggs, *TCS* II, pp. 77f.), well known from Inanna's Descent and the éš.dam hymns (Wilcke, *RlA* V, p. 78, as an alternative to é.dur.an.ki; note the writing é.bára.du$_{10}$.g̃ar.ra in *OECT* I, p. 17, 14), and from the Exaltation of Inanna (Hruška, *ArOr* 37 [1969], p. 489, 41). Rebuilt for Ungal-Nibru by Esarhaddon (Goetze, *JCS* 17 [1963], p. 129f., 3.15). Written é.bára.dur.g̃ar.ra in the hymn to the Queen of Nippur (Lambert, *Kraus AV*, pp. 200, IV 6; 202, 14; 204, 73). Mentioned as the seat of Ungal-Nibru in the Syncretistic Ištar Hymn (line 96; unpub., courtesy Lambert). Occurs in litanies to Ištar between é.ḫur.sag̃.kalam.ma and é.tùr.kalam.ma (Cohen, *Lamentations*, pp. 715f., 220.240;

Volk, *FAOS* 18, p. 135, 7a). Also listed as a sanctuary of Enlil (CTL 38). Written é.bára.⌜dúr.ga?⌝.ra in a NB prebend document (Krückmann, *TuM* 2–3 210, 2; cf. 241, 4). Cf. é.dur.an.ki 1.

111 **bára.en.nun**, "Dais of the Watch," a shrine known from a *šubtu* list (at Ur? *Topog. Texts* no. 26 C, 3′).

112 **bára.g̃ír.nun.na**, "Dais of the Princely Path," part of é.ninnu at G̃irsu (Steible, *FAOS* 9/I, Gud. 54, 4; Falkenstein, *AnOr* 30, pp. 123f.).

113 **bára.ki.sikil.la**, "Dais, Pure Place," seat of Anu in his Sublime Garden (at Ur?), built by Ur-Nammu (Steible, *FAOS* 9/II, UrN 5). Perhaps not a ceremonial name.

114 **bára.maḫ**, "Exalted Dais," a shrine or epithet of the ziqqurrat of Anu at Uruk, é.šár.ra 1.

115 **bára.nam.lugal.la**, "Dais of Kingship," seat of Anu in the cella of the *bīt rēš* at Uruk, known from a LB ritual and prayer (*RAcc.*, pp. 70, 7–8, = *pa-rak-ku šar-ru-tu*; 72, rev. 7; cf. Falkenstein, *Topographie*, pp. 18f.).

116 **bára.ri.a**, see é.bára.a.ri.a

117 **é.bára.si.ga**, "House, Low Dais," the sanctuary of a goddess, mentioned in the lament im.ma.al gù.dé.dé (Cohen, *Lamentations*, p. 614, 180). In Ur III documents the TN is found at Lagaš, Ur and Ḫurim (references collected in *PSD* B, p. 145), though not always as a ceremonial name. Ḫurim, near Lagaš, is a cult-center of Ninmar, provided with temples dedicated to Inanna and $^{d}$lamma (see Edzard and Farber, *Rép. géogr.* II, pp. 79f.). Since the document *RTC* 399 clearly distinguishes between two sanctuaries é.bára.si.ga ḫu.rìm$^{ki}$ (ix 5) and é $^{d}$inanna ḫu.rìm$^{ki}$ (vii 30), one could speculate that the former is likely to have been the residence of either Ninmar or Lamma.

118 **é.bára.sír.ra**, "House, Flat(?) Dais," a sanctuary of Damgalnunna, mentioned in the lament im.ma.al gù.dé.dé (Cohen, *Lamentations*, p. 614, 188).

119 **bára.šà.díš.ša$_4$**, "Dais of the Perfect One," seat of Lugalirra in é.me.lám.su.lim.gùr.ru (at Ur? *Topog. Texts* no. 26 A, 1).

120 **bára.sur.KU**, seat of Marduk in é.šár.ra at Aššur (*Topog. Texts* no. 21, obv. 33′).

121 **é.bára.u$_6$.de**, "House, Dais of Wonder," one of the twin ziqqurrats of Dumuzi at Akkade (TL no. 4, 11; no. 5, 3′).

122 **é.BI.du$_6$.du$_6$.da**, a sanctuary attested in a late liturgical fragment (*SBH* 34, rev. 14). Its place in the litany suggests that it must be a variant of é.g̃á.du$_6$.da.

123 **é.BI.É.bàn.da**, a sanctuary attested in a late liturgical fragment (*SBH* 34, rev. 15). The name is obscure; perhaps simply é.bi é.bàn.da, "that house, the little house."

124 **é.bur.an.na**, see é.šu.bur.an.na

125 **é.bur.dù.dù**, "House which Prepares the Jars," a sanctuary of Šara (CTL 453).

126 **é.bur.$sa_7$.$sa_7$** "House of Beautiful Jars" 1, part or by-name of é.maḫ of Šara at Umma (Proto-*Kagal* 206; CTL 452; Temple Hymns 303).

127 **é.bur.$sa_7$.$sa_7$** 2, temple of Šara at Babylon (*Topog. Texts* nos. 1 = *Tintir* IV 33; 4, 33).

128 **é.bur.$sa_7$.$sa_7$** 3, temple of a deity of the court of Sîn (CTL 280).

129 **bur.sag̃**, "Foremost Jar," chapel in é.ninnu at G̃irsu where regular offerings were made, built by Uruinimgina (Steible, *FAOS* 5/I, Ukg 4, ii 1; 8, ii′ 4′; etc.), also known to Enmetena (ibid., Ent 33, ii 2′).

130 **(é).bur.šu.šú.a**, also written (é).bur.šú.šú.a, "House of Covered (*or* Standing) Jars," sanctuary in the temple complex of Enlil at Nippur (Proto-*Kagal* 180; CTL 40; *Topog. Texts* no. 18 = Nippur Compendium § 6, 9′). Outside the lists the TN is known from the Tummal Inscription (Sollberger, *JCS* 16 [1962], p. 43, 11), a MB metrological text (Bernhardt and Kramer, *OrNS* 44 [1975], p. 98, 46: bur.šú.a), and liturgical texts (IV $R^2$ 24, no. 2, 21; Cohen, *Lamentations*, p. 350, 41–42: paired with é.ká.maḫ). Cf. ki.bur.šú.a as an epithet of a temple courtyard (ibid., pp. 98, 69; 351, 68).

131 **é.búr.[x]**, a sanctuary of Ištar (CTL 345).

132 ***bīt burmī***, "House of Coloured Decorations" 1, see é.gùn.a

133 ***bīt burmī***? 2, sanctuary built by Šalim-aḫum at Aššur's request according to a dedicatory inscription found in the OA temple of Ištar at Aššur (Grayson, *RIMA* 1, p. 14 = Farber, *RIM Annual Review* 9 [1991], p. 13, 9: *bīt bu-ur*!?*-mi*). Probably a shrine of Ištar, like TN 1.

134 ***da.abzu.a**, "Corner of *Apsû*," a shrine in the é.kur complex at Nippur, where it is a place of judgement (written da.ab.su.a: Cohen, *Lamentations*, pp. 98, 67; 351, 66).

135 **é.da.di.ḫé.g̃ál**, "House of Abundant Tribute(?)," part of é.sag̃.íl at Babylon, mentioned by Agum-kakrime, Esarhaddon and Nabonidus as the place where the king presented tribute to Marduk (V *R* 33, v 43: é.e.da.di.ḫé.g̃ál; Borger, *Esarh.*, § 59, 13: A.DÉ.di.ḫé.g̃ál; Bezold, *PSBA* 11 [1889], pp. 103ff., pl. 2, 31; V *R* 65, ii 51; also Mayer, *Gebetsbeschwörungen*, p. 460, 8; *SBH* VIII, v 29–30: cultic calendar).

136 **da.$^{giš}$ḫa.lu.úb**, "Corner of the *Ḫaluppu*-tree," a shrine in the é.kur complex at Nippur (Cohen, *Lamentations*, pp. 98, 56: da.$^{giš}$ḫa.lu.ba; 351, 56). See also é.NÍG̃.lu.úb.a, $du_6$.da.ḫa.lu.úb.ba.

137 **é.da.imin**, "House of Seven Corners," sanctuary of Ištar at Uruk (CTL 317), which became a name of the city (*MSL* XI, pp. 54, 18; 63, 11′; Kilmer, *JAOS* 83 [1963], p. 428, *Malku* I 214).

138 **é.da.rí**, "Eternal House," TN or epithet known from Proto-*Kagal* 218. Note é.da.rí.kalam.ma in a Sumerian prayer to Ninisinna (*OECT* V 8, 25).

139 **é.dadag.lál**, temple at Raqnana according to the Syncretistic Ištar Hymn (*KAR* 109, rev. 4). The cult-center of this town is called, obscurely, é.gal.*ta-bi-ri* in the syncretistic hymn to Nanāy, where however the goddess is *mubbibat ḫiṭ*[*âti*] *šākinat nūri*, "cleanser of sins, provider of light," epithets that imply knowledge of the TN (Reiner, *JNES* 33 [1974], pp. 230, 19; cf. 236). No doubt this is the same temple as that listed for Ištar at Raqnana in TL no. 3, 29′ (TN undeciphered).

140 ***bīt dalīli***, "House of Fame," a sanctuary at Nippur whose residents are listed in the Divine Directory of Nippur (*Topog. Texts* no. 18 = Nippur Compendium § 14, v 22–23: Nissaba, Kusu, Ningal, Šamaš and Bēl-ālīya).

141 **é?.dalla.ùru**, "House of the Lofty Hero(?)," a shrine in é.rab.ri.ri (at Babylon? *Topog. Texts* no. 12, 1′).

142 **é.dam**, "House of the Wife," shrine(?) built by Ur-Nanše (Steible, *FAOS* 5/I, UrN 25, v 4; 27, iv 3; etc.).

143 ***é.danna**, see é.dim.an.na

144 **é.dar.a**, see é.gùn.a

145 **é.dàra.an.na**, "House of the Ibex of Heaven," cella of Zarpanītum in é.sag̃.íl at Babylon (*Topog. Texts* nos. 6, 7; 28, 8′; 39, rev. i a 1; CTL 235); commonly follows é.te.mén.an.ki in litanies (Cohen, *Eršemma*, pp. 29, 13; 114, 25; 118, 35.2:14; 127, 18; *Lamentations* passim, index p. 750; Langdon, *BL* no. 56, obv. 18; George, *RA* 82 [1988], p. 159, 36; etc.). See also ká.ḫi.li.sù.

146 **(é).dàra.kù.ga**, "House of the Pure Ibex," sanctuary of Nanna-Suen, as found in a cultic lament (Cohen, *Lamentations*, pp. 211, 82 // 219, 12).

147 **é.di.ku$_5$**, "House of the Judge," a temple or shrine paired with é.di.ku$_5$.kalam.ma in an OB legal document (*CT* 2 1, 29 // 6, 39).

148 **é.di.ku$_5$.dá**, "House of the Judge," a temple of Šamaš (CTL 284), found in a votive inscription for Ammī-ṣaduqa (Frayne, *RIME* 4, p. 428, 2001:4; note é.di.ku$_5$.da in l. 25), and in the cultic lament u$_4$.dam gù.dé.dé.aš (Cohen, *Lamentations*, p. 434, 105); = é.di.ku$_5$?

149 **é.di.ku$_5$.gal**, "House of the Great Judge," socle (*manzāzu*) of Šamaš in é.rab.ri.ri (at Babylon? *Topog. Texts* no. 12, 8′; correct the translation "seat" to "station"!).

150 **(é).di.ku$_5$.ka.aš.bar.si.sá**, "House of the Judge who Pronounces a Just Verdict," a shrine in é.sag̃.íl at Babylon (*Topog. Texts* no. 1 = *Tintir* II 45, p. 280, K 3446+, rev. 1: royal ritual); the TN is probably to be restored in the cultic lament u$_4$.dam gù.dé.dé.aš (Cohen, *Lamentations*, p. 432, 60, = *bīt dayyāni ša purus*[*sê ušteššeru*]).

151 **é.di.ku$_5$.kalam.ma**, "House of the Judge of the Land" 1, temple of Šamaš at Babylon (Proto-*Kagal* 220; CTL 283; *Topog. Texts* nos. 1 = *Tintir* IV 38; 38, 29; *BRM* IV 25, 8: offering calendar), known in the OB period (*AbB* II 73, rev. 3′: Abī-ešuḫ; *CT* 2 1, 29 // 6, 39, with é.di.ku$_5$; cf. Apil-Sîn year 17f.), and restored by Nebuchadnezzar II (*PBS* XV 79, ii 36;

etc.). Follows é.babbar.ra of Sippar in litanies (Langdon, *BL* nos. 36, 7′; 186, rev. 5; Cohen, *Eršemma*, p. 113, 20; *Lamentations* passim, index p. 750). See *Topog. Texts*, pp. 327–29.

152 **é.di.ku$_5$.kalam.ma** 2, temple of Šamaš, rebuilt by Damiq-ilīšu (year 8). Probably = é.di.ku$_5$.kalam.ma 1. Others suggest a location at Isin itself (Kraus, *JCS* 3 [1951], p. 88; Edzard, *Zwischenzeit*, p. 158[842]), or even Nippur (Prang, *JCS* 27 [1975], pp. 160f.).

153 **é.di.ku$_5$.maḫ**, "House of the Exalted Judge" 1, socle of Muštēšir-ḫablim in á.sud.a of é.sag̃.íl at Babylon (*Topog. Texts* no. 1 = *Tintir* II 34′).

154 **é.di.ku$_5$.maḫ** 2, a sanctuary found in liturgical texts in litanies of the temples of Sîn (Cohen, *Lamentations*, p. 211, 81; *CT* 42 9, pl. 20, i 24–25?).

155 **é.di.ku$_5$.maḫ** 3, a temple of Ilaba (TL no. 3, 20′).

156 **é.di.maḫ**, "House of the Exalted Verdict," a shrine in é.sag̃.íl at Babylon (*Topog. Texts* no. 1 = *Tintir* II 16″).

157 **é.dil.e.maḫ**, see é.tílla.maḫ

158 **é.dim.an.ki**, "House, Bond (*lit.*: Pole) of Heaven and Underworld," a sanctuary at Borsippa (Cohen, *Lamentations*, p. 611, 113), possibly = é.dim.an.na 2.

159 **é.dim.an.na**, "House, Bond of Heaven" 1, a sanctuary of Sîn, found in liturgical texts among his temples at Ur (Cohen, *Lamentations*, pp. 211, 78 // 219, 7: é.di.ma.a[n.na]; *CT* 42 9, pl. 20, i 22–23: é.idim.an.na). Probably occurs in *Kagal* Boğ. I F 20: [e]-ti-na*-na = *bi-it ši-i-in* (against *MSL* XIII, p. 152, é.danna, but see Lamentation over Sumer and Ur 186; reading with Moran, *JCS* 26 [1974], p. 55[1]). In OB personal names: Wilcke, *OLZ* 66 (1971), 546[2]; Frankena, *Symbolae Böhl*, p. 149 (also é.idim.an.na).

160 **é.dim.an.na** 2, temple of Sîn in the é.zi.da complex at Borsippa, rebuilt by Nebuchadnezzar II (I *R* 55, iv 63). Also found in a NB cultic administrative fragment, *VAS* 24 112, rev. 10′.

161 **é.dim.gal.an.na**, "House, Great Bond (*lit.*: Mooring-Pole) of Heaven" 1, a temple of Sud (CTL 64; *TCL* XV 1, 4: lament), rebuilt by Enlil-bāni (Frayne, *RIME* 4, p. 84, 6; exemplars found at Isin and near Šuruppak).

162 **é.dim.gal.an.na** 2, a sanctuary of Nanna-Suen known from a cultic lament (Cohen, *Lamentations*, pp. 211, 79 // 219, 11).

163 **é.dim.gal.an.na** 3, a sanctuary of Aya (CTL 293).

164 **é.dim.gal.an.na** 4, a temple mentioned in the Syncretistic Ištar Hymn (l. 79; unpub., courtesy Lambert). Since it follows the section on Kutha we would expect it either to be in or near that city, or to be a secondary cult-center of Nergal (= é.TN 5?).

165 ***é.dim.gal.an.na** 5, a temple at Uzarpara near Uruk (*Kagal* Boğ. I G 11: ⌜e⌝-dim-kal-la-a-na), possibly the unnamed temple built there for Nergal (= é.TN 4?) by Anam in the reign of Sîn-gāmil (Frayne, *RIME* 4, p. 467, 9).

166 **é.dim.gal.kalam.ma**, "House, Great Bond of the Land," temple of Ištarān/Anu-rabû in Dēr (*MSL* XI, p. 142, vii 29; CTL [477]; TL no. 2, [13]; no. 3, 33′; Temple Hymns 423; *KAR* 109, rev. 14: Syncretistic Ištar Hymn; Reiner, *JNES* 33 [1974], p. 227, 39: similar hymn to Nanāy; Wiseman, *Iraq* 31 [1969], p. 177, 34′: *lipšur*-litany; *Šurpu* II 160; etc.: Sjöberg, *TCS* III, pp. 131f.). Patronized by Šulgi (year 11, no TN), rebuilt by Kurigalzu (Smith, *JEA* 18 [1932], p. 29). Invoked in a Kassite greeting formula (*BE* XVII/1 89, 5). Destroyed by Elam in the time of Enlil-nādin-šumi (Grayson, *Chronicles*, p. 176, 15). Cult restored by Esarhaddon (Borger, *Esarh.*, §§ 40, 8; 47, 20). Completed by Aššurbanipal (Bauer, *Asb.*, p. 76, iii 19; pl. 19, K 1769+, ii 17 // Thompson, *Prisms*, pl. 15, iii 15: Prism T; *AAA* 20 [1933], p. 84, 69; etc.).

167 ***é.dim.galam.ma**, "House, Skilfully-Wrought Bond," see *é.dim.kalam.ma

168 ***é.dim.kalam.ma**, "House, Bond of the Land," temple of Ištar, according to *Kagal* Boğ. I G 12: [e]-dim-ga-lam-ma (which might also represent *é.dim.galam.ma).

169 **é.dím.ba.ba.re**, obscure TN(?) found in the cultic lament úru àm.i.ra.bi (Cohen, *Lamentations*, p. 543, 95).

170 **é.DÍM.ga.an.na**, TN or epithet known from the big OB forerunner to *Hh* XXI (*MSL* XI, p. 142, vii 32).

171 **é.dìm.ma**, "House of the Pillar," shrine in the temple complex of é.kur at Nippur (Proto-*Kagal* 190; Hymn to E-kur: Kramer, *RSO* 32 [1957], p. 97, 23), also mentioned in liturgical texts in the standard litany of TNs of Nippur (Cohen, *Eršemma*, p. 111, 14; *Lamentations*, pp. 350, 40; 391, 181; Krecher, *Kultlyrik*, pp. 53, 10; 83; V *R* 52, no. 2, obv. 53 // *KAR* 375, ii 62; etc.). Note lexical entry é.dìm.ma = *bīt šar-ru* (group vocab. V *R* 16, iv 52; read *bīt šèr*[!]*-ru* by *AHw*, p. 1217).

172 **DU.DU.mes.lam**, seat of Uraš in é.šár.ra at Aššur (*Topog. Texts* no. 21, obv. 14′).

173 **é.DU.GA.NI**, a sanctuary(?) mentioned in a commentary on a state ritual (Livingstone, *Mystical Works*, p. 126, 8).

174 **du$_6$.bára.gal.maḫ**, "Mound, Great Exalted Dais," cultic location in the temple complex of Ur, known from a hymn to Rīm-Sîn I (*UET* VI 103 = Charpin, *Le clergé d'Ur*, pp. 282f., 35–39, where it is further described as ki.ùr úri$^{ki}$.ma).

175 **du$_6$.⸢da⸣.ḫa[!](KÙ).lu.úb[!](LU).ba**, "Mound, Corner of the *Ḫaluppu*-tree," listed in Proto-*Kagal* 173; cf. da.$^{giš}$ḫa.lu.úb. Possibly du$_6$ is misread for kisal.

176 **é.du$_6$.⟨kalam?⟩.ma**, "House, Mound of the Land(?)," a sanctuary of Ištar (CTL 375).

177 **du$_6$.ki.sikil**, "Mound, Pure Place," seat of Enmešarra and Enbilulu in é.sag̃.íl at Babylon (*Topog. Texts* no. 1 = *Tintir* II 30), on the procession route of Marduk (Cavigneaux, *Textes scolaires*, p. 175, 79.B.1/30, 4; cf. *KAR* 142, i 3 // *CT* 46 53, ii 14, where the same shrine is given as ki.tuš.ki.sikil and ki.kù.sikil).

178 **du$_6$.kù**, "Pure Mound" 1, cosmic seat of the king of the gods in the divine assembly, whence destinies are determined (= *parak šīmāti*); primeval home of the Anunnaki (Laḫar and Ašnan; Borger, *JCS* 21 [1967], p. 3, 3: *bīt rimki*; Syncretistic Ištar Hymn 37, unpub., courtesy Lambert; *BRM* IV 7, 37: prayer; cf. van Dijk, *Götterlieder* II, p. 134).

179 **du$_6$.kù** 2, shrine of Enlil (in ub.šu.ukkin.na) in é.kur at Nippur (Proto-*Kagal* 184; Sjöberg, *TCS* III, p. 50; Kramer, *RSO* 32 [1957], p. 97, 22: Hymn to E-kur; Cohen, *Eršemma*, p. 111, 13; *Lamentations*, p. 350, 38–39, qualified as [du$_6$.kù] ki nam.tar.tar.re, "where destinies are determined"; Krecher, *Kultlyrik*, pp. 53, 9; 83; *CT* 42 38, pl. 45, a 12: du-ku ki-ku-mu; etc.). Listed twice among gods and other parts of Enlil's cult-center in an Ur III offering list (*TCL* II 5501, i 12; ii 28).

180 **du$_6$.kù** 3, full name du$_6$.kù-ki.nam.tar.tar.(re).e.dè, "D., where Destinies are Determined," the seat of Marduk as Lugaldimmerankia in ub.šu.ukkin.na of é.sag̃.íl at Babylon (*Topog. Texts* no. 1 = *Tintir* II 17′, p. 288, K 3446+, obv. 16: royal ritual), restored by Aššurbanipal (Millard, *Iraq* 30 [1968], pl. 24, 127994, 6′; courtesy Borger), and Nebuchadnezzar II (I *R* 54, ii 54; 55, v 12–13). Its by-name was *parak šīmāti*, "Dais of Destinies."

181 **du$_6$.kù** 4, a shrine in é.ninnu at G̃irsu (Temple Hymns 245).

182 **é.du$_6$.kù** 5, a shrine of Enki/Ea in é.abzu at Eridu (Temple Hymns 4; cf. the equation of cosmic realms in Kilmer, *JAOS* 83 [1963], p. 429, *Malku* I 290: du$_6$.kù = *ap-su-u*).

183 **é.du$_6$.kù** 6, seat of Ea, probably in é.umuš.a of é.sag̃.íl at Babylon (*Topog. Texts* nos. 1 = *Tintir* II 5; 43, 6′–7′).

184 **é.du$_6$.kù** 7, a sanctuary of Ištar (CTL 374), possibly the du$_6$.kù at her cult-center Raqnana attested in the Syncretistic Ištar Hymn (*KAR* 109, rev. 5).

185 **é.du$_6$.kù.ga** 8, seat of Lugaldukuga in the Chariot House of é.sag̃.íl at Babylon (*Topog. Texts* no. 1 = *Tintir* II 16).

186 **é.du$_6$.kù.ga** 9, a sanctuary of Zababa at Kiš (*Topog. Texts* no. 22, 9′).

187 **du$_6$.maḫ**, "Exalted Mound" 1, shrine in é.kur at Nippur, as attested in an OB liturgical hymn to Enlil (Cohen, *Lamentations*, p. 350, 43–44).

188 **du$_6$.maḫ** 2, two stations in é.sag̃.íl at Babylon, occupied by Ababa and Antadurunnu, the temple's gatekeepers (*Topog. Texts* no. 1 = *Tintir* II 29′–30′).

189 **du$_6$.níg̃.luḫ.$^{u}$SAR**, a shrine in the temple complex of Enlil at Nippur, paired with é.du$_6$.númun.búr (Proto-*Kagal* 182; var. du$_6$.níg̃.$^{u}$númun).

190 **(é).du$_6$.(ᵘ)númun.búr**, "House, Mound of Rushes," sanctuary in the temple complex of Enlil at Nippur (Proto-*Kagal* 181, var. buru$_{14}$; *Topog. Texts* no. 19 = Nippur TL 23′), also found in the Tummal inscription (Sollberger, *JCS* 16 [1962], p. 42, 6: var. . . . bur.ra; built by Gilgameš), OB liturgical hymns to Enlil (Cohen, *Lamentations*, pp. 98, 58: du$_6$!.nú.mu.un.bur; 351, 58: du$_6$!.númun.[bú]r), and a MB metrological text (Kramer and Bernhardt, *OrNS* 44 [1975], p. 98, 46: du$_6$!.númun.buru$_{14}$).

191 **du$_6$.sag̃.dil**, "Secret(?) Mound," by-name or part of the temple of Šuzi-anna in g̃á.gi.maḫ at Nippur (CTL 66; Temple Hymns 85). Mentioned in the cultic lament e.lum gu$_4$.sún (Cohen, *Lamentations*, p. 276, 75).

192 **é.du$_6$.sag̃.gara$_{10}$**, "House, Foremost Mound of Cream," sanctuary of Bēlet-ṣēri at Uruk, known from a Seleucid prebend document (*TCL* XIII 244, 3.19 = Rutten, *Babyl.* 15 [1935], p. 233; paired with é.$^{giš}$kiri$_6$.dili.bad).

193 **du$_6$.su$_8$.ba**, see du$_6$.šuba

194 **du$_6$?.šà.abzu**, "Mound in the Midst of *Apsû*," lobby of a gate in é.sag̃.íl at Babylon (*Topog. Texts* no. 7, 18′).

195 **(é).du$_6$.šuba**, "House, Mound of the Shepherd" 1, shrine of Dumuzi in é.mùš. (kalam.ma) at Bad-tibira. Commonly found in Dumuzi texts and litanies, often written du$_6$.su$_8$.ba (Inanna and Bilulu 181; *VAS* II 1, iii 11; *BE* XXX/1 1, ii 10; Langdon, *BL* no. 8, obv. 11; Cohen, *Eršemma*, p. 90, 10; *Lamentations*, pp. 194, 25; 277, 85; 564, 179; 683, 13; etc.).

196 **du$_6$.šuba** 2, seat of Dumuzi in é.sag̃.íl at Babylon (*Topog. Texts* no. 1 = *Tintir* II 22).

197 **du$_6$.šuba** 3, an epithet of Nippur (*Topog. Texts* no. 18 = Nippur Compendium § 4, 15′), which may imply the existence there of a sanctuary of this name.

198 **é.$^{anše}$du$_{24}$.ùr**, "Donkey House," stable of the divine donkey-herd Ensignun, built by Ur-Baba (Steible, *FAOS* 9/I, UrB 1, vi 3; 8, ii 3). Part of é.ninnu at G̃irsu (Falkenstein, *AnOr* 30, p. 126).

199 **é.du$_{24}$.ùr.zi.le**, name or epithet of the preceding entry, as built by Enmetena (Steible, *FAOS* 5/I, Ent 79, iii 1).

200 **é.dub.ba**, "Storage House" 1, temple of Zababa at Kiš (*MSL* XI, p. 142, viii 39; CTL 480; TL no. 2, [10]; *Topog. Texts* no. 22, 7′; Temple Hymns 454; cf. McEwan, *Iraq* 45 [1983], pp. 119f.), rebuilt by Nabopolassar and Nebuchadnezzar II (*PBS* XV 79, iii 76). Often read é.kišib$_{(3)}$.ba. Common in liturgical texts, often paired with é.me.te.ur.sag̃ in standard litanies of TNs (Cohen, *Eršemma*, pp. 143, 4; 145, 9; *Lamentations*, index p. 751, s.v. é.kišib.ba; Maul, *Eršaḫunga* no. 37, 8; *OrNS* 60 [1991], pp. 314f., 23.33, among temples of Ninurta as Utaulu: eršemma; MacMillan, *BA* V/5 6, rev. 13; *CT* 42 12, pl. 22, 6; Pallis, *Akîtu*, pl. 11, 22; etc.), mentioned in the Syncretistic Ištar Hymn (l. 67; unpub., courtesy Lambert), and the syn-

cretistic hymn to Nanāy (Reiner, *JNES* 33 [1974], p. 225, 20). See also é.me.te.ur.sağ.

200a **é.dub.ba** 2, temple of Bēl of Šaṭer, a town of Bīt-Amukanu (Durand, *Textes babyloniens*, pl. 38, obv. 2; NB prebend).

201 **é.dub.ba.gu.la**, "Large Storage House," a building in Lagaš-Ĝirsu which housed a sanctuary of Nissaba (*MVN* VI 301, obv. ii 23; Ur III).

202 **é.DUB.gal.é.kur.ra**, seat of Ninimma represented by a brick found in the sanctuary of Ningal at Ur, é.ĝi$_6$.pàr.kù 1, made by Sîn-balāssu-iqbi (*UET* I 181). Probably best emended to é.dub.⟨sar⟩.gal . . . , in view of Ninimma's status as the scholar of Enlil's court.

203 **(é).dub.lá.maḫ**, "House, Exalted Door-Socket" 1, court of judgement at Ur dedicated to Nanna-Suen (*Kagal* Boğ. I F 19: [e]-du-ub-la-al-ma-aḫ; Lamentation over Sumer and Ur 438), rebuilt by Amar-Suen (Steible, *FAOS* 9/II, AS 12, with the epithet é.u$_6$.de.kalam.ma, "house, wonder of the land") and, following the return of Nanna's cult-statue from Anšan, by Šu-ilīšu (Frayne, *RIME* 4, p. 16, 12). Further rebuilt as a temple of Sîn by Kurigalzu (*UET* I 157–58). Mentioned among other temples of Sîn in liturgical texts (*CT* 42 9, pl. 20, i 26; Langdon, *BL* no. 27, 7′).

204 **é.dub.lá.maḫ** 2, a sanctuary at Bīt-Suenna near Nippur, probably part of é.kiš.nu.ĝál 3 (*Topog. Texts* no. 18 = Nippur Compendium § 6, 14′).

205 **é.dub.lá.maḫ** 3, a sanctuary built by Nāqimum of the Mananā dynasty, no doubt for Sîn (years ab: Charpin, *RA* 72 [1978], p. 30; at Urum, later Ilip: p. 17). Other kings of the dynasty repaired and patronized a cult-center of Sîn and Ningal (Ḫalium years d.e.h.i; Mananā years d.e.i; Sūmû-Yamutbala years a.b.f.g.h; unidentified king year x).

206 **é.dub.sağ$^?$.[ . . . ]**, "House, Ancient [ . . . ]," a sanctuary of Nanna-Suen known from a cultic lament (Cohen, *Lamentations*, p. 219, 8).

207 **é.dúb.dúb.x[ . . . ]**, "House which Provides Rest [( . . . )]," cella of the Akītu temple at Aššur, rebuilt by Sennacherib (Meissner and Rost, *Senn.*, pl. 16, 4, coll.; cf. Livingstone, *N.A.B.U.* 1990/87. Note also é.dúb.dúb.bu in Proto-*Kagal* 109). See also [é.( . . . )]x.ug$_5$.ga.

208 **dúbur.kur.gal**, "Foundation of the Great Mountain," seat of Šukurgallu in é.šár.ra at Aššur (*Topog. Texts* no. 21, obv. 17′; rev. 27′).

209 **é.dúbur$^?$.ní.gùr.ru**, "House, Dread Foundation(?)," sanctuary of Ištar at ZA-*a*-x[ (x)] (CTL 379).

210 **é.dùg**, "Pleasant House," bedchamber (é.ná) of Ninĝirsu in é.ninnu at Ĝirsu (Falkenstein, *AnOr* 30, p. 125).

211 **é.dug$_4$.ga**, "House of Speaking" 1, cella of Nergal at Kutha (TL no. 6, 21).

212 **é.dug$_4$.ga** 2, a shrine of the guardian angel Lamma, known from a cultic lament (Cohen, *Lamentations*, p. 614, 178).

213 **é.dug$_4$.ga** 3, a sanctuary of Marduk or Nabû known from a šu.íl.la prayer (Cooper, *Iraq* 32 [1970], p. 59, 8a).

214 **é.dumu.nun.na**, "House of the Son of the Prince" 1, temple of Sîn at Uruk, known from a ritual (*BRM* IV 6, 33), and evidently listed in *Kagal* Boğ. I (F 14: [é.TN = e-tu-mu-n]u-na = *bi-it ši-i-in*).

215 **é.dumu.nun.na** 2, a shrine in é.sag̃.íl at Babylon (*Topog. Texts* no. 1 = *Tintir* II 50).

216 **é.dumu.nun.na** 3, socle of Madānu in á.sud.a of é.sag̃.íl at Babylon (*Topog. Texts* no. 1 = *Tintir* II 33′).

217 **é.dun$_x$(ÍL).na**, "House of the Axe(?)," temple of Ištar at Maškan-[ . . . ] (CTL 361).

218 **(é).dur.an.ki**, "House, Bond of Heaven and Underworld" 1, sanctuary of Ištar at Nippur (Proto-*Kagal* 233; *MSL* XI, p. 142, vii 15; *Topog. Texts* no. 18 = Nippur Compendium § 6, 5′; [CTL 339]), rebuilt by Šulgi (Steible, *FAOS* 9/II, Š 20; 75). In the éš.dam hymns é.TN is an alternative of é.bára.dúr. g̃ar.ra (Wilcke, *RlA* V, p. 78). Also known from liturgical texts (Cohen, *Eršemma*, p. 66, 13; *Lamentations*, pp. 98, 62; 351, 64). Listed among TNs of Enlil in *Kagal* Boğ. I E 16–17 and CTL 36, and, as èš.nibru$^{ki}$, attributed to Enlil by Gudea (Steible, *FAOS* 9/I, Gud. 12, 4). A name of Nippur as center of the universe (*Topog. Texts*, p. 261). See also èš.dur.an.ki.

219 **é.dur.an.ki** 2, the ziqqurrat at Larsa (TL no. 4, 19), = é.dur.an.na.

220 **é.dur.an.na**, "House, Bond of Heaven," ziqqurrat of Šamaš at Larsa (TL no. 5, 17′), rebuilt by Nabonidus (Bezold, *PSBA* 11 [1889], pp. 103ff., pl. 5, 7; etc.). Also é.dur.an.ki 2.

221 **é.ʿdurʾ.si.sá**, see é.gú.si.sá 2

222 **é.dur.šu.a[n.na?]**, "House, Bond of Lofty(?) Strength," a sanctuary associated with the goddess Bizilla in an unpublished NB fragment, BM 99743, 1′ (quoted in the note on TL no. 6, 15).

223 **dúr.an.na**, "Abode of Heaven," seat of the dragon Ušumgal in é.sag̃.íl at Babylon (*Topog. Texts* no. 1 = *Tintir* II 23).

224 **dúr.an.ki.a**, "Abode of Heaven and Underworld," seat of Ea in ub.šu. ukkin.na of é.sag̃.íl at Babylon (*Topog. Texts* no. 1 = *Tintir* II 20′)

225 **é.dúr.g̃ar.g̃éštu.diri**, see é.umuš.g̃ar . . .

226 **é.dúr.gi.na**, "House, Established Abode," temple of Bēl-ṣarbi (Lugal-asal) in Bāṣ (TL no. 3, 44′), rebuilt by Nebuchadnezzar II (V *R* 34, ii 29; etc.). In NA texts the town is known as Šapazzu (George, *SAA Bulletin* 1 [1987], p. 32, 8: hymn; Bauer, *Asb.*, p. 76, iii 23). For PN é.TN-*ibni* see Joannès, *N.A.B.U.* 1987/99.

227 **é.dúr.ḫé.nun.na**, "House, Abode of Plenty" 1, part or by-name of é.šùd. dè.g̃iš.tuku of Adad at Aššur (*Topog. Texts* no. 20 = Götteradreßbuch 155: Assyrian TL).

228 **é.dúr.ḫé.nun.na** 2, part or by-name of é.kìlib.kur.kur.ra.dul$_6$.dul$_6$ of Adad at Kurbaʾil (*Topog. Texts* no. 20 = Götteradreßbuch 180: Assyrian TL), known also from the greeting formula of a NA letter (Parpola, *LAS* 2, p. 262: BM 79099, 7, cited after Millard, also Deller, *OrNS* 56 [1987], p. 181).

229 **é.dúr.ka.nag̃.g̃á**, "House, Abode of the Land," a sanctuary attested in a cultic lament for Dumuzi (Cohen, *Lamentations*, p. 564, 181).

230 **é.dúr.ki.g̃ar.ra**, "House, Well-Founded Abode," temple of Dagān at Isin, rebuilt by Ur-Dukuga (Frayne, *RIME* 4, p. 95, 21; year c).

231 **é.dúr.ki.[ . . . ]**, a sanctuary at Nippur (*Topog. Texts* no. 18 = Nippur Compendium § 6, 6′).

232 **é.dúr.kù**, "House, Pure Abode" 1, a sanctuary of Šala, probably in é.u$_4$.gal.gal at Karkara, mentioned in a *lipšur*-litany (Nougayrol, *JCS* 1 [1947], p. 330, 5′ // Wiseman, *Iraq* 31 [1969], p. 176, 16′).

233 **é.dúr.kù.ga** 2, a temple of Gula in a litany (*CT* 44 17, rev. 18).

234 **é.dúr.kù.ga** 3, dais of the Igigi at Babylon (*Topog. Texts* no. 1 = *Tintir* IV 28; cf. V 85).

235 **é.dúr.maḫ**, "House, Exalted Abode," seat of Enlil in ub.šu.ukkin.na of é.sag̃.íl at Babylon (*Topog. Texts* no. 1 = *Tintir* II 19′).

236 **é.e.da.di.ḫé.g̃ál**, see é.da.di.ḫé.g̃ál

237 **é.e.sír.galam.ma**, "House, Skillfully-Built Street," see é.e.sír.kalam.ma

238 **é.e.sír.kalam.ma**, "House of the Street of the Land," temple of Pisag̃unuk in west Babylon (*Topog. Texts* no. 1 = *Tintir* IV 39, var. é.e.sír.galam.ma).

239 **é.ᵈ*Ea-bāni***, "House, Ea is (its) Builder," a temple listed in TL no. 3, 45′.

240 **é.è.an.ki**, temple at Malgium, mentioned in the Syncretistic Ištar Hymn (l. 103; unpub., courtesy Lambert). Probably a variation on é.an.ki.

241 **é.è.umuš.a**, see é.umuš.a

242 **é.edin**, "Steppe House," a shrine built by Ur-Nanše of Lagaš (Steible, *FAOS* 5/I, UrN 24, iii 7, written a.edin); in Proto-*Kagal* 207, following é.bur.sa$_7$.sa$_7$, this TN is probably an error for é.maḫ 6.

243 **é.edin.dim$^?$.maḫ**, "Steppe House, Exalted Bond," provisional reading of a TN found in the incipit of a šu.íl.lá prayer to Zarpanītum (Mayer, *Gebetsbeschwörungen*, p. 425, after von Soden).

244 **é.edin.na**, "House of the Steppe," temple of Ištar as Bēlet-Sippar at Sippar (CTL 365), rebuilt by Nabopolassar (Winckler, *ZA* 2 [1887], p. 172, ii 8).

245 ***bītu ellu***, "Pure House," a sacred chamber attested at Nippur in the MB period, both within é.šu.me.ša$_4$ of Ninurta and as an independent structure (Bernhardt and Kramer, *OrNS* 44 [1975], p. 98, 18.34; metrological text).

246 **é.en.nun.g̃á.g̃á**, "House which Appoints the Watch," a shrine in é.gar$_6$.kù (at Ur? *Topog. Texts* no. 26 B, 2).

247 **en.zag.kù.ga**, seat of Urmašum in é.rab.ri.ri (at Babylon? *Topog. Texts* no. 12, 12′).

248 **é.engur.ra**, "House of the Sweet Waters" 1, literary by-name of é.abzu of Enki at Eridu (see Sjöberg, *TCS* III, pp. 54f.; CTL [180]), passim in Sumerian literature (note Hallo, *CRRA* 17, p. 125, Nissaba and Enki 40, = [*é-en-g*]*u-ur*), also well attested in cultic laments (Cohen, *Lamentations*, index p. 750; note p. 614, 192, as residence of Inanna; *SBH* 34, rev. 5; Langdon, *BL* no. 123, 5′; etc.).

249 **(é).engur.ra** 2, seat of Ea, probably in é.umuš.a of é.sag̃.íl at Babylon (*Topog. Texts* nos. 1 = *Tintir* II 4; 43, 6′; *CT* 53 60, rev. 6′).

250 **é.engur.ra** 3, temple of Nanše at Sulum near Lagaš, built by Enmetena (Steible, *FAOS* 5/I, Ent 1, ii 7; 8, iv 3; 44; etc.), desecrated by Lugalzaggesi (ibid., Ukg 16, vi 6), and rebuilt by Gudea (9/I, Gud. 33, 8: é.$^{an}$engur zú.lum$^{ki}$).

251 **é.engur.ra.an.na**, see é.me.ur$_4$.an.na

252 **é.ér.gig**, "House of Bitter Lament," a sanctuary of Gula (in é.gal.maḫ at Isin?), as found in a cultic lament (Cohen, *Lamentations*, p. 256, 46, qualified as é ér.ra pel.lá, "desecrated house of lament").

253 **é.ér.ra**, "House of Lament," a sanctuary of Dumuzi and Belili (CTL 444.466).

254 **é.érim.ḫaš.ḫaš**, "House which Smites the Wicked," temple of Nergal (at Ur?), rebuilt by Rīm-Sîn I (Frayne, *RIME* 4, p. 277, 12). See also é.kù.ga.

255 **é.eš.ad**, TN or epithet known from the big OB forerunner to *Hh* XXI (*MSL* XI, p. 142, viii 19).

256 **é.eš.bar.an.ki**, "House of Decisions of Heaven and Underworld," seat of Šamaš in é.sag̃.íl at Babylon (*Topog. Texts* no. 1 = *Tintir* II 38).

257 **é.eš.bar.$^{d}$en.líl.lá**, "House of Decisions of Enlil," bath-house of Aššur in é.šár.ra 2 at Aššur (*Topog. Texts* no. 20 = Götteradreßbuch 147: Assyrian TL).

258 **é.eš.bar.me.luḫ.ḫa**, "House of Decisions, which Cleans the *Me*'s," temple of Ninšubur at G̃irsu (CTL 462).

259 **eš.bar.me.si.sá**, "(House) which Keeps in Order Decisions and *Me*'s," seat of Nabû in ub.šu.ukkin.na of é.sag̃.íl at Babylon (*Topog. Texts* no. 1 = *Tintir* II 23′).

260 **é.eš.bar$^{?}$.si.sá**, "House which Keeps Decisions in Order," sanctuary of Enki at Ur, built by Rīm-Sîn I (Frayne, *RIME* 4, p. 279, 25: var. of é.g̃éštu.šu.du$_7$).

261 **é.eš.bar.zi.da**, "House of True Decisions," temple of Ninsianna (at Ur?), rebuilt by Rīm-Sîn I (Frayne, *RIME* 4, p. 298, 33; placed at Isin by Renger, *Studien Falkenstein*, p. 143). Note also an unnamed temple of DN built by Šulgi (Steible, *FAOS* 9/II, Š 67).

262 **é.éš.dam.kù**, "House, Sacred Brothel," temple of Inanna at G̃irsu (CTL 383), well known from Inanna's Descent and the éš.dam hymns (Wilcke, *RlA* V, p. 78). Cf. non-specific use of the TN in Ninmešarra 137.

263 **é.éš.gàr**, "House of the Work Assignment," seat of Uttu in é.sag̃.íl at Babylon (*Topog. Texts* no. 1 = *Tintir* II 13″).

264 **èš.abzu**, "House, *Apsû*," also èš.e.abzu, variant of (é).abzu both as temple and cosmic domain: Temple Hymns 15; *UET* VI 67, 2.56: hymn to Nanna; 101, 8.23.38: hymn to Ḫaya; VIII 33, 17′: Amar-Suen chronicle; Enki's Journey 8.127; Green, *JCS* 30 (1978), pp. 132ff., Eridu Lament 1:26; 3:18; 7:2; litanies: *Šurpu* II 150; George, *RA* 82 (1988), p. 159, 32; incantations: *VAS* XVII 14, 2; *STT* 198, 25; 199, rev. 22′; etc.

265 **é.èš.bàn.da**, "House, Little Chamber" 1, seat of Šuzianna represented by a brick found in the sanctuary of Ningal at Ur, é.g̃i$_6$.pàr.kù 1, made by Sîn-balāssu-iqbi (*UET* I 175, 1: é.èš.{ras.}.bàn.da, against Gadd's é.abzu?.bàn.da and Ebeling's é.ab.zu.bàn.da (*RlA* II, p. 258). The erased sign is like MUNUS, possibly d⟨am⟩: cf. Šuzianna's status in *An* I as Enlil's dam bàn.da, "junior wife").

266 **èš.bàn.da** 2, seat of Nanše at the gate ká.maḫ in é.sag̃.íl at Babylon (*Topog. Texts* no. 1 = *Tintir* II 43, p. 280, K 3446+, obv. 20: royal ritual; *CT* 46 53, ii 20).

267 **èš.bur**, "House of Jars," sanctuary of Inanna of Eridu (nin (kù).nun.na), built (at Ur?) by Ur-Nammu (Steible, *FAOS* 9/II, UrN 17; no TN: 6; cf. Ur 24, 1). See also é.tilmun.na.

268 **èš.dur.an.ki**, "House, Bond of Heaven and Underworld," sanctuary provisioned by Zambīya (Frayne, *RIME* 4, p. 92, 6). Perhaps = é.dur.an.ki. For èš.dur.an.ki as a name of Nippur see Šulgi D 375 (Klein, *Šulgi*, p. 86); Nippur Lament 5.

269 **é.èš.ér.ke$_4$**, sanctuary of Marduk in Sippar-Aruru, known from a votive inscription of Aššur-etel-ilāni (Ebeling, *AnOr* 12, pp. 71f., 6–7). In a lexical text Sippar-Aruru (< OB Sippar-Yaḫrurum, Zadok, *Rép. géogr.* VIII, p. 124) is equated with the Babylonian Dūr-Šarru-kīn (*MSL* XI, p. 54, 26, cited above in the note on list no. 3, 24′–9′). This town is the location of é.še.ri.ga of Šidada, and the suspicion is that é.èš.er.ke$_4$ is a variant or corruption of that TN.

270 **é.èš.gal**, "House, Big House," temple of Ištar (CTL 315) and Nanāy, one of the principal units of the late temple complex at Uruk (*BRM* IV 6, 22.26.39; see further Falkenstein, *Topographie*, pp. 30ff., reading é.iri$_{12}$.gal), which gave its name to a quarter of the city (*VAS* XV 27, 3–4:

*erṣeti*$^{ti}$ é.èš.gal *šá i-qab-bu-ú kap-ri šá bīt ilī*$^{meš}$ *šá uruk*$^{ki}$, "district of é.TN, which they call the 'Village of the temples of Uruk' "; cf. 13, 2; 22, 3; 27, 4). The temple is listed as a sanctuary of Anu in a late liturgical hymn (Cohen, *Lamentations*, p. 729, 9). In other literature: Klein, *Šulgi*, p. 138, Šulgi X 55; Enmerkar and the Lord of Aratta 51.61.62. The reading é.iri$_{12}$.gal still rests on the syllabic writing ga-ša-an i-ri-ga-al a-ma ku-ul-la-ba in a single late copy of a litany (// gašan èš.gal ama kul.aba$_4$$^{ki}$: now Cohen, *Lamentations*, pp. 286, 224 = 361, 240). There are other oddities in the syllabic text, and I do not accept that it can be given final authority (contrast the evidence of another syllabic text, *VAS* II 3, ii 21: ka-ša-an AB-ga-la ku-la-ba!). Probably the writing i-ri-ga-al arose through confusion with the well-known name of the Netherworld ("Great City": iri$_{11/12}$.gal, ÈŠ×GAL = *erṣetu*), which has of course nothing to do with the temple of Uruk.

271 **èš.gal.maḫ**, "Exalted Big House," part of g̃á.nun.maḫ at Ur, rebuilt for Nanna-Suen by Sîn-iddinam (Frayne, *RIME* 4, p. 170, 14).

272 **èš.g̃ar**, "House which is Set up," seat of Qingu in é.sag̃.íl at Babylon (*Topog. Texts* no. 1 = *Tintir* II 21).

273 **èš.gú.tùr**, part or by-name of é.ab.šà.ga.lá of Ninmar in Guabba (Temple Hymns 285: èš.kù.ŠILAM), built by Ur-Baba (Steible, *FAOS* 9/I, UrB 1, v 11: èš.gú.tùr) and Gudea (Gud. 72, 12: no TN, but note that he calls the precinct of Ninmar at Guabba gú.ab.ba.tùr$^{ki}$: lines 8–9).

274 **èš.gú.zi**, "House whose Neck is Raised up," literary alternative to é.sag̃.íl of Marduk at Babylon, first known from the reign of Adad-apla-iddina (Bahija Khalil Ismail, *Sumer* 37 [1981], p. 114, 3: èš.gú.zi.da; Finkel, *Studies Sachs*, p. 144; also *Topog. Texts* no. 5, 31–33; cf. p. 295).

275 **èš.ḫuš**, "Dread House," a sanctuary known from an unplaced year name of Ḫammurapi (year n: Stol, *OB History*, p. 43).

276 **é.èš.ki.te(n)**, "House, Place of Refreshment," a sanctuary of Nanna-Suen (at Ur?), rebuilt by Kudur-Mabuk (Frayne, *RIME* 4, pp. 208, 14; 209, 19).

277 **èš.kù.ŠILAM**, see èš.gú.tùr

278 **èš.li.li.diri.ga**, "House of Profuse Progeny," seat of Antu as Ninzalle in the temple complex at Uruk (*Topog. Texts* no. 25, obv. 6′).

279 **èš.maḫ**, "Exalted House" 1, by-name for the earth and underworld, including the netherworld and the realm of Ea, in opposition to the heavens (see George, *Iraq* 48 [1986], pp. 133, B 4; 136).

280 **(é).èš.maḫ** 2, sanctuary of Ea in Eridu (CTL 185), or a by-name for Ea's cult-center there (pars pro toto), commonly attested in liturgical texts, often in Damgalnunna's epithet ama TN (Cohen, *Lamentations*, pp. 135, 249; 157f., 67.101; 265, 6; 299, 34; 305, 156; also 403, 6′; 407, 81; 486, 124; 623, 355?.357; Maul, *Eršaḫunga* no. 10, 5; George, *RA* 82 [1988], pp. 159f., 33.51; *OECT* VI, pl. 8, K 5001, rev. 8; 26, K 9310, i 6: incantation; etc.), and

elsewhere (II *R* 58, no. 6, 45: *mīs pî*; *CT* 36 32, 3: hymn; Temple Hymns 18; Enki and the World Order 148; etc.). See also é.maḫ 16.

281 **èš.maḫ** 3, part of the *bīt rēš* of Anu at Uruk, known from LB rituals (Falkenstein, *Topographie*, p. 24).

282 **(é).èš.maḫ** 4, temple of Ea in west Babylon (*Topog. Texts* nos. 1 = *Tintir* IV 35; V 100; 3, rev. 15′; Pallis, *Akîtu*, pl. 8, 2). See *Topog. Texts*, pp. 326f.

283 **èš.maḫ** 5, seat of Ea at the gate ká.maḫ in é.sag̃.íl at Babylon (*Topog. Texts* no. 1 = *Tintir* II 42; temple ritual, K unpub.).

284 **(é).èš.maḫ** 6, a shrine in é.kur at Nippur (Proto-*Kagal* 185; CTL 30), with which Nuska and Sadarnunna are associated (Temple Hymns 49.57; van Dijk, *Götterlieder* II, p. 109, iv 5; Sjöberg, *JAOS* 93 [1973], p. 352, 4.6; note also a throne of TN in an early OB offering list: Heimerdinger, *Kramer AV*, p. 228, v 30′). Also a by-name for é.kur: *RIME* 4, p. 67, ii 8′: Ur-Ninurta; *SRT* 11, obv. 8; Falkenstein, *Götterlieder* I, p. 13, 40; van Dijk, *Götterlieder* II, p. 108, 8; Civil, *JAOS* 88 [1968], p. 4, Enlil's Chariot 2; *JAOS* 103 [1983], pp. 54, 74; 57, 146: Enlil and Sud; etc.).

285 **é.èš.me.dag̃al.la**, "House, Chamber of the Widespread *Me*'s," temple of Dagān at Ur, rebuilt for Gungunum by Išme-Dagān's daughter, Enannatumma (Frayne, *RIME* 4, p. 115, 13; qualified as é.šútum.kù.ga.ni, "his pure storeroom").

286 **èš.nam.UD**, a sanctuary of Šulpae found in a cultic lament (Cohen, *Lamentations*, p. 733, 60); restore in CTL 163?

287 **èš.šà.abzu**, "House in the Midst of *Apsû*," a chamber of é.sag̃.íl at Babylon (*Topog. Texts* no. 1 = *Tintir* II 11″).

288 **èš.urugal$_x$(ÈŠ×GAL.gal)**, "House, Great City," temple of Ereškigal in Kutha, rebuilt by Nebuchadnezzar II (*PBS* XV 79, ii 94; iii 1). Urugal (or Irigal, = *erṣetu*) is a by-name of the netherworld over which Ereškigal presides.

289 **é?.GA.DI**, sanctuary of Ningal off the Sublime Court of the main temple complex at Ur (*UET* VI 402, 22; cf. Charpin, *Le clergé d'Ur*, pp. 326ff.).

290 **é.ga.ì.nun.ḫé.du$_7$**, "House Suited for Milk and Ghee," seat of Ištar as Telîtu, probably in é.umuš.a of é.sag̃.íl at Babylon (*Topog. Texts* no. 1 = *Tintir* II 6).

291 **é.ga.ì.nun.šár.šár**, "House which Provides a Profusion of Milk and Ghee," temple of Nin-Eigara at Šadunni mentioned in the Syncretistic Ištar Hymn (l. 85, var. é.ga.nun.na.šár.šár; unpub., courtesy Lambert).

292 **é.ga.ra.ni**, see é.ì.gára

293 ***g̃á.balag̃.g̃á**, ES ma.balag̃.g̃á, "Chamber of the Harp," a shrine of Gula, as found in a cultic lament (Cohen, *Lamentations*, p. 256, 48, qualified as ma balag̃.nun.na, "chamber of the princely harp").

294 **g̃á.bur.ra**, "Chamber of Jars" 1, temple of Ningublag at Kiabrig (Temple Hymns 150; Lamentation over Sumer and Ur 201). Written G̃Á×BUR.ME in an ED geographical list (McEwan, *JCS* 33 [1981], p. 56[6])? Foundations laid by Ur-Nammu (year 17, no TN). Cult probably removed to Ur after Ur III (Charpin, *Le clergé d'Ur*, p. 222). See also é.gu$_4$.du$_7$.šár.

295 **(é).g̃á.bur.(ra)** 2, temple of Ningublag, known from inscriptions found at Ur: rebuilt by Warad-Sîn (Frayne, *RIME* 4, pp. 207, 9′; 251, 22), and Kurigalzu (*VAS* I 55, 5; *UET* I 164). Mentioned by Lipit-Ištar, who confirms its location at Ur (Frayne, *RIME* 4, p. 58, 21; cf. Charpin, *Le clergé d'Ur*, p. 222).

296 **é.g̃á.du$_6$.da**, temple of Šuzianna in g̃á.gi.maḫ at Nippur (Temple Hymns 77), also found in liturgical texts (Cohen, *Lamentations*, pp. 98, 61; 351, 63: umma.du$_6$.da). Other variants of the TN appear to be é.ama$_5$.du$_6$.dam and é.BI.du$_6$.du$_6$.da; see also é.ki.ág̃.g̃á.šu.du$_7$. A temple of Šuzianna at Nippur is listed without name in a MB metrological text (Bernhardt and Kramer, *OrNS* 44 [1975], p. 98, 41).

297 **(é).g̃á.gi.maḫ**, "House, Exalted Harem," female quarters (*gagû*) in the temple complex of Enlil at Nippur, sacred to Šuzianna (CTL 67; Temple Hymns 86).

298 **(é).g̃á.$^{giš}$apin.na**, "House, Chamber of the Plough," part of é.kur at Nippur, attested in an OB liturgical hymn to Enlil (Cohen, *Lamentations*, p. 350, 51–52) and the Hymn to E-kur (Kramer, *RSO* 32 [1957], p. 97, 27).

299 **(é).g̃á.g̃iš.šú.a**, "House, Chamber of the Stool" 1, cella of Ninlil in é.ki.ùr at Nippur (CTL 61; Proto-*Kagal* 183; Kramer, *RSO* 32 [1957], p. 97, 13: Hymn to E-kur; cf. Falkenstein, *Götterlieder* I, p. 33). Furnished with a throne for Enlil by Išme-Dagān (year f: é.g̃á.g̃iš.šu$_4$.a), its kisal.maḫ is mentioned by Ur-Ninurta (Frayne, *RIME* 4, p. 67, vi 11′), Enlil-bāni (ibid., p. 86, 18) and Kudur-Mabuk (ibid., p. 267, 16, where it is the scene of the ritual humiliation of an enemy). Passim in Sumerian literature (cf. Loding, *AfO* 24 [1973], p. 49). Also in liturgical texts (Cohen, *Eršemma*, p. 111, 17: Emesal ma.mu.šú.a; *Lamentations*, pp. 276, 57?; 349, 29: bedchamber of Enlil and Ninlil; Krecher, *Kultlyrik*, pp. 53, 7; 82; etc.). Note a stool (g̃iš.šu$_4$.a) listed among the cultic fittings of Ninlil's sanctuary at Nippur in an Ur III offering list (*TCL* II 5501, ii 18).

300 **é.g̃á.g̃iš.šú.a** 2, see é.gán.g̃iš.šú.a

301 **é.g̃á.gú.x**[ . . . ], shrine(?) mentioned by Enanedu, Warad-Sîn's sister (Frayne, *RIME* 4, p. 230, 19:3′).

302 **g̃á.nun.kù**, see é.gar$_6$.kù

303 **(é).g̃á.nun.maḫ**, "House, Exalted Storehouse" 1, treasury of Nanna-Suen at Ur, rebuilt by Nūr-Adad (Frayne, *RIME* 4, p. 140, 7; qualified as é.me.te.ì.nun.ga.àra), Sîn-iddinam (ibid., p. 170, 8; qualified as èš.gal.maḫ níg̃.ga.ra), and Kudur-Mabuk (ibid., pp. 214, 9; 216, 28: é kù.babbar.kù.sig$_{17}$

ùru.èrim.dugud [d]suen.na.ka; Warad-Sîn year 6), and again by Kurigalzu (*UET* I 162–63) and Marduk-nādin-aḫḫē (*UET* I 306). Probably = é.nun. maḫ 1. According to OB disbursements of offerings from Ur Ningal also had a building of this name (Figulla, *Iraq* 15 [1953], pp. 88ff.; note both buildings together: p. 116, *UET* V 787, 6.8).

304 **é.g̃á.nun.maḫ** 2, part of é.kur at Nippur found in liturgical texts (Cohen, *Eršemma*, p. 111, 16; *Lamentations*, pp. 350, 34; 391, 182: ma.nun. maḫ; Krecher, *Kultlyrik*, pp. 53, 6; 82; V *R* 52, no. 2, obv. 55?; etc.). Note also a g̃á[!](GÁN).nun.maḫ in é.an.na at Uruk (Enmerkar and the Lord of Aratta 324).

305 **é.g̃á.nun.na**, "House of the Storeroom," part of é.kur at Nippur mentioned in two OB liturgical hymns to Enlil (Cohen, *Lamentations*, pp. 98, 63.65; 351, 61: e.g̃á.nun.na), and in a later parallel litany (*SBH* 34, rev. 12). In all three texts the TN follows é.šu.me.ša$_4$ of Ninurta.

306 **é.gaba.ri.nu.tuku**, "House without a Rival," a sanctuary of Ištar (CTL 376).

307 **é.gada.a.ri.a**, "House Draped in Linen," a sanctuary of Ninšubur (CTL 461).

308 **é.gal.an.ki.a**, "Palace of Heaven and Underworld," a shrine of Anu (and/or Ištar?) at Uruk paired with é.èš.gal in a liturgical hymn (Cohen, *Lamentations*, p. 729, 9; Falkenstein, *Topographie*, pp. 34f.).

309 **é.gal.an.na**, "Palace of Heaven," epithet of or shrine within é.G̃ÉŠTU. [d]NISSABA, mentioned in Enmerkar and the Lord of Aratta (l. 322).

310 **é.gal.an.[zu?]**, "Sagacious House," a temple of Ea (CTL 191).

311 **é.gal.bar.ra**, "Outer Palace," a building (at Larsa) furnished with statues of Kudur-Mabuk and Warad-Sîn by Rīm-Sîn I (years 2.5). Possibly a mortuary temple?

312 **é.gal.edin**, "Palace of the Steppe" 1, a temple at Uruk, known from a LB legal document (*BRM* II 12, 2). Misreading of é.gal.maḫ 4?

313 **é.gal.edin** 2, Akītu temple of Ištar at Milqia, repaired by Aššurbanipal (Pinches, *Wedge-Writing*, p. 17, obv. 6; cf. *RAcc.*, p. 112). Also a Sargonic toponym (Foster, *Umma*, p. 65; later *MVN* VI 510, obv. 3; Edzard et al., *Rép. géogr.* I, p. 41).

314 **é.gal.gu.la**, "Big Palace," apparently the temple of Enzak on Failaka, ancient Agarum (Glassner, in J.-Fr. Salles [ed.], *Failaka*, pp. 33ff., nos. 2, 3, 33; cf. p. 48).

314a **é.gal.ḫal.ḫal**, "Palace of Secrets," a temple of NB Uruk known only from the name of a quarter of the city (Pohl, *AnOr* 8, no. 3, 2: *erṣet* é.TN). Presumably = é.IG.ḫal.an.ki and é.MI.ḫal.la.ke$_4$.

315 **é.gal.kèš[ki].a**, "Palace of Keš," see é.kèš

316 **é.gal.lam.mes**, see é.mes.lam 3

317 **é.gal.$^{d}$lamma.lugal**, "Palace of the King's Guardian Deity," a temple mentioned in the Syncretistic Ištar Hymn (l. 65; unpub., courtesy Lambert). To judge from its place in that text, between Dilbat and Kiš, it lay in a town not far from Babylon. See also é.galam.ma.lugal.

318 **é.gal.maḫ**, "Exalted Palace" 1, temple of Gula, as Ninisinna, in Isin (CTL [504]). Cult statue set up by Lipit-Ištar (year c), rebuilt after a long period of dereliction by Kurigalzu (I *R* 4, no. 14/2; Walker and Wilcke, *Isin* II, pp. 96ff.: variants read Ninurta for Gula) and Kadašman-Enlil (ibid., p. 98: *kissû* wall). Restored by Adad-šuma-uṣur (ibid., p. 99), Meli-šipak (p. 99) and Adad-apla-iddina (for $^{d}$nin.ezen.na: Edzard and Wilcke, *Isin* I, p. 90, 10: é.gal.máḫ), and apparently again by Nebuchadnezzar II (*Isin* II, p. 101). Mentioned by Zambīya (Frayne, *RIME* 4, p. 92, 8). Provisioned by Ur-Dukuga (ibid., p. 95, 12, but paired with é.šu.me.ša$_4$, so possibly the reference is to é.TN 6 instead), by Sîn-māgir (ibid., p. 98, 5) and Damiq-ilīšu (ibid., pp. 103, 11; 104, 13; 105, 12); patronized by Ḫammurapi (CḪ ii 54). Passim in Sumerian literature. Listed in liturgical texts, usually between Isin and é.rab.ri.ri in one of the standard litanies of TNs (Cohen, *Eršemma*, pp. 114, 27; 140, 34; *Lamentations*, index p. 750; Maul, *Eršaḫunga* no. 37, 4; Krecher, *Kultlyrik*, index p. 232; *CT* 15 25, 22). Also mentioned in the syncretistic hymn to Nanāy (Reiner, *JNES* 33 [1974], p. 225, 15–16), in Anzû III 137 (residence of Pabilsağ), and in a *lipšur*-litany (Wiseman, *Iraq* 31 [1969], p. 177, 45′). Divine residents listed in a late cultic text (Nougayrol, *RA* 41 [1947], p. 35, 12–27).

319 **é.gal.maḫ** 2, temple of Gula in the é.sağ.íl complex at Babylon (*Topog. Texts* nos. 1 = *Tintir* IV 5; 3, obv. 13′–14′). Probably the unnamed temple of Ninisinna ($^{d}$nin.si.in.na) built by Sūmû-abum (year 4). The TN is also found in association with é.sağ.íl in a *lipšur*-litany, where it is the residence of Iqbi-damiq (Nougayrol, *JCS* 1 [1947], p. 330, 9′ // Wiseman, *Iraq* 31 [1969], p. 177, 20′; also Craig, *ABRT* I 58, 25). See *Topog. Texts*, pp. 305f. Probably = é.ḫur.sağ.sikil.la.

320 **é.gal.maḫ** 3, temple of Gula as Ninisinna at Ur, built by Warad-Sîn (Frayne, *RIME* 4, p. 205, 16). In Šulgi hymns attributed to Ninegal (Klein, *Šulgi*, pp. 144, X 141; 196, A 57), so perhaps identical with the unnamed sanctuary of this goddess built by Ur-Nammu (Steible, *FAOS* 9/II, UrN 18).

321 **é.gal.maḫ** 4, temple of Ninisinna at Uruk, rebuilt by Sîn-kāšid (Frayne, *RIME* 4, p. 457, 11). Dedicated to other manifestations of Gula: Ninsun in SB Gilgameš (III 15.20), and Bēlet-balāṭi in a LB legal document (*BRM* II 36, 5; cf. é.gal.edin 1).

322 **é.gal.maḫ** 5, by-name of the temple of Gula at Aššur (*Topog. Texts* no. 20 = Götteradreßbuch 173: Assyrian TL). See é.sa.bad 4.

323 **é.gal.maḫ** 6, a sanctuary listed among shrines of the temple complex of Enlil at Nippur in liturgical texts (Cohen, *Lamentations*, p. 350, 32; *Eršemma*, p. 111, 18; Krecher, *Kultlyrik*, pp. 53, 8; 83; etc.), and in the

Hymn to E-kur (Kramer, *RSO* 32 [1957], p. 97, 17). Probably the sanctuary of Gula as Ninurta's wife; cf. the sequence x.gal.ma[ḫ . . . ] / é $^{d}$nin.[ì.si.in$^{ki}$.na?] in an early OB offering list (Heimerdinger, *Kramer AV*, p. 226, iv 27′–28′), and note also the pairing of é.šu.me.ša$_4$ and é.gal.maḫ by Ur-Dukuga (Frayne, *RIME* 4, p. 95, 11–12; or é.TN 1?). Also in the early OB offering list *PBS* VIII/1 13, obv. 15 (Damiq-ilīšu); prebend sale: *OECT* VIII 8, 3 (Samsu-iluna).

324 ***é.gal.mes.lam**, see é.mes.lam 4

325 **é.gal.nun.na**, "Palace of the Prince," sanctuary (at Eridu?) mentioned in a liturgical text (Cohen, *Lamentations*, p. 81, 130).

326 **é.gal.ri.ri**, see é.rab.ri.ri

327 **é.gal.*ta-bi-ri***, see é.dadag.lál

328 **é.gal.ti.ra.áš**, see é.ti.ra.áš

329 **é?.galam.an.ki.a.šu.du$_7$**, "Skilfully-Built House, Perfect in Heaven and Underworld," a shrine in é.sağ.íl at Babylon (*Topog. Texts* no. 1 = *Tintir* II 47).

330 **é.galam.ma$^!$.dím.ma**, "Skilfully-Built House," temple of Igidu at Akšak (TL no. 3, 37′).

331 **é.galam.ma.lugal**, "Skilfully-Built House of the King," a temple listed in TL no. 3, 18′. See also é.gal.$^{d}$lamma.lugal.

332 **é.galam.mes**, see é.mes.lam 4

333 **é.ğalga.sù**, "House Filled with Counsel" 1, shrine of Baba in é.tar.sír.sír at Ğirsu (Proto-*Kagal* 204; Temple Hymns 265; Hymn to Baba for Išme-Dagān: Römer, *Königshymnen*, p. 237, 24; cf. Falkenstein, *AnOr* 30, p. 146), mentioned in liturgical texts (Cohen, *Lamentations*, pp. 611, 92; 613, 158).

334 **é.ğalga.sù** 2, cella of Baba at Kiš (*Topog. Texts* no. 22, 4′; TL no. 6, 2; CTL [492]).

335 **é.ğalga.sù** 3, a sanctuary of Ištar the Queen (CTL [324]).

336 **é.ğalga.ùru.na**, "House of Lofty Counsel," temple of Enlil at Dūr-Enlil, destroyed by Agum III (Grayson, *Chronicles*, p. 156, rev. 18).

337 **é.gán.ğá.du$_7$.du$_7$**, the ziqqurrat at Marad (TL no. 4, 17; no. 5, 20′: du.du).

338 **é.gán.ğiš.šú.a**, sanctuary of Ninlil in é.šár.ra 2 at Aššur (*Topog. Texts* no. 20 = Götteradreßbuch 148: Assyrian TL), provided with a divine gate-keeper by Tiglath-pileser I (Grayson, *RIMA* 2, p. 20, 34: no TN; cf. p. 34, 23–24). See also é.ğá.ğiš.šú.a.

339 **é.gán.kalam.ma**, "House, Field of the Land," a temple of Enlil mentioned in the Lugalannemundu inscription (Güterbock, *ZA* 42 [1934], p. 41, A ii 18). Read é.ama$_5$.kalam.ma? (Sjöberg).

340 **é.gán.nun.kù**, see é.gar$_6$.kù

341 **gán.nun.maḫ**, see é.g̃á.nun.maḫ 2

342 **é.gán.nun.[na]**, "House, Field of the Prince," a temple of Ea (CTL 192).

343 **é.g̃ar.rin.na**, see é.a.girin.na

344 **é.gar$_6$**, "House, Boudoir," TN or epithet known from Proto-*Kagal* 171 (common noun) and 196.

345 **é.gar$_6$.kù**, or agrun.kù, "House, Sacred Boudoir," designation of the sanctuary of Ningal in the g̃i$_6$.pàr at Ur (cf. Charpin, *Le clergé d'Ur*, pp. 212f.), occasionally used as a ceremonial name, e.g., by Nūr-Adad (Frayne, *RIME* 4, p. 144, 33), who rebuilt it, and in a late shrine list (*Topog. Texts* no. 26 B, 2). Mentioned by Warad-Sîn (*RIME* 4, p. 225, 3:6′). In Sumerian literature: Kramer, *AS* 12, pp. 18ff.: Ur Lament 16.50.113.323; *UET* VI 67, 59: hymn to Nanna; Sjöberg, *JCS* 29 (1977), p. 9, rev. 17′: hymn to Nanna; *JCS* 34 (1982), p. 70, 16: hymn to Ninšubur; *ZA* 63 (1973), p. 32, 36: hymn to Nanna as Ašimbabbar; *OECT* VI, pl. 26, K 9310, i 15′: incantation. An ancient misreading as g̃á.nun.kù probably resulted in the entry é.gán. nun.kù in the Ningal section of CTL (l. 275). Note also é.gar$_6$.kù (as a common noun) in Proto-*Kagal* 172.

346 ***é.gar$_6$ . . .**, see also é.nun . . .

347 **é.g̃arza**, see é.ki.tuš.g̃arza and é.mar.za

348 **é.g̃arza-*kidudê***, "House of Rites and Rituals," temple of Ištar as Šarrat-nipḫi at Aššur (*Topog. Texts* no. 20 = Götteradreßbuch 168: Assyrian TL).

349 **é.gašan.an.na**, "House of the Lady of Heaven," also written é.gašan. $^{d}$*anu*, cella of Antu in the *bīt rēš* at Uruk (Falkenstein, *Topographie*, pp. 6, 24).

350 **é.gašan.an.ta.g̃ál**, "House of the Lady on High," temple of Ninlil at Dūr-Kurigalzu (CTL 62), built by Kurigalzu (Baqir, *Iraq*, Suppl. 1944, fig. 17; Suppl. 1945, p. 3; etc.).

351 **é.gašan.kalam.ma**, "House of the Lady of the Land," temple of Ištar-Ninlil at Arbil (*Topog. Texts* no. 20 = Götteradreßbuch 178: Assyrian TL), rebuilt with its ziqqurrat by Shalmaneser I (Grayson, *RIMA* 1, p. 204, 11′). Mentioned by Aššur-dān I (ibid., p. 308, 2). Refurbished by Esarhaddon (Borger, *Esarh.*, § 21, 8; cf. § 97, 8), and Aššurbanipal (Piepkorn, *Asb.*, p. 28, 20; Thompson, *AAA* 20 [1933], p. 82, 42; Streck, *Asb.*, pp. 92, 20; 150, 47; Bauer, *Asb.*, p. 111: index; Pinches, *Wedge-Writing*, p. 17, 4: no TN; etc.). See also Menzel, *Tempel* I, p. 6. For rituals of the temple see Livingstone, *Mystical Works*, pp. 116ff.

352 **é.gašan.tin.na**, "House of the Lady of Life," a temple (of Gula?) mentioned in the Syncretistic Ištar Hymn (l. 89; unpub., courtesy Lambert).

353 **gaz.si.sum.m[u?]**, seat of Nergal in the slaughterhouse of é.šár.ra at Aššur (*Topog. Texts* no. 21, obv. 16′).

354 **é.ĝéšbu.ba.**KIB-***gunû*.ma**, a sanctuary at Ur where offerings were made in the month of the Akītu (*UET* III 189, 11; 191, 19; IX 1050, 2; see McEwan, *OrNS* 52 [1983], p. 225).

355 **é.ĝéštu**, "House of Wisdom," sanctuaries of Ea (CTL 194; at Eridu: Green, *JCS* 30 [1978], p. 136, Eridu Lament 4:11; hymn to Enki for Ur-Ninurta: *CT* 36 32, 13) and Nissaba (Gudea, Cyl. A xvii 15; Nissaba and Enki: Hallo, *CRRA* 17, p. 125, 45; Ur-Ninurta B 36f.), not always clear which (Enlil-diriše 334; Šulgi C 35; see further Green, *JCS* 30 [1978], pp. 152f.).

356 **é.ĝéštu.diri**, "House of Surpassing Wisdom," socle of Indagar in é.saĝ.íl at Babylon (*Topog. Texts* no. 1 = *Tintir* II 28′).

357 **é.ĝéštu.kalam.ma.sum.mu**, "House which Dispenses Wisdom in the Land," a sanctuary of Ea (CTL 196).

358 **é.ĝéštu$^{\text{min}}$.maḫ**, "House of Sublime Wisdom," a shrine at Babylon known from a cultic calendar (*SBH* VIII iv 13).

359 **é.ĝéštu.maḫ.šu.du$_7$**, "House of Perfect Sublime Wisdom" 1, a sanctuary of Ea, probably at Ur (CTL 197), = é.ĝéštu.šu.du$_7$? See also é.múštug.maḫ.šu.du$_7$.

360 **é.ĝéštu.maḫ.šu.du$_7$** 2, temple of Ea in the é.šár.ra complex at Aššur (*Topog. Texts* no. 20 = Götteradreßbuch 151: Assyrian TL).

361 **[é.ĝéštu?].maḫ.[ . . . ].sum.mu**, temple of Ea at Uruk (CTL 199), built by Sîn-kāšid (Frame, *RIME* 4, p. 456, 11; no TN). Possibly to be restored as [é.ĝéštu.ní].maḫ.[kalam.ma].sum.mu: see above, the note on CTL 199.

362 **é.ĜÉŠTU.$^{\text{d}}$NISSABA**, "House of the Wisdom of Nissaba" 1, shrines of Nissaba at Eridu and Uruk (Green, *JCS* 30 [1978], p. 136, Eridu Lament 4:11; further references on p. 152. Note also: Civil, *JAOS* 103 [1983], p. 54, Enlil and Sud 79; Kapp, ZA 51 [1955], p. 78, Enlil-bāni A 53–54: epithet of é!.za.gìn; Šulgi B 309; *Lugale* 716, M$_2$). See *Diri* V 300, glossed [x]-ra-a; Proto-*Kagal* 222; *Kagal* Boğ. I G 4: [é.TN = e-x-x]-in-ga-ra = *bi-it ni-im-ni-ga*[*l*] (i.e., Nanibgal, but see é.nam.en.ĝar.ra for an alternative restoration).

363 **é.ĜÉŠTU.$^{\text{d}}$NISSABA** 2, seat of Nissaba in é.saĝ.íl at Babylon (*Topog. Texts* no. 1 = *Tintir* II 12″).

364 **é.ĝéštu.šu.du$_7$**, "House of Perfect Wisdom," temple of Enki at Ur, built by Rīm-Sîn I (Frayne, *RIME* 4, p. 279, 25; cf. year 8). A temple of the same name occurs in a cultic lament (Cohen, *Lamentations*, p. 432, 61, glossed mu-uš-túg). Cf. é.ĝéštu.maḫ.šu.du$_7$ 1.

365 **é.ĝéštu.tukur.ra.sum.mu**, "House which Dispenses Weighty Wisdom," a sanctuary of Ea (CTL 195).

366 **é.gi.dim.dim**, sanctuary of Enlil at KI.[ . . . ] (CTL 46; Craig, *ABRT* I 58, 20: *lipšur* litany). Also mentioned in liturgical texts, where however it is probably a shrine in é.kur at Nippur, with the qualification é i.bí nu.bar.re,

"house (inside) which none may see" (Cohen, *Lamentations*, pp. 97, 21; 349, 18: é.i.bí.dim.dim, var.: [é].gi.dím.dím, [ . . . ].dìm.dìm).

367 **é.gi.dù**, see é.igi.$du_8$

368 **é.gi.$gun_4$.kù**, "Sacred Terrace-House," a sanctuary of Ištar of Hosts (CTL 323, reading provisional).

369 **gi.$gun_4$.na($^{ki}$).(kù)** 1, by-name of é.sag̃.íl of Ištar at Zabalam, rebuilt by Warad-Sîn (Frayne, *RIME* 4, pp. 217, 9: gi.$gun_4$.na.kù; 219, 10.19: gi.$gun_4^{ki}$.kù). Also found in Inanna's Descent and the éš.dam hymns (Wilcke, *RlA* V, p. 78), a love song of Dumuzi and Inanna (*CT* 58 13, 15), and Lamentation over Sumer and Ur 149.

370 **é.gi.$gun_4$.na** 2, sanctuary of Supalītu (Ištar of Zabalam) at Muru (CTL 322).

371 **é.gi.$gun_4$.na** 3, sanctuary of Ištar at Marad (CTL 355; TL no. 3, 22′).

372 **é.gi.gun(u)$_4^{ki}$** 4, a sanctuary (in the é.an.na complex?) at Uruk (*Topog. Texts* no. 25, obv. 3′).

373 **gi.$gun_4$.na** 5, ziqqurrat temple of Nippur rebuilt by Aššurbanipal (Streck, *Asb.*, p. 353, no. 4 = Gerardi, *Studies Sjöberg*, p. 209, 15.21: $^{é}$*gi-gu-nu-ú*; *PBS* XV 74, 10: é.gi.gùn.n[a]; for Enlil). Often used of the Nippur ziqqurrat in Sumerian literary and liturgical texts (see *CAD* G, pp. 68f.), but probably only as a common noun: the true TN is given by Ur-Nammu and Aššurbanipal as ḫur.sag̃.galam.ma, q.v.

374 **é.gi.kù.ga**, "House of the Pure Reed," TN listed in the OB lexical list from Isin (p. 4, IM 96881, ii′ 5′).

375 **é.gi.rin**, "Pure House," the ziqqurrat at Dūr-Kurigalzu (TL no. 4, 7; no. 5, 4′: [é.g]i.⌜x⌝).

376 **é.gi.šu.nu.gi**, a sanctuary at Uruk, mentioned with é.an.na in a NB letter (*YOS* III 8, 27). Possibly to be read é.*gi-ku*!*-nu-gi*, < é.gi.$gunu_4$ 4?

377 **é.g̃$i_6$.pàr** "*Giparu*-House" 1, shrine of the divine En priest (CTL 175, in the section on Bēlet-ilī), for example in é.sag̃.íl at Babylon and in é.šár.ra at Aššur (*Topog. Texts* nos. 1 = *Tintir* II 6′; 21, obv. 22′). The (é).g̃$i_6$.pàr, also written (é).g̃$i_6$.$par_4$, is the name given to the chambers of the sacred marriage occupied by the "human partner in the rite, the *ēnu* or the *ēntu*" (*CAD* G, p. 84, s.v. the common noun *giparu*). Thus it is also a shrine of the deity so personified: e.g., of Ningal in Sîn's temples at Ur and Ḫarrān (é.TN 2, 4), and of Dumuzi at Uruk (é.TN 5).

378 **(é).g̃$i_6$.pàr** 2, temple of the high-priestess (*ēntu*) of Nanna-Suen at Ur (cf. Charpin, *Le clergé d'Ur*, pp. 192ff.), rebuilt by Enanedu in the reign of her brother, Rīm-Sîn I (Frayne, *RIME* 4, p. 300, 26.31: g̃$i_6$.pàr.kù.ga), and by Nabonidus for his daughter Ennig̃aldi-Nanna (*YOS* I 45, ii 6). See also g̃$i_6$.pàr.kù 1, é.kar.zi.da 1.

379 **é.g̃i$_6$.pàr** 3, temple of the high-priestess (*ēntu*) of Ningublag at Ur (cf. Charpin, *Le clergé d'Ur*, pp. 220ff.), rebuilt by Lipit-Ištar for his daughter Enninsunzi (Frayne, *RIME* 4, p. 58, 14). A g̃i$_6$.pàr of Ningublag (at Kiabrig?) also appears in a liturgical hymn to Enlil (Cohen, *Lamentations*, p. 352, 106; cf. Langdon, *BL* no. 27, 10′).

380 **é.g̃i$_6$.pàr** 4, seat of Ningal at Ḫarrān, probably in é.ḫúl.ḫúl, known to Aššurbanipal (Streck, *Asb.*, p. 288, 10).

381 **(é).g̃i$_6$.pàr** 5, part of é.an.na occupied by the high-priest (*ēnu*) of Ištar, built by Amar-Suen (Steible, *FAOS* 9/II, AS 14; cf. 7). Common in liturgical texts (Cohen, *Eršemma*, p. 66, 2–9: g̃i$_6$.par$_4$.kù; *Lamentations*, pp. 104, 218; 164, 236; 265, 19; 541, 6; 543, 65; 672, 41–42; 689, 108; 711, 134; 714, 189; etc.). In Sumerian literature the g̃i$_6$.pàr.kù at Uruk is often mentioned: Lamentation over Sumer and Ur 151f., cf. 183 (at Sirara), 191 (Gaeš: see é.kar.zi.da), 204 (Kiabrig), 249 (Eridu); Enmerkar and Lord of Aratta 14.45; Kramer, *JCS* 21 (1967), p. 116, 211: é.TN èš.é.an.na.mu: Ur-Nammu's Death; Enmerkar and Ensuḫkešdanna [52].90; Ninmešarra 66; Gilgameš and the Bull of Heaven 9′; etc. See also [é . . . ]x.kù.

382 **é.g̃i$_6$.pàr** 6, sanctuary at Sippar attested in a liturgical hymn to Adad (Cohen, *Lamentations*, p. 434, 112: note the parallel é.nam.maḫ at Babylon in line 111).

383 **é.g̃i$_6$.pàr.en.na**, "*Giparu*-House of the En-Priest," temple of the high-priest (*ēnu*) of Ištar at Uruk, repaired by Anam (Frayne, *RIME* 4, p. 472, 1:10; 2:16). Probably = é.g̃i$_6$.pàr 5.

384 **(é).g̃i$_6$.pàr.imin.(na/bi)**, "House of Seven *Giparu*'s," ziqqurrat of Ištar at Uruk (TL no. 4, 20; no. 5, 18′; CTL 318; *Topog. Texts* no. 25, obv. 4′). Also in laments, etc., usually paired with é.an.na (Cohen, *Eršemma*, p. 66, 14; *Lamentations*, pp. 707, 53; 715, 217; note *CT* 15 25, 24, g̃i$_6$.par$_4$.imin paired with Larak; Langdon, *BL* no. 156, 1). Became a name of Uruk (*MSL* XI, pp. 54, 19; 63, 12′; Kilmer, *JAOS* 83 [1963], p. 428, *Malku* I 215: *mi-pa-ru* imin).

385 **g̃i$_6$.par$_4$.kù**, "Pure *Giparu*-House" 1, sanctuary of Ningal at Ur, rebuilt by Ur-Nammu and Amar-Suen (Steible, *FAOS* 9/II, UrN 19; AS 13; var. wr. g̃i$_6$.par$_4$.ku). A new g̃i$_6$.pàr of Ningal was built by Sîn-balāssu-iqbi for the priestess Ninlille-nitadam-kiag̃g̃a-Suen (*UET* I 171). Probably = é.g̃i$_6$.pàr 2. Note also the unnamed temple of Ningal built by Kurigalzu on the ziqqurrat terrace at Ur, commemorated in *UET* VIII 99 (and I 156?). See also é.gar$_6$.kù.

386 **g̃i$_6$.pàr.kù** 2, temple of the high-priestess (*ēntu*) of Lugalbanda at Uruk, rebuilt by Sîn-kāšid for his daughter Nīši-īnīšu (Frayne, *RIME* 4, p. 455, 12). See also é.g̃i$_6$.pàr 5.

387 **g̃i$_6$.pàr.kù.ga** 3, temple of the high-priestess (*ēntu*) of Šamaš at Larsa, as installed by Nūr-Adad (van Dijk, *JCS* 19 [1965], p. 9, 201; cf. Nūr-Adad year c).

388 **ĝi$_6$.par$_4$.kù.ga** 4, see é.kar.zi.da 1

389 **é.ĝi$_6$.pàr.kù** 5, a shrine in é.saĝ.íl at Babylon (*Topog. Texts* no. 1 = *Tintir* II 15′).

390 **é.ĝi$_6$.[pàr.kù?]** 6, temple of the *atû*-priest (CTL 176).

391 **é.gibil**, "New House," temple(?) in Pre-Sargonic and Ur III documents (Westenholz, *JCS* 26 [1974], p. 72; *MVN* VI, p. 412: index; etc.). See also é.gu.la 7.

392 **é.gíd.da**, "Long House," temple of Ninazu at Enegi (*MSL* XI, p. 142, viii 41; CTL [554]; Temple Hymns 181; Enlil and Ninlil 116; Lamentation over Sumer and Ur 206; prebends: *YOS* XI 64, 20). Also known from liturgical texts, in which both Ninazu and Nergal are umun.é.TN (Cohen, *Lamentations*, pp. 286f., 229.242 = 361ff., 245.258; cf. umun á.gíd.da: pp. 238f., 312.325 = 307f., 186.199).

393 **é.ĝidru**, "House of the Sceptre" 1, shrine(?) of Ninĝirsu built by Ur-Nanše (Steible, *FAOS* 5/I, UrN 24, iv 3; 29, iii 3; etc.), Uruinimgina (ibid., Ukg 12, 10′) and Gudea, who gives it the epithet é.ub.imin, "house of seven niches" (9/I, Gud. Stat. D, ii 11; E, i 16; G, i 13; etc). According to Falkenstein, part of é.ninnu at Ĝirsu (*AnOr* 30, pp. 131f.), according to Sauren, in Lagaš and NINA$^{\text{ki}}$ (*OrNS* 38 [1969], p. 217[5]). Also Bauer, *AWL*, p. 349, ix 3: in Sirara?; *ITT* 1065, rev. 7.

394 **é.ĝidru** 2, administrative building at Umma, rebuilt by Lugalannatum of Umma in the reign of Sium of Gutium (Gelb and Kienast, *FAOS* 7, p. 297, Gutium 3), and well known from administrative documents. Cf. Farber, *ArOr* 45 (1977), p. 152[20]; Foster, *Umma*, p. 227. A sacred function cannot be excluded.

395 **é.$^{\text{ĝiš}}$ĝidru.kalam.ma.si.sá**, see é.ĝidru.kalam.ma.sum.mu 2

396 **é.ĝidru.kalam.ma.sum.mu** 1, see é.$^{\text{ĝiš}}$níĝ.ĝidar.kalam.ma.sum.ma

397 **é.ĝidru.kalam.ma.sum.mu**, "House which Bestows the Sceptre of the Land" 2, temple of Nabû of the *ḫarû* at Aššur (*Topog. Texts* no. 20 = Götteradreßbuch 158: Assyrian TL, var. é.$^{\text{ĝiš}}$ĝidru.kalam.ma.si.sá, "House which Sets in Order the Sceptre of the Land"). The temple of Nabû at Aššur was rebuilt by Sîn-šarra-iškun (Donbaz and Grayson, *Clay Cones* = *RIM Suppl.* 1, p. 56, 7; no TN).

398 **é.$^{\text{ĝiš}}$gigir.$^{\text{d}}$en.líl.lá**, "Chariot-House of Enlil," seat of Enmešarra in é.šár.ra at Aššur (*Topog. Texts* no. 21, obv. 12′; rev. 31′).

399 **é.ĝír.lá.til.la**, "House of the Exterminating(?) Butcher," a shrine in é.saĝ.íl at Babylon (*Topog. Texts* no. 1 = *Tintir* II 15″).

400 **é.ĝír.nun.(na)**, "House of the Princely Path," shrine of Ninĝirsu in é. ninnu at Ĝirsu (written ĝír.nun: Steible, *FAOS* 5/I, Ean 60, ii 11; Ent 35, iii 2; Lugalanda 15, iii′ 3′; cf. Falkenstein, *AnOr* 30, p. 151). Already known to the ED zà.mí hymns (Biggs, *OIP* 99, p. 49, 118).

401 **é.g̃ìr.gir$_{17}$.zal**, "House of the Path of Joy," TN or epithet known from the big OB forerunner to *Hh* XXI (*MSL* XI, p. 142, viii 31).

402 **é.gir$_4$?.kù**, "House of the Pure Oven," seat of Nuska in é.sag̃.íl at Babylon (*Topog. Texts* no. 1 = *Tintir* II 32).

403 **é.gir$_{17}$.zal**, "House of Joy," temple or shrine known from the big OB forerunner to *Hh* XXI (*MSL* XI, p. 142, vii 21, among temples of Ištar).

404 ***é.gir$_{17}$.zal.an.ki**, "House of Joy of Heaven and Underworld," temple of Šamaš at Mari, built by Yaḫdun-Līm (Frayne, *RIME* 4, p. 607, 105; written e-gi(var. ZI)-ir-za-la-an-ki, = *bīt tašīlat šamê u erṣetim*).

405 **é.gir$_{17}$.zal.l[e? . . . ]**, a sanctuary of Nanna-Suen known from a cultic lament (Cohen, *Lamentations*, p. 219, 10).

406 **é.gir$_{17}$.zal.z[i$^?$]**, "House of True(?) Joy," a temple of Ištar (CTL 398).

407 **é.g̃issu.bi.du$_{10}$.ga**, "House whose Shade is Pleasant," a sanctuary of Sîn (CTL 271, reading provisional), probably also to be restored in a litany of his TNS (*BL* no. 27, 8′: èš é.g̃issu.[ . . . ]). According to the Syncretistic Ištar Hymn (l. 81; unpub., courtesy Lambert) the temple was located at Damru (du$_{10}$.g̃ar$^{ki}$: on the toponym see *MSL* IX, p. 171, correcting *Hh* IV 338; Groneberg, *Rép. géogr.* III, p. 50), a town near Babylon known from other sources as a cult-center of the Moon God (Craig, *ABRT* I 58, 9: $^{d}$*sîn*(30) *bēl*(en$^!$) GN; see further Charpin, *RA* 72 [1978], p. 19[26]). TN also mentioned in the syncretistic Hymn to Borsippa, in association with Kusu (BM unpub.).

408 **(é).g̃iš.bàn.da**, "House of G̃išbanda," temple of Ning̃išzida at G̃išbanda, often paired with é.gíd.da of Ninazu (*MSL* XI, p. 142, viii 42; above, p. 4, IM 96881, iii′ 11′?; Temple Hymns 190; Lamentation over Sumer and Ur 210–11), also known from the cultic lament edin.na ú.sag̃.g̃á (Cohen, *Lamentations*, pp. 676, 154; 684, 33).

409 **é.g̃iš.ḫur.an.ki.a**, "House of the Ordinances of Heaven and Underworld" 1, temple of Bēlet-Ninua (Ištar of Nineveh) at Babylon (*Topog. Texts* nos. 1 = *Tintir* IV 32; V 101; 3, rev. 12′; 4, 32; 15, rev. 10′; Borger, *Esarh.*, §§ 53, rev. 41; 54, 11). In the offering calendar *BRM* IV 25 // *SBH* VII where the latter reads *bīt Bēlet-Ninua* (obv. 21) the former offers é.ḫur.sag̃.an.ki.a (l. 45), no doubt a corruption of é.TN.

410 **é.g̃iš.ḫur.an.ki.a** 2, temple of Bēlat-Ninūa at Aššur (*Topog. Texts* no. 20 = Götteradreßbuch 171: Assyrian TL). Probably identical with the unnamed temple of Ninevite Ištar (Ninuaʾītu) restored by Shalmaneser I and Tukultī-Ninurta I (Grayson, *RIMA* 1, pp. 196, 6–7; 264, 5).

411 **(é).g̃iš.ḫur.an.ki.a** 3, seat of Anu in ub.šu.ukkin.na of é.sag̃.íl at Babylon (*Topog. Texts* no. 1 = *Tintir* II 18′).

412 **é.g̃iš.ḫur.an.ki.a** 4, a shrine of Anu at Uruk, paired with é.an.ki in a liturgical hymn (Cohen, *Lamentations*, p. 729, 11). Presumably in ub.šu. ukkin.na of *bīt rēš* (cf. é.TN 3).

413 **é.g̃iš.ḫur.an.na**, "House of the Ordinances of Heaven," socle of Ennung̃aḫedu in é.sag̃.íl at Babylon (*Topog. Texts* no. 1 = *Tintir* II 27′).

414 **é.g̃iš.ḫur.bi.GALAM.GALAM**, "House whose Ordinances are Skilfully Contrived," Akītu temple at Kiš (TL no. 6, 9; restore in *Topog. Texts* no. 23, 1′), which gave its name to a quarter of the city (*OECT* X 6, 2: *erṣeti*$^{ti}$ *kiš*$^{ki}$ *šá qé-reb* é.g̃iš.ḫur.bi.GALAM.GALAM; Ššu; GN and TN obviously inverted! Note also ibid. 231, 1: *bīt a-ki-tum* at Kiš; Artax.).

415 **é.G̃IŠ.kalam.ma**, see é.igi.kalam.ma

416 **é.g̃iš.lá.an.ki**, "House of the Auditor of Heaven and Underworld," temple of Nabû of Accounting in east Babylon (*Topog. Texts* no. 1 = *Tintir* IV 12; CTL 240; Lambert, *Matouš Festschrift* II, p. 100, 19 and note: Nabû hymn; Cavigneaux, *Textes scolaires*, pp. 37ff., passim: colophons from the temple of Nabû of the *ḫarû*). Also written é.g̃iš.lá.ak.a.: see *Topog. Texts*, p. 309.

417 **é.g̃iš.lam.šár.šár**, "House where Heaven and Underworld Mingle," ziqqurrat of Adad at Aššur (*Topog. Texts* no. 20 = Götteradreßbuch 188: Assyrian TL). For the building history of the ziqqurrats of the double temple of Anu and Adad see é.me.lám.an.na.

418 **é.g̃iš.nu$_{11}$.gal**, see é.kiš.nu.g̃ál

419 **é.g̃iš.tuku**, see é.a.ra.zu.g̃iš.tuku

420 **é.g̃iš.túl.lá**, a sanctuary of Šamaš (CTL 286).

421 **g̃išgal.dig̃ir.e.ne**, "Station of the Gods," seat of the Igigi in é.šár.ra at Aššur (*Topog. Texts* no. 21, rev. 7′).

422 **g̃išgal.$^{d}$imin.bi**, "Station of the Divine Heptad," shrine of the Divine Heptad (Sebettu) in é.rab.ri.ri (at Babylon? *Topog. Texts* no. 12, 11′).

423 **g̃išgal.sag̃.g̃á**, "Foremost Station," seat of Šamaš (alternatively Ninurta as $^{d}$*uta*-[*u*$_{18}$-*lu*]) in é.sag̃.íl at Babylon (*Topog. Texts* no. 1 = *Tintir* II 9′).

424 **é.gu.la**, "Big House" 1, temple of Gula in Borsippa, rebuilt by Nebuchadnezzar II (Ball, *PSBA* 10 [1888], pp. 368ff., ii 47; etc.).

425 **é.gu.la** 2, a shrine of Ninlil in é.kur at Nippur (p. 4, IM 96881, ii′ 8′; *PBS* X/4 1, i 15′: Nippur Lament 32; CT 42 40, pl. 46, a obv. 15?; further references: Kraus, *AfO* 20 [1963], p. 154; Sjöberg, *AfO* 24 [1973], p. 37). Also in early OB offering lists: Heimerdinger, *Kramer AV*, p. 228, v 35′; vi 24′; *PBS* VIII/1 13, obv. 16: Damiq-ilīšu; prebend sale: *OECT* VIII 7, 1 (Samsu-iluna).

426 **é.gu.la** 3, a temple at Diniktu (TL no. 3, 27′), mentioned in the Syncretistic Ištar Hymn (*KAR* 109, rev. 10), and in the similar hymn to Nanāy (Reiner, *JNES* 33 [1974], p. 228, 42).

427 **é.gu.la** 4, a temple at *šá-an-da-lip-úr*$^{ki}$, mentioned in the Syncretistic Ištar Hymn (l. 83; unpub., courtesy Lambert).

428 **é.gu.la** 5, a sanctuary of Ninsun known from her name [$^{d}$n]in.é.gu.la = *be-let* é.g[u.la.(ke$_4$)], as entered in a god list (von Weiher, *Uruk* III 109, 2).

429 **é.gu.la$^{ki}$** 6, a temple which gave its name to a settlement (*MSL* XI, p. 132, v 32).

430 **é.gu.la** 7, a term that describes small chapels of various deities in Ur III offering lists from Lagaš: Hussey, *HSS* 4 54, obv. 2 (Ningirsu); 7 (Baba); rev. 16 (Ninḫursağ); 17 (G̃atumdug); 145, 3 (Ningirsu). Parallel terms in the same texts are é.MURUB$_4$/NISAĞ (Baba) and é.gibil (Ningirsu, G̃atumdug).

431 ***é.gu.la** 8, see (*bīt*) *qulê*

432 **é.$^{giš}$gu.za**, "House of the Throne," TN or epithet known from the big OB forerunner to *Hh* XXI (*MSL* XI, p. 142, vii 31).

433 **é.gu.za.alim.maḫ**, see é.gu.za.lá.maḫ

434 **é.gu.za.lá.maḫ**, "House of the Exalted Chamberlain," temple of Ningišzida at Babylon (*Topog. Texts* no. 1 = *Tintir* IV 13). Written é.gu.za. alim.maḫ, "House, Throne of the Exalted Bison," in a mythological text (BM unpub., courtesy Lambert).

435 **é.gú.si.sá**, "House which Provides Justice for the Wronged" 1, seat of the divine weapon Muštēšir-ḫablim in é.sağ.íl at Babylon (*Topog. Texts* no. 1 = *Tintir* II 8″).

436 **é.gú.si.sá** 2, a sanctuary at Sippar (of Muštēšir-ḫablim in é.babbar.ra?), known from an edict of Šamaš-šuma-ukīn (Steinmetzer, *ArOr* 7 [1935], p. 315 = *AnOr* 12, p. 305, 6, reading *ina* é.gú!.si.sá *pa-*[*paḫ*? $^{d?}$]*muš-te-šir$_4$-ḫab-lim*).

437 **é.gù.bi.du$_{10}$.ga**, "House whose Voice is Pleasing," socle of Papsukkal in the *bīt rēš* of Anu at Uruk, known from a LB ritual (*RAcc.*, p. 66, 26). Cf. in *An* I the name of Papsukkal's sheriff $^{d}$é.gù.bi.du$_{10}$.ga (*KAV* 50, i 6; cf. *TCL* XV 10, 415).

438 **é.gu$_4$.du$_7$.šár**, "House of Numerous Perfect Oxen," temple of Ningublag at Kiabrig (Temple Hymns 147), in CTL 276 corrupted to é.pa$_4$.ul.ḫé.

439 **é.gub.ba**, "Established House," a shrine known from a *šubtu* list (at Ur? *Topog. Texts* no. 26 C, 1′).

440 **é.gub.ba.an.ki**, "Established House of Heaven and Underworld," the ziqqurrat at Dilbat (TL no. 4, 16); another list has a variant name that might be [é.te.me.e]n.an.ki (no. 5, 21′).

441 **gul.la.ir.ra**, "Ruined and Pillaged," seat of Bēl-labrīya in é.šár.ra at Aššur (*Topog. Texts* no. 21, obv. 11′). A sanctuary of $^{d}$en.libir.ra at Aššur was rebuilt by Tiglath-pileser I (Grayson, *RIMA* 2, p. 26, 87: no TN).

442 **é.gùn.a**, "Coloured House," sanctuary of Ištar which gave name to a court of the palace at Mari (Charpin, *AEM* I/2 298, 46, reading é.dar.a; elsewhere translated as *bīt birmī* or *burmī*: Birot, *ARM* IX 29, 7; Durand, *AEM* I/1 74, 25). See also *bīt burmī*.

443 **é.gùn.za.gìn**, "Coloured House of Lapis Lazuli," a TN or epithet known from Proto-*Kagal* 195.

444 **é.gúr.ḫur.sag̃**, "House which Subdues the Mountains," seat of Ninurta's weapon Kurgigimšaša in é.sag̃.íl at Babylon (*Topog. Texts* no. 1 = *Tintir* II 27; also royal ritual, K 3446+, rev. 7: ibid., p. 276).

444a **é.gúrum.ma**, "House which Subdues," a sanctuary of Ninurta known only from his name ᵈlugal.é.TN in *An* I 204 (Lambert, *RlA* VII, p. 137).

445 **ḫa.lam.mar.àm.ak**, shrine of Enlil and Šamaš in é.šár.ra at Aššur (*Topog. Texts* no. 21, obv. 32′).

446 ***é.ḫa.lu.úb.a**, see é.NÍG̃.lu.úb.a

447 **é.ḫa.mun**, a sanctuary of Nissaba (Cohen, *JAOS* 95 [1975], p. 602, 7; further refs. p. 604; Sjöberg, *TCS* III, p. 84).

448 **é.ḫal.an.ki**, "House of the Secrets of Heaven and Underworld" 1, seat of Zarpanītum in her cella (é.dàra.an.na) in é.sag̃.íl at Babylon (*Topog. Texts* nos. 1 = *Tintir* II 7; 20 = Assyrian TL 182; Bauer, *Asb.*, pl. 58, rev. 12; Erra I 128; Syncretistic Ištar Hymn 38, unpub., courtesy Lambert). Doors restored by Nabonidus (é.ḫal!(AN).an.ki: Messerschmidt, *MVAG* I/1, p. 78, viii 32).

449 **é.ḫal.an.ki** 2, seat of Ea in é.sag̃.íl at Babylon (*Topog. Texts* no. 1 = *Tintir* II 20).

450 **é.ḫal.an.[kù]**, a temple of Ea (CTL 193) and by-name for his cosmic domain (= *apsû*, see the commentary on CTL).

451 **é.ḫal.ḫal.la**, "House of Secrets(?)," sanctuary of a goddess in the cultic lament im.ma.al gù.dé.dé (Cohen, *Lamentations*, p. 614, 186).

452 **é.ḪAR.ra.na**, see é.me.ur$_4$.an.na

453 **é.ḫé.g̃ál**, "House of Abundance," a shrine in é.sag̃.íl at Babylon (*Topog. Texts* no. 1 = *Tintir* II 17″). TN also known to the big OB forerunner to *Hh* XXI, *MSL* XI, p. 142, viii 37.

454 **é.ḫé.g̃ál.kalam.ma**, "House of the Abundance of the Land," epithet of an.ta.sur.ra in inscriptions of Uruinimgina (Steible, *FAOS* 5/I, Ukg 1, i 7; 11, 6).

455 ***é.[ḫé].g̃ál.la**, in an inscription of Sîn-kāšid (Kärki, *StOr* 49, Sk 9, 8), now read é.[šà].ḫúl.la.

456 **é.ḫé.nun.(na)**, "House of Plenty," temple of Adad in Uruk, known from a LB ritual (*RAcc.*, p. 67, 26, residence of Mēšarru), and liturgical texts (Maul, *Eršaḫunga* no. 21, 11; Cohen, *Lamentations*, pp. 431, 45; 433, 97).

457 **é.ḫi.li**, "House of Luxuriance," temple of Utu at Ur, rebuilt for Gungunum by Išme-Dagān's daughter, Enannatumma (Frayne, *RIME* 4, p. 117, 18; qualified as é.šútum.kù.ga.ni, "his pure storeroom").

458 **é.ḫi.li.ak?.a**, "House which Makes(?) Luxuriance," a temple known from a topographical fragment (*Topog. Texts* no. 30, 5′).

459 **é.ḫi.li.an.na**, "House of the Luxuriance of Heaven," shrine of Nanāy in é.an.na at Uruk, rebuilt by Nazi-Maruttaš, Erība-Marduk and Esarhad-

don, cult reinstated by Aššurbanipal (Borger, *Esarh.*, §§ 49–50; see also Streck, *Asb.*, p. 58, 123; Thompson, *Prisms*, p. 35, 31; etc.). Possibly the temple of Nanāy into which Irdanene of Uruk sent a statue of Anam (year a). Also known from a LB ritual (*RAcc.*, p. 66, 4); its garden is mentioned in a house deed (*VAS* XV 13, 3.6: é.ḫi.il.an.na; cf. Falkenstein, *Topographie*, p. 41). Cf. the name of the processional barge $^{giš}$má.ḫi.li.an.na, which belonged to Ištar (*MSL* V, p. 178, *Hh* IV 329). See also é.ḫi.li.kù.ga.

460 **é.ḫi.li.diri.ga**, "House of Surpassing Luxuriance," seat of Nanāy at the Gate of Wonder (ká.$u_6$.de) in the temple complex at Uruk (*Topog. Texts* no. 25, obv. 7′).

461 **é.ḫi.li.g̃ar**, "House Endowed with Luxuriance," TN found in NA literary texts as a name of Zarpanītum's cella in é.sag̃.íl at Babylon: variation on ká.ḫi.li.sù (George, *SAA Bulletin* I/1 [1987], pp. 34f.).

462 **é.ḫi.li.$^{d}$*Ištar***, "House of Luxuriance of Ištar," temple of Ištar as the goddess Ulsigga at Dunni-sāʾidi (*KAR* 109, obv. 11: syncretistic Ištar hymn). Otherwise Ištar is known in this town as Bēlet-ṣēri (Ebeling, *TuL* no. 2, i 16).

463 **é.ḫi.li.kalam.ma**, "House of the Luxuriance of the Land," temple of Ašratum at Babylon (*Topog. Texts* nos. 1 = *Tintir* IV 17; 4, 17; offering calendar: *BRM* IV 25, 38). Identification with the excavated temple D II: George, *Sumer* 44 (1985–6), p. 15. See *Topog. Texts*, pp. 312f.

464 **é.ḫi.li.kù.ga**, "House of Pure Luxuriance," bed-chamber (é.nir, q.v.) in é.ḫi.li.an.na of Nanāy in é.an.na at Uruk (*RAcc.*, p. 66, 4).

465 **é.ḫi.li.sig$_5$.ga**, "House of Beautiful Allure," seat of the divine hairdressers Katunna and Ṣilluš-ṭāb in é.rab.ri.ri (at Babylon? *Topog. Texts* no. 12, 17′).

466 **é.ḫi.li.x.x**, a temple of Panig̃ing̃arra (CTL 166).

467 **é.ḪI.[ . . . ]**, temple of Kakkala/Kakkuda at Aḫud (CTL 478).

468 **é.ḪUB.ba**, TN(?) occurring in an epithet of Ištar in liturgical texts (Cohen, *Lamentations*, pp. 240, 340 = 309, 214). Note an Iščali year name, mu bàd é.ḪÚB.ba$^{ki}$ (NBC 7342, tablet = Ibni-šadūʾī, year ca.?).

469 **é.ḫúl.[la]** (or é.ḫúl.[ḫúl]?), "Joyful House," a shrine in é.sag̃.íl at Babylon (*Topog. Texts* no. 1 = *Tintir* II 5″).

470 **é.ḫúl.ḫúl**, "House which Gives Joy" 1, temple of Sîn at Ḫarrān, rebuilt by Shalmaneser III, Aššurbanipal (Streck, *Asb.*, p. 170, 37; Thompson, *AAA* 20 [1933], p. 83, 60; also in 64, with a *bīt á-ki-tu*; etc.) and Nabonidus (V *R* 64, i 8; etc.). In existence in the OB period (Durand, *AEM* I/1 24, 12; no TN).

471 **é.ḫúl.ḫúl** 2, see é.ḫúl.la

472 **é.ḫúl.ḫúl.dir.dir.ra**, "House of Surpassing Joys," temple of Sîn at Aššur (*Topog. Texts* no. 20 = Götteradreßbuch 156: Assyrian TL). The double

temple of Sîn and Šamaš was rebuilt by Aššur-nārārī I (Grayson, *RIMA* 1, p. 85, 3:4–5; no TN), Tukultī-Ninurta I (p. 266, 29–30, no TN; cf. p. 296, 1006:3′), and Aššurnaṣirpal II (no TN: *RIMA* 2, pp. 325, 3′; 340, 11; cf. 219, 90).

473 **é.ḫur.sag̃**, "House of the Mountains" 1, name or epithet of Ninḫursag̃'s temple at ḪI.ZA[ki] (Temple Hymns 494).

474 **é.ḫur.sag̃** 2, temple of the deified Šulgi at Ur (*MSL* XI, p. 142, viii 21; Temple Hymns 132), built by Šulgi (Steible, *FAOS* 9/II, Š 5; year 10). Elsewhere in Sumerian literature: Šulgi B 377; Tree and Reed 30 (quoted in Castellino, *Two Šulgi Hymns*, p. 240); Sjöberg, *JCS* 29 (1977), p. 9, rev. 18′: hymn to Nanna. Originally a secular building (Hallo, *HUCA* 33 [1962], p. 29[214]; cf. Limet, *CRRA* 20, p. 81). Also known as é.nam.ti.la (references collected by Michalowski, *Lamentation*, p. 81). See also é.ḫur.sag̃.g̃á 1.

475 **é.ḫur.sag̃.an.ki.a**, "House, Mountain of Heaven and Underworld," see é.g̃iš.ḫur.an.ki.a 1

476 [**é.ḫu**]**r.sag̃.an.na**, "House, Mountain of Heaven," temple listed in a litany of Ninurta in the position normally occupied by é.me.ur$_4$.an.na (*VAS* 24 30, rev. 5′; dittography from é.ḫur.sag̃.ti.la below?).

477 ***é.ḫur.sag̃.g̃á**, "House of the Mountains" 1, temple listed in *Kagal* Bog̃. I G 13: [é.TN] = ⌜e⌝-ḫu-ur-ša-an-ga = *bi-it šu-ul-pé* (the DN is apparently Šulpae, if not a corruption of Šulgi: cf. é.ḫur.sag̃ 2).

478 **é.ḫur.sag̃.g̃á** 2, see é.ùru.sag̃.g̃á

479 **é.ḫur.sag̃.gal.kur.kur.ra**, "House of the Great Mountain of the Lands," cella of Aššur in é.šár.ra at Aššur. Embellished by Sargon II (*KAH* I 37–42; 71), rebuilt by Sennacherib (*KAH* II 124) and Esarhaddon (Borger, *Esarh.*, §§ 53, rev. 46; 57, rev. 12; etc.), and completed by Aššurbanipal (Streck, *Asb.*, p. 146, 10; Thompson, *Prisms*, p. 29, 14; etc.). Appears in a MA liturgical hymn to Aššur (Cohen, *Lamentations*, p. 344, 35), alongside é.ḫur.sag̃.kur.kur.ra.

480 **é.ḫur.sag̃.galam.(ma)**, "House, Skilfully-Built Mountain," cella of Enlil on the ziqqurrat at Nippur, commonly found in Ur III offering lists, in which it is written ḫur.sag̃.ga.lam.ma (*TCL* II 5501, i 4; ii 8; iii 9; 5513, obv. 12; Legrain, *TRU* 256, 6; 293, 4; 324, 3; 336, 6; 339, 6; Kang, *Drehem* 172, 19; van de Mieroop and Longman, *RA* 79 [1985], p. 22, 8:9; etc.; note also OB lists: *PBS* VIII/1 13, obv. 10: Damiq-ilīšu; Heimerdinger, *Kramer AV*, p. 227, rev. i 9′: ḫur.sag̃.[ . . . ]). It is also found in a liturgical hymn to Enlil (Cohen, *Lamentations*, p. 349, 25, qualified as an.da sá.a, "which vies with heaven"), and in a brick of Aššurbanipal (Gerardi, *RIM Annual Review* 4 [1986], p. 37, 11; construction therein of a baked-brick fitting: l. 10, A.GÀR+DIŠ). Elsewhere in Sumerian literature: *SRT* 11, 22.29: TN gi.gun$_4$.na ki.tuš.kù kur.gal.la, "terrace-house, pure abode of the Great Mountain," preceding g̃á.g̃iš.šú.a (Ur-Nammu; cf. Falkenstein, ZA 48

[1944], pp. 87f.); Kramer, *RSO* 32 (1957), p. 97, 9: Hymn to the E-kur. As an epithet of other sanctuaries see Sjöberg, *ZA* 63 (1973), p. 32, 38: Ur; and also é.kun$_4$.an.kù.ga.

481 **é.ḫur.sag̃.gu.la**, "House, Big Mountain," *bīt šaḫūri* of Aššur in é.šár.ra at Aššur (*Topog. Texts* no. 20 = Götteradreßbuch 145: Assyrian TL; cf. van Driel, *Cult of Aššur*, pp. 34f.). Known to Aššurnaṣirpal I (*KAR* 107, 44 // 358, 31 // *KAH* II 139, rev. 11: hymn to Ištar), rebuilt by Sennacherib (*KAH* II 124, 17: *bīt šá-ḫu-ru*), Esarhaddon (Borger, *Esarh.*, § 2, v 37, = *bīt šadî rabî*) and completed by Aššurbanipal (Streck, *Asb.*, p. 146, 15; Thompson, *Prisms*, p. 29, 19; etc.). Appears in a MA liturgical hymn to Aššur (Cohen, *Lamentations*, p. 344, 39, partly restored). See also é.kur 2.

482 **(é).ḫur.sag̃.kalam.ma**, "House, Mountain of the Land" 1, temple of Ištar in Ḫursag̃-kalamma at Kiš (Proto-*Kagal* 230; *MSL* XI, p. 142, vii 18; CTL 366; also as GN: TL no. 4, 13; no. 7 b 2), patronized by Ḫammurapi (CḪ ii 67). Well known from Inanna's Descent and the éš.dam hymns (Wilcke, *RlA* V, p. 78; McEwan, *RA* 76 [1982], p. 188). Also in the syncretistic hymn to Nanāy (Reiner, *JNES* 33 [1974], p. 226, 21; as GN?). Here Ištar is seen as a manifestation of Ninlil, as witnessed by TL no. 6, 12–13; no. 7 b 4; a *lipšur*-litany (Wiseman, *Iraq* 31 [1969], p. 177, 42′); and a cultic calendar (*BRM* IV 25, 34 // *SBH* VII, 15). Later apparently known as é.kur.ní.zu.

483 **é.ḫur.sag̃.kalam.ma** 2, a sanctuary of Enlil (CTL 28), probably = é.ḫur.sag̃.galam.ma.

484 **é.ḫur.sag̃.kalam.ma** 3, a sanctuary on the bank of the íd.KAL.$^{d}$*la-ta-ra-ak*.šè known from a votive inscription from the reign of Burnaburiaš (*BE* I 33, 23; ed. Legrain PBS XV, p. 32[1]; cf. Brinkman, *MSKH*, p. 45[84]).

485 **é.ḫur.sag̃.kù.ga**, "House, Pure Mountain," a temple of Gula in Babylon, according to late documents (*Topog. Texts* no. 38, 11; *BRM* I 99, 28 // *CT* 49 150, 25).

486 **é.ḫur.sag̃.kur.kur.ra**, "House, Mountain of the Lands," name of Aššur's cella in his temple at Aššur (*Topog. Texts* no. 20 = Götteradreßbuch 146: Assyrian TL; cf. van Driel, *Cult of Aššur*, p. 35). First mentioned by Adad-nārārī I (Grayson, *RIMA* 1, pp. 134, 48; 154, 17′). Extensively rebuilt by Shalmaneser I, who uses the TN (alongside é.kur 2?) for the temple as a whole and records previous rebuildings by Ušpia, Erišum I and Šamšī-Adad I (ibid., pp. 182ff., 6.112.164; 189, 5; 190, 6; 192, 19; 194, 19). Other early restorers were Šalim-aḫum, Aššur-nārārī I, Tukultī-Ninurta I and Aššur-rēša-iši I (for the building history of the temple complex of Aššur see van Driel, *Cult of Aššur*, pp. 1–31; Grayson, *RIMA* 1–2, passim). The TN appears in a bilingual of Tukultī-Ninurta I (Lambert, *Iraq* 38 [1976], p. 91, 11), and in a MA liturgical hymn to Aššur (Cohen, *Lamentations*, p. 344, 33), alongside the expanded form commonly used in Sargonid times, é.ḫur.sag̃.gal.kur.kur.ra. Also known to Tiglath-pileser I (Grayson,

*RIMA* 2, pp. 13, 26; 33, 10), Erība-Adad II (ibid., p. 114, 5″) and Aššur-dān III (Donbaz and Grayson, *Clay Cones* = *RIM Suppl.* 1, p. 53, 4). See also é.am.kur.kur.ra, é.šár.ra 2.

487 **é.ḫur.sag̃.si.ga**, "House, Silent Mountain," seat of Meslamtaea in é.me.lám.su.lim.gùr.ru (at Ur? *Topog. Texts* no. 26 A, 2).

488 **é.ḫur.sag̃.sikil.la**, "House, Pure Mountain," temple of Gula-Ninkarrak in east Babylon, rebuilt by Nebuchadnezzar II (I *R* 55, iv 40; etc.), survived into the Arsacid period (*BRM* I 99, 27 // *CT* 49 150, 24). Probably = é.gal.maḫ 2.

489 **é.ḫur.sag̃.ti(l).la**, "House which Exterminates the Mountains," temple of Ninurta in Babylon (*Topog. Texts* nos. 1 = *Tintir* IV 19; 4, 19; 9, 5′.7′; 38, 18), rebuilt as é.PA.GÌN.ti.la by Nabopolassar (Weissbach, *Misc.* no. 9, 22). Seat of the Asakku demon in gate of TN: *KAR* 142, ii 2. Also in rituals (*RAcc.*, p. 133, 213; Lambert, *Love Lyrics*, p. 104, iii 4; *CT* 51 99, 6–7), a cultic calendar (*BRM* IV 25, 21), and liturgical texts, where it is occasionally inserted in the standard litany of TNs of Ninurta (Maul, *Eršaḫunga* no. 31 + K 17441, obv. 10; *OrNS* 60 [1991], p. 314, 16: eršemma; Cohen, *Lamentations*, p. 461, 87: é.ḫur!.sag̃!.ti.la, coll.; *VAS* 24 30, rev. 6′). See *Topog. Texts*, pp. 313f.

490 **é.ḪUR.šà.ba**, see é.ur$_5$.šà.ba

491 **é.ḫuš**, "Fearsome House," sanctuary of Ning̃irsu in Lagaš-G̃irsu (Falkenstein, *AnOr* 30, p. 167), built by Enmetena (a.ḫuš: Steible, *FAOS* 5/I, Ent 1, i 20; 8, iii 2; etc.; by-name or epithet é.igi.zi.bar.ra), looted by Lugalzaggesi (ibid., Ukg 16, ii 2). Written é.ḫuš$^{ki}$ in the offering list *ITT* 4582, 8.

492 **é.ḫuš.ki.a**, "Fearsome House of the Netherworld," by-name of Nergal's cult-center at Kutha which follows (é).mes.lam in Temple Hymns 464 (var.) and probably in Proto-*Kagal* 215 and CTL [565].

493 **é.*ibbi*-$^{d}$*Anum***, "House, Anu Called it into Being," temple of Uraš at Dilbat (CTL 481; TL no. 2, 9), rebuilt by Sābium (year 9, written é.*i-bi-a-nu-um*, é.*i-bé-n*[*u-um*]), Aššur-etel-ilāni (Walker, *CBI* no. 87), and Nebuchadnezzar II (V *R* 34, ii 31; *PBS* XV 79, iii 9: é.*i-bí*-an.na; etc.). Mentioned in the Syncretistic Ištar Hymn (*KAR* 109, obv. 25) and Anzû III 133 (Moran, *AfO* 35 [1988], p. 29; George, *BSOAS* 54 [1991], p. 146). Common in liturgical texts, usually paired with Dilbat in the standard litany of TNs and GNs (Maul, *Eršaḫunga* no. 37, 15; *OrNS* 60 [1991], p. 315, 28.34: eršemma; Cohen, *Lamentations*, index p. 750; note p. 267, vi 17: [é.*i*]-*bí*-an.na; MacMillan, *BA* V/5 6, rev. 16; etc.).

494 **é.i.bí.dim.dim**, variant of é.gi.dim.dim.

495 **é.i.bí.šu.galam**, "House in Front of Šu-galam," sanctuary found in the standard litany of temples of Ninurta (Maul, *Eršaḫunga* no. 31 + K 17441, obv. 9; *OrNS* 60 [1991], p. 314, 13: eršemma; Cohen, *Lamentations*, pp. 180, 154, reading é.i.bí.šu.ubi; 441, 10?; *VAS* 24 30, rev. 5′). The reading

galam is assured by comparison with older šu.ga.lam at G̃irsu. Emesal form of é.igi.šu.galam.

496 **é.i.bí.šuba**, shrine of Ninurta which appears as a variant of é.i.bí.šu.galam in the standard litany of his TNs in liturgical texts, following é.šà.maḫ and é.me.ur$_4$.an.na (Cohen, *Lamentations*, pp. 441, 10?; 458, 11; 461, 86). šuba appears to be a secondary interpretation of šu.ubi(GALAM), probably arising from a confusion of the TN with i.bí.šuba, "bright-eyed," an epithet of Ištarān common in cultic laments (ibid., index p. 761).

497 **é.i.lu.zi.ù.li**, temple of Ištar(?) of the Seas (CTL 439). i.lu and ù.li are both exclamations of lament, otherwise one might read é.kun$_4$.zi.ù.li, "House, True Threshold of Lamentation."

498 **é.ì.dub.ba**, "House of Storage Bins," sanctuary of Aya at Aššur, listed among TNs of Šarrat-nipḫi (*Topog. Texts* no. 20 = Götteradreßbuch 168a: Assyrian TL). Possibly takes its name from the granary é.ì.dub in the cloister of the *nadītu*'s at Sippar (Harris, *JESHO* 6 [1963], pp. 129f.; Biggs, *JNES* 28 [1969], p. 134).

499 **é.ì.gára**, "House of Butterfat" 1, temple of Nin-Eigara (*MSL* XI, p. 142, vii 26, among temples of Ištar), garbled as é.ga.ra.ni of her husband Ningublag in CTL 278.

500 **é.ì.gára** 2, temple dairy at G̃irsu (Falkenstein, *AnOr* 30, p. 128; *MVN* VI, p. 412: index).

501 **é.ì.gára.sù**, "House Filled with Butterfat," temple of Dumuzi (at Ur?), rebuilt by Rīm-Sîn I (Frayne, *RIME* 4, p. 276, 12).

502 **é.ì.rá.rá**, "House of the Parfumier," a temple (at Ur?) built by Rīm-Sîn I (Frayne, *RIME* 4, p. 280, 8′).

503 **ib.é.an.na**, sanctuary of Lagaš-G̃irsu, desecrated by Lugalzaggesi (Steible, *FAOS* 5/I, Ukg 16, iv 5). Possibly to be emended to ib.⟨gal⟩ é.an.na, with ibid., AnLag 17: $^{d}$inanna ib.gal é.[ . . . ].

504 **(é).ib.gal** 1, temple of Inanna as Nin-Ibgal at Umma (Proto-*Kagal* 226; *MSL* XI, p. 142, vii 24; Krecher, *RlA* V, p. 8, 2–3), known also from Inanna's Descent and the éš.dam hymns (Wilcke, *RlA* V, p. 78, var. é.za.gìn.na). In liturgical texts also (Cohen, *Eršemma*, p. 67, 39; *Lamentations*, p. 614, 168, as a residence of Ašnan and Kusu).

505 **(é).ib.gal** 2, temple complex of Inanna in Lagaš (Falkenstein, *AnOr* 30, pp. 160f.; Krecher, *RLA* V, p. 8, 1), built by Ur-Nanše (Steible, *FAOS* 5/I, UrN 25, ii 7; 28, iii 1; etc.) and Enannatum I (ibid., En I 9, iii 4; 10–17; etc.). On the route of divine procession from G̃irsu to Lagaš (Sauren, *OrNS* 38 [1969], p. 217). See also é.an.na 2 and ib.é.an.na.

506 **é.ib.gal** 3, part or epithet of the temple of Keš (Keš Temple Hymn 31).

507 **é.íd.lú.ru.gú**, "House of the River Ordeal," temple of the river god, Id (CTL 243; *Topog. Texts* no. 28, 7′). For é.TN as a general epithet see Römer, *Königshymnen*, p. 186; Sjöberg, *TCS* III, p. 60.

508 **é.íd.lú.ru.gú.[ . . . ]**, a temple of Id (CTL 244).

509 **é.íd.lú.ru.gú.kalam.ma**, "House of the River Ordeal of the Land," shrine of Ningal in the g̃i$_6$.pàr at Ur, listed in an OB forerunner to *Hh* XXI (*MSL* XI, p. 142, vii 14, following é.kar.zi.da), rebuilt by Ṣillī-Adad and Warad-Sîn (Frayne, *RIME* 4, pp. 201, 11; 204, 14). A connection between the TN and sacred marriage rites is suspected (Weadock, *Iraq* 37 [1975], p. 118; Charpin, *Le clergé d'Ur*, pp. 213f.). See also é.gar$_6$.kù.

510 **é.idim.an.na**, variant of é.dim.an.na.

511 **é.idim?.[sag̃?].g̃á**, "House of the Foremost Spring(?)," seat of the Tigris and Euphrates in é.sag̃.íl at Babylon (*Topog. Texts* no. 1 = *Tintir* II 33).

512 **IG.a.kù.ga**, seat of Id and Kiša by the well in é.šár.ra at Aššur (*Topog. Texts* no. 21, obv. 15′).

513 **é.IG.ḫal.an.ki**, temple at Uruk known only from the city quarter *erṣet* é.TN (*BIN* II 130, 2; cf. Falkenstein, *Topographie*, pp. 51f.). Cf. é.gal.ḫal.ḫal, é.MI.ḫal.la.ke$_4$/ka.

514 **é.$^{g̃iš}$ig.imin**, "House of Seven Doors," shrine in or epithet of é.an.na at Uruk, as found in the cultic lament úru àm.i.ra.bi (Cohen, *Lamentations*, p. 552, 27′). Probably a variant of é.ub.imin.

515 **ig.sag̃.sum.dili.na**, shrine in é.šár.ra at Aššur (*Topog. Texts* no. 21, obv. 4′).

516 **é.igi.du**, "House of the Leader," seat of Lillu in èš.šà.abzu of é.sag̃.íl at Babylon (*Topog. Texts* no. 1 = *Tintir* II 11″).

517 **é.igi.du$_8$.a**, "House whose Eye is Open," temple of Inanna at Kullab (éš.dam hymns: Wilcke, *RlA* V, p. 78), placed in Kutha by the Canonical Temple List (l. 388), probably because of confusion of the TN with gú.du$_8$.a$^{ki}$. Note the variant spelling é.gi.dù.[a] in a cultic lament (Langdon, *BL* no. 156, 3).

518 ***é.igi.ḫuš.a**, see é.igi.TUM.a

519 **é.igi.íl($^{ki}$)**, "House whose Eye is Raised," ED and later place name, near Lagaš, deriving from a temple (Farber, *RA* 69 [1975], p. 190).

520 **é.igi.kalam.ma**, "House, Eye of the Land" 1, temple of Ninurta as Lugal-Maradda at Marad (Proto-*Kagal* 212; *MSL* XI, p. 142, viii 43; *Kagal* Boğ. I F 7, = *bi-it ni-nu-*[*ur-ti*]; CTL 469; TL no. 2, [12]; no. 3, 21′; Temple Hymns 407; etc.: see Sjöberg, *TCS* III, p. 127). Built by Lipit-ilī for his father Narām-Sîn (Gelb and Kienast, *FAOS* 7, p. 103, NS A 1, 24: no TN), by Kadašman-Enlil and Kadašman-Turgu (Beckman, *RIM Annual Review* 5 [1987], p. 1, 8), Nebuchadnezzar II, who reports the earlier work of Narām-Sîn (*YOS* I 44, i 25; Durand, *N.A.B.U.* 1987/103; etc.), and Nabonidus (*CT* 36 23, 27). Mentioned in the Syncretistic Ištar Hymn (line 87; unpub., courtesy Lambert) and Anzû III 148 (é.GIŠ.kalam.ma). Also found in a litany, among sanctuaries of Ninurta (Maul, *Eršaḫunga* no. 31 + K 17441, obv. 11).

521 **é.igi.kalam.ma** 2, a temple of Ištar (as Nanāy? CTL 436).

522 **é.igi.[kù?]**, "House of the [Pure(?)] Eye," a temple of Ea (CTL 186).

523 **é.igi.šu.ʻDU$_8$ʼ**, see é.igi.šu.galam

524 **é.igi.šu.galam**, "House in Front of Šu-galam," a shrine of Ninurta at Nippur (p. 4, IM 96881, ii′ 11′: é.ŠU.IGI.galam; probably Proto-*Kagal* 193–94 contains the pair é.šu.me.ša$_4$, é.igi.šu.galam). Listed as part of é.šu.me.ša$_4$ in the MB metrological text of Nippur (Bernhardt and Kramer, *OrNS* 44 [1975], p. 97, 15). Very possibly this was the cella of Ninurta itself (note also ká.igi.šu.galam in é.šu.me.ša$_4$ in Frayne, *RIME* 4, p. 46, 15′: Išme-Dagān). In hymns to Ninurta: Sjöberg, *Kramer AV*, p. 412, 8; Falkenstein, *Götterlieder* I, p. 83 = *STVC* 34, iv 3: collated by Sjöberg, loc. cit., p. 422). In an early OB offering list: Heimerdinger, *Kramer AV*, p. 227, ii 23′. See also é.i.bí.šu.galam.

525 **é.igi.TUM.a**, chapel in the temple of Ninimma at Nippur (*Topog. Texts* no. 18 = Nippur Compendium § 14, v 12). Emend to é.igi.ḫuš$^!$.a, "House of the Angry Eye"?

526 **é.igi.zi.bar.ra**, "House Seen with a Steadfast Eye," name or epithet of é.ḫuš in inscriptions of Enmetena.

527 **é.igi.zu.u$_{18}$.ru**, "House, your Eye is Lofty," part or by-name of é.akkil of Ninšubur at Akkil (*MSL* XI, p. 142, viii 13; CTL 460: uru$_{16}$; Temple Hymns 221).

528 **iku$_x$(AŠ.IKU)**, "Field," seat of Ea, probably in é.dàra.an.na of é.sag̃.íl at Babylon (*Topog. Texts* no. 1 = *Tintir* II 11), also known from a Kedorlaomer text (Jeremias, *MVAG* 21, p. 86, 15).

529 **é.IM.ḫur.sag̃**, a ziqqurrat at Nippur (TL no. 4, 5; no. 5, 5′). Written IM.ḫur.sag̃ in a litany of Enlil (IV $R^2$ 27, no. 2, 15–18). Read é.tu$_{15}$.ḫur.sag̃, "House of the Mountain Wind" (cf. the note above on CTL 42)? Cf. é.ní.te.ḫur.sag̃, also ḫur.sag̃.galam.

530 **IM.ŠID.kur.ra**, seat of Lāgamāl in é.šár.ra at Aššur (*Topog. Texts* no. 21, obv. 9′).

531 **é.IM.x.[x]**, sanctuary of Ištar at Dūr-[ . . . ] (CTL 351).

532 **é.inim.bi.du$_{10}$.ga**, see é.gù.bi.du$_{10}$.ga

533 **é.inim.kù.ga**, "House of the Pure Word," a sanctuary of Zababa at Kiš (*Topog. Texts* nos. 22, 6′; 24, 3′?). Included in a litany of TNs of Kiš in a cult-song to Madānu (Maul, *Eršaḫunga* no. 37, 11).

534 **é.ir.in.DU**, seat of Pabilsag̃ in é.rab.ri.ri (at Babylon? *Topog. Texts* no. 12, 10′).

535 **ir.su.un**, seat of Kalkal in é.šár.ra at Aššur (*Topog. Texts* no. 21, obv. 30′).

536 **é.iri$_{12}$.gal**, see é.èš.gal

537 **é.išib.[ba]**, "House of the Purification Priest," shrine of the divine Lumaḫ priest (CTL 174).

538 **(è).iti$_6$.kù.ga**, "House of the Pure New Moon," a sanctuary of Nanna-Suen known from a cultic lament (Cohen, *Lamentations*, p. 211, 80; a parallel text has é.ta.é.kù.ga.x: p. 219, 9).

539 **(é).itima.kù**, "House, Sacred Bed-Chamber," a shrine of Enlil (CTL 44), bed-chamber of Ninlil at Nippur, also known from the Hymn to E-kur (Kramer, *RSO* 32 [1957], p. 96, 4: é.itim.ma) and liturgical texts (Cohen, *Lamentations*, pp. 97, 20; 349, 17: qualified as é u$_4$ nu.zu, q.v.; cf. 129, [106–7]; note also itima.ku$_4$ u$_4$ nu.zu of Aruru at Keš: Green, *JCS* 30 [1978], p. 138, 12′: Eridu Lament).

540 **é.itu.da**, "House of the Month," sanctuary of Nanāy at Ur, rebuilt by Sūmû-El (Frayne, *RIME* 4, p. 133, 7).

541 **é.itu.da.buru$_{14}$**, "House of the Harvest Month," listed among shrines of the é.kur complex at Nippur in the Hymn to E-kur (Kramer, *RSO* 32 [1957], p. 97, 16) and a liturgical hymn to Enlil (Cohen, *Lamentations*, p. 350, 33).

542 **é.itu.da.buru$_{14}$.maḫ**, "Exalted House of the Harvest Month," listed among shrines of the é.kur complex at Nippur in the Hymn to E-kur (Kramer, *RSO* 32 [1957], p. 97, 18).

543 ***é.iz.zi.šu.tag.ga**, "House of Decorated Walls," a temple (of Šulpae?) known from *Kagal* Boğ. I G 14: [é.TN = e]-i-zi-šu-ut-ta-ga = *bi-it šu-ul-pé.*

544 **é.ka.aš.bar.(ra)**, "House of Decisions" 1, sanctuary of Gula as Ungal-Nibru in é.šu.me.ša$_4$ at Nippur (Lambert, *OrNS* 36 [1967], p. 124, 128: é.TN *bīt purussê*; hymn). The sanctuary of the Queen of Nippur ($^{d}$nin-nibru) in é.šu.me.ša$_4$ is listed without name in the MB metrological text of Nippur (Bernhardt and Kramer, *OrNS* 44 [1975], p. 98, 16).

545 **é.ka.aš.bar** 2, a socle in é.sağ.íl at Babylon (*Topog. Texts* no. 1 = *Tintir* II 26′).

546 **(é).ka.aš.bar.kalam.ma**, "House of the Decisions of the Land," seat of Šamaš in ub.šu.ukkin.na of é.sağ.íl at Babylon (*Topog. Texts* no. 1 = *Tintir* II 21′; *BRM* IV 25, 9: offering calendar).

547 **é.ka.aš.bar.sum.mu**, "House which Gives Decisions," sanctuary of Panunna, vizier of Šamaš (CTL 294).

548 **é.ka.dím.ma**, temple of Belili at Babylon (*Topog. Texts* nos. 1 = *Tintir* IV 36, vars. é.ká.dím.ma and é.ká.edin.na; 3, rev. 16′).

549 **(é).ka.du$_8$.ḫa**, "House which Opens the Mouth," a sanctuary at Ĝirsu in the time of Gudea, apparently part of é.munus.gi$_{16}$.sa (Falkenstein, *AnOr* 30, p. 151; Steible, *FAOS* 9/II, pp. 82f.). Note also an é.ka.du$_8$ at Bašime (*TCL* V 6038, viii 33; Ur III).

550 **é.ka.kéš.ḪU.ḪU**, socle of Papsukkal in the Grand Court of the *bīt rēš* of Anu at Uruk, known from a LB ritual (*RAcc.*, p. 66, 17).

551 **é.KA×LI.KA×LI**, see é.tu$_6$.tu$_6$

552 **é.ká.dím.ma**, see é.ka.dím.ma

553 **é.ká.edin.na**, "House, Gate of the Steppe," see é.ka.dím.ma

554 **é.ká.gu.la**, "House, Big Gate," dais of the Anunnaki at Babylon (*Topog. Texts* no. 1 = *Tintir* IV 29; cf. V 85), also known from rituals (Lambert, *Love Lyrics*, pp. 102ff., ii 6–7, iii 3–4).

555 **ká.ḫi.li.sù**, "Gate Sprinkled with Luxuriance," by-name of é.ḫal.an.ki, the seat of Zarpanītum in é.sağ.íl at Babylon, in inscriptions of Aššurbanipal and Nebuchadnezzar II. Strictly the name of the gate of her cella, é.dàra.an.na, so not itself a TN. See *Topog. Texts*, pp. 394f.

556 **é.ká.maḫ**, "House, Exalted Gate," gate-room listed among shrines of the é.kur complex at Nippur in liturgical texts (Cohen, *Eršemma*, p. 111, 15; *Lamentations*, p. 350, 41: paired with bur.šú.šú.a; Krecher, *Kultlyrik*, p. 53, 5), and in the Hymn to E-kur (Kramer, *RSO* 32 [1957], p. 97, 6).

557 **é.ká.silim.ma**, "House, Gate of Well-Being," gate-room listed among shrines of the é.kur complex at Nippur in the Hymn to E-kur (Kramer, *RSO* 32 [1957], p. 97, 7). ká.silim.ma is a well-known gate of é.kur (e.g., Curse of Akkade 125; *SRT* 11, 22).

558 **ká.su.lim.ma**, "Gate of Radiance," name used by Agum-kakrime (V *R* 33, v 37) and in a bilingual of Nebuchadnezzar I (IV $R^2$ 20, no. 1, 19–20) for the cella of Marduk in é.sağ.íl at Babylon, usually é.umuš.a; variation on ká.silim.ma, the gate of é.umuš.a.

559 **é.ká.šà.abzu**, "House, Gate in the Midst of *Apsû*," a lobby between two courtyards of é.sağ.íl at Babylon (*Topog. Texts* no. 7, 17′).

560 **é.kal**, "Precious House," shrine of Ninğirsu, built by Uruinimgina (Steible, *FAOS* 5/I, Ukg 11, 42); or é.ğá? see Jerrold S. Cooper, *Presargonic Inscriptions* (New Haven, 1986), p. 80[1].

561 **é.KAL.dù.a**, a sanctuary of Enlil (CTL 29).

562 **é.kalam.ta.ní.gùr.ru**, "House which Inspires Dread in the Land," temple of Ištar of Zabalam (CTL 400, om. ní), rebuilt by Warad-Sîn (year 6, var. é.níğ.gùr.ru.kalam.ma); cf. é.sağ.íl 2. Ištar's temple at Zabalam was also rebuilt by Šar-kali-šarrī (year h, no TN). See also é.še.er.zi.gùr.ru, é.zi.kalam.ma.

563 **é.kankal**, see é.ki.kal

564 **kar.ab.ba**, "Quay of the Sea," seat of Asalluḫi in é.šár.ra at Aššur (*Topog. Texts* no. 21, obv. 7′).

565 **é.kar.gíd.da**, "House, Long Quay," a temple known from a topographical fragment (*Topog. Texts* no. 30, 5′). Note as a toponym in Ur III: de Genouillac, *TSA* no. 7, rev. vi 19.

566 **é.kar.ra**, "House of the Quay" 1, temple in Tilmun (TL no. 7 a 8′), of Enzak and Meskilak according to the syncretistic hymn to Nanāy (Reiner, *JNES* 33 [1974], pp. 225, 13; cf. 227, 31). Mentioned in a votive inscription

(of Nebuchadnezzar II) from Failaka (Glassner, in J.-Fr. Salles [ed.], *Failaka*, pp. 46f., no. 46, 1; Šamaš of Larsa as resident?).

567 **é.kar.ra** 2, a sanctuary of a goddess in the lament im.ma.al gù dé.dé (Cohen, *Lamentations*, p. 614, 182).

568 **kar.za.gìn.na**, "Pure Quay" or "Quay of Lapis Lazuli" 1, sacred quay at Eridu, later also at Nippur, Ur and Lagaš (*YOS* XI 42, 11: OB ritual; *RAcc.*, p. 24, rev. 11: incantation; *VAS* II 75, 8: ka-ar-za-gi-na; Ferrara, *Nanna's Journey*, pp. 128f.). The prototype of é.TN 2.

569 **é.kar.za.gìn.na** 2, temple of Ea within the complex of é.sag̃.íl at Babylon (*Topog. Texts* nos. 1 = Tintir IV 3; 2, 3; 3, obv. 7′–9′). Rebuilt by Aššurbanipal (Streck, *Asb.*, p. 246, 65), and provided with a new throne by Nabonidus (Messerschmidt, *MVAG* I/1, p. 78, viii 23). Location for rituals of *mīs pî* and *pīt pî* (*BBSt* 36, iv 25; Borger, *Esarh.*, §§ 57, rev. 22; 60, 10f.; Streck, *Asb.*, p. 268, 19). Included in a litany of TNs of Ea in his eršaḫung̃a (Maul, *Eršaḫunga* no. 10, 9). See *Topog. Texts*, pp. 300–303.

570 **(é).kar.zi.da**, "House, True Quay" 1, temple of Nanna-Suen at Gaeš (*MSL* XI, p. 142, vii 13; Temple Hymns 160), rebuilt for Ningal as Lady of Ur (Nin-Urimma) by Šulgi (Steible, *FAOS* 9/II, Š 17; cf. years 9.36). Provided with a g̃i.par$_4$.(kù.ga) and en priestess, Enagazianna, by Amar-Suen (ibid., AS 6; 8; 11; 21; cf. year 9). Note phonetic orthography ka-ar-zi-[da] in *VAS* II 75, 7. See further D. Loding, *Studies Jones*, pp. 30f. Possibly corrupted in *Kagal* Boğ. I F 21: [é.TN = e]-⌜x⌝-al-mi-id-du = *bi-it ši-i-in.*

571 **é.kar.zi.da** 2, a temple at Nippur (*Topog. Texts* no. 19 = Nippur TL 22, restored on the basis of Akk. translation, *bītu ēṭir na*[*pišti*]).

572 **é.kar.zi.d[a?]** 3, sanctuary of Nabû, the scriptorium (é.úmun.a = *bīt mummi*) of the Street of the Šamaš Gate, according to a NA docket from Aššur (*KAV* 146, 2).

573 **é.kas.kas.$^{d}$lamma.[ . . . ]**, a temple (of Damkina?) at Eridu listed in TL no. 7 a 4′.

574 **é.KAS$_4$.gi.na**, sanctuary of Marduk (CTL 234), probably to be read é.suḫuš!.gi.na, "House of Firm Foundations."

575 **é.kaš.dé.a**, "House where Beer is Poured," TN or epithet known from a hymn to Damgalnunna (*SLTNi* 65, ii 8).

576 **é.($^{g̃iš}$)kéš.da.kalam.ma**, "House, Bond of the Land," part or by-name of é.mes.lam at Kutha (Temple Hymns 457; *MSL* XI, p. 142, viii 34, om. g̃iš).

577 **é.kéš.nun.gal**, see é.kiš.nu.g̃ál

578 **é.kèš$^{ki}$**, "House of Keš," temple of Ninḫursag̃ at Keš (Temple Hymns 94.99; Keš Temple Hymn passim; hymn to Nintu: Wilcke, *AS* 20, p. 235, 1.4), rebuilt by Ur-Nammu (Steible, *FAOS* 9/II, UrN 14). Site of Rīm-Sîn II's elevation to to kingship (year B). Appears in liturgical texts as é.gal kèš$^{ki}$.a, in parallel with é.maḫ adab$^{ki}$ (Cohen, *Lamentations*, pp. 733, 51; 735, 102). See further Gragg, *TCS* III, pp. 159ff.

579 **é.KÉŠDA.sag̃.ús.sa**, usually read é.šìr.sag̃.ús.sa, sanctuary of Nabû listed in liturgical texts in a standard litany of TNs, following é.ur$_4$.me.imin. an.ki (Cohen, *Lamentations*, index p. 752; Langdon, *BL* nos. 26, 5′; 56, obv. 22: é.SAR.ús.sa; 73, rev. 40; Meek, *BA* X/1, no. 10, rev. 12; etc.). é.x[ (x) d]a.ús.sa, the temple of Nabû of the *ḫarû* listed in CTL 239, is probably a version of the same TN.

580 **é.ki.a**, see é.an.ki

581 **é.ki.ág̃.g̃á.a.ni**, "His Beloved House," a cella (of é.su.lim.an.na?) at Kiš (*Topog. Texts* no. 22, 13′; TL no. 6, 7).

582 **é.ki.ág̃.g̃á.šu.du$_7$**, "Perfect Beloved House," a temple known only from a late cultic list of divine residents (Nougayrol, *RA* 41 [1947], p. 35, 1), where it is likely to be a bed-chamber of Enlil and his junior wife Šuzianna, so at Nippur (cf. é.kur.igi.g̃ál). Probably it should be restored as a temple of Šuzianna in CTL 65.

583 **ki.aga.kù.ga**, "Place of the Pure Crown," socle of Ea in the Grand Court of the *bīt rēš* of Anu at Uruk, known from a LB ritual (*RAcc.*, p. 100, 9).

584 **ki.aga.zi.da**, "Place of the True Crown," socle of Enlil in the Grand Court of the *bīt rēš* of Anu at Uruk, known from a LB ritual (*RAcc.*, p. 100, 8).

585 **ki.aratta$^{ki}$**, "Place of the Noble," seat of Anu, probably in é.umuš.a of é.sag̃.íl at Babylon (*Topog. Texts* no. 1 = *Tintir* II 2).

586 **é.ki.bi.kù.ga**, see é.ki.tuš.kù.ga

587 **ki.dag̃al**, "Wide Place," a shrine in é.kur at Nippur (Proto-*Kagal* 189; Cohen, *Lamentations*, p. 275, 33?).

588 **ki.du$_6$.kù.ga**, "Place, Pure Mound," seat of Šulpae[sia] or Šulpae[utulam] in é.rab.ri.ri (at Babylon? *Topog. Texts* no. 12, 4′).

589 **[é.k]i$^?$.du$_7$.du$_7$**, see é.šu.gán.du$_7$.du$_7$

590 **ki.du$_{10}$.ga**, "Pleasant Place," a shrine (at Ur?) known from a *šubtu* list (*Topog. Texts* no. 26 B, 1).

591 **ki.dúr.g̃ar**, "Place of the Seat," a shrine (at Ur?) known from a *šubtu* list (*Topog. Texts* no. 26 C, 2′)

592 **ki.dúr . . .** , see ki.tuš . . .

593 **ki.gal.la**, "Great Place," seat of Ning̃išzida in é.sag̃.íl at Babylon (*Topog. Texts* no. 1 = *Tintir* II 24).

594 **é.ki.g̃ar.dub.nam.tar.tar.re.dè.kišib.gur$^?$.sag̃.dil$^!$**, "House, Edifice where the Tablet of Destinies is Sealed in Secret," the City Hall of Aš-šur, listed in the Assyrian TL among temples of Nabû (*Topog. Texts* no. 20 = Götteradreßbuch 159).

595 **é.ki.g̃ar.UD.x[ x]**, possible temple name in a broken OB cone fragment (Frayne, *RIME* 4, p. 322, 5).

596 **é.ki.imin.GA**, a sanctuary known from the Lament to Sud (*TCL* XV 1, 3). Possibly to be emended to é.ki.imin.bi, "House, Place of Seven"?

597 **ki.ir.du$_{10}$**, see *kirḫi*

598 **é.ki.kal**, "House, Precious Place," temple of Lugalbanda (and Ninsun) at Kullab (CTL 470), rebuilt by Sîn-kāšid (Frayne, *RIME* 4, p. 454, 11, reading é.kankal).

599 **é.ki.kù.an.na**, "House, Pure Place of Heaven," see é.ki.kù.nun.na

600 **é.ki.kù.nun.na**, "House, Princely Pure Place," temple of Inšušinak at Susa, rebuilt by Indattu-Inšušinak (*SAKI*, p. 180, 2) and Indattu II (ibid., p. 182, 4 a-b; variant é.ki.kù.an.na).

601 **ki.kù.sikil**, "Pure Sacred Place," a shrine in é.sağ.íl at Babylon, = du$_6$.ki.sikil.

602 **é.ki.me.sikil**, "House, Place of Pure *Me*'s," a shrine in é.šár.ra at Aššur (*Topog. Texts* no. 21, rev. 6′).

603 **é.ki.ná.šà.tén.na**, "House, Bed-Chamber which Soothes the Heart," a sanctuary at Larak, mentioned in the Syncretistic Ištar Hymn (l. 91; unpub., courtesy Lambert).

604 **é.ki.nam**, "House, Place of Destinies" 1, temple of Bēlat-ekalli at Aššur (*Topog. Texts* no. 20 = Götteradreßbuch 165: Assyrian TL). An unnamed temple of this goddess was built for Amar-Suen by the governor Zarriqum (Steible, *FAOS* 9/II, AS 15 = Grayson, *RIMA* 1, p. 9). Courtyard repaired by Adad-nārārī I (ibid., p. 163, 30:4; no TN).

605 **é.ki.nam.ma** 2, TN or epithet associated with Anu at Keš in a liturgical text (*PBS* X/2 2, 10).

606 **ʻkiʼ.númun.búr**, see é.du$_6$.númun.búr

607 **ki.nir**, "High Place," a shrine built by Ur-Nanše (Steible, *FAOS* 5/I, UrN 25, iii 6; 28, iii 3; etc.). Cf. ki.nu.nir$^{ki}$ ? see Edzard, *Rép. géogr.* I, p. 90; *RlA* V, pp. 603f.

608 **é.ki.si.ga**, "House, Silent Place," temple of Dagān at Terqa built by Šamšī-Adad I (Grayson, *RIMA* 1, p. 60, 6 = *bīt qūltīšu*).

609 **é.ki.sì.ga**, "House of Funerary Offerings," sanctuary of Sud found in the cultic lament im.ma.al gù dé.dé (Cohen, *Lamentations*, p. 610, 66; p. 612, 136).

610 **ki.si.ĝar**, "Place of the Latch," seat of Etalak in the temple complex at Uruk (*Topog. Texts* no. 25, rev. 6′).

611 **é.ki.sikil.bi.kar.za.gìn.na**, "House whose Pure Place is a Quay of Lapis Lazuli," a sanctuary of Ištar (CTL 385).

612 **ki.šà.du$_{10}$.ga**, "Place where the Heart is Pleased," a shrine in é.sağ.íl at Babylon (*Topog. Texts* no. 1 = *Tintir* II 28).

613 **é.ki$^{?}$.šà$^{?}$.ḫúl$^{?}$**, "House, Place of the Happy Heart," TN listed in the OB lexical list from Isin (p. 4, IM 96881, ii′ 2′).

614 **ki.šen.šen.na**, "Place of Battle" or "Shining Place," a seat of Ištar in the lower courtyard of the temple complex at Uruk (*Topog. Texts* no. 25, obv. 5′).

615 **ki.šú**, "Place of Subjection," part of the temple complex at Uruk (*Topog. Texts* no. 25, obv. 11′).

616 **ki.šú.kù**, "Pure Place of Subjection," a shrine in é.saĝ.íl at Babylon (*Topog. Texts* no. 1 = *Tintir* II 14′).

617 **ki.tilmun$^{ki}$.na**, "Place of the Noble," seat of Enlil, probably in é.umuš.a, Marduk's cella in é.saĝ.íl at Babylon (*Topog. Texts* no. 1 = *Tintir* II 2).

618 **(é).ki.tuš.akkil.lé**, "House, Abode of Lamentation," shrine of Šulšagana (CTL [499]) at G̃irsu (in é.ninnu? Falkenstein, *AnOr* 30, p. 152), built by Uruinimgina (Steible, *FAOS* 5/I, Ukg 1, ii 5; 6, v 14′; etc.) and Gudea (9/I, Gud. 75, rev. 1).

619 **é.ki.tuš.bi.du$_{10}$**, "House whose Abode is Pleasant," temple of Nergal at Uzarpara, built by Damiq-ilīšu of Isin (Frayne, *RIME* 4, p. 105, 18).

620 **é.ki.tuš.gal.an.na**, "House, Great Abode of Heaven," a temple at Kiš (*Topog. Texts* no. 23, 3′).

621 **é.ki.tuš.ĝarza**, "House, Abode of the Regulations," temple of Ištar as Bēlet-Eanna by the city wall in west Babylon (*Topog. Texts* no. 1 = *Tintir* IV 41, var. é.ĝarza), rebuilt by Nebuchadnezzar II (V *R* 34, ii 9; etc.). See *Topog. Texts*, pp. 330f.

622 **é.ki.tuš.$^{ĝiš}$ĝeštu**, "House, Abode of Wisdom," temple of the Mother Goddess Bēlet-ilī built by Ipiq-Ištar, presumably in Malgium (Frayne, *RIME* 4, p. 670, 36).

623 **é.ki.tuš.gi.na**, "House, Established Abode," a temple whose administrator (*qīpu*) is a witness in a LB document dated at Šušan (*VAS* VI 155, 20; Darius 29; cf. Joannes, *N.A.B.U.* 1989/78). Perhaps = é.dúr.gi.na.

624 **é.ki.tuš.gir$_{17}$.zal**, "House, Abode of Joy" 1, temple of Ištar as Bēlet-Eanna in east Babylon (*Topog. Texts* nos. 1 = *Tintir* IV 22; V 95–96; 3, rev. 3′; 4, 22; *KAR* 109, obv. 21: syncretistic Ištar hymn; Strassmaier, *Nbk* 247, 12 // 416, 4). See *Topog. Texts*, pp. 316–18.

625 **é.ki.tuš.gir$_{17}$.zal** 2, temple of Ištar at Ilip (CTL 390: ki.bal.maš.dà$^{ki}$), built by Apil-Sîn (unplaced year, no TN: Charpin, *RA* 72 [1978], p. 18[21]; cf. Ḫammurapi year 17).

626 **é.ki.tuš.ḫé.ĝál.ti.la**, "House, Abode of Life-Giving Abundance," sanctuary of Adad at Babylon, restored by Nebuchadnezzar I (Böhl, *BiOr* 7 [1950], p. 43, 11); probably a shrine in é.nam.ḫé.

627 **ki.tuš.ḫun.ĝá**, "Restful Abode," a shrine in é.saĝ.íl at Babylon (*Topog. Texts*, p. 280, K 3446+, obv. 20: royal ritual).

628 **ki.tuš.inim.du$_{10}$.ga.lá**, "Abode which Bears a Pleasing Word," seat of Zannaru in the temple complex at Uruk (*Topog. Texts* no. 25, obv. 12′).

629 **ki.tuš.ki.sikil**, "Abode, Pure Place," a shrine in é.sağ.íl at Babylon, = du$_6$.ki.sikil.

630 **é.ki.tuš.kù.ga**, "House, Pure Abode," ziqqurrat of Ištar at Nineveh, rebuilt by Šamšī-Adad I (Grayson, *RIMA* 1, pp. 53f., ii 18.iii 15 = *ḫuruš ni-ṣirtīša*; for é.ki.tuš = *uršu* see *BWL*, p. 269, 5) and, following an earthquake, by Shalmaneser I (Grayson, *RIMA* 1, p. 208, 8: *sequrrata*, no TN), lastly by Aššurbanipal, who calls it é.ki.bi.kù.ga, "House whose Site is Pure" (Thompson, *AAA* 20 [1933], p. 82, 36).

631 **é.ki.tuš.maḫ**, "House, Exalted Abode," name or epithet of the cella of Nanna-Suen in é.kiš.nu.ğál at Ur, according to Abī-sarē (Frayne, *RIME* 4, p. 122, i 9′).

632 **ki.tuš.silim$^?$.ma**, "Abode of Well-Being," seat of the Daughters of Uruk at ki.šú in the temple complex at Uruk (*Topog. Texts* no. 25, obv. 11′).

633 **é.ki.tuš.šà.te.en**, "House, Abode which Soothes the Heart," temple of Zababa at Ur, built by Warad-Sîn (Frayne, *RIME* 4, p. 248, 28).

634 **ki.únu.ga**, "Place of the Food Offering" 1, a shrine in é.sağ.íl at Babylon (*Topog. Texts* no. 1 = *Tintir* II 14″).

635 **ki.únu.ga** 2, seat of Ištar in é.ği$_6$.pàr.imin.bi at Uruk (*Topog. Texts* no. 25, obv. 4′).

636 **(é).ki.ùr**, "Levelled Place" 1, shrine of Ninlil in é.kur at Nippur (Proto-*Kagal* 188; CTL [57]; *Topog. Texts* nos. 18 = Nippur Compendium § 8, 28′; 19 = Nippur TL 2′–10′; Temple Hymns 44; Civil, *JAOS* 103 [1983], pp. 50, 10; 52, 37: Enlil and Sud; and passim in Sumerian literature). Mentioned by Ur-Ninurta (Frayne, *RIME* 4, p. 67, ii 7′) and Burnaburiaš, who built its kissa.a.maḫ (van Dijk, *TLB* II 20, 9; cf. *BE* I 68, i 13). Commonly found between é.kur and é.nam.ti.la in liturgical texts, often also with the description ki.gal (Cohen, *Eršemma*, pp. 111, 12; 113, 18; 127, 8; *Lamentations*, passim: see index pp. 751, 764; Krecher, *Kultlyrik*, pp. 53, 4; 81; IV $R^2$ 27, no. 2, 25–27; MacMillan, *BA* V/5 6, rev. 9; V *R* 52, no. 2, obv. 50; etc.). Also *Šurpu* II 144–45. The component parts of é.ki.ùr in the MB period are listed in a metrological text (Bernhardt and Kramer, *OrNS* 44 [1975], p. 97, 9–12). Apparently written é.ka.⌜ur⌝.ra in a MB letter (Biggs, *JCS* 19 [1965], p. 98, 7, alongside é.kur and é.šu.me.ša$_4$). See also é.tum. ma.al.

637 **é.ki.ùr** 2, chapel of Ninlil in the temple of Ninimma at Nippur (*Topog. Texts* no. 18 = Nippur Compendium § 14, v 12).

638 **é.ki.ùr** 3, shrine of Ninlil in é.šár.ra at Aššur (*Topog. Texts* nos. 20 = Götteradreßbuch 149: Assyrian TL; 21, obv. 18′).

639 **ki.ùr** 4, at Ur (probably a common noun), see du$_6$.bára.gal.maḫ.

640 **ki.ùr.kù.ga**, "Pure Levelled Place," seat of $^{d}$gu$_{7}$.bi.sig.sig and Tiʾāmat in é.sag̃.íl at Babylon (*Topog. Texts* no. 1 = *Tintir* II 31); written ki.ùru.kù.ga in a royal ritual (ibid., p. 278 = *ašru ellu naklu*).

641 **ki.ús.$^{d}$nammu**, a shrine in é.sag̃.íl at Babylon mentioned by Nabonidus (Messerschmidt, *MVAG* I/1, p. 79, viii 55; see further *Topog. Texts*, p. 416). Probably borrowed from é.kur at Nippur, among shrines of which we can restore [ki].ús.$^{d}$nammu in a liturgical hymn to Enlil (*VAS* II 8, i 28; Cohen, *Lamentations*, p. 349, 30, reads [x].ta.$^{d}$nammu, but comparison of the first preserved sign with the many examples of TA and with UŠ in i 34 clinches the reading in favour of the latter).

642 **ki.zalag.ga**, "Bright Place" 1, a shrine in é.sag̃.íl at Babylon (*Topog. Texts* no. 1 = *Tintir* II 29; unpub. Kislīmu ritual).

643 **ki.zalag.ga** 2, a shrine in the Grand Court of the *bīt rēš* of Anu at Uruk, known from a LB ritual (*RAcc.*, p. 69, 1).

644 **ki.zalag.ga** 3, shrine of the divine torch in é.zi.da at Borsippa (Nassouhi, *AfK* 2 [1924–25], p. 100, i 7: Aššurbanipal).

645 ***bīt*** $^{(d)}$***kidmuri***, temple of Ištar *šarrat* $^{(d)}$*kidmuri*, "Queen of the (divine) *k.*," at Kalaḫ, rebuilt by Aššurnaṣirpal II and also known from later documents (Grayson, *RIMA* 2, p. 304, 19; cf. pp. 291, 58; 352, 2; 360, 3; also Menzel, *Tempel* I, pp. 102f.). The meaning of *kid*$_{9}$(KAD)-*mu-ri*, also written *kid-mu-ri*, *kid-mur-ri*, *ki-di-mu-ri*, is unclear (cf. Menzel, loc. cit.; George, *AfO* 32 [1985], p. 89).

646 **é.kìlib.kur.kur.ra.dul$_{6}$.dul$_{6}$**, "House which Overwhelms All Lands," temple of Adad as Bēl-Kurbaʾil at Kurbaʾil (*Topog. Texts* no. 20 = Götteradreßbuch 179: Assyrian TL).

647 ***kirḫi***, "Enclosure Wall," two seats, of Enlil (right) and Anu (left), probably in é.dàra.an.na of é.sag̃.íl at Babylon (*Topog. Texts* no. 1 = *Tintir* II 9–10). An alternative reading of the TN is perhaps ki.ir.du$_{10}$, "Place of Sweet Fragrance."

648 **é.$^{g̃iš}$kiri$_{6}$.dili.bad**, "House, Garden of *Maštakal*-Herb," sanctuary of Bēlet-ṣēri at Uruk, known from a Seleucid prebend document (*TCL* XIII 244, 3.19; paired with é.du$_{6}$.sag̃.gara$_{10}$).

649 **(é).$^{g̃iš}$kiri$_{6}$.maḫ**, "House, Grand Garden" 1, sanctuary of the sacred garden in the temple complex of Enlil at Nippur (Proto-*Kagal* 178), also found in the Tummal inscription (Sollberger, *JCS* 16 [1962], p. 44, 16), in a liturgical hymn to Enlil (Cohen, *Lamentations*, p. 350, 37: OB), and in the MB metrological text of Nippur (Bernhardt and Kramer, *OrNS* 44 [1975], p. 98, 45). Note the speculative writings ki.ir.rù.maḫ and ki.ér.maḫ in the Nippur Compendium (*Topog. Texts* no. 18, § 6, 7′–8′).

650 **$^{g̃iš}$kiri$_{6}$.maḫ** 2, sacred garden (at Ur?) planted for An and furnished with a dais by Ur-Nammu (Steible, *FAOS* 9/II, UrN 5).

651 **$^{giš}$kiri$_6$.maḫ** 3, sacred garden at Babylon, known only from the rituals of the Divine Love Lyrics (BM unpub.).

652 **é.kisal$^?$.am.ma**, "House, Court of the Wild Bull," site of a monumental inscription of Narām-Sîn, according to its colophon (Gelb and Kienast, *FAOS* 7, p. 261, NS 5, colophon 1).

653 **é.kiš.nu.g̃ál** 1, also written é.g̃iš.nu$_{11}$.gal, temple of Nanna-Suen at Ur (TL no. 2, [6]; *Kagal* Boğ. I F 13: [e-gi-iš]-nu-un-kal; Temple Hymns 102.110), rebuilt by Narām-Sîn and no doubt Ur-Nammu (no TN: Walker, *CBI* no. 3; Steible, *FAOS* 9/II, UrN 1, 3; 26, 9; 47, i 12; etc., but cf. é.temen.ní.gùru), who was known to Utu-ḫeg̃al as ama.[(a).tu] é.TN (ibid., Uḫ 6, ii 3–4). Worked on by kings of Isin and Larsa (see Edzard, *Zwischenzeit*, p. 52), by Kurigalzu (*UET* I 152–54; 161; etc.), Marduk-nādin-aḫḫē (*UET* I 306, 8; VIII 101), Adad-apla-iddina (*UET* I 166–67), and Nebuchadnezzar II (V *R* 34, ii 35; etc.). Mentioned by Gungunum (Frayne, *RIME* 4, p. 116, 5: é.kiš$^{ki}$.nu.g̃ál; cf. years 10.11.14.26), Abī-sarē (ibid., p. 123, v 10; cf. year 3). Patronized by Nūr-Adad (ibid., p. 142, 12.55), Sîn-iddinam (ibid., p. 169, 21), Warad-Sîn (ibid., pp. 216, 12; 226, 3:10′; 4:9′; etc.), Rīm-Sîn I (ibid., p. 284, 4; cf. year 3) and Ḫammurapi (CḪ ii 21). Ground-plan sought by Sîn-balāssu-iqbi (*UET* I 172, iv 5), who also claims to have provisioned the temple (*UET* I 169, i 9: written é.kéš.nun.gal; 170, 8). Passim in Sumerian literature especially. Mentioned in the Syncretistic Ištar Hymn (*KAR* 109, obv. 8). In the standard list of cult-centers in liturgical texts, usually following Ur (Cohen, *Lamentations*, pp. 149, 196; 211, 76; 242, 375 = 311, 249; 615, 196; *CT* 42 9, pl. 20, i 21; Langdon, *BL* nos. 27, 6′; 156, 4; etc.). See further Charpin, *Le clergé d'Ur*, pp. 325ff., "Topographie de l'Ekišnugal."

654 **é.kiš.nu.g̃ál** 2, temple of Sîn at Babylon (*Topog. Texts* nos. 1 = *Tintir* IV 24; 3, rev. 5′–6′; 4, 24), mentioned in year names of Ḫammurapi (year 3: throne and bára.maḫ) and Samsu-iluna (year 5: throne), rebuilt by Abī-ešuḫ (year h; cf. 28.p) and Nebuchadnezzar II (*CT* 37 13, 42; etc.). Survived into the Seleucid period (Grayson, *Chronicles*, p. 120, obv. 7.9). Prebend: Peiser, *Verträge* 91, 4 (Nbn 12). In the late period the TN is usually written é.g̃iš.nu$_{11}$.gal. See *Topog. Texts*, pp. 319f.

655 **é.kiš.nu.g̃ál** 3, temple of Sîn at Bīt-Suenna, near Nippur (*Topog. Texts* no. 18 = Nippur Compendium § 6, 11′–13′; divine residents of an unnamed temple of Sîn at Nippur are listed in § 14, v 7–8). The cult of Sîn at Nippur was patronized by Šulgi (year 14, no TN).

656 **é.kiš.[ . . . ]**, a temple at Kiš (*Topog. Texts* no. 23, 15′). Perhaps simply é.kiš[$^{ki}$].

657 **$^{na4}$kišib.sikil.la**, "Pure Seal," seat of Ištarān in the treasury of é.šár.ra at Aššur (*Topog. Texts* no. 21, obv. 21′).

658 ***é.kišib.ba**, see é.dub.ba

659 **é.KU.a**, see é.umuš.a.

660 **é.KU.sağ.GA.NI**, see é.du$_6$.sağ.gara$_{10}$

661 **é.kù**, "Pure House" 1, seat (*arattû*) of Ištar in é.maš.maš at Nineveh restored by Aššurnaṣirpal II (Grayson, *RIMA* 2, p. 309, 36).

662 **é.kù** 2, shrine of Šulmānītu in the temple of Ištar at Aššur, rebuilt by Tukultī-Ninurta I (Grayson, *RIMA* 1, p. 260, 20; cf. p. 261, 5–6: *bēt* $^{d}$DI-*nite* written over erased Bēlat-Akkade).

663 **é.kù.ga** 3, temple of Nergal (at Ur?), rebuilt by Warad-Sîn (Frayne, *RIME* 4, p. 247, 23). Possibly only an epithet of é.me.te.ir$_9$.ra or é.érim.ḫaš.ḫaš.

664 **kù.bára.**[ . . . ], temple of Ištar at Zabalam rebuilt by Narām-Sîn, but according to later tradition, by Šar-kali-šarrī (Gelb and Kienast, *FAOS* 7, pp. 52, NS year 8; 86, NS 2, 7 // 276, Škš C 1, 6).

665 **é.kù.ki.ná**, "Pure House, Bed-Chamber," a sanctuary of Šamaš (CTL 290).

666 **é.kù.mul.mul**, "Shining Pure House," a sanctuary of Šamaš (CTL 291).

667 **é.kù.nun.na**, "Princely Pure House," sanctuary of Inanna at Eridu according to Inanna D 63 (as given by M. W. Green, *Eridu in Sumerian Literature* [unpub. Ph.D., Chicago, 1975], p. 210), restored in CTL 341. Unnamed temples of Inanna nin.kù.nun.na are also known at URU×KÁR$^{ki}$ (built by Ur-Baba: Steible, *FAOS* 9/I, UrB 1, iv 9; 8, iii 2), and probably at Ur (rebuilt by Ur-Nammu: Steible, *FAOS* 9/II, UrN 6; all exemplars from Ur: = èš.bur?).

668 **é.kù.x**, a temple listed in the OB lexical list from Isin (p. 4, IM 96881, iii′ 10′).

669 **é.ku$_6$.nu.gu$_7$**, "House where Fish is not Eaten," sanctuary of Ninurta listed among gods and other parts of Enlil's cult-center at Nippur in Ur III offering lists (*TCL* II 5501, iii 1; *PDT* I 523, 9; 636, 2); cf. Salonen, *StOr* 19/2 (1953).

670 **ku$_7$.nim.ma**, a shrine in é.šár.ra at Aššur (*Topog. Texts* no. 21, rev. 22′).

671 **kun.sağ**, part of é.kur at Nippur (Cohen, *Lamentations*, pp. 97, 24; 349, 21). Presumably the temple's main threshold (i.e., kun$_4$; cf. Sjöberg, *Mondgott*, p. 117, n. 19. In *STVC* 60 = Šulgi R 17 read now kun.sağ pú.kur.ra: Klein, *Bar-Ilan Studies Artzi*, p. 114).

672 **é.kun$_4$.an.kù.ga**, "House, Pure Stairway of Heaven," the ziqqurrat of Šamaš at Sippar (TL no. 4, 8; no. 5, 7′), rebuilt by Samsu-iluna (no TN, u$_6$.nir gi.gun$_4$.na.maḫ, "ziqqurrat, exalted terrace-house": Frayne, *RIME* 4, p. 377, 68 // 83–85; year 18), Ammī-ṣaduqa (year 17+d: VAT 5909: no TN, but note the epithet u$_6$.nir ⟨ḫur⟩.sağ galam!.ma, "ziqqurrat, artificial mountain"), Neriglissar (van Dijk, *TLB* II 22, 21′; no TN), and Nabonidus (V *R* 64, iii 4).

673 **kun$_4$.ká.tilla$_4$.é.šár.ra**, "Threshold, Outer Gate of E-šarra," seat of Zababa in é.šár.ra at Aššur (*Topog. Texts* no. 21, rev. 20′).

674 **kun$_4$.kur.ra.ke$_4$ *abul* $^d$*Ištar***, "The Ištar Gate is the Threshold of the Mountain," a dais of Marduk at Babylon (*Topog. Texts* no. 1 = *Tintir* V 48).

675 **(é).kun$_4$.sa.tu**, "House, Threshold of the Mountain," temple of Numušda at Kazallu (Proto-*Kagal* 213; *MSL* XI, p. 142, viii 17; Temple Hymns 404; *VAS* XVII 38, 39: hymn to Numušda; see Sjöberg, *TCS* III, p. 126). Patronized by Šulgi (year 12, no TN), and Sîn-iqīšam (year 2, no TN). Note also unnamed temples of Numušda in year names of Sūmû-ditāna (year b, from Kiš) and Sūmû-numḫim of Šadlaš (Simmons, *JCS* 14 [1960], pp. 85ff., from Marad).

676 **é.kun$_4$.zi.ù.li**, see é.i.lu.zi.ù.li

677 **é.kur**, "House, Mountain" 1, temple of Enlil at Nippur (p. 4, IM 96881, ii′ 3′; Proto-*Kagal* 176; *Kagal* Boğ. I E 11; TL no. 2, 1; no. 7 b 14; *Topog. Texts* nos. 18 = Nippur Compendium § 5; 19 = Nippur TL 1′), rebuilt, restored or repaired by among others Narām-Sîn and Šar-kali-šarrī (Gelb and Kienast, *FAOS* 7, pp. 52, NS year 8; 55, Škš years 5–9; 101, NS 17; 107, NS B 3; 113ff.: Škš 1, 8; 2, 10; 4, 5; 282, Škš C 3, 10), Ur-Nammu (Steible, *FAOS* 9/II, UrN 16; cf. 3; 28, i 8), Kadašman-Enlil I/II (Biggs, *AS* 17, no. 52), Burnaburiaš (probably: Brinkman, *MSKH*, p. 106[29]), Adad-šuma-uṣur (*BE* I 81), Meli-šipak (Brinkman, *MSKH*, p. 253; no TN?), Ḫašmar-galšu (ibid., pp. 326; 379, no. 2; *YOS* IX 67), Nebuchadnezzar I (Brinkman, *PKB*, pp. 113 with n. 624; 326), Esarhaddon (Borger, *Esarh.*, §§ 40, 18; 41, 12) and Aššurbanipal (*BE* I 82). Patronized by Amar-Suen (sag̃.ús é $^d$en.líl.ka: Steible, *FAOS* 9/II, AS passim), Ur-Ninurta (Frayne, *RIME* 4, p. 67, ii 8′: é.kur èš.maḫ; 17′), Enlil-bāni (ibid., p. 88, iii 11), Ur-Dukuga (ibid., pp. 94, 9; 95, 2:6), Sîn-iqīšam (ibid., p. 191, iii 13), Warad-Sîn (ibid., pp. 216, 11; 233, 7; etc.), Ḫammurapi (CḪ i 62), Burnaburiaš (Arnaud, *Sumer* 32 [1976], p. 101, 9), Kudur-Enlil (Brinkman, *MSKH*, p. 191; no TN?), etc. Given the epithet èš.nam.ti.la, "house of life" (cf. é.nam.ti.la 1) by Rīm-Sîn I (year 23). Passim in Sumerian literature especially. Commonly attested in liturgical texts, usually between nibru$^{ki}$ and ki.ùr (Cohen, *Eršemma*, pp. 111, 11; 113, 18; 118, 35.2:3; 127, 7; *Lamentations*, passim, often qualified as é šà.ge pàd.da, "house chosen in the heart": index p. 751–52; Krecher, *Kultlyrik*, pp. 53, 3; 81; MacMillan, *BA* V/5 6, rev. 7; V *R* 52, no. 2, obv. 47–49; etc.). Mentioned twice in the Syncretistic Ištar Hymn (lines 35.93; unpub., courtesy Lambert). Also in the syncretistic hymn to Nanāy (Reiner, *JNES* 33 [1974], p. 225, 17). The component parts of é.kur in the MB period are given in a metrological text (Bernhardt and Kramer, *OrNS* 44 [1975], p. 97, 1–8). See also é.kur.igi.bar.ra, é.kur.igi.g̃ál, é.kur.za.gìn.

678 **é.kur** 2, by-name of the temple of the god Aššur at Aššur. The TN is first used by Shalmaneser I, who rebuilt it for Nunamnir, i.e., Enlil (ibid., pp. 193, 5; 194, 19, alongside é.ḫur.sag̃.kur.kur.ra of Aššur; 200, 7; cf. 192, 3; 207, 4), and later by Tukultī-Ninurta I (ibid., pp. 240, 12; 272, 51: with the

epithet *šadî rabî* here cf. é.ḫur.sag̃.gu.la; 279f., 1.5). See é.ḫur.sag̃.kur.kur.ra and é.šár.ra 2.

679 **é.kur** 3, temple of Enlil "outside Babylon," mentioned in the inscription of Gaddaš (i.e., Gandaš; Winckler, *Untersuchungen*, p. 156, 6:4). Possibly refers to é.nam.ti.la in west Babylon.

680 **é.kur** 4, chapel of Enlil in the temple of Ninimma at Nippur (*Topog. Texts* no. 18 = Nippur Compendium § 14, v 12).

681 **é.kur.ɢɪš.[. . . ]**, a temple of Enlil listed in *Kagal* Boğ. I E 13. In the light of the gloss e-gur-na-aš-ki this is probably a mistake for é.kur.na$_4$.za.gìn.

682 **é.kur.igi.bar.ra**, "House, Mountain which Sees," a temple of Enlil built by Kurigalzu (*BE* I 38; year name in Brinkman, *MSKH*, p. 402). Probably a variation on é.kur 1.

683 **é.kur.igi.g̃ál**, "House, Mountain Endowed with Sight," a shrine in the storehouse of é.kur at Nippur (p. 4, IM 96881, ii′ 7′; Proto-*Kagal* 177; *Kagal* Boğ. I E 12), dedicated to both Enlil and Ninlil (CTL 37.59), where a throne of Enlil was installed by Nebuchadnezzar I and Simbar-šipak (Goetze, *JCS* 19 [1965], p. 123, 6.9; Grayson, *Chronicles*, p. 181, 13; cf. Brinkman, *PKB*, p. 152 with n. 920). In early OB offering lists (*PBS* VIII/1 13, obv. 5: Damiq-ilīšu; 33, 2.8.12: Rīm-Sîn I; written é.kur.ra.igi.g̃ál in Heimerdinger, *Kramer AV*, pp. 226, iii 22′; 228, iv 24′; vi 21′), and prebend sales, etc. (*OECT* VIII 9, 1; 10, 1; *PBS* VIII/2 133, 7–10; all Samsuiluna). In the MB metrological text of Nippur é.ᴛɴ is listed immediately after the temple complex of Enlil, Ninlil and Ninurta (Bernhardt and Kramer, *OrNS* 44 [1975], p. 98, 20). According to the cultic commentary of Nippur the marriage of Enlil and Šuzianna was consummated here (*OECT* XI 69, i 12′–14′, 10th Ayyāru; cf. é.ki.ág̃.g̃á.šu.du$_7$).

684 **é.kur.maḫ**, "House, Exalted Mountain" 1, ziqqurrat at Ḫursag̃-kalamma (TL no. 4, 13; no. 5, 11′; no. 6, [14]), presumably of Ištar-Ninlil.

685 **é.kur.maḫ** 2, a temple of Ninazu according to Anzû III 139.

686 **é.kur.me.sikil**, "House, Mountain of Pure *Me*'s," a sanctuary of Ištar (CTL 358).

687 **é.kur.me.šár.ra**, "House, Mountain of All the *Me*'s," temple of Aššur at Kār-Tukultī-Ninurta built by Tukultī-Ninurta I (Grayson, *RIMA* 1, pp. 274, 114; 276, 54: é.⌜x.x⌝.šá.[r]a!; 278, 27).

688 **é.kur.na$_4$.za.gìn**, see é.kur.($^{na}$4)za.gìn

689 **é.kur.nam.ti.la**, "House, Mountain of Life," a temple of Enlil listed in *Kagal* Boğ. I E 14. Perhaps simply a conflation of é.kur (line 11) and é.nam. ti.la (line 15).

690 **é.kur.ní.zu**, "House, Fearsome Mountain," sanctuary of Ninlil at Ḫursag̃-kalamma (Walker, *CBI* no. 75: Merodach-baladan; TL no. 6, [12]), also mentioned in the Syncretistic Ištar Hymn (l. 74; unpub., courtesy Lambert). Probably the later name of é.ḫur.sag̃.kalam.ma of Ištar (cf. McEwan, *Iraq* 45 [1983], p. 120).

691 **é.kur.ra**, "House of the Mountain," temple of Bunene in Sippar, rebuilt by Nabonidus (Bezold, *PSBA* 11 [1889], pp. 103f., pl. 1, 30). Possibly an incomplete variant writing of é.tukur.ra.

692 **é.kur.ra.igi.g̃ál**, see é.kur.igi.g̃ál

693 **é.kur.(${}^{na_4}$)za.gìn**, "House, Mountain of Lapis Lazuli," part of é.kur at Nippur, or even its full name, common in Sumerian literature, sometimes written é.kur é.za.gìn (Falkenstein, *Götterlieder* I, pp. 13ff., 37.64.77.91a; also p. 43; Römer, *Königshymnen*, pp. 236f., 12.54: hymn to Baba for Išme-Dagān; Civil, *JAOS* 103 [1983], p. 57, 147: Enlil and Sud; *STVC* 75, rev. i 12′: Lipit-Ištar and the Plough; Šulgi A 88; *KAR* 16, obv. 39–40: cult-song; Sjöberg, *ZA* 63 [1973], p. 18, 9′: hymn to Nuska; *UET* VI 118, iii 14–15: hymn to Nippur; etc.). Mentioned by Ur-Ninurta (Frayne, *RIME* 4, p. 67, vi 4′) and Burnaburiaš (*BE* I 68, ii 23). See also é.kur.G̃IŠ.[ . . . ].

694 **é.kúr.kúr.ru**, sanctuary at Bīt-Suenna near Nippur (*Topog. Texts* no. 18 = Nippur Compendium § 6, 15′). Reading uncertain.

695 **é.kurun.na**, "House of Liquor," seat of Siraš in é.rab.ri.ri (at Babylon? *Topog. Texts* no. 12, 7′).

696 **é.kúrun.na**, see é.TIN.na

697 **é.kúš**, TN or epithet known from the big OB forerunner to *Hh* XXI (*MSL* XI, p. 142, viii 25).

698 **[é.l]a$^?$.la**, "House of Delight," a temple listed in CTL 601.

699 **é.làl.DU**, temple of Nindara at ke.ès.(sá)$^{ki}$, rebuilt by Gudea (Steible, *FAOS* 9/I, Gud. 37, 8), after the desecration by Lugalzaggesi (5/I, Ukg 16, v 4; no TN); possibly the unnamed sanctuary earlier built by Enannatum I (ibid., En I 20, ii 2) and Ur-Baba (9/I, UrB 1, v 3), though this may equally well have been the temple in G̃irsu. Also in a list of cultic personnel (Gelb, *StOr* 46 [1975], p. 48, rev. i 5–8; Ur III, no TN).

700 **é.làl.g̃ar**, a temple of Ea (CTL 187), named after his cosmic abode, làl.g̃ar or làl.ḫar (see the commentary on CTL).

701 **é.làl.ì.nun-*ù*-g̃eštin**, "House of Honey, Ghee and Wine," a shrine of Enlil at Nippur (in é.kur?) where offerings were made, rebuilt by Amar-Suen (Steible, *FAOS* 9/II, AS 10).

702 **é.lam.ma**, "House of the Netherworld," TN or epithet known from a liturgical hymn to Nergal (Cohen, *Lamentations*, pp. 502, 10; 507, 99).

703 **é.lam.mes**, see é.mes.lam 3

704 **é.líl.l[á$^?$]**, "House of Wind(?)," a shrine of the temple complex at Uruk, known from a late ritual (*RAcc.*, p. 73 = Lackenbacher, *RA* 71 [1977], p. 40, obv. 9′).

705 **é.lú.maḫ**, shrine of the divine Lumaḫ priest (CTL 173), for example in é.sag̃.íl at Babylon (*Topog. Texts* no. 1 = *Tintir* II 7′).

706 **é.lugal.g̃alga.si.sá**, "House of the King who Lets Counsel Flourish," ziqqurrat of Sîn at Ur (TL no. 5, 16′: [é.luga]l.g̃á.g̃á.si.sá), rebuilt by Sîn-balāssu-iqbi (*UET* I 168; 170), and Nabonidus, who reports earlier work of Ur-Nammu and Šulgi (I *R* 68, no. 1, i 5; etc.). See also é.temen.ní.gùr.ru.

706a **é.lugal.gu$_4$.si.sá**, see the entry below for the DN Lugalgusisa.

707 **é.lugal.kalam.ma**, "House of the King of the Land," TN or epithet known from the big OB forerunner to *Hh* XXI (*MSL* XI, p. 142, viii 44). Perhaps emend to é.rab$^!$.kalam.ma, "House, Shackle of the Land"?

708 **ma.balag̃.g̃á**, see *g̃á.balag̃.g̃á

709 **ma.gú.en.na**, "Chamber of the Supreme Council," sanctuary of $^d$ab.ba.Ú in the Ur Lament (Kramer, *AS* 12, pp. 18f., 25.58).

710 **ma.mu.šú.a**, Emesal form of é.g̃á.g̃iš.šú.a.

711 **é.má.gur$_8$**, "House of the Barge," epithet or part of the cult-center of Nanna-Suen at Ur (Cohen, *Lamentations*, p. 149, 195; coll.).

712 **mà . . .**, see g̃á . . .

713 **é.maḫ**, "Exalted House" 1, temple of the Mother Goddess (Nintu, Nin-maḫ, Ninḫursag̃, Bēlet-ilī) in An = *Anum*, where it seems to be the temple of Keš not Adab (probably the two cults are conflated; cf. Moran, *Kramer AV*, p. 338). Sometimes also associated with Keš rather than Adab in liturgical texts (Cohen, *Eršemma*, p. 128, 28 B; *Lamentations*, pp. 106, 259; Scheil, *RA* 17 [1920], p. 50, 3; *PBS* X/2 2, 3–5; *CT* 36 47, 41; cf. Krecher, *Kultlyrik*, p. 200, n. 559), but the distinction cannot always be made. See also é.kèš$^{ki}$.

714 **é.maḫ** 2, temple of the Mother Goddess at Adab (Temple Hymns 367.371a), built by Eiginimpae of Adab (Steible, *FAOS* 5/II, pp. 190, ii 1; 191, 6), patronized by Ḫammurapi (CḪ iii 69), rebuilt by Kurigalzu (Luckenbill, *OIP* 14 44–47). Common in litanies (Cohen, *Lamentations*, pp. 210, 61; 612, 134; 733, 52; 735, 103; Thureau-Dangin, *RA* 19 [1922], p. 181, 15). Also called é.nam.zu, é.sar.ra?

715 **é.maḫ** 3, temple of the Mother Goddess at Babylon (*Topog. Texts* nos. 1 = *Tintir* IV 18; 4, 18), rebuilt by Aššurbanipal (Streck, *Asb.*, p. 240, 5:13) and Nebuchadnezzar II (V *R* 34, ii 6; etc.). See *Topog. Texts*, p. 313.

716 **é.maḫ** 4, temple of Ninḫursag̃ at G̃irsu, built by Ur-Baba (Steible, *FAOS* 9/I, UrB 1, iv 1; no TN) and Gudea (ibid., Stat. A, ii 5; cf. i 8; L, iv′ 2″; 9/II, p. 71? No TN: Gud. 69–70). Also *MVN* VI 272, obv. 2; = é.maḫ 8?

717 **é.maḫ** 5, temple of Ninsun at Ur, rebuilt by Ur-Nammu (Steible, *FAOS* 9/II, UrN 15; cf. 2; also year 6). Mentioned in an OB disbursement of offerings (Figulla, *Iraq* 15 [1953], p. 89, *UET* V 775, 3).

718 **é.maḫ** 6, temple of Šara at Umma (CTL 451; Proto-*Kagal* 207?), first noted in the votive inscription of Barairnun, wife of G̃iššakidu of Umma (Steible, *FAOS* 5/II, p. 268, 1.9), and often mentioned in Sumerian

literature (Temple Hymns 307–9; Lamentation over Sumer and Ur 156; Kramer, *AS* 12, p. 18, Ur Lament 20; Sjöberg, *StOr* 46 [1975], p. 309, 16′: bal.bal.e), as well as in administrative documents from Umma (e.g., Englund, *Acta Sum* 14 [1992], p. 87, 19, where it is distinct from é $^{d}$šára; Ur III). Possibly listed for Ištar in TL no. 3, 30′. See also é.bur.sa$_7$.sa$_7$, é.šà.ge.pàd.da.

719 **é.maḫ** 7, shrine in é.ninnu at G̃irsu (Steible, *FAOS* 9/I, Gud. Stat. B, iv 51; cf. Falkenstein, *AnOr* 30, pp. 129f.), apparently of Nanše (Steible, *FAOS* 5/I, Ean 62, IV i 2′). Also a residence of Šulutul (Bauer *AWL*, pp. 442, iv 15; 450: in Sirara?).

720 **é.maḫ** 8, shrine in é.tar.sír.sír at G̃irsu (Falkenstein, *AnOr* 30, p. 146).

721 **é.maḫ** 9, temple of Nanna-Suen, rebuilt by Sūmû-abum (year 5ff.). Probably an epithet of one of Sîn's temples in Babylon, é.ní.te.en.du$_{10}$ or é.g̃iš.nu$_{11}$.gal 2. Note also the TN in use as an epithet of é.kiš.nu.g̃ál at Ur in Sîn-iddinam A 6 (*CT* 42 45, pl. 48, b 6; also in a litany: 9, pl. 20, i 24–25?).

722 **é.maḫ** 10, see é.me.sikil.(la) 2

723 **é.maḫ** 11, part or by-name of Ninurta's é.šu.me.ša$_4$ at Nippur (Temple Hymns 67); see also é.maḫ.di.

724 **é.maḫ** 12, part or by-name of Ninurta's é.šu.me.ša$_4$ at Aššur (*Topog. Texts* no. 20 = Götteradreßbuch 152a.177: Assyrian TL).

725 **é.maḫ** 13, a sanctuary of Enlil (CTL 32), possibly = é. maḫ 11.

726 **é.maḫ** 14–15, temples of Ištar listed in TL no. 3, 30′.39′. As originally deciphered by Jacobsen a building inscription of Sūmû-Amnānim of Šadlaš reports the building of an é.maḫ in the Diyala region (Frayne, *RIME* 4, p. 695). But the reading is open to doubt since Jacobsen now renders the concluding lines of the brick in question as é.gibil *ù* é.mìn *i-pu-uš* (*OIP* 98, pp. 93f.). Cf. also é.maḫ at or near Dēr in the Syncretistic Ištar Hymn (rev. 18; unpub., courtesy Lambert), and é.maḫ 6.

727 **é.maḫ** 16, variant of èš.maḫ 2 in ama é.TN, the epithet of Damgalnunna (Cohen, *Lamentations*, pp. 99, 102; 275f., 23.67; 279, 132; 284, 202 = 359, 218; Lamentation over Sumer and Ur 247; Green, *JCS* 30 [1978], p. 132, 15: Eridu Lament; note also the TN as an epithet of é.engur.ra in Enki's Journey to Nippur 58).

728 **é.maḫ** 17, a sanctuary listed in the OB lexical list from Isin (p. 4, IM 96881, iii′ 5′).

729 **é.maḫ** 18, variant of, or mistake for, é.me.sikil.la of Amurru at Babylon (*Topog. Texts* no. 1 = *Tintir* IV 37, MS v).

730 **é.maḫ$^{ki}$** 19, temple which gave its name to a settlement (*MSL* XI, p. 132, v 31), probably near Larsa (*TCL* X 115, 25′: uru$^{ki}$ é.maḫ; OB).

731 **é.maḫ.di**, "House Most Lofty," a sanctuary of Ninurta (Cohen, *Lamentations*, pp. 180, 155; 458, 12); variant of é.maḫ 11.

732 **é.maḫ.gir$_{17}$.zal**, "Exalted House of Joy," temple of Mār-bīti in the vicinity of Babylon or Borsippa known from colophons of Parthian-period tablets (Hunger, *Kolophone*, nos. 166, 5; 449, 8 = Maul, *OrNS* 60 [1991], p. 316, 22). Also appears in the syncretistic Hymn to Borsippa (BM unpub.).

733 **é.maḫ.maḫ**, "House Most Sublime," a temple of Ištar listed in TL no. 3, 41′.

734 **é.maḫ.ti.la**, "Exalted House which Gives Life" 1, also written é.maḫ.til.la, cella of Nabû in é.zi.da at Borsippa, as repaired by Nebuchadnezzar II (V *R* 34, ii 4, etc.). Commonly follows é.zi.da in the standard litany of TNs in liturgical texts (Cohen, *Eršemma*, pp. 29, 11; 114, 24; 118, 35.2:12; 127, 16; *Lamentations*, passim: index p. 751; Langdon, *BL* nos. 26, 1′; 56, obv. 15; George, *RA* 82 [1988], pp. 159f., 35.52; Reiner, *JNES* 15 [1956], p. 144, 10; IV $R^2$ 29, no. 1, 29–30; Cooper, *Iraq* 32 [1970], p. 59, 8; etc.). Also *Topog. Texts* no. 28, 4′?

735 **é.maḫ.ti.la** 2, a seat of Marduk in é.sag̃.íl at Babylon (*Topog. Texts* no. 1 = *Tintir* II 10″).

736 **é.máḫ.ti.la**, see é.al.ti.la

737 **é.malga.sù**, see é.g̃alga.sù

738 **é.mar.uru$_5$**, "House of the Deluge," temple of $^{d}$inanna mu.ur$_5^{ki}$ (Ištar of Muru?), built at Isin by Lamassatum, Lipit-Ištar's mother (Frayne, *RIME* 4, p. 59, 13, qualified as é.šutum ki.ág̃.g̃á.ni, "her beloved storeroom").

739 **é.mar.za**, "House of Rites," a sanctuary mentioned in the cultic lament im.ma.al gù.dé.dé (Cohen, *Lamentations*, p. 614, 172). Emesal version of é.g̃arza.

740 **é.maš**, temple of Ulmaššītum (Ištar of Akkade) in Malgium, built by Takil-ilissu (Frayne, *RIME* 4, p. 673, 26). Error for é.ul.maš?

741 **é.maš.da**, a sanctuary of the goddess $^{d}$e.re.da/ereš.da, known from a litany (Cohen, *Lamentations*, pp. 288, 244 = 363, 260).

742 **é.maš.maš**, also é.mes.mes (or é.mèš.mèš), temple of Ištar-Ninlil at Nineveh (CTL 393: é.mes.mes; *Topog. Texts* no. 20 = Götteradreßbuch 150: Assyrian TL). Partly rebuilt by Maništūšu, then Šamšī-Adad I (Grayson, *RIMA* 1, p. 53, i 8; see é.me.nu.è). Patronized by Ḫammurapi (CḪ iv 61: é.mes.mes). Restored by Aššur-uballiṭ I (cf. Grayson, *RIMA* 1, p. 116) and, after an earthquake, Shalmaneser I (ibid., pp. 209, 7; 217, 29:1; cf. without TN pp. 206, 6; 208, 8), then again by Tukultī-Ninurta I (no TN: pp. 284, 3; 285, 3), and Aššur-rēša-iši I (no TN: pp. 311, 9; 313, 4). Rebuilt by Tiglath-pileser I (*RIMA* 2, p. 59, 24′: no TN), Šamšī-Adad IV (ibid., p. 119, 2:5, 3:3′: no TN), and Aššurnaṣirpal II (pp. 309, 31; 332, 2; 333, 7; etc.; see also é.kù 1). Refurbished(?) by Esarhaddon (Borger, *Esarh.*, §§ 29, 6; 64, rev. 5) and Aššurbanipal (Streck, *Asb.*, pp. 92, 20; 150, 47; etc.; see also é.gašan.

kalam.ma 2). Known to Sennacherib as é.mes.mes (*KAH* II 124, 4). See further Menzel, *Tempel* I, pp. 116ff.

743 **é.máš.da.ri**, "House of Animal Offerings" 1, temple of Bēlet-Akkade (Ištar of Agade) in Babylon (*Topog. Texts* no. 1 = *Tintir* IV 16), rebuilt by Nabonidus (Smith, *RA* 22 [1925], p. 59, 33; etc.). Written é.maš.da.ri in the offering calendar *BRM* IV 25, 40. See *Topog. Texts*, p. 312.

744 **é.máš.da.ri** 2, a shrine in é.sağ.íl at Babylon (*Topog. Texts* no. 1 = *Tintir* II 49).

745 **é.máš.da.ri** 3, temple of Ištar listed in TL no. 3, 43′, apparently not the temple of Babylon.

746 **é.me**, see é.me.$^{d}$inanna

747 **é.me.an.na**, "House of the *Me*'s of Heaven," a sanctuary of Gula (at Isin?), as found in a cultic lament (Cohen, *Lamentations*, p. 256, 51, qualified as ù.šu.dé.a).

748 **é.me$^{?}$.bi.šè.dağal.la**, "House, Spacious for its *Me*'s," a sanctuary of Enlil (CTL 26).

749 **é.me$^{?}$.bi.šè.dù.a**, "House, Built for its *Me*'s," a sanctuary of Enlil and Ninlil (CTL 25.60).

750 **é.me.bi.za[lag.ga?].ní.su.zi.b[ar.ra]**, "House whose *Me*'s are Shining(?), Emitting Fearsome Radiance," a sanctuary of a deity of Adad's court (CTL 312).

751 **é.me.bi[r.ra?]**, "House of Scattered(?) *Me*'s," a shrine in é.šár.ra at Aššur (*Topog. Texts* no. 21, obv. 2′).

752 **me$^{?}$.dàra.nam.duḫ.a**, seat of the Divine Ladies ($^{d}$gašan$^{meš}$ = Bēlētu?) in é.šár.ra at Aššur (*Topog. Texts* no. 21, obv. 35′).

753 **é.me.du$_{10}$.du$_{10}$.ga**, "House of Pleasing *Me*'s," sanctuary of which Ninurta is the divine pa$_{4}$.šeš (Sjöberg, *OrSuec* 22 [1973], p. 117, 8′).

754 **é.me.galam.ma**, "House of Skilfully-Contrived *Me*'s," Akītu temple of Ištar at Akkade, rebuilt by Kurigalzu (*CT* 9 3, b 7).

755 **é.me.ḫuš.gal.an.ki**, "House of the Great Awesome *Me*'s of Heaven and Underworld," temple of Igalimma (CTL [498]) at Ğirsu (Falkenstein, *AnOr* 30, p. 153), built by Uruinimgina (Steible, *FAOS* 5/I, Ukg 1, ii 2; 6, v 11′; etc.) and Gudea (9/I, Gud. 19, 8).

756 **é.me.$^{d}$inanna**, "House of *Me*'s of Inanna," temple of Assyrian Ištar (Ištar-Aššurītu) at Aššur (*Topog. Texts* no. 20 = Götteradreßbuch 164: Assyrian TL). The temple was extant in the OAkk period (Grayson, *RIMA* 1, p. 7, 7: votive inscription of Ititi, no TN), and was rebuilt by Ilu-šumma (no TN: ibid., pp. 15, 13; 17, 22), reportedly by Sargon I, then by Puzur-Aššur III (no TN: ibid., 91, 5) and Adad-nārārī I (no TN: ibid., pp. 139, 19′; 150, 5ff.: *ḫuršu, bēt šuḫūri*, chapel of Išḫara). Further rebuildings are claimed by Shalmaneser I (ibid., p. 195, 5; no TN), Tukultī-Ninurta I

(p. 255, 38: é.me *bīt parṣī*) and Aššur-rēša-iši I (p. 318, 7; no TN). Rebuilt by Tiglath-pileser I (*RIMA* 2, p. 26, 86: no TN; cf. pp. 20, 36; 34, 23–24), towers repaired by Šamšī-Adad IV (ibid., p. 118, 4: no TN).

757 **é.me.kìlib.ba.sag̃.íl**, "House which Lifts on High All the *Me*'s," temple of Ninšubur (at G̃irsu?), rebuilt by Rīm-Sîn I (Frayne, *RIME* 4, p. 289, 30). An unnamed temple of Ninšubur was earlier built by Gudea (Steible, *FAOS* 9/I, Gud. 73, rev. 1, from Uruk; 74, 6, from G̃irsu).

758 **é.me.kìlib.šu.du$_7$**, "House which Perfects All the *Me*'s," temple of Ninimma at Nippur (CTL 109; *LKA* 76, 3–4: Sons of Nippur). The residents of Ninimma's temple are listed in the Divine Directory of Nippur (*Topog. Texts* no. 18 = Nippur Compendium § 14, v 11–13; no TN). A temple of Ninimma at Nippur is listed without name in a MB metrological text (Bernhardt and Kramer, *OrNS* 44 [1975], p. 98, 42).

759 **é.me.kìlib.ur$_4$.ur$_4$**, "House which Gathers All the *Me*'s," temple of Ištar as the Queen of Larsa at Babylon (*Topog. Texts* nos. 1 = *Tintir* IV 25; 3, rev. 7′; 4, 25).

760 **é.me.kù.kù.ga**, "House of Pure *Me*'s," by-name of é.abzu at Eridu, as rebuilt by Nūr-Adad (see é.abzu 1).

761 **é.me.lam.an.na**, "House of the Radiance of Heaven," seat of Šamaš in the court of é.zalag.ga at Uruk (*Topog. Texts* no. 25, obv. 10′). See also é.me.lám.an.na.

762 **é.me.lám**, "House of Radiance," TN known from Ur III documents (Hussey, *HSS* 4 127, 4; *MVN* VI 115, obv. 4; 143, rev. 6; etc.).

763 **é.me.lám.an.na**, "House of the Radiance of Heaven" 1, temple of Nuska at Nippur (Proto-*Kagal* 218b?; CTL 103; *Topog. Texts* no. 19 = Nippur TL 17′–19′), also known from liturgical texts (Maul, *Eršaḫunga* nos. 35, obv. 5; 113, 5). The temple of Nuska at Nippur is listed without name in a MB metrological text (Bernhardt and Kramer, *OrNS* 44 [1975], p. 98, 21). See also é.me.lám.ḫuš 1.

764 **é.me.lám.an.na** 2, temple of Nuska in Ḫarrān, rebuilt by Aššurbanipal (Bauer, *Asb.*, pp. 36–40, passim; Thompson, *Prisms*, p. 32, 49; Streck, *Asb.*, p. 150, 66; etc.).

765 **é.me.lám.an.na** 3, ziqqurrat of Anu at Aššur (*Topog. Texts* no. 20 = Götteradreßbuch 187: Assyrian TL). The ziqqurrats of the double temple of Anu and Adad at Aššur were built by Šamšī-Adad I and restored by an unidentified king (Grayson, *RIMA* 1, p. 81, ii′ 2, no TNs: Šamšī-Adad III or Aššur-rēša-iši I?), and rebuilt by Tiglath-pileser I (*RIMA* 2, p. 28, 87: no TNs). See also é.me.lam.an.na.

766 **é.me.lám.bi.kur.kur.ra.(a).dul$_5$**, "House whose Radiance Covers the Lands," name or epithet of the temple of an.ta.sur.ra in inscriptions of Enmetena (Steible, *FAOS* 5/I, Ent 8, vi 2; 23, 40), and of the Chariot

House (of é.ninnu at G̃irsu?) in an inscription of Uruinimgina (ibid., Ukg. 10, ii 4; cf. 11, 40).

767 **é.me.lám.ḫuš**, "House of Awesome Radiance" 1, temple of Nuska at Nippur (*MSL* XI, p. 142, viii 16; Proto-*Kagal* 191.218c?; CTL 104; Temple Hymns 48; *An* I: *CT* 24 24, 64; Sjöberg, *JAOS* 93 [1973], p. 352, 9: Hymn to Sadarnunna), also occupied by his agent Girra (CTL 108; bilingual prayer to Girra, *MDP* 57, p. 41, ii 30′; cf. p. 49, but in ii 31′ read [*é-me*]-*lé-em-ḫu-*⌜*uš*⌝: Moran, private communication). See also é.me.lám.an.na 1.

768 **é.me.lám.ḫuš** 2, a shrine in é.sag̃.íl at Babylon (*Topog. Texts* no. 1 = *Tintir* II 12′).

769 **é.me.lám.ḫuš** 3, seat of Lugalirra and Meslamtaea in é.rab.ri.ri (at Babylon? *Topog. Texts* no. 12, 15′).

770 **é.me.lám.kur.kur.ra**, "House of the Radiance of the Lands," name or epithet of the Chariot-House (of é.ninnu at G̃irsu?) in an inscription of Uruinimgina (Steible, *FAOS* 5/I, Ukg 11, 40). Variant of é.me.lám.bi.kur. kur.ra.(a).dul$_5$.

771 **é.me.lám.ma**, "House of Radiance," a shrine in é.sag̃.íl at Babylon (*Topog. Texts* no. 1 = *Tintir* II 13′).

772 **é.me.lám.maḫ**, "House of Exalted Radiance," ziqqurrat of Enlil at Ḫursag̃-kalamma (TL no. 4, 14; no. 5, 12′; no. 6, [17]). Probably one should restore é.me.lám.[maḫ] in a temple list of Kiš (*Topog. Texts* no. 23, 18′).

773 **é.me.lám.su.lim.gùr.ru**, "House Clad in Fearsome Radiance," temple of Meslamtaea (at Ur? CTL 578; *Topog. Texts* no. 26 A).

774 **é.me.nu.è**, "House of the *Me*'s which do not Leave," shrine of Ištar at Nineveh, in the immediate vicinity of é.maš.maš, rebuilt by Šamšī-Adad I (Grayson, *RIMA* 1, p. 53, i 7), who reports a previous building by Maništūšu.

775 **é.me.sì.(ga).kalam.ma.šár.ra**, "House of All the Given *Me*'s of the Land," temple of Anunnîtum at Babylon (*Topog. Texts* no. 1 = *Tintir* IV 14; variant of é.sag̃.g̃á.šár.ra).

776 **é.me.sikil.(la)**, "House of Pure *Me*'s" 1, temple of Amurru (CTL 472; *MSL* XI, p. 142, viii 35–36: é.me.sikil, é.me.sikil.la), rebuilt by Damiq-ilīšu (Frayne, *RIME* 4, p. 104, 19; qualified as é.šútum ki.ág̃.g̃á.ni, "his beloved storeroom"). Possibly = é.me.sikil.la 2 (or at Isin? Renger, *Studien Falkenstein*, pp. 142f.).

777 **é.me.sikil.la** 2, temple of Amurru in west Babylon (*Topog. Texts* nos. 1 = *Tintir* IV 37, var. é.maḫ; 3, rev. 17′; 38, 31).

778 **é.me.te**, "Worthy House," TN or epithet of a sanctuary of Enki (Cohen, *Lamentations*, p. 78, 82).

779 **é.me.te.ba.la.aš.é.gi$_4$.a.g̃ál.la.(na)**, "House, Worthy of Office, Provided with a Bride," sanctuary of Aššur and Šerua mentioned in the syncretistic hymn to Nanāy (Reiner, *JNES* 33 [1974], p. 230, 17).

780 **é.me.te.è**, "House, Fitting for Coming Forth," a sanctuary of Šamaš (CTL 287).

781 **é.me.te.ì.nun.ga.àra**, "House, Fitting for Ghee and Cheese," by-name or epithet of é.g̃á.nun.maḫ 1.

782 **é.me.te.ir$_9$.ra**, "House, Worthy of the Mighty One," temple of Nergal (at Uruk?), rebuilt by Kudur-Mabuk (Frayne, *RIME* 4, p. 206, 23). Also known to the big forerunner of *Hh* XXI (*MSL* XI, p. 142, viii 32). See also é.kù.ga.

783 **é.me.te.nu.g̃ál**, "House, Worthy of Light," seat of Dipar in a window of é.šár.ra at Aššur (*Topog. Texts* no. 21, obv. 6′).

784 **é.me.te.nun.e**, "House, Worthy of the Prince," temple (of Tešub?) at Kaḫat, known from an OB metrological text, = *bītum sí-ma-at ru-bi-a-am* (sic! Charpin, *MARI* I, p. 139, 27). Probably this is the unnamed temple of Adad at $^{uru}$*ka*$^?$*-ḫat* built by Shalmaneser I (Grayson, *RIMA* 1, p. 204, 15′).

785 **é.me.te.ur.sag̃**, "House, Worthy of the Hero" 1, cella of Zababa in é.dub.ba at Kiš (*Topog. Texts* no. 22, 5′; *PBS* XV 79, iii 74: Nebuchadnezzar II), though in earlier times the TN is used for the temple as a whole (as p. 4, IM 96881, iii′ 6′; CTL 479; cf. McEwan, *Iraq* 45 [1983], p. 119). Rebuilt by Sūmû-la-El (year 30) and Ḫammurapi (Frayne, *RIME* 4, pp. 343, 6; 344, 8; year 36; cf. CḪ ii 62), and probably Kurigalzu (Walker, *CBI* no. 70; no TN), repaired by Adad-apla-iddina (ibid., no. 72). Patronized by Ammī-ditāna (year 34) and Ammī-ṣaduqa (year 15). Paired with é.dub.ba in the Syncretistic Ištar Hymn (l. 68; unpub., courtesy Lambert). Mentioned in a *lipšur*-litany (Nougayrol, *JCS* 1 [1947], p. 330, 16′ b // Wiseman, *Iraq* 31 [1969], p. 177, 28′). Commonly found in the standard litany of TNs of Ninurta in liturgical texts, usually following é.dub.ba (Cohen, *Lamentations*, index p. 751; *Eršemma*, pp. 143, 5; 145, 10; Maul, *Eršaḫunga* no. 37, 9; *OrNS* 60 [1991], p. 314, 24: eršemma; *CT* 42 12, pl. 22, 7; MacMillan, *BA* V/5 6, rev. 15; etc.).

786 **é.me.te.[ur.sag̃?]** 2, a temple of Panig̃ing̃arra (CTL 165).

787 **é.me.ur.an.na**, see é.me.ur$_4$.an.na

788 **é.me.ur$_4$**, "House which Gathers the *Me*'s," two sanctuaries of Ištar listed separately in the Canonical Temple List (lines 349.396), the second probably at Mari: see é.me.ur$_4$.ur$_4$ 4.

789 **é.me.ur$_4$.an.na**, "House which Gathers the *Me*'s of Heaven," shrine of Ninurta in é.šu.me.ša$_4$ at Nippur (p. 4, IM 96881, ii′ 12′; *Kagal* Boğ. I F 8, = *bi-it ki-ra-a*; Temple Hymns 61, var. é.me.ur.an.na). Often appears in the standard litany of TNs of Ninurta in liturgical texts, between é.šà.maḫ and é.i.bí.šu.galam (Maul, *Eršaḫunga* no. 31 + K 17441, 8: é.mur.ra.na; *OrNS* 60 [1991], p. 314, 12: eršemma; Cohen, *Lamentations*, pp. 458, 10; 461, 85: é.ur$_4$!.ra.an.na (coll.); 469, 10; see also é.ḫur.sag̃.an.na).

790 **me.ur$_4$.g̃iš.**DU, seat of the Anunnaki in é.šár.ra at Aššur (*Topog. Texts* no. 21, obv. 26′).

791 **é.me.ur$_4$.imin.an.ki**, see é.ur$_4$.me.imin.an.ki

792 **é.me.ur$_4$.ur$_4$**, "House which Gathers the *Me*'s" 1, temple of Ištar at Larsa (éš.dam hymns: Wilcke, *RlA* V, p. 78), rebuilt by Gungunum (year 16, no TN), and by Kudur-Mabuk and Rīm-Sîn I (Frayne, *RIME* 4, pp. 273, 14; 303, 27; cf. R-S year 4, which records the building at Larsa of temples of Ištar, Sîn and Ea). Its main outer gate was provided with statues of lions by Sūmû-El (year 4, no TN). Note dual entries for this TN in the temple lists (*MSL* XI, p. 142, vii 27–28; CTL 348: Ištar; 435: Nanāy?).

793 **é.me.ur$_4$.ur$_4$** 2, temple of Nanāy, apparently at Uruk, rebuilt by Sîn-gāmil (Frayne, *RIME* 4, p. 466, 9) and restored by Anam (Falkenstein, *Bagh. Mitt.* 2 [1963], p. 80, 22.28: Anam Hymn). Probably part of é.an.na 1.

794 **é.me.ur$_4$.ur$_4$** 3, temple of Nanāy at Babylon (*Topog. Texts* nos. 1 = *Tintir* IV 30; 3, rev. 10′; 4, 30; 38, 35). Also found in an offering calendar (*BRM* IV 25, 48 // *SBH* VII, obv. 24), and an unpublished temple ritual (BM 32656, iv 3′).

795 **é.me.ur$_4$.ur$_4$** 4, temple of Ištar at Mari or Aššur, = *bītum muḫammim parṣī* (Charpin, *MARI* 3, p. 46, 16: Šamšī-Adad I). Cf. é.me.(dinanna), é.me.ur$_4$, é.ur$_4$.ur$_4$, é.gùn.a.

796 **é.me.zi.da**, "House of True *Me*'s," a sanctuary of Ea (Proto-*Kagal* 174; CTL 200?, at Adab?), built by Enlil-bāni (year i).

797 **é.mè.a**, "House of Combat," temple of Inanna at gù.dam[ki] according to two éš.dam hymns (Wilcke, *RlA* V, p. 78). Note also é.mè-(ak) in Inanna and Ebiḫ 131 (Limet, *OrNS* 40 [1971], p. 15, 9).

798 **é.men.gal**, "House of the Great Crown," part or epithet of the temple of Keš (Keš Temple Hymn 33).

799 **é.mes**, "House of the Warrior" 1, temple of Lil, the son of Bēlet-ilī (CTL 169), already known to the big OB forerunner to *Hh* XXI (*MSL* XI, p. 142, vii 34).

800 **é.mes** 2, a sanctuary of Marduk (CTL 230).

801 **é.mes.i.i.ki.šár.ra**, "House which Sends the Warrior Forth, of the Universe," variant or alternative name of é.šid.dù.ki.šár.ra.

802 **é.mes.lam** (or é.mèš.lam), "House, Warrior of the Netherworld" 1, temple of Nergal (as Erra, Meslamtaea, etc.) at Kutha (Proto-*Kagal* 214; *MSL* XI, p. 142, vii 35; CTL [564]; TL no. 2, [11]; no. 6, 20), rebuilt by Šulgi (Steible, *FAOS* 9/II, Š 4a-b), Apil-Sîn (year 6f.; cf. Sîn-muballiṭ year 16) and Ḫammurapi (year 40, = Akk. *šanat mi-iš-la-mi*: Stol, *OB History*, p. 33; cf. CḪ iii 6; Frayne, *RIME* 4, pp. 346, 33; 811, 8′?), restored by Aššurbanipal (Streck, *Asb.*, p. 186, 24; Nassouhi, *AfK* 2 [1924–25], p. 100, i 13; etc.), and Nebuchadnezzar II (*PBS* XV 79, ii 85–86; etc.). Still functioning in the Seleucid period (Grayson, *Chronicles*, p. 117, 5). Sumerian literature: van Dijk, *Götterlieder* II, p. 13, 19: cult-song to Nergal for Šulgi;

Sjöberg, *ZA* 63 [1973], p. 5, 66: ditto for Šu-ilīšu; *TCL* XVI 46, 17 // *OECT* V 25, 108: literary letter to Rīm-Sîn I. Mentioned in the Syncretistic Ištar Hymn (l. 77; unpub., courtesy Lambert), and in a *lipšur*-litany (Wiseman, *Iraq* 31 [1969], p. 177, 36′). Also in liturgical texts, commonly in the standard litany of TNs of Ninurta, following Kutha (Cohen, *Lamentations*, index p. 751; Maul, *Eršaḫunga* nos. 34, 6; 37, 13; *OrNS* 60 [1991], p. 315, 26: eršemma; *VAS* 24 30, rev. 8′; also Pallis, *Akîtu*, pl. 11, 25; etc.).

803 **(é).mes.lam** 2, temple (of Nergal?) at Maškan-šāpir, patronized by Ḫammurapi (CḪ iv 6).

804 **é.mes.lam** 3, temple of the Divine Twins (diĝir.min.a.bi, i.e., Meslamtaea and Lugalirra) at Dūrum near Uruk (Hallo, *Études Garelli*, p. 386, 53, cf. pp. 379f.; literary letter of Sîn-kāšid's daughter Ninšatapadda to Rīm-Sîn I). Either an abbreviation of é.mes.lam.me.lám.íl.la, or a name for the whole temple complex.

805 ***é.mes.lam** 4, temple of Nergal at Tarbiṣu, built by Sennacherib (III *R* 3, no. 13: é.lam.mes; I *R* 7, no. 8 C-D: é.gal.lam.mes), and provided with a standard by Aššurbanipal (Thompson, *Prisms*, pl. 15, ii 27: é.galam.me[s]; cf. Pinches, *Wedge-Writing*, p. 17, 10: no TN).

806 **é.mes.lam.me.lám.íl.(la)**, "E-meslam which Bears Radiance," temple of Meslamtaea of Dūrum near Uruk, rebuilt by Sîn-kāšid (Frayne, *RIME* 4, p. 462, 8–9; cf. year a: mu BÀD.(AN)$^{ki}$). Listed in the big OB forerunner to *Hh* XXI (*MSL* XI, p. 142, vii 36). In *Kagal* Boğ. I G 5–6 the TN, rendered [e-m]i-iš-lam-mi*-šu-zi-ra-an-ni (= TN+ani? cf. Moran, *JCS* 26 [1974], pp. 55[1], 57f., who interprets it as é.mes.lam + *šu-ṣí-ra-an-ni*), has been corrupted with its twin temple (l. 7), é.ní.ḫuš.gùru.su.zi.íl.la of Lugalirra. See also é.mes.lam 3.

807 **é.mes.lam.ní.gùr.ru**, "E-meslam which is Clad in Terror," temple of Uqur at Ĝirsu (CTL 576).

808 **é.mes.mes**, see é.maš.maš

809 **é.MI(gi$_6$?).ḫal.la.ke$_4$/ka**, a temple at Uruk known only from the city quarter *erṣet* é.TN (Falkenstein, *Topographie*, pp. 51f.). Cf. é.gal.ḫal.ḫal, é.IG.ḫal.an.ki.

810 **é.mi.tum.ma.al**, "Harem(?), Tummal," shrine of Ninlil at Nippur (CTL [58]). Occurs in liturgical texts in the standard litany of TNs of Nippur (Cohen, *Lamentations*, pp. 178, 40; 391, 180; V *R* 52, no. 2, obv. 52 // *KAR* 375, ii 58; etc.). Also Hymn to the Mattock 39 (var. a.mi . . . ).

811 **é.mu.maḫ**, "House of the Exalted Name," part or by-name of é.ḫur.saĝ of Šulgi (Temple Hymns 119), listed twice in the big OB forerunner to *Hh* XXI (*MSL* XI, p. 142, viii 18.20).

812 **é.mu.pàd.da**, "House Chosen by Name," a temple of Ninurta and Gula at Ḫilpu on the Euphrates, known from two votive inscriptions of a Kassite period priest (Sollberger, *JAOS* 88 [1968], pp. 192f.)

813 **é.mu.ri.a.na.ba.AK**, sanctuary of Nanna at Ur, rebuilt by Šu-Suen (Steible, *FAOS* 9/II, ŠS 7). Cf. Brinkman, *OrNS* 38 (1969), p. 316[4]; Edzard and Farber, *Rép. géogr.* II, p. 134.

814 **é.mu.uš.túg.šu.du$_7$**, see é.g̃éštu.šu.du$_7$

815 **é.mud.kalam.ma**, "House, Creator of the Land," variant of é.mud.kur.ra in Inanna's Descent 49.

816 **é.mud.kur.ra**, "House, Creator of the Mountain Lands," shrine, perhaps the cella, of Sîn in é.kiš.nu.g̃ál at Ur (Hallo, *JCS* 20 [1966], p. 139, 14; Sjöberg, *ZA* 63 [1973], p. 37, [24].28.32: song to Suen; Inanna's Descent 49.193); rebuilt by Rīm-Sîn II (year A). This or the previous entry can be restored among TNs of Sîn in a liturgical text (*BL* no. 27, 9′: še.eb é.mud. [. . . ]).

817 **é.mul**, "House of the Star," a sanctuary of Nabû (CTL 242).

818 **é.mul.ág̃**, TN or epithet known from OB lists (Proto-*Kagal* 221; *MSL* XI, p. 142, viii 14). Its position in Proto-*Kagal*, between sections on Šamaš and Nissaba, encourages comparison with é.mul.mul, and therefore attribution to Nissaba.

819 **é.mul.ág̃.gùn.a**, TN or epithet known from the big OB forerunner to *Hh* XXI (*MSL* XI, p. 142, viii 15).

820 **é.mul.mul**, "House of Stars," temple of Nissaba at Ereš (Temple Hymns 529). See also é.za.gìn 3.

821 **[é.(x).mul.m]ul**, a sanctuary of Ea (CTL 201).

822 **munsub.è**, "(House where) the Shepherd Comes Forth," seat of Dumuzi in é.šár.ra at Aššur (*Topog. Texts* no. 21, obv. 36′; first sign glossed mu-un-ṣu-ub). The translation rests on the equations $^{\text{mu-su-ub}}$mùnsub = *re-é-um* (*MSL* III, p. 151, S$^{b}$ B 366) and $^{\text{su-ub}}$sùb *šá* mu$_6$.sùb = *r.* (XIV, p. 491, A VIII/1 82). The word munsub is presumably a compound of mu$_6$ (or mua), "young man," and su$_8$.ba, "shepherd," and so in this usage is better read musub, with the lexical glosses.

823 **é.munus.gi$_{16}$.sa**, "House of the Bejewelled Woman," temple of Ninmar at G̃irsu (Falkenstein, *AnOr* 30, pp. 153f.; Gelb, *StOr* 46 [1975], pp. 47f., i 11; ii 3.52; *MVN* VI 93, rev. 6; 198, obv. 3: granary; etc.), rebuilt by Ur-Ning̃irsu I (Steible, *FAOS* 9/I, UrN I 4; cf. also Gud. Stat. R, iv 3), and Šulgi (Steible, *FAOS* 9/II, Š 21; 24; cf. 26, ii 11). Steible places Ur-Ning̃irsu I's foundation in Guabba, without further explanation (*FAOS* 9/I, p. 127).

824 **é.mur.ra.na**, see é.me.ur$_4$.an.na

825 **é.MURUB$_4$**, see é.gu.la 7

826 **é.múš**, see é.mùš

827 **é.múš.za.gìn.na**, "House, Foundation of Lapis Lazuli," a sanctuary of Dumuzi (CTL 442). Also appears in the syncretistic Hymn to Borsippa (BM, unpub.).

828 **é.múš.[ . . . ]**, a temple at Kiš (*Topog. Texts* no. 23, 14′).

829 **é.mùš.(kalam.ma)**, also é.múš.(kalam.ma), "House, Foundation (of the Land)," temple of Dumuzi (CTL 440), as Lugal-Emuš, and Inanna, and also of Lulal, in Bad-tibira (Temple Hymns 213); note in OS lugal é.mùš $^{d}$ama.ušum.gal (Westenholz, *OSP* I 3, ii′ 3–4). Rebuilt by Enmetena, with the help of Lugalkinešdudu of Uruk (Steible, *FAOS* 5/I, Ent 45–74; 79, iv 8). Common in liturgical and Dumuzi texts (Cohen, *Eršemma*, pp. 63, 4; 79, 113; 90, 12; *Lamentations*, pp. 194, 26; 611, 101: é.múš?; *VAS* X 123, rev. i 10; etc.). The fuller version of the TN is found in lists (*MSL* XI, p. 142, viii 23: OB forerunner to *Hh* XXI; CTL 441: múš), Inanna's Descent and the éš.dam hymns (Wilcke, *RlA* V, p. 78), and other literarature (Sjöberg, *TCS* III, p. 95; *JCS* 40 [1988], p. 168, ii 12: muš; note *VAS* II 1, iii 12: e-mu-uš$^{!}$-ka-na-ma; Langdon, *BL* no. 8, obv. 13: é.umuš.ka.nağ.ğá; etc.).

830 **é.múštug.maḫ.šu.du$_7$**, "House of Perfect Sublime Wisdom," a temple of Ea (Maul, *Eršaḫunga* no. 10, 7). Emesal version of é.ğéštu.maḫ.šu.du$_7$.

831 **é.na.ám.tar.ra**, "House which Determines Destinies," part of é.an.na at Uruk or an epithet of its gate ká.maḫ (Cohen, *Eršemma*, p. 66, 19).

832 **é.nam.BAD** = é.nam.til, a variant of é.nam.ti.la.

833 **é.nam.bára.nun.na**, "House of Responsibility, Princely Dais," sanctuary of Gula (at Isin?), as found in a cultic lament (Cohen, *Lamentations*, p. 256, 52, qualified as ki.ús.sa).

834 **é.nam.bi.zi.da**, "House whose Destiny is True," a temple of Nabû (CTL 237), also known from one of the standard litanies of TNs in liturgical texts, in which it is paired with é.ur$_4$.me.imin.an.ki (Cohen, *Lamentations*, index p. 751; Meek, *BA* X/1 10, rev. 10; Langdon, *BL* nos. 26, 3′; 56, obv. 19: é.nam.bi.é.zi.da; George, *RA* 82 [1988], p. 159, 37; etc.).

835 **é.nam.du.du**, sanctuary(?) known from an Ur III document (*MVN* VI 142, rev. 10).

836 **é.nam.en.ğar.ra**, "House which Establishes Dominion," a sanctuary of Ninimma (CTL 110), probably a variant of é.nam.me.ğar.ra. Restored by Moran in *Kagal* Boğ. I G 4, reading [é.TN = e-na-am]-in-ga-ra = *bi-it ni-im-ni-m*[*a*] (*JCS* 26 [1974], p. 58[9]).

837 **é.nam.en.na**, "House of Dominion" 1, cella (*papāḫu*) of Anu in the *bīt rēš* at Uruk (*YOS* I 52: Anu-uballiṭ; *BRM* IV 7, 1: New Year festival; cf. Falkenstein, *Topographie*, pp. 18ff.), also known from a liturgical hymn to Anu (Cohen, *Lamentations*, p. 729, 7).

838 **é.nam.en.na** 2, shrine in or epithet of é.rab.ri.ri in a cultic lament (Cohen, *Lamentations*, p. 256, 42).

839 **é.nam.ḫé**, "House of Plenty" 1, temple of Adad in Babylon (*Topog. Texts* nos. 1 = *Tintir* IV 40, var. é.nam.maḫ; 38, 28: NB document; 39, ii b 4; 40, 8′: ritual; *KAR* 109, obv. 19: syncretistic Ištar hymn; *BRM* IV 25, 6: offering calendar), sometimes written é.nam.maḫ (e.g., *VAS* 24 110,

rev. 12′: ritual; also below). Rebuilt by Sūmû-la-El (year 7ff.; no TN), Ḫammurapi (year 28), and Nebuchadnezzar II (V *R* 34, ii 8; etc.). Patronized by Samsu-iluna (year 27, no TN), Abī-ešuḫ (year aa) and Ammī-ṣaduqa (year 13), known to Nebuchadnezzar I (Böhl, *BiOr* 7 [1950], p. 43, 11). Seat of the Asakku demon opposite TN: *KAR* 142, ii 6 (EN.nam.ḫé). Also in liturgical texts, usually following é.u$_4$.gal.gal.la in the standard litany of TNs of Adad (Maul, *Eršaḫunga* nos. 18, 8; 19–20, 8; 21, 8; Cohen, *Lamentations*, pp. 431; 42; 433, 94: é.nam.ḫé, coll.; 434, 115) or, as é.nam. maḫ, between é.di.ku$_5$.kalam.ma and é.rab.ri.ri (ibid., pp. 242, 380 = 311, 254; also p. 434, 111; Craig, *ABRT* I 58, 23). See *Topog. Texts*, pp. 329f. See also é.ki. tuš.ḫé. g̃ál.ti.la.

840 **é.nam.ḫé** 2, temple of Adad and Apladad at Anat, rebuilt by Ninurta-kudurrī-uṣur (Cavigneaux and Bahija Khalil Ismail, *Bagh. Mitt.* 21 [1990], p. 341, 8; cf. p. 345, 28), who reports the earlier patronage of the cult of Adad at Anat by Ḫammurapi of Babylon (ibid., p. 393, 7).

841 **é$^?$.nam.ḫé.**PAP.TIN$^?$**.dili.na**, a shrine in é.sag̃.íl at Babylon (*Topog. Texts* no. 1 = *Tintir* II 48).

842 **é.nam.ḫé.[ . . . ]**, sanctuaries of members of Adad's court (CTL 309–11).

843 **é.nam.maḫ**, "House of Loftiness," variant orthography for é.nam.ḫé.

844 **é.nam.me.g̃ar.ra**, TN or epithet known from Proto-*Kagal* 201. Probably = é.nam.en.g̃ar.ra of Ninimma.

845 **é.nam.nun.na**, "House of Princeliness," sanctuary of Nanna-Suen (at Ur?), rebuilt by Sîn-iddinam (Frayne, *RIME* 4, p. 172, 28).

846 **é.nam.tag.ga.duḫ.a**, "House which Undoes Guilt," temple of Amurru (CTL 473) in east Babylon (*Topog. Texts* no. 1 = *Tintir* IV 6); cult-statue renewed by Esarhaddon (Borger, *Esarh.*, § 53, rev. 40). Mentioned in the eršaḫung̃a to Amurru (Maul, *Eršaḫunga* no. 29, 9).

847 **é.nam.tar.kalam.ma**, "House of the Destinies of the Land," a sanctuary of Šamaš (CTL 285).

848 **é.nam.ti.la**, "House of Life" 1, sanctuary of Enlil (*Kagal* Boğ. I E 15), probably in é.kur 1 (cf. èš nam.ti.la as an epithet of é.kur in Rīm-Sîn I year 23), commonly found in liturgical texts in the standard litany of TNs of Nippur following é.kur, ki.ùr, etc. (Cohen, *Eršemma*, p. 113, 18; 118, 35.2:5; 127, 9; *Lamentations*, passim: index p. 751; V *R* 52, no. 2, obv. 51; also Craig, *ABRT* I 58, 23, = é.TN 2?). Elsewhere in Sumerian literature: Winter and Summer 67–68: *ISET* II pl. 67, ii′ 15′.18′; Römer, *Königshymnen*, pp. 54, Enlil-diriše 284; 237, 34: hymn to Baba for Išme-Dagān; Sjöberg, *JCS* 34 [1982], p. 75, 24: royal hymn; etc.

849 **é.nam.ti.la** 2, temple of Enlil as Bēl-mātāti at Babylon (*Topog. Texts* nos. 1 = *Tintir* IV 34; V 100, var. é.nam.til; 3, rev. 13′–14′; 4, 34; 38, 25: NB document; 40, 7′: ritual). Mentioned in the Syncretistic Ištar Hymn (*KAR* 109, obv. 18). Provided with a warehouse by Ḫammurapi (Frayne, *RIME*

4, p. 337, 24; cf. year 18). Patronized by Ammī-ditāna (years 19.28.34; cf. 31: throne of Ninurta), Ammī-ṣaduqa (years 5.8.14) and Samsu-ditāna (year 8, no TN), probably also Burnaburiaš (Arnaud, *Sumer* 32 [1976], p. 101, 10). See *Topog. Texts*, pp. 325f. See also é.kur 3.

850 **é.nam.ti.la** 3, temple, apparently of Ea and Damkina (at Malgium?), surrounded with an abutment wall by Takil-ilissu (Frayne, *RIME* 4, p. 671, 12; also p. 670, 17: Ipiq-Ištar).

851 **é.nam.ti.la** 4, part or by-name of é.sa.bad of Gula at Aššur (*Topog. Texts* no. 20 = Götteradreßbuch 176: Assyrian TL).

852 **[é].nam.ti.la** 5, possibly a temple of Šimaliya in the syncretistic hymn to Nanāy (Reiner, *JNES* 33 [1974], p. 230, 12).

853 **é.nam.ti.la** 6, a sanctuary of Marduk (CTL 233).

854 **é.nam.ti.la** 7, by-name of é.ḫur.sag̃ 2.

855 **é.nam.zu**, "House of Knowledge," temple of Bēlet-ilī at Adab (TL no. 3, 26′; Syncretistic Ištar Hymn: *KAR* 109, rev. 12), mentioned in a *lipšur*-litany (Wiseman, *Iraq* 31 [1969], p. 177, 44′), also repeatedly in the Lugalannemundu text (Güterbock, *ZA* 42 [1934], pp. 41, A ii 25.28; 42, A iii 33′; 43, A iv 31′).

856 **ne.sag̃.maḫ**, see é.nisag̃.maḫ

857 **ni-da-naNÍG̃.ZU.g̃éštu**, "(House of) Learning and Understanding," seat of Ninimma in the library of é.šár.ra at Aššur (*Topog. Texts* no. 21, obv. 27′; rev. 30′).

858 **é.NI.gu.la**, see é.a.mir.kù

859 **é.ní.dúb.bu**, "House which Gives Rest," temple of Nintinugga (at Isin?), rebuilt by Enlil-bāni (Frayne, *RIME* 4, p. 83, 10).

860 **é.ní.gal.abzu**, "House of the Awesome Splendour of *Apsû*," a sanctuary (at Nippur?), mentioned in the Syncretistic Ištar Hymn (l. 101; unpub., courtesy Lambert).

861 **é.ní.gal.kur.kur.ra.dir.dir.ra**, "House whose Awesome Splendour Fills the Mountain Lands," temple of Adad as Bēl of Zabban (*Topog. Texts* no. 20 = Götteradreßbuch 183: Assyrian TL).

862 **é.ní.gal.kur.kur.ra.dul.la**, "House whose Awesome Splendour Covers the Mountain Lands" 1, temple of Adad at Dunnu (TL no. 3, 34′).

863 **é.ní.gal.kur.kur.ra.dul$_6$.la** 2, a temple at Zabban (*Topog. Texts* no. 20 = Götteradreßbuch 184: Assyrian TL), no doubt of Adad.

864 **é.ní.gal.su.lim.gùr.ru**, "House Clad in Awesome Splendour and Radiance," a temple of Ištar (CTL 397).

865 **é.ní.gùr.(ru)**, "House Clad in Terror" 1, dais (at Nippur?) on which Išme-Dagān erected a statue of himself (Frayne, *RIME* 4, p. 37, 26, qualified as bára.kal.kal.la, "most precious dais"). A sanctuary of this name is

associated with gašan nibru$^{ki}$, i.e., Ištar as Queen of Nippur, in a liturgical text (IV *R*$^2$ 27, no. 4, 61–62; cf. Moran, *Kramer AV*, p. 337[16]).

866 **é.ní.gùr.ru** 2, a temple of Paniĝinĝarra (CTL 167).

867 **é.ní.ḫur.saĝ**, see é.IM.ḫur.saĝ

868 **é.ní.ḫuš.gùru.su.[lim/ši].íl.la.ni**, "House Clad in Awesome Terror, Bearing Radiance," a temple known from the big OB forerunner to *Hh* XXI (*MSL* XI, p. 142, vii 37, coll. Moran, *JCS* 26 [1974], p. 55[2]: the missing sign is too short to be zi). Nevertheless, probably no more than a variation on é.ní.ḫuš.gùru.su.zi.íl.(la).

869 **é.ní.ḫuš.gùru.su.zi.íl.(la)**, "House Clad in Awesome Terror, Bearing Radiance," temple of Lugalirra of Dūrum near Uruk, rebuilt by Sîn-kāšid (Frayne, *RIME* 4, p. 460, 8–9; cf. year a?). In *Kagal* Boğ. I G 7–8: [e]-⌜x⌝-ḫu-uš-kur-ra-šu-zi-ra-an-ni = TN+ani? (cf. Moran, *JCS* 26 [1974], pp. 57f., explaining the TN as é.ní.ḫuš.gùru + *šu-ṣí-ra-an-ni*). See also the twin temple, é.mes.lam.me.lám.íl.la of Meslamtaea.

870 **é.ní.te.en.du$_{10}$**, also é.ní.te.en.na, "House of (Pleasant) Rest," temple of Sîn in east Babylon (*Topog. Texts* no. 1 = *Tintir* IV 9), patronized by Ammī-ditāna (year 30), Ammī-ṣaduqa (year 17, where it is also é.maḫ) and Samsu-ditāna (year d). Appears among other sanctuaries of Sîn in liturgical texts (Cohen, *Lamentations*, pp. 149, 197; 211, 77; 242, 376 = 311, 250; Langdon, *BL* nos. 27, 6′; 156, 5; Craig, *ABRT* I 58, 20). Probably listed in *Kagal* Boğ. I F 23: [é.TN = e-ni-te]-ed-du = *bi-it ši-i-in.*

871 **é.ní.te.ḫur.saĝ**, "House of Fear of the Mountain," a shrine of Enlil (CTL 42), probably = é.IM.ḫur.saĝ.

872 **ni$_9$...**, see nìĝin ...

873 **é.nidba.níĝ.kur$_4$.ra**, "House of Sumptuous Food Offerings," a shrine in é.šár.ra at Aššur (*Topog. Texts* no. 21, rev. 3′).

874 **é.níĝ.érim.ḫul.e.dè**, "Houses which Destroys Evil," seat of Ninurta's weapon Kurzigimmumu in é.saĝ.íl at Babylon (*Topog. Texts* no. 1 = *Tintir* II 26; royal ritual: K 3446+, rev. 4: ibid., p. 276).

875 **é.níĝ.érim.nu.dib**, "House which Lets not Evil Pass," socle of Madānu in the Grand Court of é.saĝ.íl at Babylon (*Topog. Texts* no. 1 = *Tintir* II 31′).

876 **é.níĝ.érim.nu.si.sá**, "House which Lets not Evil Flourish," socle of Nergal in the Grand Court of é.saĝ.íl at Babylon (*Topog. Texts* no. 1 = *Tintir* II 32′).

877 **é.níĝ.gi.na**, "House of Truth," temple of Ninĝišzida at Ur, rebuilt by Sîn-iqīšam (Frayne, *RIME* 4, p. 196, 8) and Rīm-Sîn I (ibid., p. 285, 41).

878 **é.($^{ĝiš}$níĝ).ĝidar.kalam.ma.sum.ma**, "House which Bestows the Sceptre of the Land" 1, temple of Nabû of the *ḫarû* in east Babylon (*Topog. Texts* no. 1 = *Tintir* IV 15; CTL 238: é.ĝidru.kalam.ma.sum.mu), rebuilt by

Nebuchadnezzar II (V *R* 34, ii 7; etc.). Included a chapel of Tašmētum (Messerschmidt, *MVAG* I/1, p. 78, vii 23: Nabonidus). Mentioned during the reign of Simbar-šipak by the Religious Chronicle, and visited by Cambyses when crown-prince (Grayson, *Chronicles*, pp. 111, 25; 135, 10). For the TN in colophons and its identification with the excavated temple D I see Cavigneaux, *Sumer* 37 (1981), pp. 118–26; George, *Sumer* 44 (1985–86), pp. 12ff. See *Topog. Texts*, pp. 310–12.

879 **é.(gišníĝ).ĝidar.kalam.ma.sum.ma** 2, see é.ĝidru.kalam.ma.sum.mu

880 **é.níĝ.gùr.ru.kalam.ma**, a variant or corruption of é.kalam.ta.ní.gùr.ru in the sixth year name of Warad-Sîn (*UET* V 300, rev. 9).

881 **é.níĝ.ki.šár**, temple(?) mentioned in an Ur III document (Schollmeyer, *MAOG* 4 [1928–29], p. 188, rev. 5).

882 **é.níĝ.lu.lu**, "House of Teeming Flocks," a temple of Ninĝeštinanna (CTL 463), and Dumuzi (CTL 450).

883 **é.NÍĜ.lu.úb.a**, TN or epithet known from Proto-*Kagal* 199. Emend to é.ḫa!.lu.úb.a, "House of the *Ḫaluppu*-Tree"?

884 **é.níĝ.si.sá**, "House of Justice," a sanctuary(?) at Namkarum, "the pre-eminent place of the gods," built by Lipit-Ištar when he promulgated his law code (Frayne, *RIME* 4, p. 54, 20).

885 **é.nìĝin.ĝar.ra**, "House, Established Chamber" 1, temple of Ištar at Šuruppak (*MSL* XI, p. 142, vii 33; CTL 356), known as (é).nìĝin.ĝar.kù in Inanna's Descent and an éš.dam hymn (Wilcke, *RlA* V, p. 78). Note Ištar as gašan ( . . . ) nìĝin.mar.kù.ga // g[a.ša.a]n ni.èm.ĝar.kù.ga in a cultic lament (Cohen, *Lamentations*, pp. 656, 160; 661, 140′). On the epithet nìĝin.ĝar (which contracts to $ni_9$.ĝar or, better, $niĝ_6$.ĝar) used of other temples of Inanna see Krecher, *Kultlyrik*, pp. 128ff.; Sjöberg, *TCS* III, pp. 92f.; also Farber-Flügge, *Inanna und Enki*, pp. 28, 33; 56, 47. The contraction of the TN to é.$niĝ_6$.ĝar.ra perhaps accounts for the gloss é.nu.ĝálé.nìĝin.ĝar.ra èš.maḫ in a practice tablet (Gurney, *AAA* 22 [1935], pl. 14, K 3241, 8).

886 **é.nìĝin.ĝar.ra** 2, part of the sanctuary of Gula at Isin (Temple Hymns 388); Emesal form (é).nìĝin.mar.(ra) used in Sîn-iddinam's letter to Ninisinna (*OECT* V 30, 7, among temples of Larak), and in cultic laments (Cohen, *Lamentations*, pp. 255ff., 9.36.59, qualified as é $du_8$.$du_8$.a, "house of profusion"; 621, 319; Krecher, *Kultlyrik*, pp. 55, 29; 128f.).

887 **é.nìĝin.na**, "House of the Chamber," a shrine in é.saĝ.íl at Babylon (*Topog. Texts* no. 1 = *Tintir* II 6″).

888 **é.nim.ma**, "High House," a shrine mentioned in broken context by Enanedu, Warad-Sîn's sister (Frayne, *RIME* 4, p. 229, 16:10′). Possibly one should restore [dnin].é.nim.ma, whose chapel in a temple of Ninmar was built by Rīm-Sîn I (year 8). For é.TNki as an OB toponym see Stol, *OB History*, pp. 19f.

889 **é.nim.ma.an.kù**, "High House of Pure Heaven," a temple at Bubê near Dēr, dedicated to Ninurta or a similar deity (Anzû III 150).

890 **é.nim$_x$(NÌĞIN).mar.ra**, Emesal form of é.nìĝin.ĝar.ra.

891 **é.nin.bi.šè.túm**, "House Worthy of its Lady," a temple of Ninlil (at Ur?), rebuilt by Rīm-Sîn I (Frayne, *RIME* 4, p. 283, 40).

892 **é.nin.bi.túm**, "House Worthy of its Lady," a temple of Ninšubur (at Ur?), rebuilt by Rīm-Sîn I (Frayne, *RIME* 4, p. 282, 29). Possibly only an epithet of é.á.áĝ.ĝá.sum.mu.

893 **nin.ĝar**, see é.nin$_9$.e.ĝar.ra

894 **é.nin$_9$.e.ĝar.ra**, "House Founded by the Sister," a temple of Ninĝirsu at Sirara (Falkenstein, *AnOr* 30, p. 162), built by Ur-Nanše (nin.ĝar: Steible, *FAOS* 5/I, UrN 24, iv 1; 33, iv 1). The "twin" of é.šeš.šeš.e.ĝar.ra.

895 **é.ninda.ba.du$_8$.a**, "House where Bread Portions are Baked," sanctuary of Amurru at Aššur (*Topog. Texts* no. 20 = Götteradreßbuch 172: Assyrian TL), rebuilt by Tiglath-pileser I (Grayson, *RIMA* 2, p. 26, 87: no TN). Probably part of the temple complex of Gula (George, *Iraq* 50 [1988], pp. 32ff.).

896 **é.ninda.dù.a**, temple of Ištar at LIBIR.RA$^{ki}$ (CTL 382).

897 **é.ninnu**, "House of Fifty (White *Anzû*-Birds)," temple of Ninĝirsu at Ĝirsu (Proto-*Kagal* 202; above, p. 4, IM 96881, iii′ 3′; CTL [484]; Temple Hymns 240.261), full name é.ninnu.anzu$^{mušen}$.bábbar (Falkenstein, *AnOr* 30, pp. 116ff.). Built by Mesalim and Ur-Nanše (Steible, *FAOS* 5/I, UrN 2–17, etc., no TN; 5/II, p. 215, 4: no TN). Mentioned by Enannatum I (5/I, En I 18, 16; 19, 2), rebuilt by Enmetena (ibid., Ent 80; cf. 16, iv 8; 34, 19), Uru-inimgina (ibid., Ukg 1, iii 8′; 10, iv 8), Ur-Baba (9/I, UrB 1, iii 6; etc.), most famously by Gudea (Cyls. and passim; also year 7, without TN), also by Ur-Ninĝirsu II (*FAOS* 9/I, UrN II 1–3; 6), Nammaḫni (ibid., Nam. 8, ii 1) and Šulgi (9/II, Š 15; no TN: 23). Provisioned by Warad-Sîn (Frayne, *RIME* 4, p. 233, 15) and Ḫammurapi (CḪ iii 46). In liturgical texts, usually in the standard litany of TNs of Ninurta (Cohen, *Lamentations*, pp. 441, 6; 458, 6; 469, 6; 472, 85; *Eršemma*, pp. 106, 4; 122, 3, with var. é.nin$_5$(NIMIN).ù; 139, 11; etc.). Elsewhere in Sumerian literature: Lamentation over Sumer and Ur 160; hymn to Baba for Išme-Dagān: Römer, *Königshymnen*, p. 236, 22 (qualified as uru.kù, q.v.); etc.

898 **é.ninnu.anzu$^{mušen}$.bábbar**, see é.ninnu

899 **é.nir**, bed-chamber of Antu in the *bīt rēš* at Uruk (*RAcc.*, p. 68, 6; cf. Falkenstein, *Topographie*, pp. 25f.). Probably é.nir (for which see also é.ḫi.li.kù.ga) represents *é.a.nir = *bīt tānēḫi*, "House of Weariness."

900 **é.nir.ĝál-$^{d}$*Anim***, see é.nir.ĝál.an.na 1

901 **é.nir.ĝál.an.na**, "House of the Prince of Heaven" 1, cella of Ištar in é.an.na at Uruk, rebuilt by Esarhaddon (Borger, *Esarh.*, § 48, 11). Known to Aššurbanipal as é.nir.ĝál-($^{d}$)*a-nim* (*YOS* I 42 // Lutz, *UCP* 9/VIII, 6).

902 **é.nir.g̃ál.an.na** 2, a shrine in é.sag̃.íl at Babylon (*Topog. Texts* no. 1 = *Tintir* II 46).

903 **é.nir.g̃ál.an.na** 3, seat of Nabû in é.rab.ri.ri (at Babylon? *Topog. Texts* no. 12, 2′).

904 **é.nir.maḫ-ki.u$_8$.zé.eb.ba.mu**, "My Exalted E-nir, Place of Pleasant Sleep," a bed-chamber in the temple complex at Uruk (*Topog. Texts* no. 25, obv. 8′). Cf. é.ḫi.li.kù.ga, é.nir.

905 **é.NISAG̃**, see é.gu.la 7

906 **é.nisag̃.maḫ**, "Exalted First House," a shrine of Enlil in é.kur at Nippur (Proto-*Kagal* 186, written ne.sag̃.maḫ; CTL 33; also Cohen, *Lamentations*, pp. 276, 56?; 302, 97?). Possibly to be restored in an early OB offering list (Heimerdinger, *Kramer AV*, p. 227, rev. ii 5′: ne.sag̃.[ . . . ]).

907 **é.nita.kala.ga**, "House of the Mighty Hero," a temple, perhaps at Kiš (*Topog. Texts* no. 22, 1′).

908 **é.nu.bànda**, "House of the Captain," TN or epithet(?) known from the big OB forerunner to *Hh* XXI (*MSL* XI, p. 142, viii 27).

909 ***é.nu.g̃ál.an.na**, see é.pa$_4$.g̃ál.an.na

910 **é.nu.nir.ki.tuš.maḫ**, see é.u$_6$.nir.ki.tuš.maḫ

911 **é.nu.tur.ra**, "House of the Young Man," a sanctuary of Ninḫursag̃ known from the Lamentation over Sumer and Ur 207.

912 **é.nu.úr.ma**, "House of Pomegranates," temple of Ištar at Maškanātu (CTL 380).

913 **é.nu$_{11}$.gal.an.na**, "House of the Great Light of Heaven" 1, temple of Ištar at Lagaš (CTL 387; above, p. 4, IM 96881, iii′ 12′?).

914 **[nu$_{11}^{?}$.g]al.an.na** 2, a seat of Ištar in é.sag̃.íl at Babylon (*Topog. Texts* no. 1 = *Tintir* II 3′).

915 **é.nun.an.na**, "House of the Prince of Heaven," part or epithet of é. babbar.ra of Šamaš at Sippar (Temple Hymns 480; Kutscher, *Kramer AV*, p. 307, 9: Sum. hymn to Utu).

916 **é.nun.maḫ**, "House of the Exalted Prince" 1, *bīt ḫilṣi* of Ningal inside é.g̃iš.nu$_{11}$.gal at Ur, rebuilt by Nabonidus (I *R* 68, no. 6, 3; etc.). Also found in an eršaḫung̃a of Ningal (Maul, *RA* 85 [1991], p. 71, obv. 3′). Probably = é.g̃á.nun.maḫ 1.

917 **é.nun.maḫ** 2, temple of Nuska at Babylon (*Topog. Texts* nos. 1 = *Tintir* IV 31, var. é.nu.maḫ; 3, rev. 11′).

918 **é.nun.maḫ** 3, temple of Ištar at Ḫudada (TL no. 3, 28′), older Eššeb (Syncretistic Ištar Hymn: *KAR* 109, rev. 8).

919 **é.nun.na**, "Princely House" 1, a temple of Ištar somewhere in north Mesopotamia (CTL 394).

920 **é.nun.na** 2, sanctuary of Ninmaḫ (Frayne, *RIME* 4, p. 261, 1003:4, dalla é.TN; Warad-Sîn?). Possibly to be read as the common noun, agrun.na, "boudoir."

921 **é.nun.ud.da**, "Princely House, Station(?)," a sanctuary of Ningublag (CTL 277).

922 **é.NUN.( . . . )**, see also é.gar$_6$.( . . . )

923 **é.PA**, see é.g̃idru

924 **é.PA.GÌN.ti.la**, temple of Ninurta at Babylon, see é.ḫur.sag̃.ti.la.

925 **é.pa.paḫ**, "House, Cella," cella of Anu and Ištar in é.an.na at Uruk, built by Sîn-kāšid (Frayne, *RIME* 4, p. 453, 10). Note also é.pa.paḫ among shrines of Ninlil in a Šulgi text (*CT* 42 40, pl. 46, a obv. 13: é.TN ki ⌜u$_6$⌝.de kur.kur.ra; Falkenstein, *Iraq* 22 [1960], p. 140, 12, read é.PA.ḪUŠ.ki . . . ). Not certainly a true TN.

926 **é.pa$_4$.g̃ál.an.na**, a sanctuary of Šamaš (CTL 289), perhaps to be read é.nu$^!$.g̃ál.an.na, "House of the Great Light of Heaven" (nu.g̃ál for nu$_{10}$.gal, as in other TNs).

927 **é.pa$_4$.ul.ḫé**, see é.gu$_4$.du$_7$.šár

928 **é.pàd.da**, "Chosen House," a temple of Adad, in liturgical texts listed after é.nam.ḫé in the standard litany of TNs of Adad (Maul, *Eršaḫunga* nos. 18, 9; 19–20, 9; 21, 9; Cohen, *Lamentations*, pp. 431, 43; 433, 95). The temple evidently lent its name to its home town, pàd.da$^{ki}$, which was fortified for Adad by Samsu-iluna (Frayne, *RIME* 4, p. 381, 38 // 36), and is listed as one of seven cult-centers of Adad in the Archive of Mystic Heptads (*KAR* 142, i 17; cf. iii 24).

929 **é.pàd.da.nu.nus**, "Chosen House of the Woman," a sanctuary of Sadarnunna (CTL 107), possibly also found in the Hymn to Sadarnunna (Sjöberg, *JAOS* 93 [1973], p. 352, 8: ⟨é⟩.⌜pàd$^?$.da$^?$.nu.nus.e⌝?). Presumably at Nippur.

930 **é.pirig̃**, "House of the Lion," a seat (of Madānu?) in é.sag̃.íl at Babylon (*Topog. Texts* no. 1 = *Tintir* II 7″).

931 **é.pirig̃.babbar**, "House of the White Lion," a sanctuary of Marduk (CTL 229).

932 **(*bīt*) *qulê***, sanctuary at Babylon, known from a dais list (*Topog. Texts* no. 9, 10′: ⟨*bīt*⟩ *q.*), and temple rituals (Lambert, *Love Lyrics*, pp. 102ff., i 4; ii 6.24, var. *a-qu-le-e-a*: *CAD* Q, s.v.; iii 1–3; BM 32656, iv 16′.18′). Probably better read as a loan-word, i.e., *equlû* < Sum. *é.gu.la, "Big House."

933 **é.rab.di$_5$.di$_5$**, see é.rab.ri.ri

934 ***é.rab.kalam.ma**, see é.lugal.kalam.ma

935 **é.rab.ri.ri**, "House of the Shackle which Holds in Check" 1, sanctuary of Pabilsag̃ (or Dikumaḫ) as consort of Gula, as listed in liturgical texts, usually paired with é.gal.maḫ in the standard litany of TNs of Ninurta

(Cohen, *Eršemma*, pp. 114, 27; 140, 345; *Lamentations*, index p. 752; Maul, *Eršaḫunga* no. 37, 3; *OrNS* 60 [1991], p. 314, 19: eršemma; *VAS* 24 30, rev. 7′; etc.; note the writing é.ráb.ri.ri: *SBH* 52, obv. 14.16). Possibly to be read é.rab.di$_5$.di$_5$ (cf. Krecher, *WO* 4 [1967–68], p. 266). See *Topog. Texts*, pp. 303–5.

936 **é.rab.ri.ri** 2, temple of Madānu as consort of Gula in Babylon (*Topog. Texts* nos. 1 = *Tintir* IV 4; 2, 4; 3, obv. 10′–12′; 12: divine residents; 39, ii b 1).

937 **é.rab.ri.ri** 3, cella of Madānu at Kiš (*Topog. Texts* no. 22, 10′; TL no. 6, 3).

938 **é.rab.ri.ri** 4, a temple of Ennugi (CTL 111), probably at Nippur. The temple of Ennugi at Nippur is listed without name in a MB metrological text (Bernhardt and Kramer, *OrNS* 44 [1975], p. 98, 38).

939 **é.rab.ša$_5$.ša$_5$**, "House which Snaps the Shackle," a temple of Ennugi (CTL 112).

940 ***(bīt) rēš***, "Head Temple," temple of Anu and Antu in the later temple complex at Uruk, rebuilt twice in the Seleucid era (Falkenstein, *Topographie*, pp. 4ff.), first of Anu's sanctuaries as listed in the bilingual liturgical hymn *BRM* IV 8 (Cohen, *Lamentations*, p. 729, 7: é.*re-eš* // *bīt re-eš*). Possibly a development of é.sag̃ of Lugalbanda, with the temple's original owner demoted to a subordinate position when Anu and Antu moved in from é.an.na (for Lugalbanda in the *rēš* temple see Falkenstein, *Topographie*, pp. 21, 33[14], 36[3]). The procession of Anu from the *rēš* temple to the Akītu temple is the subject of the complete LB ritual tablet, *BRM* IV 7, and this may have been an original function of Lugalbanda's temple (an association of é.sag̃ and *akītu* may survive at Babylon, see é.sag̃ 2).

941 ***bētum rīmum***, "House, Wild Ox," temple of Aššur at Aššur built by Erišum I (Grayson, *RIMA* 1, pp. 20, 16; 32, 11–12), rebuilt for Enlil by Šamšī-Adad I as é.am.kur.kur.ra.

942 **é.sa.ba.ad**, see é.sa.bad 1, 3

943 **é.sa.bad**, "House of the Open Ear" 1, sanctuary of Gula (*Topog. Texts* no. 39, rev. i a 3) at Isin and perhaps also at Larak, found in a cultic lament following é.gal.maḫ and é.aš.te (Cohen, *Lamentations*, pp. 256f., 49: é.sa.ba.ad; 57); also in Sîn-iddinam's letter to Ninisinna (*OECT* V 30, 7).

944 **é.sa.bad** 2, temple of Gula in west Babylon (*Topog. Texts* no. 1 = *Tintir* IV 42; *KAR* 109, obv. 20: syncretistic Ištar hymn; *BRM* IV 25, 17: offering calendar), rebuilt by Aššurbanipal (Millard, *Iraq* 30 [1968], p. 108, 13′), and Nebuchadnezzar II (I *R* 55, iv 40; cf. Wadi Brisa A ix 34 // B vi 10, var. é.sa.bàd). Mentioned by Esarhaddon (Borger, *Esarh.*, § 54, 10), the temple survived to Arsacid period (archive of Rahimesu: *CT* 49 153, 8; 161, 2; McEwan, *Iraq* 43 [1981], pp. 132, 3.26.29; 136, 5). Also found in rituals (Lambert, *Love Lyrics*, p. 104, iii 15; *Topog. Texts* no. 40, 9′; BM 78076, 9). See *Topog. Texts*, pp. 331f.

945 **é.sa.bad** 3, a temple which gave its name to a settlement (near Kiš? *MSL* XI, pp. 14, *Hh* XXI/4 10, = *bi-it* ᵈ*gu-la*; OB forerunner: 131, iii 37; also Grayson and Sollberger, *RA* 70 [1976], p. 112, G 25 // M 14, var. é.sa. ba.ad: Narām-Sîn). TL no. 3, 17′?

946 **é.sa.bad** 4, temple of Gula at Aššur (*Topog. Texts* no. 20 = Götteradreßbuch 174–75: Assyrian TL), rebuilt by Adad-nārārī II, who reports earlier work of Tukultī-Ninurta I (Grayson, *RIMA* 2, p. 154, 128: no TN). Source of copies of medical texts (Hunger, *Kolophone*, no. 202, 1).

947 **é.sa.bàd**, see é.sa.bad 2

948 **é.sa.pàr**, "House of the Net" 1, a temple or shrine of Nungal, known from the big OB forerunner to *Hh* XXI (*MSL* XI, p. 142, viii 40).

949 **é.sa.pàr** 2, a temple of Bēlet-ekalli, probably at Dilbat (Nougayrol, *JCS* 1 [1947], p. 330, 19′ // Wiseman, *Iraq* 31 [1969], p. 177, 31′: *lipšur*-litany; Cohen, *Lamentations*, pp. 232, 195 = 448, 167; CTL [483]). Note also diĝir. é.sa.$par_4$ as an interpreter of Ištar (*TCL* XV 10, 242; *An* IV: *CT* 24 33, 23: ᵈe.sa.$par_4$).

950 **é.sa.sum.ma**, a TN or epithet associated with Gula at Isin or Larak in Sîn-iddinam's letter to Ninisinna (Hallo, *Kramer AV*, p. 214, 7; following é.nìĝin.mar, ⟨é⟩.aš.te and é.sa.bad).

951 **é.sá.ĝar.ra**, "House which Gives Counsel," sanctuaries of Enlil (and Sîn?) at Ešnunna, known from year names of Ibāl-pî-El II (years 8.v = Jacobsen, *OIP* 98, p. 97, 16).

952 **é.saĝ**, "Foremost House" 1, temple of Lugalbanda (at Kullab? CTL 471); see also (*bīt*) *rēš*. Note the DN ᵈlugal.é.saĝ.ĝá in *An* VI 49 (Lambert, *RlA* VII, p. 138).

953 **é.saĝ** 2, temple of Lugalbanda in the quarter Kullab at Babylon (*Topog. Texts* nos. 1 = *Tintir* IV 27; 3, rev. 9′). If the same building is meant, the description in a NB legal document of the temple as é.saĝ *a-ki-tum* (? = *bīt rēš akīti*, "starting place of the *akītu*": *VAS* V 5, 4), does not agree with the known progress of the Akītu festival at Babylon, which began at Marduk's cella in é.saĝ.íl (*KAR* 142, i 1 // *CT* 46 53, ii 12; cf. *RAcc.*, p. 147). Probably it reflects a function of é.saĝ 1 and the *rēš* temple at Uruk (see (*bīt*) *rēš*).

954 **é.saĝ** 3, seat of the Queen of the Treasury (Šarrat-nakkamte) in é.šár.ra at Aššur (*Topog. Texts* no. 21, obv. 29′).

955 **é.saĝ.abzu.ta.an.ús**, "Foremost House, Supporting Heaven from *Apsû*," a temple of Ninurta or a similar god, found in litanies (Maul, *OrNS* 60 [1991], p. 314, 17: eršemma; *VAS* 24 30, rev. 6′, copy é.saĝ.kalam.ma.ta. an.ús).

956 **é.saĝ.dil**, "House of Secrets" 1, a ziqqurrat at Nippur (TL no. 4, 6; no. 5, 6′), dedicated to Enlil (CTL 24). Located in the Grand Court (kisal.maḫ) of é.kur according to a brick inscription of the NB priest Ninurta-šuma-

iddin which reports its destruction (*PBS* XV 69; cf. Landsberger, *ZA* 38 [1929], p. 115).

957 **é.sag̃.dil** 2, sanctuary of Gula at Isin, known from the Pabilsag̃ Tale (*PBS* XIII 44, i 11) and a cultic lament (Cohen, *Lamentations*, p. 256, 50, qualified as é bára.nun.na, "house, princely dais").

958 **é.sag̃.dil** 3, a shrine at Ur mentioned in an inscription of Sîn-balāssu-iqbi, qualified as é ḫal.la.ta dù.a, "house built in secret" (*UET* I 169, 29).

959 **é.sag̃.dil.an.na.$^{giš}$g̃idru.tuku**, "House of the Heavenly Secrets, Holding a Sceptre" 1, temple of Papsukkal at Babylon (*Topog. Texts* no. 1 = *Tintir* IV 10).

960 **é.sag̃.dil.an.na.$^{giš}$g̃idru.tuku** 2, seat of Ninšubur in é.rab.ri.ri (at Babylon? *Topog. Texts* no. 12, 6′).

961 **é.sag̃.dig̃ir.(re).e.ne**, "Foremost House of the Gods," temple of Ninurta at Dūr-Kurigalzu, built by Kurigalzu (Baqir, *Iraq*, Suppl. 1944, figs. 18–19).

962 **é.sag̃.dìm.me.er.e.ne**, "Foremost House of the Gods," a sanctuary known from a bilingual hymn to Ning̃irsu (*KAR* 97, 7). Emesal version of the name of the preceding temple, and probably identical with it.

963 **é.sag̃.**DUL, a temple of Ning̃eštinanna (CTL 464). Cf. é.sag̃.ug$_5$.

964 **é.sag̃.g̃á.an.[na/ki]**, "Foremost House of Heaven (and Underworld)," a shrine in é.sag̃.íl at Babylon (*Topog. Texts* no. 1 = *Tintir* II 4″).

965 **é.sag̃.g̃á.šár.ra**, "Foremost House of the Universe," temple of Anunnîtum at Babylon (*Topog. Texts* no. 1 = *Tintir* IV 14; variant é.me.sì.(ga).kalam.ma.šár.ra). Built by Šar-kali-šarrī (Gelb and Kienast, *FAOS* 7, p. 54, Škš year 3; no TN).

966 **é.sag̃.gi$_4$.a.ni.du$_{10}$**, "House, its(!) Closing is Pleasant," temple of Iškur rebuilt by Ubār-Adad in the reign of Ilum-gāmil of Uruk (Frayne, *RIME* 4, p. 469, 11). Part of Sîn-kāšid's é.u$_4$.gal.gim.ki.ḫuš.[ . . . ]?

967 **é.sag̃.íl**, "House whose Top is High" 1, also written é.sag̃.gíl, temple of Marduk at Babylon (Proto-*Kagal* 225; *MSL* XI, p. 142, viii 29; CTL 228; TL no. 2, 3; *Topog. Texts* nos. 1 = *Tintir* IV 1; 2, 1; 3, obv. 1′–2′; 5; 20 = Götteradreßbuch 181: Assyrian TL; metrology: nos. 13; 14), rebuilt by Sābium (year 10), destroyed by Sennacherib and rebuilt by Esarhaddon (passim), completed and refitted by Aššurbanipal (Streck, *Asb.*, p. 146, 17; Thompson, *Prisms*, p. 29, 21; etc.); further restored by Nebuchadnezzar II (passim), Neriglissar (*CT* 36 19, 9) and Antiochus I (V *R* 66). Cult-statue removed to Assyria following the looting of é.sag̃.íl by Tukultī-Ninurta I (Grayson, *Chronicles*, pp. 175f., 5–6), and again, to Elam, at the end of the Kassite period; retrieved by Nebuchadnezzar I (III *R* 38, no. 2; IV *R*$^2$ 20, no. 1; *VAS* 24 87; etc.; cf. George, *BiOr* 46 [1989], 382f.). Patronized by Sūmû-la-El (year 22: bára.maḫ, no TN), Ḫammurapi (CḪ ii 12), Samsu-iluna (years 6.7), Ammī-ditāna (years 5.7.14.24), Ammī-ṣaduqa (year 4) and

Samsu-ditāna (years 6.12.14.17.e). See further Renger, *Studien Falkenstein*, p. 139, s.v. Babylon: Marduk. Visited by Kurigalzu and Adad-šuma-uṣur (Finkel, *AnSt* 33 [1983], p. 78, rev. 5; Grayson, *BHLT*, p. 68, 22). Survived well into the Arsacid period (e.g., *CT* 49 154, 13; 155, 8; McEwan, *Iraq* 43 [1981], p. 138, 11). Also in liturgical texts, commonly in the standard litany of TNs after tin.tir$^{ki}$ (Cohen, *Eršemma*, pp. 29, 8; 113, 22; 118, 35.2:9; 127, 13; 136, 5.9; *Lamentations*, passim: index p. 752; Maul, *Eršaḫunga* nos. 37, 6; 104, rev. 1′; George, *RA* 82 [1988], p. 159, 34; etc.). Mentioned in the Syncretistic Ištar Hymn (ll.36, unpub., courtesy Lambert; 50: *KAR* 109, obv. 13), in the syncretistic hymn to Nanāy (Reiner, *JNES* 33 [1974], p. 226, 26), and in *lipšur*-litanies (*Šurpu* II 152–53; VIII 10–11; Nougayrol, *JCS* 1 [1947], p. 330, 8′.10′.12′ // Wiseman, *Iraq* 31 [1969], p. 176f., 19′.21′.23′), etc. See *Topog. Texts*, pp. 294–98.

968 **é.sag̃.íl** 2, temple of Ištar of Zabalam (at Uruk?), rebuilt by Warad-Sîn (Frayne, *RIME* 4, p. 219, 11: described as gi.gun$_4$$^{ki}$.kù, q.v.). See also é.kalam.ta.ní.gùr.ru.

969 **é.sag̃.íl.la** 3, temple of Ištar at Tilmun (CTL 359).

970 **é.sag̃.kal**, "House of the Leader" 1, seat of Ninurta in ub.šu.ukkin.na of é.sag̃.íl at Babylon (*Topog. Texts* no. 1 = *Tintir* II 22′).

971 **é.sag̃.kal** 2, seat of Nergal in é.rab.ri.ri (at Babylon? *Topog. Texts* no. 12, 5′).

972 **é.sag̃.kal.la** 3, a sanctuary (of Dumuzi?) at Kissig (Lamentation over Sumer and Ur 262).

973 **é.sag̃.kalam.ma.ta.an.ús**, "Foremost House, Supporting Heaven from the Land," see é.sag̃.abzu.ta.an.ús

974 **é.sag̃.sur**, the temple of an Ištar figure (CTL 438).

975 **é.sag̃.ug$_5$**, temple of Amag̃eštin, rebuilt by Enannatum I (Steible, *FAOS* 5/I, En I 9, iv 10; 20, ii 10), desecrated by Lugalzaggesi (ibid., Ukg 16, vi 11). Possibly identical with the unnamed temple of G̃eštinanna at G̃irsu built by Ur-Baba (9/I, UrB 1, vi 7) and Gudea (ibid., Gud. Stat. M, ii 5; N, ii 5; O, ii 4), though sag̃.ug$_5$ is probably to be explained as a variant of the toponym sag̃.ùb$^{ki}$, near Lagaš, with which this goddess is associated (note in a votive inscription $^{d}$g̃eštin.an.na nin sag̃$^{!}$.ùb$^{!ki!}$: ibid., Gud. 16, 1–2, following Steinkeller, *RA* 73 [1979], pp. 189f.). See also é.sag̃.DUL.

976 **é.sag̃.x.x.x**, a sanctuary (of Ninurta?) listed in the OB lexical list from Isin (p. 4, IM 96881, ii′ 13′).

977 **é.ság̃g̃a.maḫ**, "House of the Exalted Purifier," temple of Kusu (CTL 113). The temple of Kusu at Nippur is listed without name in a MB metrological text (Bernhardt and Kramer, *OrNS* 44 [1975], p. 98, 23).

978 **é.sar.(ra)**, "House of Vegetation(?)" 1, temple of Inanna at Adab (*MSL* XI, p. 142, vii 17; [CTL 342]; etc.: see Sjöberg, *TCS* III, p. 120), first known from inscriptions of pre-Sargonic kings of Adab (Steible, *FAOS* 5/II, pp. 187, 1: Medurba; 191 b 1: Lugaldalu; 192, 1: Lumma; 195–98 passim:

Anon. and Baraḫenidu?) and Mesalim of Kiš (ibid., p. 216, 3). Rebuilt by Narām-Sîn (Gelb and Kienast, *FAOS* 7, p. 101, NS 19: no TN). Also in Inanna's Descent and the éš.dam hymns (Wilcke, *RlA* V, p. 78; McEwan, *RA* 76 [1982], p. 188), and a love song of Dumuzi and Inanna (*CT* 58 13, 16).

979 **é.sar.ra** 2, part of the complex of é.kur at Nippur (Cohen, *Lamentations*, p. 349, 16; note Ninurta and é.sa.ra in the hymn *OECT* V 5, 3).

980 **é.sar.ra** 3, sanctuary attested at Sargonic Umma (Foster, *Umma*, p. 227: index).

981 **é.SAR.ús.sa**, see é.KÉŠDA.sağ.ús.sa

982 **é.síg.ùz**, "House of Goat Hair," temple of Ištar at Guabba (CTL 389). Possibly also of Sud (CTL 63). The TN occurs twice in the cultic lament im.ma.al gù.dé.dé, where it is associated with Ištar of Zabalam and the goddess ${}^{d}$a.tu.ur$_5$.ra (Cohen, *Lamentations*, pp. 610, 78; 613, 146: é.síg.ùz.ra; cf. Lambert, *JNES* 49 [1990], p. 76).

983 **sig$_4$.kur.šà.ga**, "Brick, Mountain of the Heart," by-name for the cult-center of Šara at Umma (é.maḫ 6), as found in Inanna's Descent 328–29; Lamentation over Sumer and Ur 155; Sjöberg, *JCS* 34 [1982], p. 68, iii 8′ and note.

984 **é.sig$_4$.me.šè.du$_7$**, also written é.sig$_4$.me.šè.túm, "House, Brick Worthy of the *Me*'s," temple of Inanna at Isin (Proto-*Kagal* 229; CTL [344]), well known from Inanna's Descent and the éš.dam hymns (Wilcke, *RlA* V, p. 78).

985 **é.sig$_4$.me.šè.túm**, see é.sig$_4$.me.šè.du$_7$

986 **é.sig$_4$.x.[x]**, sanctuary of Ištar at Dūr-[ . . . ] (CTL 352).

987 **é.sikil.(la)**, "Pure House" 1, temple of Ninazu-Tišpak in Ešnunna (*MSL* XI, p. 142, viii 30; CTL 474.[555]; TL no. 3, 36′; Temple Hymns 425.445), rebuilt by Šulgi (Steible, *FAOS* 9/II, Š 3; 7), Bilalama (Frayne, *RIME* 4, p. 492, 8; year a) and Ibāl-pî-El II (year 6; cf. 11.u). No doubt the temple of Ninazu or Tišpak patronized variously by Ipiq-Adad (years b.c), Narām-Sîn (year v), Dannum-tāḫāz (years y.z), Dādūša (year 4) and Sîn-abūšu (year x). Written é.si.kil.la in the boundary stone of Nazi-Maruttaš (*MDP* 2, pl. 17, iv 29). Mentioned in the Syncretistic Ištar Hymn (*KAR* 109, rev. 3), in Anzû III 149, and in a *lipšur*-litany (Wiseman, *Iraq* 31 [1969], p. 177, 32′).

988 **é.sikil** 2, shrine in the é.kur temple complex at Nippur, as listed in a liturgical hymn to Enlil (Cohen, *Lamentations*, p. 349, 20, qualified as ki na.ám.sikil.e, "place of purity").

989 **é.sikil.la** 3, a temple of Ninazu, not in Ešnunna (TL no. 3, 40′).

990 **é.silim.[ . . . ]**, a temple at Kiš (*Topog. Texts* no. 23, 16′).

991 ***bīt sipittê***, "House of Lament," a building at Babylon which is the site of rituals conducted by personnel of Bēlet-Bābili (Lambert, *Love Lyrics*, p. 104, iii 1; BM 32656, iv 12′).

992 **é.sìrara$^{ki}$**, temple of Nanše at Sirara in NINA$^{ki}$ (Temple Hymns 281; Falkenstein, *AnOr* 30, p. 163; Heimpel, *JCS* 33 [1981], pp. 84, 46; 92, 178: Nanše Hymn), built by Ur-Nanše (Sollberger, *JCS* 21 [1967], p. 282, 154: Lagaš king list), Uruinimgina (Steible, *FAOS* 5/I, Ukg 1, iii 10′) as well as Gudea (é.sirara$_6$: *FAOS* 9/1, Stat. I, iii 1; P, iii 2; Gud. 29–32; etc.). Claimed by Inanna in an éš.dam hymn (*PBS* V 157, i 17).

993 **é.sískur**, "House of the Sacrifice" 1, temple of the Akītu of Marduk outside Babylon, rebuilt by Nebuchadnezzar II (I *R* 55, iv 7; etc.; = *bīt ikribī*). Cf. *bīt ik-rib* as an epithet of the Akītu temple of Anu at Uruk (*BRM* IV 7, 24).

994 **é.sískur** 2, temple listed in TL no. 3, 47′, apparently not the temple of Babylon.

995 **é.su.gal.(la)**, "House of the Great Niche(?)," one of the twin ziqqurrats of Dumuzi in Ištar's cult-center at Akkade (TL no. 4, 10; no. 5, [2′]), also found in the syncretistic hymn to Nanāy (Reiner, *JNES* 33 [1974], p. 227, 34). See also *é.zu.zal.

996 **é.su.lim.an.na**, "House of the Awesome Radiance of Heaven," temple of Ištar as Bēlet-Eanna at Kiš (CTL 367; TL no. 6, 6; *Topog. Texts* no. 22, 12′).

997 **é.su.lim.$^{d}$en.líl.le**, "House of the Awesome Radiance of Enlil," temple of Uqur at G̃irsu (CTL 577).

998 **é.su.lim.gùr.ru.e.dè**, "House Clad in Awesome Radiance," a temple of Lugalirra and Meslamtaea (CTL 579).

999 **é.su.lim.ḫuš.ri.a**, "House Imbued with Dread Awesome Radiance" a sanctuary (at Dūr-Kurigalzu? CTL 106).

1000 **é.sù.ga.a**, "Joyful House," epithet or part of é.maḫ at Adab (Temple Hymns 370). Cf. the big OB forerunner to *Hh* XXI, *MSL* XI, p. 142, vii 25, é.sù.ga.

1001 **é.sù.sù.g̃ar.ra**, "House where Meals are Set out" 1, temple of Supalītu (Ištar of Zabalam), probably at Uruk (*Topog. Texts* no. 25, obv. 2′; CTL 320).

1002 **é.sù.sù.g̃ar.ra** 2, another temple of Ištar (CTL 364).

1003 **é.su$_8$.ba**, "House of the Shepherd," a sanctuary known from a bal.bal.e of Nanna (*TuM NF* 4 7, 102), = *é.šuba.

1004 **é.su$_{11}$.lum.ma**, "House of Dates," temple of Ištar at Napsanu-Sulumma (CTL 360; see the commentary ad loc.).

1005 **é.sud**, "Distant House," a temple of Ištar (as Nanāy? CTL 437).

1006 ***é.suḫuš.gi.na**, see é.KAS$_4$.gi.na

1007 **é.sukud.da**, "High House," a sanctuary of Ištar (in Kār-Bēl-mātāti? CTL 377), also known from the cultic lament im.ma.al gù.dé.dé (Cohen, *Lamentations*, p. 611, 100).

1008 **é.šà**, "House of the Heart" or "Inner Chamber," a sanctuary of Ningirsu furnished with a garden by Enmetena (Steible, *FAOS* 5/I, Ent 16, ii 5; 42, iv 2; etc.; cf. Ukg 38, 2).

1009 **é.šà.an**, "House of the Midst of Heaven," temple of Anu at Aššur (*Topog. Texts* no. 20 = Götteradreßbuch 153: Assyrian TL). The double temple of Anu and Adad was repaired by Adad-nārārī I (Grayson, *RIMA* 1, p. 153, 4.11: no TNs) and rebuilt by Aššur-rēša-iši I (ibid., pp. 317, 7–8; 318, 8:2: no TNs). Tiglath-pileser I also rebuilt it, along with its two ziqqurrats, in his accession year, and reports an earlier building of Šamšī-Adad III demolished by Aššur-dān I (Grayson, *RIMA* 2, pp. 28, 60.83; 65, 3; Adad temple only: 66, 3; cf. 20, 36; 79, 2′?: no TNs). Note a NA metrological fragment describing parts of the Anu temple (Weidner, *AfO* 8 [1932–33], p. 43; in obv. 1 read *bēt* $^{d}$*a-nim*, not Adad!). See also é.šùd.dè.giš.tuku of Adad.

1010 **é.šà.ba**, "House of the Heart," sanctuaries of Baba, and Sud (or Aya) as Sudag, found in liturgical texts (Krecher, *Kultlyrik*, pp. 54, 11; 124; Cohen, *Eršemma*, p. 139, 9; *Lamentations*, pp. 240, 337; 255f., 6.33; 289, 255 // 309, 211; 621, 316). The epithet dumu é.TN is used of Enbune/Enbule in similar texts (ibid., pp. 235, 271 = 304, 145; 283, 192 = 358, 208), and in *An* II in connection with the entourage of the Mother Goddess (unpub.).

1011 **é.šà.ba.an.na**, "House of the Heart of Heaven," temple of Ištar at Mari, as known to Yasmaḫ-Addu (Frayne, *RIME* 4, p. 616, 2). Written é.šà.ba.na in CTL 395.

1012 **é.šà.di$_{5}$.ḫi.li.ba**, "House, Instructor of the Netherworld(?)," a shrine in é.šár.ra at Aššur (*Topog. Texts* no. 21, rev. 19′).

1013 **é.šà.du$_{10}$.ga**, "House which Pleases the Heart" 1, seat represented by a brick found in the sanctuary of Ningal at Ur, é.gi$_{6}$.pàr.kù 1, made by Sîn-balāssu-iqbi (*UET* I 178).

1014 **é.šà.d[u$_{10}$.ga]** 2, a sanctuary of Ištar (CTL 347).

1015 **šà.ga.a**, "(House) in the Midst," seat of Nanāy in é.šár.ra at Aššur (*Topog. Texts* no. 21, obv. 23′).

1016 **é.šà.ga.bi.du$_{10}$.ga**, "House whose Interior is Pleasing," a sanctuary of Sîn (CTL 272).

1017 **é.šà.ge.pàd.da**, "House Chosen in the Heart," temple of Šara (CTL 454) at Umma, rebuilt by Šu-Suen and Ibbi-Suen (Steible, *FAOS* 9/II, ŠS 4; 8–9; cf. ŠS year 9, IS year 1a, no TN). See also é.bur.sa$_{7}$.sa$_{7}$, é.maḫ 5; é.šà.pàd.da.

1018 **é.šà.ḫúl.la**, "House of the Happy Heart" 1, temple of Ištar as Nanāy at Kazallu (CTL 346), also known from Inanna's Descent and an éš.dam hymn (Wilcke, *RlA* V, p. 78). The temple of this name restored by Sîn-kāšid (Frayne, *RIME* 4, p. 452, 6:8), and rebuilt by Kudur-Mabuk and Rīm-Sîn I (ibid., p. 275, 14) was probably in Uruk, however.

1019 **é.šà.ḫúl.la** 2, temple of Nergal at $^{uru}$Í[D.SUMUN.D]AR (TL no. 3, 35′: emend to $^{uru}$Mê-[Turn]a$^{!}$ ? See the commentary ad loc.). See also é.TN 3.

1020 **é.šà.ḫúl.la** 3, temple of Nergal at Sirara in Mê-Turna built by Aššurbanipal (Fawzi Rashid, *Sumer* 37 [1981], p. 80 (Arabic section), 2), also mentioned in the syncretistic hymn to Nanāy (Reiner, *JNES* 33 [1974], p. 228, 48). See also é.TN 2.

1021 **é.šà.maḫ.(a/àm)**, "Exalted Inner Chamber," a sanctuary of Ninurta at Nippur (p. 4, IM 96881, ii′ 10′; *Kagal* Boğ. I F 6), known also from liturgical texts, where it follows é.šu.me.ša$_4$ in the standard litany of TNs of Ninurta (Maul, *Eršaḫunga* no. 31 + K 17441, obv. 7; *OrNS* 60 [1991], p. 314, 11: eršemma; Cohen, *Lamentations*, pp. 180, 154; 441, 9; 458, 9; 461, 84; 469, 9; *VAS* 24 30, rev. 4′; etc.).

1022 **(é).šà.pàd.da**, "House Chosen in the Heart," a sanctuary of Nanše at Lagaš (Falkenstein, *AnOr* 30, pp. 161f.; Sauren, *OrNS* 38 [1969], p. 217), built by Enmetena (Steible, *FAOS* 5/I, Ent 1, ii 20; 8, vii 3; 23, 19; etc.), desecrated by Lugalzaggesi (Ukg 16, iv 11).

1023 **é.šà.RI.ḫi.li.ba**, see é.šà.di$_5$.ḫi.li.ba

1024 **é.šà.sur.ra**, "House of the Womb," temple of Išḫara at Babylon (*Topog. Texts* nos. 1 = *Tintir* IV 20, var. é.*sa-as-su-ru*; 3, rev. 1′; 4, 20). Also written é.šà.tùr.ra (Strassmaier, *Nbk* 247, 7; Peiser, *Verträge* 107, 10: é.šà.tùr *bīt* DN!). Identified with the excavated temple Z: cf. George, *Sumer* 35 (1979), p. 229; 44 (1985), p. 12. See *Topog. Texts*, pp. 314–16.

1025 **é.šà.te.na**, "House which Soothes the Heart," a temple of Inanna known from an éš.dam hymn, which places it in [x (x) d]a$^{ki}$ (i.e., Marad? *OECT* I, pl. 15f., iii 29–iv 1).

1026 **é.šà.te.zu**, "House which Knows the Soothing of the Heart," a temple of Ninšubur known from Šulgi M (*SLTNi* 76, rev. 6; quoted by van Dijk, *Götterlieder* II, p. 53)

1027 **é.šà.tùr.ra**, see é.šà.sur.ra

1028 **[é.š]à$^{?}$.zu.gal.kalam.ma**, "House, Great Midwife(?) of the Land," a sanctuary of Enlil (CTL 27).

1029 **é.šà.zukum$^{kum}$**, a shrine of Enlil (CTL 43), possibly a corruption of é.du$_6$.númun.búr.

1030 **[é?].ša$_6$.$^{d}$en.líl.lá**, "Lovely House(?) of Enlil," the inner sanctum (*kummu*) of Nuska: see the commentary on CTL 105.

1031 **é.šaga.ér.ra**, "House which Weeps for the Wronged," chapel of Iqbi-damiq in the temple of Bēlat-ekalli at Aššur (*Topog. Texts* no. 20 = Götteradreßbuch 167: Assyrian TL).

1032 **é.šaga.ra**, "House which Smites(?) the Wronged," temple of Ištar at Dadmuš (CTL 381; TL no. 3, 25′).

1033 **é.šar.ra**, see é.sar.ra, é.šár.ra

1034 **é.šár.ra**, "House of the Universe" 1, temple of Enlil, both as a cosmic abode (*En. el.* IV 145, V 120, VI 66; Borger, *Esarh.*, p. 21, 49; Weissbach, *WVDOG* 59, p. 42, iii 28: Nbp; *Topog. Texts* nos. 1 = *Tintir* IV 2; 16, i 10′; cf. no. 57, 9; Köcher, *ZA* 53 [1959], p. 238, 2: hymn to Borsippa; *STT* 73, 5.25: cosmic bond of é.TN), and also as a part of é.kur at Nippur (CTL [22]; the Syncretistic Ištar Hymn 34–35 pairs the two TNs: unpub., courtesy Lambert; further refs. by Sjöberg, *TCS* III, p. 119), whence it was borrowed at Aššur (é.šár.ra 2). In liturgical texts it often appears, typically in the standard litany of TNs of Ninurta, where it follows é.ninnu (Cohen, *Lamentations*, pp. 97, 19 // 349, 16: var. é.šar.ra; 284, 207 = 359, 223; 343, 16–19; 441, 7; 458, 7; 469, 7; 472, 86; note also Niraḫ as the temple's sheriff, udug // *rābiṣ* é.TN: 235, 265 = 304, 139; 282, 187 = 357, 203; Ninlil as téš // *bal-ti* é.TN: IV $R^2$ 27, no. 2, 25–26).

1035 **é.šár.ra** 2, name of the temple complex of Aššur at Aššur in later times (*Topog. Texts* nos. 20 = Götteradreßbuch 144: Assyrian TL; 21: shrine list; cf. van Driel, *Cult of Aššur*, p. 36). TN known to Aššur-bēl-kala (Grayson, *RIMA* 2, p. 94, 5′), repaired by Aššur-dān II (ibid., p. 139: cones in courtyard wall, no TN). Gate of Enpi repaired and refurbished by Tukultī-Ninurta II (pp. 172, 27; 184, 14:3). TN mentioned by Aššurnaṣirpal II (p. 219, 90), who restored the towers of the Kalkal Gate (p. 386, 4ff.). Provisioned by Šamšī-Adad V and Adad-nārārī III (I *R* 29, 31; 35, no. 1, 3). Mentioned by Sargon II (Winckler, *Sammlung* II, no. 1, 37); extensively rebuilt by Sennacherib (*KAH* II 124; etc.) and Esarhaddon, who reports the earliest building of Ušpia, and subsequent rebuildings by Erišum I, Šamšī-Adad I and Shalmaneser I (Borger, *Esarh.*, § 2; *AfO* 18 [1957–58], p. 113, § 10[a]). For a history of the Aššur temple see van Driel, *Cult of Aššur*, pp. 1–31. Site of the restoration of divine statues (Lambert, *Festgabe Deller* = AOAT 220, p. 162, 10; Esarh.). See also é.kur 2 and é.ḫur.sag̃.kur.kur.ra.

1036 **é.šár.ra** 3, ziqqurrat of the *bīt rēš* of Anu at Uruk (Falkenstein, *Topographie*, pp. 27ff.; Cohen, *Lamentations*, p. 729, 8: paired with bára.maḫ).

1037 **é.šár.ra** 4, epithet of é.maḫ at Adab (Temple Hymns 367, var. é.šár.šár).

1038 **é.šár.šár**, see é.šár.ra 4

1039 **é.še.er.zi.gùr.(ru)**, "House Clad in Splendour," temple of Ištar at Zabalam (*MSL* XI, p. 142, vii 23; CTL 399, om. zi; Temple Hymns 315).

1040 **še.er.zi.ki.šár.ra**, "(House of) the Splendour of the Universe," a seat of Šamaš in é.sag̃.íl at Babylon (*Topog. Texts* no. 1 = *Tintir* II 15).

1041 **é.še.numun**, "House of Barleycorn," temple of Lulal at Apak (TL no. 6, 29).

1042 **é.še.ri.ga**, "House which Gleans Barley," temple of Šidada at Dūr-Šarrukīn in Babylonia (TL no. 3, 24′; *Topog. Texts* no. 39, ii b 3), also mentioned by Esarhaddon (Borger, *Esarh.*, § 64, rev. 41). See also é.èš.ér.ke$_4$.

1043 **é.šeg̃$_9$.bar**, "House of Wild Boar," a temple of Ea (CTL 189), synonym of *Apsû.*

1044 **é.šeš.e.g̃ar.ra**, "House Established by the Brother," temple of Ninšeš-eg̃arra at Bad-tibira, built by Ur-gigir, son of Ur-nig̃in of Uruk (Steible, *FAOS* 9/II, p. 321). Ninšešeg̃arra is possibly Dumuzi's sister, G̃eštinanna, at least at Bad-tibira (Kutscher, *Bar-Ilan Studies Artzi*, p. 33[15]).

1045 **é.šeš.g̃ar**, a temple of Ea (CTL 188).

1046 **šeš.g̃ar** 2, see é.šeš.šeš.e.g̃ar.ra

1047 **é.šeš.šeš.e.g̃á/g̃ar.ra**, "House Established by the Brothers," temple of Nanše at G̃irsu, built by Ur-Nanše (šeš.g̃ar: Steible, *FAOS* 5/I, UrN 19; 23b; etc.; no TN: 20a; 22a; etc.), given new doors by Enmetena (šeš.g̃ar.ra: ibid., Ent 27, 2; cf. Sollberger, *ZA* 50 [1952], pp. 22ff.), and rebuilt by Šulgi (Steible, *FAOS* 9/II, Š 13; 22). Part of é.ninnu, according to Falkenstein, *AnOr* 30, pp. 130f. The "twin" of é.nin.e.g̃ar.ra.

1048 **é.šid.dù**, "House of the Director," a seat (of Nabû?) in é.sag̃.íl at Babylon (*Topog. Texts* no. 1 = *Tintir* II 3″).

1049 **é.šid.dù.an.na.ki**, "House of the Director of Heaven and Underworld," cella of Nabû in é.zi.da at Borsippa, refurbished by Nebuchadnezzar II (Koldewey, *WVDOG* 15, p. 54, fig. 97 = *VAB* IV, Nbk 44, 3!; *Topog. Texts* no. 28, 5′).

1050 **é.šid.dù.ki.šár.ra**, "House of the Director of the Universe," temple of Nabû in west Babylon (*Topog. Texts* no. 1 = *Tintir* IV 43, var. é.mes.i.i.ki.šár.ra).

1051 **é.ŠID.kù.ga**, "House of the Pure Recitation(?)," a temple known from a hymnal excerpt (*VAS* 24 38, 3).

1052 **é.šìr.sag̃.ús.sa**, see é.KÉŠDA.sag̃.ús.sa

1053 **é.šu.bil.lá**, "House of the Mat," a sanctuary of Ištar at Dūr-[ . . . ] (CTL 353).

1054 **é.šu.bur.an.na**, pantry of é.šár.ra at Aššur (*Topog. Texts* no. 20 = Götteradreßbuch 185: Assyrian TL, var. é.bur.an.na). Also é.bur.an.na, "House of the Heavenly Jars," in a prayer to Tašmētum (*KAR* 122, rev. 3).

1055 **é.šu.$^{d}$en.líl.le**, "House (Created) by the Hand of Enlil," a sanctuary at Nippur (CTL 105), listed between temples of Nuska and his consort Sadarnunna.

1056 **šu.ga.lam**, part of é.ninnu at G̃irsu (Falkenstein, *AnOr* 30, pp. 140f.; "die sich erhebende 'Hand'"). Cf. é.igi.šu.galam.

1057 **é.šu.gán.du$_7$.du$_7$**, ziqqurrat at Ur (TL no. 4, 18; šu.gán is probably an ancient misreading of aga: see é.aga.du$_7$.du$_7$).

1058 **šu.gi$_4$.gi$_4$.nigin.šu.a.bi**, seat of the Anunnaki in é.sag̃.íl at Babylon (*Topog. Texts* no. 1 = *Tintir* II 25).

1059 **é.šu.gur.ra**, "House of the Turban," temple(?) known from a Sargonic year name (Gelb and Kienast, *FAOS* 7, p. 59, Anon. 10).

1060 **é.ŠU.IGI.galam**, see é.igi.šu.galam

1061 **é.šu.luḫ.bi.kù.ga**, "House whose Cleansing Ritual is Pure" 1, courtyard (of é.su.lim.an.na?) at Kiš (TL no. 6, 8; *Topog. Texts* 22, 14′: é.šu.luḫ.ḫa.kù).

1062 **šu.luḫ.bi.kù.ga** 2, a shrine in é.sag̃.íl at Babylon (*Topog. Texts* no. 1 = *Tintir* II 44; ibid., p. 280, K 3446+, obv. 20: royal ritual; *CT* 46 53, ii 19).

1063 **é.šu.luḫ.ḫa.túm.ma**, "House Worthy of the Cleansing Ritual," a temple of Ninšar (CTL 115), probably at Nippur. The sanctuary of Ninšar at Nippur is listed without name in a MB metrological text (Bernhardt and Kramer, *OrNS* 44 [1975], p. 98, 40).

1064 **é.šu.luḫ.ḫa.kù**, see é.šu.luḫ.bi.kù.ga 1

1065 **é.šu.me.ša$_4$** 1, temple of Ninurta at Nippur (Proto-*Kagal* 193; IM 96681, ii′ 9′; TL no. 2, [8]; *Topog. Texts* nos. 18 = Nippur Compendium § 6, c; 19 = Nippur TL 11′–16′; Temple Hymns 68.75), known from ED times on (Sigrist, *BiMes* 11, p. 6). Cult statue of Ninurta set up by Išme-Dagān (year m), and also Ninurta's fifty-headed mace (Frayne, *RIME* 4, p. 46, 14′). TN provisioned by Ur-Dukuga (ibid., p. 95, 11). Passim in Sumerian literature. Mentioned in the Syncretistic Ištar Hymn (line 95; unpub., courtesy Lambert), and in a *lipšur*-litany (Nougayrol, *JCS* 1 [1947], p. 330, 13′ // Wiseman, *Iraq* 31 [1969], p. 177, 24′). Also in liturgical texts, often paired with é.šà.maḫ in the standard litany of TNs of Ninurta (Maul, *Eršaḫunga* no. 31 + K 17441, obv. 6; *OrNS* 60 [1991], pp. 314f., 10.31: eršemma; Cohen, *Lamentations*, index p. 752; add pp. 98, 59: šu!.me.eš ḫé.g̃ál.la; 351, 59: é.šu!.me.ša$_4$ ḫé.ma.al: cf. *SBH* 34 rev. 10: é.šu.me.ša$_4$ ḫé.ma.al.la; Krecher, *Kultlyrik*, pp. 60, 35; 195, 4.7; MacMillan, *BA* V/5 6, rev. 11; etc.). The component parts of é.TN in the MB period are listed in a metrological text (Bernhardt and Kramer, *OrNS* 44 [1975], pp. 97f., 13–19). NB documents: Krückmann, *TuM* 2–3 200, 8; 241, 4.8; 266, 5.6; etc.

1066 **é.šu.me.ša$_4$** 2, chapel of Ninurta in the temple of Ninimma at Nippur (*Topog. Texts* no. 18 = Nippur Compendium § 14, v 12).

1067 **é.šu.me.ša$_4$** 3, temple of Ninurta in the é.šár.ra complex at Aššur (*Topog. Texts* no. 20 = Götteradreßbuch 152: Assyrian TL).

1068 **é.šu.nigin.šu.du$_7$**, "House Perfect in its Entirety" 1, a sanctuary of Nabû (*Topog. Texts* no. 28, 6′; CTL 241: [é.šu.nigin?.ḫ]é.du$_7$).

1069 **é.šu.nigin.šu.du$_7$** 2, part or by-name of the temple of Nabû at Aššur (*Topog. Texts* no. 20 = Götteradreßbuch 163: Assyrian TL).

1070 **é.šu.zi.an.na**, "House, True Hand of Heaven," temple of the goddess Anat at Anat according to an inscription of Ninurta-kudurrī-uṣur (Cavigneaux and Bahija Khalil Ismail, *Bagh. Mitt.* 21 [1990], p. 380, 8), who also reports the earlier patronage of Ḫammurapi of Babylon (ibid., p. 381, 31).

1071 ***é.šuba**, see é.su$_8$.ba

1072 **é.šùd.dè.g̃iš.tuku**, "House which Hears Prayers" 1, a temple of Kusu (CTL 114).

1073 **é.šùd.dè.g̃iš.tuku** 2, temple of Adad at Aššur (*Topog. Texts* no. 20 = Götteradreßbuch 154: Assyrian TL). An unnamed temple of Adad at Aššur was built by Erišum I (Grayson, *RIMA* 1, pp. 37, 23; 38, 10) and completed by Ikūnum (ibid., p. 42, 14). For the building history of the double temple of Anu and Adad see é.šà.an.

1074 **é.$^{kuš}$šuḫub.bi.[ . . . ]**, "House whose Boot [ . . . ]," a sanctuary built by Warad-Sîn(?), at Ur (Frayne, *RIME* 4, p. 259, 11).

1075 **é.šul$^{!}$.an.na**, "House of the Hero of Heaven," a sanctuary of Zababa at Kiš (*Topog. Texts* no. 22, 8′; tablet: é.IGI.NIR.an.na).

1076 **é.šúruppak**, by-name of Ištar's temple é.nìg̃in.g̃ar.ra at Šuruppak (CTL 357).

1077 **é.šutum.kù**, see é.šútum.kù 1 and 2

1078 **é.šutum.lugal**, "House, Storeroom of the King," seat of the king in é.šár.ra at Aššur (*Topog. Texts* no. 21, obv. 28′).

1079 **é.šútum.ki.ág̃.g̃á**, "House, Beloved Storeroom" 1, sanctuary of Aqtuppītum of ŠID.tab (kiri$_8$.tab or àk.tab?), rebuilt for Sîn-māgir by his concubine, the *nadītu* Nuṭṭuptum (Frayne, *RIME* 4, p. 99, 12). Possibly not a true name. See also é.me.sikil 1.

1080 **é.šútum.ki.ág̃.g̃á** 2, sanctuary of Ninlil at Nippur, built by Ur-Nammu (Steible, *FAOS* 9/II, UrN 21; var. šu.tum).

1081 **é.šútum.kù**, "House, Pure Storeroom" 1, temple of Inanna/Ištar at Ur, rebuilt by Ibbi-Suen (é.šutum.kù, for Ninlil and Inanna: year 18, cf. 19) and Sūmû-El (Frayne, *RIME* 4, p. 132, 7). See also é.èš.me.dag̃al.la, é.ḫi.li.

1082 **é.šútum.kù** 2, temple storehouse of Sîn at Ur, rebuilt by Gungunum (year 25, var. é.šutum.kù), and by Rīm-Sîn I (Frayne, *RIME* 4, p. 287, 26).

1083 **é.ta.é.kù.ga.x**, see é.iti$_6$.kù.ga

1084 **tab.mud.ḫum.ḫum**, seat of Ilī-abrāt in é.šár.ra at Aššur (*Topog. Texts* no. 21, obv. 5′).

1085 **(é).tar.sír.sír** 1, temple of Baba in Uru-ku at G̃irsu (p. 4, IM 96881, iii′ 2′; Proto-*Kagal* 203; CTL [491]; Temple Hymns 266; Falkenstein, *AnOr* 30, pp. 147f.), built by Ur-Nanše (é.tar: Steible, *FAOS* 5/I, UrN 18), Uruinimgina (no TN: ibid., Ukg 1, i 10; 4, i 10; etc.), and Gudea (9/I, Stat. E, ii 18; G, v 11; H, ii 1; cf. ii 3: epithet é.ḫé.du$_7$ uru.kù.ga, "House of Abundance in Uru-ku"). Reading established by the variant é.tàr.sir.sir in a *lipšur*-litany (Nougayrol, *JCS* 1 [1947], p. 330, 16′ // Wiseman, *Iraq* 31 [1969], p. 177, 27′). In Sumerian literature: Kramer, *AS* 12, pp. 18f., Ur Lament 27.57; Römer, *Königshymnen*, p. 237, 25: hymn to Baba for Išme-Dagān; *CT* 36 39, 12; *STVC* 36, rev. 6: hymn to Baba; also liturgical texts (Cohen, *Eršemma*,

p. 108, 6; *Lamentations*, p. 613, 154–55: e.TN). Cf. Baba as $^{d}$lamma.TN (e.g., Kärki, *StOr* 58, Š 28, 1; liturgies, passim). See also é.uru.kù.ga.

1086 **é.tar.sír.sír** 2, temple of Baba at Lagaš (Falkenstein, *AnOr* 30, pp. 158ff.)?

1087 **é.te.en.te.en**, "House which Cools," cella of the goddess $^{d}$*ba*-KUR (in the temple of Ninurta?) at Ša-Uṣur-Adad (Walker, *Iraq* 44 [1982], p. 72, 17′; Bēl-ibni).

1088 **é.te.me.en.an.ki**, "House, Foundation Platform of Heaven and Underworld," also written é.temen.an.ki, ziqqurrat of Marduk at Babylon (*Topog. Texts* nos. 1 = *Tintir* IV 2; 2, 2; 3, obv. 3′–6′; 13: metrology; TL no. 4, 2; no. 5, 8′; Erra I 128), rebuilt by Esarhaddon (Borger, *Esarh.*, p. 24, 28b; etc.) and Aššurbanipal (Streck, *Asb.*, p. 350, α–β), again by Nabopolassar (*BE* I 84, i 30) and completed by Nebuchadnezzar II (*BE* I 85, ii 3; etc.). Often written é.te.mén.an.ki in liturgical texts, where typically it appears in the standard litany of TNs paired with é.dàra.an.na (Cohen, *Eršemma*, pp. 29, 12; 114, 25; 118, 35.2:13; 127, 17; *Lamentations*, passim: index p. 752; Langdon, *BL* nos. 26, 2′; 56, obv. 17; George, *RA* 82 [1988], p. 159, 36; etc.). See *Topog. Texts*, pp. 298–300. The TN was probably borrowed from Eridu, where it was an epithet of é.u$_{6}$.nir (Temple Hymns 2). For another ziqqurrat possibly bearing this name see under é.gub.ba.an.ki.

1089 **é.temen.bi.nu.kúr**, "House whose Foundation Platform Is Unalterable," cella of Ištar as the Queen of Kiš at Kiš (*Topog. Texts* no. 22, 11′; TL no. 6, 4).

1090 **é.temen.ní.gùr.(ru)**, "House, Foundation Platform Clad in Terror" 1, ziqqurrat terrace of Nanna-Suen at Ur, built by Ur-Nammu and Amar-Suen (Steible, *FAOS* 9/II, UrN 10; 25; cf. 9; AS 19), repaired by Ṣillī-Adad (Frayne, *RIME* 4, p. 200, 11). Rebuilt by Warad-Sîn (ibid., pp. 234, 38; 242, 49), and Sîn-balāssu-iqbi (*UET* I 169; 183). In Sumerian literature: Lamentation over Sumer and Ur 464; Šulgi V 24; X 130; *TuM NF* 4 7, 113: bal.bal.e; Ur-Nammu's Death B, rev. 2; Cohen, *JAOS* 95 (1975), p. 597, 18. See also é.lugal.g̃algа.si.sá, é.temen.ní.íl.lá.

1091 **é.[temen?].ní.gùr.ru** 2, sanctuary of Ištar as Supalītu, the goddess of Zabalam (CTL 319).

1092 **é.temen.ní.íl.lá**, "House, Foundation Platform which Bears Terror," a sanctuary of Ur mentioned in Šulgi C 26: doubtless a variation on é.temen.ní.gùr.ru 1.

1093 **é.temen.ur.sag̃**, "House, Foundation Platform of the Hero," temple of Adad at Ešnunna, patronized by Dādūša (year 3; cf. Bahija Khalil Ismail, *Oberhuber AV*, p. 105), and Ibāl-pî-El II (year 2, no TN) and probably Sîn-abūšu (year t, no TN).

1094 ***tiʾāmat***, "Sea," seat of Marduk in é.umuš.a of é.sag̃.íl at Babylon (*Topog. Texts* no. 1 = *Tintir* II 1).

1095 **é.ti.la**, "House which Gives Life," a temple of Gula-Ninkarrak in Borsippa, rebuilt by Nebuchadnezzar II (Ball, *PSBA* 10 [1888], pp. 368ff., ii 43; etc.), also mentioned in a ritual fragment (*Topog. Texts* no. 45, obv. 6′).

1096 **ti.la.a**, seat of Alala and Belili in é.sag̃.íl at Babylon (*Topog. Texts* no. 1 = *Tintir* II 14).

1097 **(é).ti.ra.áš**, "House of Tiraš," a shrine built for Ning̃irsu by Ur-Nanše (Steible, *FAOS* 5/I, UrN 25, v 8; 28, iv 5; 41; etc.), Eannatum (ibid., Ean 2, vii 19: é.gal ti.ra.áš; Ean 5, ii 4: é.ti.ra.áš$^{ki}$) and Uruinimgina (ibid., Ukg 1, i 8; 4, i 6; etc.), for whom it is é.gal ti.ra.áš, "Palace of GN." Looted by Lugalzaggesi (ibid., Ukg 16, i 8). Among other cult-centers near Lagaš in Ur III documents and offering lists (*ITT* 695, rev. 8; Hussey, *HSS* 4 54, rev. 6; *MVN* VI 301, rev. ii 1; etc.).

1098 **é.ti.[ . . . ]**, sanctuary found among TNs of Nanna-Suen in a liturgical text (*BL* no. 27, 10′).

1099 **é.til.la.šár.šár.ra**, "House which Makes Living Things Multiply," a socle in é.sag̃.íl at Babylon (*Topog. Texts* no. 1 = *Tintir* II 25′).

1100 **é.tílla.maḫ**, "House, Exalted Open Place" 1, a sanctuary of Enlil (CTL 31) at Nippur, also known from the Hymn to E-kur (Kramer, *RSO* 32 [1957], p. 97, 26) and liturgical texts (Cohen, *Lamentations*, pp. 98, 51: é.dil.e.maḫ; 350, 49–50: qualified as ki ní te.en.te.en, "place of repose"). Note the toponym é.ti.la.maḫ$^{ki}$ in pre-Sargonic documents from Nippur (Pohl, *TuM* 5 24, i 3; 88, ii 3).

1101 **é.tilla$_x$.maḫ?** 2, see É.AŠ.AN.AMAR

1102 **é.tílla.ra**, "House which Smites the Steppe(?)," a sanctuary of Šulpae (Cohen, *Lamentations*, p. 733, 64).

1103 **é.tilmun.(na)**, "House of the Noble" or "Tilmun-House" 1, temple of Inanna/Ištar at Ur (Proto-*Kagal* 227; CTL [343]), well known from Inanna's Descent, the éš.dam hymns and other literature (Wilcke, *RlA* V, p. 78; *CT* 58 13, 18; T. Howard-Carter, *JCS* 39 [1987], pp. 99f.; Wilcke, *Isin* III, p. 109, iv′ 7′: OB royal). Furnished with a bára.si.ga by Sargon of Akkade (Gelb and Kienast, *FAOS* 7, p. 65, Srg A 1: $^{d}$INANNA.ZA.ZA, no TN). Provided with a priestess by Išme-Dagān (Frayne, *RIME* 4, p. 41, 7′); its cella (é.šu.sì.ga) was enlarged by Warad-Sîn (ibid., p. 253, 32). Mentioned among other cult-centers of Ištar in the hymn to the Queen of Nippur (Lambert, *Zikir šumim*, p. 206, 85). See also é.èš.bur.

1104 **é.tilmun.na** 2, sanctuary of Ninšubur (CTL 458).

1105 **é.tilmun.na.ŠA**, sanctuary of Ninšubur (CTL 459).

1106 **é.TIN.na**, sanctuary of Belili (CTL 468), possibly to be read é.kúrun.na, "House of Liquor."

1107 **é.$^{d}$TIR.an.na**, "House of the Rainbow," part or epithet of the temple of Keš (Keš Temple Hymn 34).

1108 **é.tir.kù.ga**, "House, Pure Forest," a sanctuary of Gula (Cohen, *Lamentations*, p. 225, 27; Krecher, *Kultlyrik*, pp. 53, 12; 85). Cf. zag.tir.ra.

1109 **é.tu$_6$.tu$_6$**, "House of Spells," TN or epithet known from Proto-*Kagal* 200.

1110 **é.$^{giš}$tukul.ka.kéš**, "House which Binds on the Weapons," TN or epithet known from the big OB forerunner to *Hh* XXI, where it appears among TNs associated with Nergal (*MSL* XI, p. 142, viii 33).

1111 **é.tukur.ra**, "Weighty House," temple of Bunene (CTL 292; é.tukur.re: Nougayrol, *JCS* 1 [1947], p. 330, 3′ = Wiseman, *Iraq* 31 [1969], p. 176, 14′; *lipšur*-litany). Metrological text: *Topog. Texts* no. 37 (no TN). See also é.kur.ra.

1112 **túl.idim.an.ki**, "Well of the Springs of Heaven and Underworld," a shrine in ub.šu.ukkin.na of é.sag̃.íl at Babylon (*Topog. Texts* no. 1 = *Tintir* II 24′).

1113 **é.tum.ma.al$^{ki}$** 1, by-name for é.ki.ùr of Ninlil at Nippur (Temple Hymns 46), borrowed from her cult-center downstream of Nippur (Wilcke, *AfO* 24 [1973], pp. 5f.; Yoshikawa, *Acta Sum* 11 [1989], pp. 285 ff.), the subject of the eponymous chronicle (Sollberger, *JCS* 16 [1962], pp. 40ff.).

1114 **é.tum.ma.al** 2, seat of Ninlil as Kutušar in é.ki.ùr of é.šár.ra at Aššur (*Topog. Texts* no. 21, obv. 18′).

1115 **é.tùn.gal**, "House of the Great Axe," temple of Ištar in Šubat-[ . . . ] (CTL 363).

1116 **(é).tùr.amaš.a**, "House of Cattle-Pen and Sheepfold," shrine of Ištar as Lillaenna mentioned in liturgical texts (Cohen, *Lamentations*, pp. 651, 6; 711, 136; 714, 191).

1117 **é.tùr.kalam.ma**, "House, Cattle-Pen of the Land," temple of Bēlet-Bābili (Ištar of Babylon) in Babylon (*Topog. Texts* nos. 1 = *Tintir* IV 8; 9, 14′; 39, ii b 2; CTL 368; *PBS* V 157, i 3: éš.dam hymn), rebuilt by Apil-Sîn (years 11.13ff.) and Ḫammurapi (year 34, for Anu, Ištar and Nanāy; cf. year 14), and by Aššurbanipal (Streck, *Asb.*, p. 228, 13). Patronized by Samsu-ilūna (Frayne, *RIME* 4, p. 392, 9′.15′; cf. ys 8.31?). Visited by Nabonidus (Grayson, *Chronicles*, p. 109, 6). Survived into the Parthian period (*BRM* I 99, 26 // *CT* 49 150, 23; McEwan, *Iraq* 43 [1981], p. 138, obv. 7). In the OB prayer *PBS* I/1 2 the temple is the abode of Ištar as Anunnîtum (see now Lambert in *Studies Sjöberg*, p. 328, 157). Mentioned in the Dumuzi text *CT* 15 28, 18, and in the Syncretistic Ištar Hymn (*KAR* 109, obv. 17). TN in rituals: Lambert, *Love Lyrics*, passim; Watanabe, *Acta Sum* 13 (1991), p. 378, 5′; *Topog. Texts* no. 57, obv. 7; BM 32656, iii 2′; iv 8′–9′. Commonly attested in liturgical texts, often in the standard litany of TNs, where it follows é.sag̃.íl (Maul, *Eršaḫunga* no. 70–71, 12′; Cohen, *Lamentations*, index p. 752; *Eršemma*, pp. 113, 22; 133, 37; 144, 22; 145, 26; etc.). *KAR* 142, ii 1 lists a seat of the Asakku demon opposite é.TN. Street of é.TN: Strassmaier, *Camb.* 431, 5–6. See *Topog. Texts*, pp. 307f.

1118 **tuš . . .**, see also dúr . . .

1119 **é.tuš.mes**, "House, Seat of the Warrior" 1, part or by-name of é.ki.nam of Bēlat-ekalli at Aššur (*Topog. Texts* no. 20 = Götteradreßbuch 166: Assyrian TL).

1120 **é.tuš.mes** 2, part or by-name of é.g̃arza-*kidudê* of Ištar as Šarrat-nipḫi at Aššur (*Topog. Texts* no. 20 = Götteradreßbuch 169–70: Assyrian TL).

1121 **é.u.dul**, "House of the Herdsman," a building in uru.kù at G̃irsu, a shrine of Baba? (Cohen, *Eršemma*, p. 139, 10; for a different interpretation of the TN cf. p. 194).

1122 **é.u.gal**, or é.umun.gal, "House of the Great Lord," temple of Enlil at Dūr-Kurigalzu, built by Kurigalzu (I *R* 4, no. 14/1, 7; Baqir, *Iraq*, Suppl. 1944, fig. 16; etc.; restored CTL 55). Note MB votive inscription of a steward (*šatammu*) of TN: Sollberger, *JAOS* 88 (1968), p. 192, 6. Also known as é.$u_4$.gal of Parsâ: TL no. 3, 42′; Erra IV 63; *STT* 20, 8′?. If Parsâ is the old name of the city rebuilt as Dūr-Kurigalzu, as is generally maintained, it is legitimate to suggest that é.$u_4$.gal, "House of the Great Storm," was reinterpreted as é.u(mun).gal at the same time. See also é.$u_5$.gal.

1123 **é.ú.nam.ti.la**, "House of the Herbs of Life," temple of Gula as Ninisinna at Larsa, rebuilt by Gungunum (year 24, no TN), and Warad-Sîn (Frayne, *RIME* 4, p. 245, 12).

1124 **ú.su**, seat of Gula in é.rab.ri.ri (at Babylon? *Topog. Texts* no. 12, 9′). Cf. é.ú.zu.

1125 **é.ú.zu**, "House which Knows Herbs," seat of Gula in é.sag̃.íl at Babylon (*Topog. Texts* no. 1 = *Tintir* II 12).

1126 **é.ù.la**, "House of Sleep(?)," temple of Ninurra, "the mother of Umma," at Umma, rebuilt by the city governor Nammaḫani in the reign of Yarlagan of Gutium (Gelb and Kienast, *FAOS* 7, p. 296, Gutium 2). Ninurra's is the second-ranking temple of Umma according to an Ur III administrative document (Englund, *Acta Sum* 14 [1992], p. 87, 16; no TN).

1127 **é.$u_4$.gal**, "House of the Great Storm" 1, a variant or older name of Enlil's temple at Dūr-Kurigalzu, see é.u.gal.

1128 **é.$u_4$.gal** 2, seat of Enlil in é.rab.ri.ri (at Babylon? *Topog. Texts* no. 12, 3′).

1129 **é.$u_4$.gal** 3, a temple of Adad (CTL 296).

1130 **é.$u_4$.gal.gal.(la)**, "House of Great Storms" 1, temple of Adad at Karkara (CTL 295), provided with an *ēntu*-priestess by Rīm-Sîn I (year 12; no TN), patronized by Utu-ḫeg̃al (Römer, *OrNS* 54 [1985], p. 280, iii 23–26; no TN), and Ḫammurapi (CḪ iii 64). Also in liturgical texts, where it is first in the standard litany of TNs of Adad (Maul, *Eršaḫunga* nos. 18, 7; 19–20, 7; 21, 7; Cohen, *Lamentations*, pp. 431, 41; 433, 93), a *lipšur*-litany (Nougayrol, *JCS* 1 [1947], p. 330, 4′ // Wiseman, *Iraq* 31 [1969], p. 176, 15′), and in the syncretistic hymn to Nanāy (Reiner, *JNES* 33 [1974], p. 227, 37: *ina Bīt-Kar-ka-ra*).

1131 **é.u$_4$.gal.gal.la** 2, seat (of Adad?) in é.sağ.íl at Babylon (*Topog. Texts* no. 1 = *Tintir* II 39).

1132 **é.u$_4$.gal.gim**, "House Like a Great Storm," a temple of Adad (CTL 297); cf. é.úg.gal.gim as an epithet of his temple in Karkara (Temple Hymns 328, var. é.u$_6$.gal.gim).

1133 **é.u$_4$.gal.gim.ki.ḫuš.[ . . . ]**, "House Like a Great Storm, [*Built in a*] Fearsome Place," temple of Iškur (at Uruk?), rebuilt by Sîn-kāšid (Frayne, *RIME* 4, p. 458, 7). Restore [ri.a] or [dù.a]? See also é.sağ.gi$_4$.a.ni.du$_{10}$.

1134 **é.u$_4$.gim.x.x**, "House Like a Storm . . . ," temple of Ašgi (CTL 171), no doubt at Keš or Adab.

1135 **é.u$_4$.nu.zu**, "House which Knows Not Daylight," by-name of é.itima.kù of Ninlil, used on its own in the Hymn to E-kur (Kramer, *RSO* 32 [1957], p. 96, 5; cf. Curse of Akkade 129).

1136 **é.u$_4$.sakar.ra**, "House of the Crescent" 1, a sanctuary of Šara (CTL 455).

1137 **é.u$_4$.sakar.ra** 2, a sanctuary of Gašan-ğagia in liturgical texts (Cohen, *Lamentations*, pp. 210, 63; 352, 102; Krecher, *Kultlyrik*, pp. 60, 36; 199, 7).

1138 **é.u$_4$.sakar** 3, sanctuaries at Ğirsu (uru.kù.ga) and URU×KÁR.kù.ga (see Selz, *FAOS* 15/I, p. 185).

1139 **é.u$_4$.šú.uš**, "House of Sundown," temple listed in Proto-*Kagal* 216 among those of Nergal: cf. his epithet lugal (var. en) u$_4$.šú.[uš] in the Temple Hymns (line 464).

1140 **é.u$_4$.u$_5$.x.dim.[ . . . ]**, TN or epithet known from the big OB forerunner to *Hh* XXI (*MSL* XI, p. 142, viii 45).

1141 **é.u$_4$.ul**, "House of Days of Old," shrine of Marduk as Bēl-mātāti, in é.sağ.íl at Babylon, known from the New Year rituals (*RAcc.*, pp. 130ff., 29.66.77, etc.; BM 41577, iii 27).

1142 **é.u$_4$.x**, a temple or shrine known from CTL 225.

1143 **é.u$_4$.[ . . . ]**, sanctuaries of Adad (CTL 299–300).

1144 **é.u$_5$.gal**, temple patronized by Burnaburiaš (Arnaud, *Sumer* 32 [1976], p. 101, 9). Listed between Enlil's temples é.kur (Nippur) and é.nam.ti.la (Nippur or, more probably, Babylon), this TN is very likely a variant of é.u.gal.

1145 **é.u$_6$.de**, "House of Wonder," TN or epithet known from Proto-*Kagal* 198.

1146 **é.u$_6$.de.gal.an.na**, "House, Great Wonder of Heaven," ziqqurrat at IM$^{ki}$ (i.e., Karkara? TL no. 4, 22; no. 5, 13′: an.g[al?]).

1147 **é.u$_6$.de.kalam.ma**, "House, Great Wonder of the Land" 1, see é.dub.lá.maḫ 1

1148 **é.u$_6$.de.kalam.ma** 2, see aš.te.ki.sikil 1

1149 **é.u$_6$.gal.gim**, see é.u$_4$.gal.gim

1150 **é.u$_6$.nir**, "House, Temple-Tower," ziqqurrat of Ea in Eridu (CTL 184; TL no. 4, 21; no. 5, 19′; no. 8, 8′?; Temple Hymns 1; see Sjöberg, *TCS* III, p. 50; Lambert, *AfO* 19 [1959–60], p. 115, A 5′). In Sumerian literature: van Dijk, *MIO* 12 (1966–67), p. 64, 3: hymn to Ḫammurapi; *UET* VI 101, 9: hymn to Ḫaya; Green, *JCS* 30 (1978), p. 158, 7: Eridu Lament Ur. Also in litanies (Maul, *Eršaḫunga* no. 10, 4; Cohen, *Lamentations*, p. 623[49]?; Langdon, *BL* no. 156, 2; George, *RA* 82 [1988], p. 159, 32; etc.), and the syncretistic hymn to Nanāy (Reiner, *JNES* 33 [1974], p. 225, 11).

1151 **(é).u$_6$.nir.ki.tuš.maḫ**, "House, Temple-Tower, Exalted Abode," ziqqurrat of Zababa at Kiš (TL no. 4, 12; no. 5, 10′), rebuilt by Ḫammurapi (year 36) and Samsu-iluna, for Zababa and Ištar (Frayne, *RIME* 4, p. 384, 9; year 22). Also in liturgical texts, where it often follows é.me.te.ur.sağ in the standard litany of TNs of Ninurta (Cohen, *Eršemma*, p. 145, 10; *Lamentations*, pp. 441, 16; 458, 16; 470, 16: nu.nir; Maul, *Eršaḫunga* no. 37, 10; *CT* 42 12, pl. 22, 7). Also known as é.an.úr.ki.tuš.maḫ.

1152 **é.u$_{18}$.lu.ğál.[ . . . ].sì.sì**, a temple at Nippur (*Topog. Texts* no. 18 = Nippur Compendium § 6, d).

1153 **é.ub.a.ra.al.li**, "House, Niche of the Netherworld," a seat of Gula in é.sağ.íl at Babylon (*Topog. Texts* no. 1 = *Tintir* II 13).

1154 **é.ub.imin**, "House of Seven Niches" 1, part or by-name of é.anna at Uruk (Temple Hymns 201; Green, *JCS* 30 [1978], p. 138, 23′: Eridu Lament; CTL 316; Cohen, *Lamentations*, pp. 544, 125; 552, 125; 563f., 165–67; *VAS* II 3, iv 16), and so also of Uruk itself (*MSL* XI, pp. 54, 17; 63, 10′; Kilmer, *JAOS* 83 [1963], p. 428, *Malku* I 213).

1155 **é.ub.imin** 2, by-name of é.PA of Ninğirsu (q.v), as built by Gudea (cf. Falkenstein, *AnOr* 30, p. 134).

1156 **ub.saḫar.ra**, "Earthen Niche" 1, a shrine at Nippur known from the OB list from Isin (p. 4, IM 96881, iv′ 4′).

1157 **ub.saḫar.ra** 2, a dais of Marduk at Babylon (*Topog. Texts* no. 1 = *Tintir* V 25).

1158 **ub.šu.ukkin.na**, "Court of the Assembly" 1, the cosmic court of the divine assembly (*En. el.* VI 162).

1159 **ub.šu.ukkin.na** 2, in é.kur at Nippur (Proto-*Kagal* 187; p. 4, OB Isin list, IM 96881, iv′ 3′; *Topog. Texts* no. 18 = Nippur Compendium § 14, iv 13: divine residents; *Angim* 89; Kramer, *RSO* 32 [1957], p. 97, 12: Hymn to E-kur; IV $R^2$ 56, ii 17: incantation; OB prebend sales: *OECT* VIII 9, 2.16; 10, 2: Samsu-iluna). Its full name is TN-me.zi.ḫal.ḫal, "which Allots the True *Me*'s" (Cohen, *Lamentations*, p. 349, 28).

1160 **ub.šu.ukkin.na** 3, in é.sağ.íl at Babylon, where its full name is TN-me.zu.ḫal.ḫal.la, "which Allots the Known *Me*'s" (*Topog. Texts* nos. 1 = *Tintir* II 16′; 8, 5′; 13 = E-sagil Tablet 3.14; Borger, *Esarh.*, p. 28, 39; I *R* 54, ii 55: Nebuchadnezzar II; royal ritual: *Topog. Texts*, p. 288, K 3446+, obv. 15.18).

1161 **ub.šu.ukkin.na** 4, in é.ninnu at G̃irsu (Falkenstein, *AnOr* 30, p. 141).

1162 **ub.šu.ukkin.na** 5, in the *bīt rēš* of Anu at Uruk, known from LB rituals (Falkenstein, *Topographie*, p. 13).

1163 **é.UD.ta.aš**, temple found in liturgical texts in the standard litany of TNs of Adad (Maul, *Eršaḫunga* nos. 18, 10; 19–20, 10; 21, 10; Cohen, *Lamentations*, pp. 431, 44; 433, 96).

1164 **é.ug.gal**, "House of the Great Lion," TN or epithet known from Proto-*Kagal* 218a.

1165 **é.UG$^{?}$.ti**, temple in Susa whose šabra official dedicated an object to Nungal for Amar-Suen (Steible, *FAOS* 9/2, p. 247, 6).

1166 **é.úg.gal.gim**, see é.u$_4$.gal.gim

1167 **é.ul.la**, "House of Rejoicing," temple of Gula as Ninkarrak at Sippar, rebuilt by Nebuchadnezzar II (*PBS* XV 79, iii 5; etc.). Note the NB offering list *VAS* VI 29, 10–11: $^{d}$g[*u-l*]*a u* $^{d}$[ . . . ] *šá* é.ul.la.

1168 **(é).ul.maš** 1, temple of Ištar at Ulmaš in Akkade (Proto-*Kagal* 231; *MSL* XI, p. 142, vii 30; CTL 362; TL no. 3, 31′; Temple Hymns 518), rebuilt by Nabonidus (*CT* 34 33, 6), who attributes the previous building to Sargon and Narām-Sîn (cf. the unattributed Sargonic year-name, Gelb and Kienast, *FAOS* 7, p. 58, Anon. 8; Curse of Akkade 7–9), and also reports the fruitless attempts at uncovering the ruins made by Kurigalzu, Esarhaddon and Aššurbanipal. Patronized by Ḫammurapi (CḪ iv 49). Well known from Inanna's Descent and the éš.dam hymns (Wilcke, *RlA* V, p. 78). Also in liturgical texts (Maul, *Eršaḫunga*, p. 353, 7′–8′; Cohen, *Lamentations*, p. 585, 508), in *lipšur*-litanies (*Šurpu* II 171; Wiseman, *Iraq* 31 [1969], p. 177, 43′), and in the syncretistic hymn to Nanāy (Reiner, *JNES* 33 [1974], p. 227, 34). NB prebend document: *VAS* V 157, 3. Note [(x) é?] $^{d}$*ul-*[*ma-ši-tu*]*m*.⌈ma⌉ in an unattributed and fragmentary Ur III royal inscription (Steible, *FAOS* 9/II, Ur 12, 3′). See also é.maš.

1169 **é.ul.maš** 2, temple of Anunnîtum at Sippar-Anunnîtum, rebuilt by Ammī-ṣaduqa (year 17+d) and Nabonidus, who reports earlier constructions of Sābium (I *R* 69, iii 28) and Šagarakti-Šuriaš (V *R* 64, iii 27).

1170 **é.ul.maš** 3, shrine of Anu and Ištar at Uruk, known from liturgical texts (IV $R^2$ 19, no. 3, 37–38; Cohen, *Lamentations*, p. 729, 10) and a LB temple ritual (Lackenbacher, *RA* 71 [1977], p. 40, 4′; cf. Falkenstein, *Topographie*, p. 40).

1171 **é.ul.šár.me.šu.du$_7$**, "House of Jubilation and Perfect *Me*'s," temple (of Baba at Dēr?), mentioned in the Syncretistic Ištar Hymn (rev. 16; unpub., courtesy Lambert).

1172 **ul$_4$.nun**, see é.g̃ír.nun

1173 **umma.du$_6$.da**, see é.g̃á.du$_6$.da

1174 **é.umun.gal**, see é.u.gal

1175 **úmun.sağ**, "Foremost Craft," seat of Bēlet-ilī at the gate ká.$u_6$.de.babbar in é.sağ.íl at Babylon (*Topog. Texts* no. 1 = *Tintir* II 41).

1176 **é.umuš.a**, "House of Command," cella of Marduk in é.sağ.íl at Babylon (*Topog. Texts* no. 6, 1, rest.; CTL 226; *KAR* 109, obv. 16, é.è.umuš.a: syncretistic Ištar hymn; *RAcc.*, pp. 130ff., 34.199.245, etc.), restored by Aššurbanipal (Streck, *Asb.*, p. 230, 14; etc.) and refurbished by Nebuchadnezzar II (George, RA 82 [1988], p. 143, 31′; and passim). Location of a seat of Tašmētum (Borger, *Esarh.*, § 53, rev. 39). See *Topog. Texts*, pp. 389f.

1177 **é.umuš.a.$^{d}$asal.lú.ḫi**, "House of Command, of Asalluḫi," seat of the Igigi in the chapel of Ninurta(?) in é.sağ.íl at Babylon (*Topog. Texts* no. 1 = *Tintir* II 17).

1178 **é.umuš.ğar.ğéštu.diri**, "House Endowed with Reason, Surpassing in Wisdom," a sanctuary known only from a Sumerian hymn (Sjöberg, *ZA* 63 [1973], p. 41, 28; read é.dúr.ğar . . . ?).

1179 **é.umuš.ka.nağ.ğá**, see é.mùš.kalam.ma

1180 **é.ùn.na**, "Mighty House," a temple of Ištar in Subartu, i.e., Assyria (CTL 392).

1181 **unu.maḫ**, "Exalted Seat," part of é.kur at Nippur, restored by Nebuchadnezzar I (Brinkman, *PKB*, p. 113[624]).

1182 **é.ur.$gi_7$.ra**, "Dog-House," sanctuary of Gula as Ninisinna (at Isin?), rebuilt by Enlil-bāni (Frayne, *RIME* 4, p. 81, 16). Probably a sacred dog kennel.

1183 **ur.máš.tùr**, "Pen of Lions and Wild Beasts," seat of Šakkan and Urmaḫ in é.šár.ra at Aššur (*Topog. Texts* no. 21, obv. 31′).

1184 **é.ʿurʾ.me.(imin).an.ki**, see é.$ur_4$.me.imin.an.ki

1185 **é.ur.sağ**, "House of the Hero," sanctuary known from a love song of Dumuzi and Inanna (*CT* 58 13, 38).

1186 **é.ur.sağ.pa.è**, "House of the Eminent Hero," sanctuary at or near Lagaš known from an Ur III offering list (*MVN* VI 301, rev. ii 19).

1187 **ur.sağ.sum.kud.da**, seat of Lātarāk and Mīšarru in a lobby of é.šár.ra at Aššur (*Topog. Texts* no. 21, obv. 13′; rev. 26′).

1188 **é.ur.sağ.[ . . . ]**, temple of Paniğinğarra at Adab (CTL 164). Note an unnamed temple of this god (as Barauleğarra) built at Adab by Rīm-Sîn I (year 6).

1189 **é.úr.bi.$du_{10}$**, "House whose Foundation is Good," TN or epithet known from the big OB forerunner to *Hh* XXI (*MSL* XI, p. 142, viii 28).

1190 **é.úr.gub.ba**, "House, Established Foundation," temple of Pisağunuk in east Babylon (*Topog. Texts* nos. 1 = *Tintir* IV 26; 3, rev. 8′).

1191 **é.úr.nam**, see é.uru.na.nam 2

1192 **ur$_4$.g̃éštu.lal**, "Gatherer of the Deaf," seat of $^{d}$en.PI in an inner gate of é.šár.ra at Aššur (*Topog. Texts* no. 21, obv. 24′).

1193 **é.ur$_4$.(me).imin.an.ki**, "House which Gathers the Seven (*Me*'s) of Heaven and Underworld," ziqqurrat of é.zi.da at Borsippa (TL no. 4, 3; no. 5, 22′), restored by Nebuchadnezzar II (I *R* 51, no. 1, i 27; etc.). Appears in liturgical texts in the standard litany of TNS, where it follows é.nam.bi.zi.da (Cohen, *Lamentations*, index p. 752; Langdon, *BL* nos. 26, 4′; 56, obv. 21; George, *RA* 82 [1988], p. 159, 37; etc.).

1194 **é.ur$_4$.ur$_4$**, "Master Bedroom," part or by-name of a temple of Nabû (at Aššur? *Topog. Texts* no. 20 = Götteradreßbuch 162: Assyrian TL).

1195 **é.ur$_5$.šà.ba**, "House, Oracle(?) of the Heart" 1, temple of Ištar as Nanāy in Borsippa (CTL 370; *Topog. Texts* no. 57, obv. 3: ritual), which gave its name to a city quarter (*VAS* V 96, 1). Also in cultic calendars (*BRM* IV 25, 48 // *SBH* VII, obv. 23; VIII, ii 18.20; or to é.ur$_5$.šà.ba 2?).

1196 **é.ur$_5$.šà.ba** 2, seat of Nanāy in é.sag̃.íl at Babylon (*Topog. Texts* no. 1 = *Tintir* II 9″; *BE* VIII/1 108, 9: Darius).

1197 **é.ur$_5$.šà.ba** 3, temple of Lisi (CTL 172), also mentioned in liturgical texts (Cohen, *Eršemma*, p. 147, 6; *Lamentations*, pp. 237, 294 = 306, 168; 360, 228; describing a temple bed-chamber: pp. 611, 102; 614, 176). At Kissa = Umma! (ibid., pp. 610, 80; 613, 148: see Lambert, *JNES* 49 [1990], p. 76).

1198 **é.uru.kù.ga**, by-name of é.tar.sír.sír of Baba in Uru-ku, the sacred quarter of G̃irsu (so really é.GN-ak; cf. Temple Hymns 263.270, and note uru.kù also used of é.ninnu); used by Ur-Baba (Steible, *FAOS* 9/I, UrB 1, iv 6; 3, 9; 8, ii 8) and Gudea (Stat. D, iii 17; Gud. 6–9), also found in Lamentation over Sumer and Ur 161 and in the cultic lament im.ma.al gù.dé.dé (Cohen, *Lamentations*, pp. 610, 86; 613, 152: úru).

1199 **(é).uru.na.nam**, "House, the Very City" 1, sanctuary in the temple complex of Enlil at Nippur (Proto-*Kagal* 179: é.úru.na.nam; CTL 41), built by Enmebaraggesi according to the Tummal inscription (Sollberger, *JCS* 16 [1962], p. 42, 1). Also a name and/or quarter of Nippur (*MSL* XI, p. 11, *Hh* XXI 8!; *Topog. Texts* no. 18 = Nippur Compendium § 6, 10′; paired with uzu!.mú.a in two OB liturgies of Nippur: Cohen, *Lamentations*, pp. 98, 54; 350, 54).

1200 **é.uru.na.nam** 2, dais of Nabû at Babylon (*Topog. Texts* nos. 1 = *Tintir* IV 21, var. é.ùru.na.nam, also é.úr.nam; 3, rev. 2′; 4, 21).

1201 **é.úru.ama.ki**, see é.ùru.an.ki

1202 **é.úru.kù**, "House, Pure City," a temple of Belili (CTL 465). See also é. uru.kù.ga.

1203 **é.úru.na.nam**, see é.uru.na.nam 1

1204 **é.úru.sag̃.g̃á**, see é.ùru.sag̃.g̃á

1205 **é.úru.[zé.eb?]**, "House, Pleasant(?) City," a temple of Ea (CTL 183).

1206 **é.ùru.an.ki**, "House which Guards Heaven and Underworld," ziqqurrat of Kutha (TL no. 5, 9′; no. 6, 24; cf. no. 4, 15: é.AN.ÙRU.ki). Written é.úru. ama.ki in the Syncretistic Ištar Hymn (l. 78; unpub., courtesy Lambert).

1207 **é.ùru.na.nam**, see é.uru.na.nam 2

1208 **(é).ùru.sag̃.g̃á**, temple of Gula at Nippur (*Topog. Texts* no. 19 = Nippur TL 24′–26′; divine residents listed in no. 18 = Nippur Compendium § 14, v 14–17; also Nougayrol, *RA* 41 [1947], p. 35, 4–11), known also from LB administrative documents (*TuM* 2–3 241, 6; McEwan, *LB Tablets*, p. 60, 48:5). Also written (é).úru.sag̃.g̃á, "House, Foremost City," as in the Syncretistic Ištar Hymn (line 98; unpub., courtesy Lambert), and in liturgical texts, in which it may sometimes refer to a shrine in é.gal.maḫ at Isin and is commonly found in epithets of Gula, as Gašantilluba-Nintinugga, and Ninurta, who are ama/umun.(é).TN (Cohen, *Lamentations*, pp. 161, 151′; 210, 67; 225, 23; 239, 328; 255f., 3.30.45: var. é.ḫur.sag̃.g̃á, qualified as ma balag̃.sag̃.g̃á, "chamber of the foremost harp"; 308, 202; 351, 65: Nippur; 471, 55; 502, 14; 507, 109; 529, 79; 621, 313: é.ùru.sag̃.g̃á; Krecher, *Kultlyrik*, pp. 60, 38; 199, 9; Langdon, *BL* no. 73, 23; etc.).

1209 **é.urugal**, "House, Netherworld," a sanctuary of Nergal known from Proto-*Kagal* 217. Possibly = èš.urugal$_x$ of Ereškigal.

1210 **é.ÚS.GÍD.DA**, "House, Lobby," a shrine of Enlil (CTL 34) at Nippur, in the é.kur complex at the Gate of Sîn (Cohen, *Lamentations*, p. 350, 36).

1211 **é.ÚS.GÍD.DA.gíd.da**, "House, Long Lobby," a shrine of Enlil (CTL 35).

1212 **é.usu.[x]**, a temple of Utaulu (CTL 170).

1213 **é.uš.ma.al.la**, seat of the divine image ($^{d}$*ṣa-lam*) in é.šár.ra at Aššur (*Topog. Texts* no. 21, rev. 21′).

1214 **é.ušumgal.an.na**, "House of the Dragon of Heaven" 1, socle of Ninkasi represented by a brick found in the sanctuary of Ningal at Ur, é.g̃i$_6$.pàr.kù 1, made for Sîn by Sîn-balāssu-iqbi (*UET* I 173–74).

1215 **é.ušumgal.an.na** 2, seat of Ninkarnunna in é.rab.ri.ri (at Babylon? *Topog. Texts* no. 12, 13′).

1216 **é.utul**, "House of the Herd," a temple of Panig̃ing̃arra (CTL 168).

1217 **é.za**, "House of Stone," name or epithet of a shrine of Ning̃irsu in Lagaš, built by Eannatum (Steible, *FAOS* 5/I, Ean 69, ii 10; cf. 5/II, p. 83).

1218 **é.za.an.gàr**, see é.AN.za.gàr

1219 **é.za.gìn.(na)**, "House of Lapis Lazuli" 1, temple of Ištar at Susa (CTL 391), rebuilt by Mê-Kūbi, daughter of Bilalama (Frayne, *RIME* 4, p. 494, 13; no TN).

1220 **é.za.gìn.(na)** 2, temple at Aratta, attributed to Inanna in the Uruk epics (Enmerkar and Ensuḫkešdanna 28.59.78.149; Enmerkar and Lord of

Aratta 560), but elsewhere to Nissaba (Hallo, *CRRA* 17, p. 125, Nissaba and Enki 32).

1221 **é.za.gìn** 3, temple of Nissaba as Nanibgal at Ereš (Civil, *JAOS* 103 [1983], pp. 50, 7; 53, 46: Enlil and Sud; Proto-*Kagal* 223), known to the Temple Hymns as é.mul.mul é za.gìn gùn.a (line 529).

1222 **é.za.gìn.(na)** 4, possible seat of Nissaba in é.kur at Nippur: Kapp, *ZA* 51 (1955), p. 78, Enlil-bāni A 53! qualified as é.G̃EŠTU.$^{d}$NISSABA; see also é.kur.za.gìn.

1223 **é.za.gìn.na** 5, a sanctuary of Dumuzi (CTL 443), = é.TN 6?.

1224 ***é.za.gìn.na** 6, by-name of é.ib.gal of Ištar at Umma used in an éš.dam hymn (*VAS* II 48, 13: é-za-gi-na), = é.TN 5?

1225 **za.gìn.mu.uš**, seat of Kusu in é.šár.ra at Aššur (*Topog. Texts* no. 21, obv. 10′).

1226 **za?.na.me.gal**, a shrine in é.šár.ra at Aššur (*Topog. Texts* no. 21, rev. 4′).

1227 **zà.du$_{8}$.á.gùb.bu**, "Left-Hand Door-Sill," a shrine in the temple complex at Uruk (*Topog. Texts* no. 25, rev. 5′).

1228 **zà.du$_{8}$.á.zi.da**, "Right-Hand Door-Sill," a shrine in the temple complex at Uruk (*Topog. Texts* no. 25, rev. 4′).

1229 **é.zag.ir$_{9}$.ra**, "House, Sanctuary of the Mighty One," temple of Ninurta or a similar god, found in litanies (Maul, *OrNS* 60 [1991], pp. 314, 18; 316, 13: eršemma; *VAS* 24 30, rev. 7′: é.zag].ir$_{9}$!.ra), and in a cultic calendar of Babylon (*SBH* VIII, ii 30).

1230 **zag.tir.ra**, "Sanctuary of the Forest," sanctuary of Gula (at Isin?), as found in a cultic lament (Cohen, *Lamentations*, p. 256, 53, qualified as zag.tir.kù.ga).

1231 **é.zalag.ga**, "Bright House," *bīt ḫilṣi* in an upper courtyard of the temple complex at Uruk (*Topog. Texts* no. 25, obv. 9′).

1232 **é.zálag.x.gal**, a temple listed in the OB lexical list from Isin (p. 4, IM 96881, iii′ 9′).

1233 **é.zi.ba.na**, a sanctuary of Šulpae known from a liturgical hymn (Cohen, *Lamentations*, p. 733, 59); restore in CTL 163?

1234 **é.zi.ba.ti.la** 1, temple of Gula in Borsippa, rebuilt by Nebuchadnezzar II (Ball, *PSBA* 10 [1888], pp. 368ff., ii 51; etc.). Mentioned in a ritual fragment as é.zi.da.ba.ti.la (*Topog. Texts* no. 45, obv. 5′).

1235 **é.zi.ba.ti.la** 2, temple (of Gula?) at Marad, mentioned in the Syncretistic Ištar Hymn (l. 88; unpub., courtesy Lambert).

1236 **é.zi.da**, "True House" 1, temple of Marduk as Tutu, later of Nabû, at Borsippa (Proto-*Kagal* 224; CTL 231.236; TL no. 2, [5]; *Topog. Texts* nos. 14, 71: metrology; 28, 1′). Variously rebuilt, repaired or restored by Ḫammurapi (Frayne, *RIME* 4, p. 355, 31; cf. CḪ iii 15), Marduk-apla-iddina I (*VAS* I 34, for Marduk), Marduk-šāpik-zēri (*LIH* I 70), Nabûšuma-imbi (Lambert, *JAOS* 88 [1968], p. 126, i b5ff.; ii b 33, for Nabû), Esarhaddon (Borger, *Esarh.*, § 64, rev. 10), Aššurbanipal (Streck, *Asb.*, p. 242, 33; Thompson, *Prisms*, p. 30, 5; Nassouhi, *AfK* 2 [1924–25], p. 100, i 4–13; etc.) and Šamaš-šuma-ukīn (Lehmann-Haupt, *Šamaššumukîn*, II, no. 3, 27: šutum$_x$(É.G̃I$_6$.NAM.AB.DU$_7$)$^{meš}$, "storerooms"), Nebuchadnezzar II (passim), and finally Antiochus I (V *R* 66). Also in liturgical texts, commonly in the standard litany of TNs, where it is paired with é.maḫ.ti.la (Cohen, *Eršemma*, pp. 29, 10; 114, 24; 118, 35.2:11; 127, 15; 136, 5.9; *Lamentations* passim: index p. 752; Maul, *Eršaḫunga* nos. 63, 5′; 110, 3′; *OrNS* 60 [1991], p. 314, 21, among temples of Ninurta: eršemma; Langdon, *BL* no. 56, obv. 13; George, *RA* 82 [1988], p. 159f., 35.52; also Pallis, *Akîtu*, pl. 10, 19). Hymn to é.zi.da: Köcher, *ZA* 53 (1959), pp. 236–40. Mentioned in the Syncretistic Ištar Hymn (*KAR* 109, obv. 23), in the syncretistic hymn to Nanāy (Reiner, *JNES* 33 [1974], p. 227, 29), and in a *lipšur*-litanies (*Šurpu* II 155; Nougayrol, *JCS* 1 [1947], p. 330, 11′ // Wiseman, *Iraq* 31 [1969], p. 177, 22′).

1237 **é.zi.da** 2, seat of Lugaldimmerankia and cella of Nabû in é.sag̃.íl at Babylon (*Topog. Texts* no. 1 = *Tintir* II 2″; *RAcc.*, pp. 140f., 346.370: New Year ritual), refurbished by Nebuchadnezzar II (I *R* 65, i 34, and passim).

1238 **é.zi.da** 3, temple of Nabû in Nineveh (*Topog. Texts* no. 20 = Götteradreßbuch 160: Assyrian TL; Streck, *Asb.*, p. 272, 2), rebuilt or restored by Adad-nārārī III, Sargon II, Esarhaddon, Aššurbanipal and Sîn-šarra-iškun (see Menzel, *Tempel* I, p. 119; II, P 12).

1239 **é.zi.da** 4, temple of Nabû in Kalaḫ (*Topog. Texts* no. 20 = Götteradreßbuch 161: Assyrian TL), built by Aššurnaṣirpal II (Grayson, *RIMA* 2, p. 291, 57: no TN), patronized and restored by Adad-nārārī III, Esarhaddon, Aššurbanipal, Aššur-etel-ilāni and Sîn-šarra-iškun (see Menzel, *Tempel* I, p. 97; II, P 10).

1240 **é.zi.da.ba.ti.la**, see é.zi.ba.ti.la

1241 **é.zi.da.gal**, "Great True House," part or epithet of the temple of Keš (Keš Temple Hymn 32).

1242 **é.zi.da.g̃iš.nu$_{11}$.gal**, "True House of Great Light," temple of Dumuzi at Babylon (*Topog. Texts* no. 1 = *Tintir* IV 11, var. é.zi.da.nu.g̃ál; CTL [449]; also in a mythological text, BM unpub., courtesy Lambert).

1243 **é.zi.da.nu.g̃ál**, see é.zi.da.g̃iš.nu$_{11}$.gal

1244 **é.zi.dè.**[( . . . )], TN found in a ritual, possibly a variant of é.zi.da 1 (*Topog. Texts* no. 57, 2).

1245 **é.zi.kalam.ma**, "House of the Life of the Land" 1, temple of Ištar at Zabalam (CTL 401), rebuilt by Ḫammurapi (Frayne, *RIME* 4, pp. 352, 7; 354, 33).

1246 **é.zi.kalam.ma** 2, a temple known from *Kagal* Boğ. I F 9 (= *bi-it ki-ra-a*, following TNs of Ninurta).

1247 **é.zi.sù.ud.gal**, "Great House of Long Life," a sanctuary of Marduk (CTL 232; TL no. 3, 19′).

1248 *__é.zu.zal__, temple of Sugallītum (Ištar of é.su.gal), found in the OB hymn to Pauleĝarra (Pinches, *JRAS Cent. Suppl.* 1924, pp. 72ff., vi 23, written *e-zu-za-al*). Error for é.su.gal?

1249 **é.x.x.[a]n.ki**, temple of Ištar at Kār-Bēl-mātāti (TL no. 3, 23′). See é.an.ki 1.

1250 **é.x.babbar.ra**, a sanctuary of Šulpae (Cohen, *Lamentations*, p. 733, 61).

1251 **[é.x.d]é.a**, a temple of Inšušinak (CTL 475). Cf. é.kaš.dé.a?

1252 **[é.x.x.e]n.an.ki**, see é.gub.ba.an.ki

1253 **[é.x].gi.na**, a sanctuary of Enlil (CTL 23)

1254 **[é.x].gigir**, a ziqqurrat at Nippur (TL no. 4, 4).

1255 **[é.x].gú?.kù.ga**, seat of Ennugi represented by a brick found in the sanctuary of Ningal at Ur, é.ĝi$_6$.pàr.kù 1, made by Sîn-balāssu-iqbi (*UET* I 182).

1256 **[é.x.(x).ḫ]é.du$_7$**, sanctuary of Nabû (CTL 241). See é.šu.nigin.šu.du$_7$.

1257 **[é].x.kalam.(ma)**, two temples listed in TL no. 3, 14′–15′.

1258 **[é . . . ]x.kár**, temple of Amagula, built by Rīm-Sîn I (Frayne, *RIME* 4, p. 299, 23).

1259 **[é.x].kár.kár**, temple of Enlil at Ur (CTL 45).

1260 **[é . . . ]x.kù**, sanctuary of Ištar at Uruk mentioned in Sargon II's E-anna inscription (*YOS* I 38, 12), = é.ĝi$_6$.pàr.kù?

1261 **é.x.maḫ**, a sanctuary listed in the OB lexical list from Isin (p. 4, IM 96881, iii′ 4′).

1262 **[é].x.maḫ.di**, temple of Anunnîtum at Akkade (TL no. 3, 32′).

1263 **[é.(x).mul.m]ul**, a sanctuary of Ea (CTL 201).

1264 **[é.x.(x).n]í.te.na**, a temple listed in CTL 602.

1265 **é.x.sum.ma**, sanctuary associated with the temple of Ninlil at Nippur in an Ur III offering list (*TCL* II 5513, rev. 6; x = e, bur?).

1266 **[é.( . . . )]x.ug$_5$.ga**, the Akītu Temple at Aššur, rebuilt by Sennacherib (Meissner and Rost, *Senn.*, pl. 16, 3; coll. against Livingstone, *N.A.B.U.* 1990/87). See also é.dúb.dúb.x[ . . . ].

1267 **[é].⌜x⌝.zu.gal.kalam.ma**, see [é.š]à?.zu.gal.kalam.ma

## *Unnamed Temples, Listed by Divine Owner*

As an appendix to the gazetteer I have thought it useful to collect, from the sources utilized in its compilation, a list of temples for which no ceremonial name is given. Naturally this list could be hugely enlarged, as explained above, by culling information from all kinds of other texts, but such an operation is beyond the scope of this book. Because on occasion there is strong suspicion that an unnamed temple can be identified with a known ceremonial name, cross-references to the gazetteer are given, and sometimes information presented below is also found in the gazetteer.

1268 Adad: temple at Aššur built by Erišum I (Grayson, *RIMA* 1, pp. 37, 23; 38, 10) and completed by Ikūnum (ibid., p. 42, 14). See é.šùd.dè.g̃iš.tuku.

1269 Adad: temple at Borsippa, rebuilt by Nebuchadnezzar II (I *R* 55, iv 59).

1270 Adad: temple at Isani built by Shalmaneser I (Grayson, *RIMA* 1, p. 204, 16′).

1271 Adad: temple at uru*ka*?-*ḫat* built by Shalmaneser I (Grayson, *RIMA* 1, p. 204, 15′). Probably = OB é.me.te.nun.e.

1272 Adad: temple of DN and Šala at Kalaḫ rebuilt by Aššurnaṣirpal II (Grayson, *RIMA* 2, pp. 286, 8; 291, 56).

1273 Adad: temple at Larsa, built by Rīm-Sîn I (Frayne, *RIME* 4, p. 272, 16; year 2).

1274 Adad: temple at Nineveh, built by Aššurnaṣirpal II (Grayson, *RIMA* 2, p. 338, 9).

1275 Adad: temple at Nippur, known from a MB metrological text (Bernhardt and Kramer, *OrNS* 44 [1975], p. 98, 31), whose residents are listed in the Divine Directory of Nippur (*Topog. Texts* no. 18 = Nippur Compendium § 14, v 9–10).

1276 Adad: temple at uru*ši*-[ . . . ], near Babylon (*Topog. Texts* no. 38, 36).

1277 Adad: temple at Tell al-Hawa, rebuilt by Shalmaneser III (George, *Iraq* 52 [1990], p. 44, 2).

1278 Adad: temple at Udada, rebuilt by Ninurta-kudurrī-uṣur (shared with Mēšaru: Cavigneaux and Bahija Khalil Ismail, *Bagh. Mitt.* 21 [1990], p. 346, 5; 359, 6; etc.).

1279 Adad: cult at URU-*gab-ba-ri*-DÙ, established by Šamaš-rēša-uṣur (with Apladad, Šala and Mēšaru: Cavigneaux and Bahija Khalil Ismail, *Bagh. Mitt.* 21 [1990], p. 399, 2).

1280 Akītu temple: at Nineveh, built by Sargon II and Aššurbanipal (Thompson, *Prisms*, p. 35, 33; cf. idem, *Archaeologia* 79 [1929], p. 120, no. 43?).

1281 Amurru: temple built by Mananā (year h).

1282 Anu and Adad: temple at Aššur rebuilt by Aššur-rēša-iši I (Grayson, *RIMA* 1, pp. 317, 7–8; 318, 8:2); ziqqurrats at Aššur (ibid., p. 81, ii′ 2: Šamšī-Adad III or Aššur-rēša-iši I?; originally built by Šamšī-Adad I); gate of temple at Aššur (*RIMA* 1, p. 153, 4.11: Adad-nārārī I). See é.šà.an, é.me.lám.an.na.

1283 Anunnîtum: temple (at Ur?) built by Šu-Suen (Steible, *FAOS* 9/II, ŠS 6).

1284 Anunnîtum: temple built by Itūr-Šamaš of Kisurra (years c.d).

1285 Asakku: shrines of this demon at cultic locations in Babylon are listed in the Archive of Mystic Heptads (*KAR* 142, ii 1–10; *Topog. Texts*, p. 285).

1286 Baraulegarra: temples at Adab and Zarbilum, built by Rīm-Sîn I (years 2.6); see é.ur.sag̃.[ . . . ].

1287 Batirītum: temple built by the Amorite chief Ayyābum (Frayne, *RIME* 4, p. 702, 6).

1288 Bēlet-ilī: temple at Nippur, whose residents are listed in the Divine Directory of Nippur (*Topog. Texts* no. 18 = Nippur Compendium § 14, v 20–21).

1289 Bēlet-ṣēri: temple listed in CTL 563 (TN lost).

1290 Bēl-ibrīya: chapel at Aššur built by Aššur-nārārī I (Grayson, *RIMA* 1, p. 84, 5).

1291 Bizilla: temple at Ḫursag̃-kalamma, listed in TL no. 6, 15.

1292 Dagān: chapel (in temple of Aššur?) rebuilt by Shalmaneser I (Grayson, *RIMA* 1, p. 197, 10).

1293 Damgalnunna: temple at Nippur built by Šulgi (Steible, *FAOS* 9/II, Š 9).

1294 Damgalnunna: chapel in the temple of Ninḫursag̃ at Ubaid, built by KUR:É (Steible, *FAOS* 5/II, AnUr 7).

1295 Damu: sanctuary at Isin in OB documents, Kraus, *JCS* 3 (1949), p. 60.

1296 Dimgalabzu: temple on the border between Lagaš and Umma, as recorded by Enmetena and Lugalzaggesi (Steible, *FAOS* 5/I, Ent 28, iv 31; 5/II, p. 330, 55; cf. Falkenstein, *AnOr* 30, pp. 67, 150).

1297 Dumuzi: temple at Kinunir near Lagaš, desecrated by Lugalzaggesi (Steible, *FAOS* 5/I, Ukg 16, v 9). Also in an Ur III list of cultic personnel (Gelb, *StOr* 46 [1975], p. 49, 13–16).

1298 Dumuziabzu, Lady of Kinunir: temple at G̃irsu built by Ur-Baba (Steible, *FAOS* 9/I, UrB 1, vi 11) and Gudea (ibid., Gud. 10, 6).

1299 Ea: temple of DN and Damkina at Kalaḫ rebuilt by Aššurnaṣirpal II (Grayson, *RIMA* 2, pp. 286, 8; 291, 55).

1300 Ea: temple built by Itūr-Šamaš of Kisurra (years f.g).

1301 Ea: temple at Larsa, built by Rīm-Sîn I (year 4).

1302 Ea: temple at Nēmed-Laguda, listed in CTL 202 (TN lost).

1303 Ea and Damkina: temple at Nippur, known from a MB metrological text (Bernhardt and Kramer, *OrNS* 44 [1975], p. 98, 33).

1304 Ea/Enki: temple at Uruk, rebuilt by Sîn-kāšid (Frayne, *RIME* 4, p. 456, 11). See further [é.g̃éštu?].maḫ.[ . . . ].sum.mu.

1305 Enki: temple at G̃irsu, built by Ur-Baba (Steible, *FAOS* 9/I, UrB 1, iv 12; 4, 8; 8, iii 6).

1306 Enki: temple on the bank of the Tigris built by Gudea (Steible, *FAOS* 9/I, Gud. 11, found at Ur), also known from an Ur III offering list (*MVN* VI 301, obv. ii 8).

1307 Enkigal: temple built by Ur-Lumma of Umma (Steible, *FAOS* 5/II, UrL 1).

1308 Enlil: temple(?) at Aššur (Grayson, *RIMA* 1, p. 98, 4: Aššur-rabi I). See é.kur 2.

1309 Enlil: sanctuaries at Dūr-Suenna, G̃irsu and é.uru.kù, listed in CTL 53–54 and 56 (TNs lost).

1310 Enlil: dais (bára) at Namnunda-kig̃arra, erected by Eannatum, destroyed by Ur-Lumma of Umma, and rebuilt by Enmetena (Steible, *FAOS* 5/I, Ent 28, ii 14.39; cf. v 12).

1311 Ereškigal: temple, presumably at Aššur, built by Ikūnum and rebuilt by Šamšī-Adad I (Grayson, *RIMA* 1, p. 55, 4).

1312 Ereškigal: temple at Umma (ki.$^{d}$utu.è) built by Lu-Utu of Umma (Steible, *FAOS* 9/II, pp. 343–44).

1313 Ešertu: sanctuary of the Divine Decad ($^{d}$10-*te*) at Aššur rebuilt by Tiglath-pileser I (Grayson, *RIMA* 2, p. 26, 88). These may be the ten divine judges of é.šár.ra listed in the Divine Directory of Aššur (Menzel, *Tempel* II 64, Götteradreßbuch 34–42).

1314 G̃atumdug: temple in Uru-ku at G̃irsu, built by Ur-Nanše (Steible, *FAOS* 5/I, UrN passim) and Enmetena (ibid., Ent 1, ii 22; 8, vi 8; 24–25; etc.). Desecrated by Lugalzaggesi (ibid., Ukg 16, iii 13), and restored by Gudea (9/1, Stat. F, ii 2, cf. iii 6; Gud. 13–15a; year 14).

1315 G̃eštinanna: temple at G̃irsu built by Ur-Baba (Steible, *FAOS* 9/I, UrB 1, vi 7): see é.sag̃.ug$_{5}$.

1316 Gubarra: temple listed in CTL 562 (TN lost).

1317 Gula: cult at Dunni-sāʾidi, near Babylon (*Topog. Texts* no. 38, 22).

1318 Gula: temple at Kalaḫ rebuilt by Aššurnaṣirpal II (Grayson, *RIMA* 2, pp. 212, 135; 286, 8; 287, 14′; 291, 56; 296, 9).

1319 Gula, as $^{d}$nin.g̃á.ug$_{5}$.ga: temple at Maškan-šāpir built by Warad-Sîn (year 13, DN written variously $^{d}$nin.g̃á.ug$_{7}$.x, $^{d}$nin.ug$_{7}$.ug$_{5}$, and $^{d}$nin.ug$_{5}$.ga: cf. Stol, *OB History*, pp. 17f.; Sigrist, *Larsa Year Names*, p. 36).

1320 Ḫaṭṭu ($^{d.giš}$g̃idru, the Divine Sceptre): temple at Nippur, known from a MB metrological text (Bernhardt and Kramer, *OrNS* 44 [1975], p. 98, 37). Note also outer and inner Courts of the Sceptre in the Divine Directory of Nippur (*Topog. Texts* no. 18 = Nippur Compendium § 14, v 1.6).

1321 Ḫaya: temple built by Sennacherib (Luckenbill, *OIP* 2, p. 147, 19).

1322 Ḫeg̃ir: temple, no doubt at G̃irsu, built by Uruinimgina (Steible, *FAOS* 5/I, Ukg 6, v 19′; 11, 29).

1323 Ḫendursag̃: temple in Uru-ku at G̃irsu built by Enannatum I (Steible, *FAOS* 5/I, En I 20, ii 5; 29, iv 3), and Gudea (9/I, Gud. 17, 6; cf. 18?).

1324 Ḫuškia: temple at Apak, listed in CTL 571 (TN lost).

1325 Ilaba: temple at Babylon built by Šar-kali-šarrī (Gelb and Kienast, *FAOS* 7, p. 54, Škš year 3).

1326 Ilu lemnu (Evil God): two shrines at Babylon (*Topog. Texts* no. 1 = *Tintir* V 88).

1327 Inanna as dnin.an.šè.lá.a: temple (at Lagaš or nearby) built by Lugirzal of Lagaš (Steible, *FAOS* 9/II, p. 335).

1328 Inanna nin.kù.nun.na, i.e., Ištar of Eridu: temple at URU×KÁRki built by Ur-Baba (Steible, *FAOS* 9/I, UrB 1, iv 9; 8, iii 2); temple rebuilt by Ur-Nammu (idem, *FAOS* 9/II, UrN 6, all exemplars from Ur; = èš.bur?).

1329 Inimmanizi: temple at Nippur, known from a MB metrological text (Bernhardt and Kramer, *OrNS* 44 [1975], p. 98, 39).

1330 Išḫara: chapel in temple of Assyrian Ištar at Aššur rebuilt by Adad-nārārī I (Grayson, *RIMA* 1, p. 150, 19).

1331 Ištar: 180 outdoor shrines at Babylon (*Topog. Texts* no. 1 = *Tintir* V 86).

1332 Ištar: temple at Ešnunna or nearby, built by Ibāl-pî-El II (year 6: Jacobsen, *OIP* 98, p. 96, 15).

1333 Ištar: temple at Nineveh (Grayson, *RIMA* 1, p. 284, 3; 285, 3: Tukultī-Ninurta I): see é.maš.maš.

1334 Ištar: temple and ziqqurrat at Talmuššu rebuilt by Shalmaneser I (Grayson, *RIMA* 1, p. 204, 6′–10′).

1335 Ištar-Akusītum: cult of Ištar at Akus(um) known from year names of the Mananā dynasty (Nāqimum year e; Unidentified a). Perhaps the Akusītum Gate at Babylon was named after the goddess not the city (cf. *Topog. Texts*, pp. 378f.)?

1336 Ištar-Aššurītu (Assyrian Ištar): temple at Aššur (Grayson, *RIMA* 1, p. 7, 7: Ititi; 15, 13; 17, 22: Ilu-šumma; 91, 5 (*bēt šuḫūri*): Puzur-Aššur III; 139, 19′; 150, 5–6 (*ḫuršu, bēt šuḫūri*, chapel of Išḫara): Adad-nārārī I; 195, 5: Shalmaneser I; 318, 9:7: Aššur-rēša-iši I). Built by Ilu-šumma, Sargon I, Puzur-Aššur III, Adad-nārārī I. See é.me.dinanna.

1337 Ištar-Kudnittu: sanctuary (in the temple of Ištar at Aššur?) rebuilt by Aššur-uballiṭ I (Grayson, *RIMA* 1, p. 113, rev. 7).

1338 Išum: sanctuary at Nippur, known from a MB metrological text (Bernhardt and Kramer, *OrNS* 44 [1975], p. 98, 27).

1339 Kanisurra: temple (at Uruk?) built by Anam in the reign of Sîn-gāmil (Frayne, *RIME* 4, p. 468, 6).

1340 Kittum: temples at Bad-tibira and Raḫabu (*AbB* II 30, 6.10).

1341 Kūbu: six shrines at Babylon (*Topog. Texts* no. 1 = *Tintir* V 87).

1342 Lakuppītu: temple at Isin listed in CTL 560 (TN lost).

1343 Lalašaga: temple listed in CTL 178 (TN lost).

1344 Lammašaga: temple built by Uruinimgina, with chapels of the minor deities Zazaru, Nipae and Urnuntaea (Steible, *FAOS* 5/I, Ukg 1, ii 7–14; 6, v 21′). A temple of the same deity and associated chapels of Zazaru, [Nipae] and Urnuntaea, at G̃irsu (Uru-ku), were later built by Ur-Ning̃irsu I, who further identifies Lammašaga as Ninsun (9/I, UrN I 6, ii 4′; cf. pp. 130f.).

1345 Lugalbanda: temple at Nippur, known from a MB metrological text (Bernhardt and Kramer, *OrNS* 44 [1975], p. 98, 35).

1346 Lugalgusisa/u: temple at Nippur, which gave its name to a city gate and quarter (Lambert, *RlA* VII, p. 141); note also é.lugal.gu$_4$.si.sá in a Persian period document (Krückmann, *TuM* 2–3 241, 5: Darius), a TN which evidently derives from the compound of é + DN. An unpublished cylinder of Esarhaddon shows that [é.($^{d}$)lugal.g]u$_4$.si.sá (l. 3) is in fact the residence of a god [DN *kaš*]-*kaš ilī*$^{meš}$ *qar-du . . . bēl tam-ḫa-ra* (l. 1; information courtesy of K. Kessler). These epithets provoke the restoration of the DN as Nergal, and thus suggest an equation Lugalgusisa = Nergal (already advanced by Tallqvist, *Götterepitheta*, pp. 353, 390, presumably because in the OB forerunner to An = *Anum* $^{d}$lugal.gu$_4$.si.su is the first of the DNs compounded with lugal that follow the section on Nergal and his family: *TCL* XV 10, 425). For Nergal's temple at Nippur see the entry against his name, below.

1347 Lugalirra: temple at Babylon in the late period, see *Topog. Texts*, p. 370. 180 shrines of DN and Meslamtaea at Babylon (*Topog. Texts* no. 1 = *Tintir* V 86).

1348 Lugalirra: temple at Luḫāṭu, near Babylon (*Topog. Texts* no. 38, 16).

1349 Lugal-ki.dun$_5$.na: temple built by Gungunum (year 18), at Kutalla according to Renger (*Studien Falkenstein*, p. 145).

1350 $^{d}$LUGAL-*ma-tim*: temple at Mari built by Išṭup-ilum (Gelb and Kienast, *FAOS* 7, pp. 361f., Mari Šak. 5–6: Bēl-mātim).

1351 Lugal-URU×KÁR$^{ki}$: temple at URU×KÁR$^{ki}$, often designated é.gal.URU×KÁR$^{ki}$, "Palace of GN," built by Enannatum I (Steible, *FAOS* 5/I, En I 20, ii 7; 29, v 4; etc.), along with its granary (20, iii 4–5: g̃anun.maḫ), and by Enmetena (ibid., Ent 1, ii 4; 8, iii 6; 26; etc.). Desecrated by Lugalzaggesi (ibid., Ukg 16, vi 2).

1352 Mamu(d): sanctuary at Imgur-Enlil (Balawat), adjacent to the palace, built by Aššurnaṣirpal II (Grayson, *RIMA* 2, p. 320, 23–24).

1353 Manzât: four shrines at Babylon (*Topog. Texts* no. 1 = *Tintir* V 88).

1354 Manzât: sanctuary at Nippur, known from a MB metrological text (Bernhardt and Kramer, *OrNS* 44 [1975], p. 98, 28).

1355 Mār-bīti: temple at Borsippa, rebuilt by Nebuchadnezzar II (V *R* 34, ii 27; etc.).

1356 Mār-bīti: temple at Ilip (*Topog. Texts* no. 38, 27).

1357 Marduk: 55 throne-daises scattered throughout Babylon (*Topog. Texts* no. 1 = *Tintir* V 1–48.83).

1358 Marduk: sanctuary at Nippur known from a MB metrological text (Bernhardt and Kramer, *OrNS* 44 [1975], p. 98, 24).

1359 Meslamtaea: sanctuary at G̃irsu built by Gudea (Steible, *FAOS* 9/I, Gud. 28, 6; cf. Stat. X, 1). See also Lugalirra.

1360 Nammu: temple built by Lugalkisalsi of Uruk (Steible, *FAOS* 5/II, Lukis 5).

1361 Nanāy: sanctuary at Ubassu, between Babylon and Borsippa, rebuilt by Nabonidus (*CT* 36 22, 7).

1362 Nanše: terrace-temple (gi.gù.na maḫ) rebuilt by Enmetena (Steible, *FAOS* 5/I, Ent. 1, iii 2; 8, vii 5; etc.)

1363 Narām-Sîn: temple at Akkade built to himself (Gelb and Kienast, *FAOS* 7, p. 82, 55: Bassetki statue).

1364 Nergal as Lugal-Gudua, "King of Kutha": sanctuary at Isin in OB documents, Kraus, *JCS* 3 (1949), p. 60; cf. above, note on CTL 560.

1365 Nergal: temple at Nippur, whose residents are listed in the Divine Directory of Nippur (*Topog. Texts* no. 18 = Nippur Compendium § 14, v 18–19). See further above, the entry for Lugalgusisa.

1366 Nergal: temple built by Tišatal and Atalšen of Urkiš (Gelb and Kienast, *FAOS* 7, pp. 382f.).

1367 Nimintabba: temple at Ur built by Šulgi (Steible, *FAOS* 9/II, Š 18).

1368 Ninagal: temple (at G̃irsu?) built by Ur-Baba (Steible, *FAOS* 9/I, UrB 1, v 6; 8, iii 10).

1369 Ninansianna: temple built by Šulgi (Steible, *FAOS* 9/II, Š 67); see é.eš. bar.zi.da.

1370 Ninazu: temple built by Gudea (Steible, *FAOS* 9/I, Gud. 92, 6).

1371 Nindara: temple at G̃irsu built by Gudea (Steible, *FAOS* 9/I, Gud. 36, 7; 38, 7; year 10), possibly the building earlier rebuilt by Enannatum I (5/I, En I 20, ii 2) and Ur-Baba (9/I, UrB 1, v 3); but see also é.làl.DU.

1372 Nindub: temple built by Gudea (Steible, *FAOS* 9/I, Gud. 39, 6), at Uruk (three exemplars) or Surghul, ancient NINA$^{ki}$ (one)?

1373 Ninegal: temple at Ur built by Ur-Nammu (Steible, *FAOS* 9/II, UrN 18). See é.gal.maḫ 3.

1374 Ning̃irida: temples listed in CTL 558–59 (TNs lost).

1375 Niñĝirsu: sanctuary at Dugru (èš.dug.ru), built by Enannatum I and Enmetena (Steible, *FAOS* 5/I, En I 29, vi 6; Ent 1, i 18; 8, ii 7; etc.). Desecrated by Lugalzaggesi (ibid., Ukg 16, iii 7: dug.ru).

1376 Ninĝirsu: reed chamber of the terrace-temple (èš.gi gi.gù.na), built by Enmetena (Steible, *FAOS* 5/I, Ent 17, 9; 18, 4; 36, iii 1; etc.). No doubt some part of the temple complex of é.ninnu at G̃irsu.

1377 Ninĝirsu: dais (bára) at Namnunda-kiĝarra, erected by Eannatum, destroyed by Ur-Lumma of Umma, and rebuilt by Enmetena (Steible, *FAOS* 5/I, Ent 28, ii 16.39; cf. v 12).

1378 Ninĝišzida: chapel in é.an.na at Uruk, built by Anam and Merodach-baladan (Gadd, *Iraq* 15 [1953], pp. 123f.).

1379 Ninĝišzida: temple at G̃irsu built by Gudea (Steible, *FAOS* 9/1, Stat. I, iii 9; P, iii 10; Gud. 67–68; etc.).

1380 Ninĝišzida: sanctuary at Isin in OB documents, Kraus, *JCS* 3 (1949), p. 60.

1381 Ninḫursaĝ: temple at G̃irsu built by Ur-Baba (Steible, *FAOS* 9/I, UrB 1, iv 1) and Gudea (ibid., Gud. Stat. A, i 8).

1382 Ninḫursaĝ: temple at Mari built by the *šakkanakku* Niwar-Mēr (Gelb and Kienast, *FAOS* 7, p. 363, Mari Šak. 8).

1383 Ninḫursaĝ: temple at Susa built by Šulgi (Steible, *FAOS* 9/II, Š 73).

1384 Ninḫursaĝ: temple at Ubaid built by Aannepadda of Ur (Steible, *FAOS* 5/II, Aan 2; 4, 2′).

1385 Ninḫursaĝ: temple at Umma built by Lu-Utu of Umma (Steible, *FAOS* 9/II, pp. 345–46).

1386 Ninḫursaĝ: dais (bára) at Namnunda-kiĝarra, erected by Eannatum, destroyed by Ur-Lumma of Umma, and rebuilt by Enmetena (Steible, *FAOS* 5/I, Ent 28, ii 15.39; cf. v 12).

1387 Nin-Ibgal: temple (at Isin?) rebuilt by Enlil-bāni (Frayne, *RIME* 4, p. 82, 19).

1388 Ninisinna: temple built by Sūmû-ditāna of Kiš (year a).

1389 Ninkarnunna: sanctuary at Nippur, known from a MB metrological text (Bernhardt and Kramer, *OrNS* 44 [1975], p. 98, 26).

1390 Ninkarrak: temple known from a Diyala year name (*CT* 48 42, left edge ii 2).

1391 Ninkasi: temple at Nippur, known from a MB metrological text (Bernhardt and Kramer, *OrNS* 44 [1975], p. 98, 36). Two temples listed in CTL 116–17 (TNs lost).

1392 Ninmada: temple listed in CTL 118 (TN lost).

1393 Ninmaḫ: sanctuary built by Enmetena as gi.gù.na tir.kù.ga, "terrace-house of Tir-ku (the pure forest)" (Steible, *FAOS* 5/I, Ent 1, ii 14–15; 8, v 3–4; etc.; cf. En I 29, v 1?). Plundered by Lugalzaggesi (ibid., Ukg 16, ii 10–12).

1394 Ninmar: temple in aš.dub.ba$^{ki}$, built by Rīm-Sîn I (year 3; cf. 8).

1395 Ninmar: temple built by Ur-Nanše (Steible, *FAOS* 5/I, UrN 26, iii 2; 29, iv 2; etc.). See é.ab.šà.ga.lá.

1396 Ninsianna: temple at Nippur, known from a MB metrological text (Bernhardt and Kramer, *OrNS* 44 [1975], p. 98, 30).

1397 Ninšagepadda: temple (at Ur?) built by Ur-Nammu (Steible, *FAOS* 9/II, UrN 38).

1398 Ninšar: temple, no doubt at G̃irsu, built by Uruinimgina (Steible, *FAOS* 5/I, Ukg I, ii [17]; 6, v [24′]; 11, 24).

1399 Ninšar: temple at Ur, built by Šulgi (Steible, *FAOS* 9/II, Š 16).

1400 Ninuaʾītu: temple at Aššur? (Grayson, *RIMA* 1, p. 196, 6–7: Shalmaneser I; 264, 5: Tukultī-Ninurta I). See é.g̃iš.ḫur.an.ki.a

1401 Ninurta: temple of Enlil and DN at Kalaḫ built for the first time by Aššurnaṣirpal II (Grayson, *RIMA* 2, pp. 285, v 7; 287, 13′; 291, 54; Ninurta only: pp. 212, 132; 296, 9; etc.).

1402 Ninurta: temple built by Šulgi (year 4); = é.šu.me.ša$_4$ at Nippur, or even é.ninnu of Ning̃irsu?

1403 Ninurta: temple built by Mana-balti-El of Kisurra (year c; cf. d.e, Ubaya years a.b).

1404 Nissaba: three temples listed in CTL 94–96, in Dūr-Kurigalzu, Nippur and elsewhere (TNs lost).

1405 Rābiṣ-āli (Watcher of the City): two shrines at Babylon (*Topog. Texts* no. 1 = *Tintir* V 88).

1406 Samnuḫa and Gubaba: temple rebuilt by Bēl-ēriš of Šadikanni, time of Aššur-rēša-iši II (Grayson, *RIMA* 2, p. 127, 17).

1407 Sebettu (Divine Heptad): twelve shrines at Babylon (*Topog. Texts* no. 1 = *Tintir* V 87).

1408 Sebettu: temple at Kalaḫ rebuilt by Aššurnaṣirpal II (Grayson, *RIMA* 2, p. 291, 57; cf. pp. 361, 1′; 380, 5–6).

1409 Sebettu: shrine at Nippur, built by the local potentate Hašmar-galšu (*YOS* IX 66).

1410 Sîn: built by Narām-Sîn of Akkade (Gelb and Kienast, *FAOS* 7, p. 101, NS 18; at G̃irsu?).

1411 Sîn: temple at Ilip? (*Topog. Texts* no. 38, 27).

1412 Sîn: temple at Kalaḫ rebuilt by Aššurnaṣirpal II (Grayson, *RIMA* 2, pp. 212, 135; 286, 8; 287, 14′; 291, 56; 296, 9).

1413 Sîn: temple at Larsa built by Rīm-Sîn I (year 4).

1414 Sîn and Šamaš: temple at Nineveh, rebuilt by Esarhaddon (Borger, *Esarh.*, § 29, Nin. I. 4; cf. § 86, ii 17) and Aššurbanipal (Thompson, *Prisms*, pl. 15, ii 18–19 // Bauer, *Asb.*, pl. 19, K 1769+, ii 19).

1415 Šamaš: temple whose building is recorded in a Diyala year name (Jacobsen, *OIP* 43, p. 195, no. 127). Another records the moving of earth to build his ziqqurrat (Greengus, *Iščali*, p. 34, no. 55).

1416 Šamaš: temple at Nippur, known from a MB metrological text (Bernhardt and Kramer, *OrNS* 44 [1975], p. 98, 25).

1417 Šarrat-nipḫi: temple at Kalaḫ rebuilt by Aššurnaṣirpal II (Grayson, *RIMA* 2, pp. 212, 135; 286, 9; 291, 57; 296, 9).

1418 Šerua, in temple of Aššur? (*ga-ni-ni*, Grayson, *RIMA* 1, p. 197, 10: Shalmaneser I).

1419 Šubula: temple listed in CTL 572 (TN lost).

1420 dŠU.GU: temple built by Puzur-Inšušinak (Gelb and Kienast, *FAOS* 7, p. 335, Elam 9).

1421 Šullat and Ḫaniš: temple built by Šulgi (Steible, *FAOS* 9/II, Š 19).

1422 Šulpae: ten temples listed in CTL 154–63 (TNs lost).

1423 Šuqamuna and Šimaliya: temple at Dūr-Kurigalzu, built by Kurigalzu (according to Jaritz, *MIO* 6 [1958], p. 211).

1424 Šu-Suen: temples at various towns, mostly built by the local governors (Steible, *FAOS* 9/II, ŠS 3 at Adab; 5; 10–11 at Ur; 12 at Ešnunna; 13 at G̃irsu). Note an Ur III document from Umma listing unnamed temples of Šulgi, Amar-Suen and Šu-Suen (Englund, *Acta Sum* 14 [1992], p. 87, rev. 3.6.9).

1425 dTAG.NUN (= Uttu?): temple built by Il of Umma (Steible, *FAOS* 5/II, Il 1).

1426 dTU (= Nintu?): temple listed in CTL 177 (TN lost).

1427 Ug-Elamma: temple listed in CTL 119 (TN lost).

1428 Ūmu: temple listed in CTL 573 (TN lost).

1429 Ungal-Nibru: temple in Nippur, rebuilt by Esarhaddon (Borger, *Esarh.*, § 39).

1430 Uqur: temple at Isin, listed in CTL 574 (TN lost).

1431 Uraš: Akītu temple (in Kiš?) rebuilt by Nabonidus (*CT* 36 22, 3).

1432 Uraš: sanctuary at Nippur known from a MB metrological text (Bernhardt and Kramer, *OrNS* 44 [1975], p. 98, 22).

1433 Utu: dais (bára) at Namnunda-kig̃arra, erected by Eannatum, destroyed by Ur-Lumma of Umma, and rebuilt by Enmetena (Steible, *FAOS* 5/I, Ent 28, ii 17.39; cf. v 12).

1434 Zababa: chapel at Aššur, built by Sennacherib (Galter, *RIM Annual Review* 2 [1984], p. 1, 3).

1435 Zababa and Ninlil?: Akītu temple at Kiš (*OECT* X 231, 1–2).

1436 Zababa: temple at tibira[ki], near Babylon (*Topog. Texts* no. 38, 15).

1437 Zāriqu: temple or chapel at Babylon in the late period, see *Topog. Texts* no. 15, obv. 5′.

1438 [d]REC 290.KU.ra: temple built by Enšakušanna of Uruk (Steible, *FAOS* 5/II, Enšak 5).

1439 [d]⌜x⌝.si: temple built for Enšakušanna of Uruk by the vizier Šunamugi (Steible, *FAOS* 5/II, Enšak 4).

## *Ceremonial Names of Royal Palaces*

A few rulers, mostly late, gave Sumerian ceremonial names to their own dwellings, and these are also collected here:

1440 **é.gal.gaba.ri.nu.tuk.a**, "Palace without an Equal," palace of Sargon II at Dūr-Šarru-kēn (Lie, *Sar.*, p. 76, 14; Winckler, *Sar.*, pl. 36, 159).

1441 **é.gal.ki.šár.ra**, "Palace of the Whole World," palace of Kurigalzu at Dūr-Kurigalzu (Brinkman, *MSKH*, p. 221, Q.2.50).

1442 **é.gal.lugal.šár.ra.kur.kur.ra** = *ekal šàr kiš-š[at mātāti*[m]][eš], "Palace of the King of All Lands," built by Tiglath-pileser I at Aššur (Grayson, *RIMA* 2, p. 45, 78).

1443 **[é.gal.lugal.ub.(da).límmu].ba** = *ekal šàr kib-rat arbāʾi*[[i]], "Palace of the King of the Four Quarters," built by Tiglath-pileser I at Nineveh (Grayson, *RIMA* 2, p. 57, 18′).

1444 **é.gal.me.šár.ra**, "Palace of the Myriad *Me*'s," = *bīt kiššati*, palace of Tukultī-Ninurta I at Kār-Tukultī-Ninurta (Grayson, *RIMA* 1, p. 270, 51).

1445 **é.gal.zag.sá.nu.tuk.a**, "Palace without a Rival," palace of Sennacherib at Nineveh (Luckenbill, *OIP* 2, pp. 100, 56; 126, b 3; written é.gal.zag.ša$_4$.nu.tuk.a: 96, 79; *ekal(lu ša) šānina lā išû*: 111, 51; 124, 40).

1446 **é.ḫur.sag̃** of Šulgi, see the main list.

1447 **é.lugal.umun.kur.kur.ra**, "House of the King, Lord of the Lands," palace of Tukultī-Ninurta I at Aššur (Grayson, *RIMA* 1, p. 245, 79).

1448 **é.me.te.nam.lugal.la**, "House Worthy of Kingship," palace of Lipit-Ištar (Frayne, *RIME* 4, p. 49, 17).

1449 **èš.gal.šid.dù.dù.a**, = *ekallu pāqidat kalāmu*, "Palace which Administers All," palace of Esarhaddon at Nineveh (Borger, *Esarh.*, p. 62, 42–43).

# Indexes to the Gazetteer

## *Divine Names*

References to deities other than those resident in each temple are selective.

Bēl-ibrīya, 1290
Belili, 13, 253, 548, 1096, 1106, 1202
Bēl-Kurbaʾil, 646
Bēl-labrīya, 441
Bēl-mātāti, 849, 1141
Bēl-ṣarbi, 226
Bizilla, 222, 1291
Bunene, 691, 1111

Dagān, 230, 285, 608, 1292
Damgalnunna, 118, 280, 575, 727, 1293–94
Damkina, 39, 573, 850, 1299, 1303
Damu, 43, 1295
Daughters of Uruk, 632
Dikumaḫ, 935
Dimgalabzu, 1296
Dipar, 783
Dumuzi, 13–14, 101, 121, 195–96, 229, 253, 377, 501, 822, 827, 829, 882, 972, 995, 1185, 1223, 1242, 1297
Dumuziabzu, 1298

Ea, 23, 30, 45, 182–83, 224, 239, 249, 279–80, 282–83, 310, 342, 355, 357, 359–61, 365, 449–50, 522, 528, 569, 583, 700, 796, 821, 830, 850, 1043, 1045, 1150, 1205, 1263, 1299–1304; *see also* Enki
$^{d}$En, 377
Enbilulu, 177
Enbule (Enbune), 1010
Enki, 30–31, 182, 248, 260, 355, 361, 364, 778, 1304–6; *see also* Ea
Enkigal, 1307
Enlil, 11, 26, 36, 38, 40, 56, 90–91, 108, 110, 130, 179, 187, 189–90, 218, 235, 257, 298–99, 305, 336, 339, 366, 373, 398, 445, 480, 483, 529, 539, 541, 561, 582, 584, 617, 647, 649, 677–83, 689, 701, 725, 748–49, 772, 848–49, 871, 906, 941, 951, 956, 988, 997, 1028–30, 1034, 1055, 1100, 1122, 1127–28, 1144, 1199, 1210–11, 1253, 1259, 1308–10, 1401
Enmešarra, 177, 398
Ennugi, 938–39, 1255
Ennundag̃alla, 41
Ennung̃aḫedu, 41, 413
$^{d}$en.PI, 1192
Ensignun, 198
Enzak, 314, 566
Ereškigal, 288, 1209, 1311–12
Erra, 802
Ešertu, 1313
Etalak, 610
Euphrates, 511

G̃anunḫedu, 41
Gašan-g̃agia, 1137
Gašantilluba, 1208
G̃atumdug, 430, 1314
G̃eštinanna, 882, 975, 1044, 1315; *see also* Amag̃eštin, Ning̃eštinanna
Girra, 767
$^{d}$G̃IŠ.ŠA[R. . .], 94
Gubaba, 1406
Gubarra, 1316
$^{d}$gu$_{7}$.bi.sig.sig, 640
Gula, 13, 92, 233, 252, 293, 318–23, 352, 424, 485, 488, 544, 747, 812, 833, 851, 886, 895, 935, 943–46, 950, 957, 1095, 1108, 1123–25, 1153, 1167, 1182, 1208, 1230, 1234–35, 1317–19; *see also* Ninisinna, Ninkarrak
Gunura, 73

Ḫaniš, 1421
Ḫaṭṭu, 1320
Ḫaya, 1321
Ḫeg̃ir, 1322
Ḫendursag̃, 1323
Ḫuškia, 1324

Id, 507–8, 512
Igalimma, 755
Igidu, 330
Igigi, 234, 421, 1177
Ilaba, 155, 1325
Ilī-abrāt, 1084

Pabilsağ, 318, 534, 935
Paniğinğarra, 466, 786, 866, 1188, 1216
Panunna, 547
Papsukkal, 49–50, 437, 550, 959
Pisağunuk, 238, 1190

Qingu, 272

Rābiṣ-āli, 1405

Sadarnunna, 284, 929, 1055
Samnuḫa, 1406
Sebettu, 422, 1407–9
Sîn (Suen), 29, 47, 81, 128, 154, 159–60, 203–6, 214, 303, 377–78, 407, 470, 472, 631, 653–55, 706, 711, 721, 816, 870, 951, 1016, 1082, 1098, 1214, 1410–14; *see also* Nanna
Siraš, 695
Sud, 161, 596, 609, 982, 1010
Sudağ, 1010
Sugallītum, 1248
Supalītu, 74, 370, 1001, 1091

ᵈ*ṣa-lam*, 1213
Ṣilluš-ṭāb, 465

Šakkan, 1183
Šala, 232, 1272, 1279
Šamaš, 84, 97–100, 140, 148–49, 151–52, 220, 256, 387, 404, 420, 423, 445, 472, 546, 566, 665–66, 672, 761, 780, 847, 915, 926, 1040, 1414–16; *see also* Utu
Šara, 125–27, 718, 983, 1017, 1136
Šarrat-kidmuri, 645
Šarrat-nakkamte, 954
Šarrat-nipḫi, 348, 498, 1120, 1417
Šerua, 779, 1418
Šidada, 269, 1042
Šimaliya, 852, 1423
Šubula, 1419
ᵈŠU.GU, 1420
Šukurgallu, 208
Šulgi, 474, 811, 1424
Šullat, 1421
Šulmānītu, 80, 662
Šulpae, 286, 477, 543, 1102, 1233, 1250, 1422
Šulpaesia, 588
Šulpaeutulam, 588
Šulšagana, 22, 618
Šulutul, 719
Šuqamuna, 1423
Šu-Suen, 1424
Šuzianna, 191, 265, 296–97, 582, 683

ᵈTAG.NUN, 1425
Tašmētum, 878, 1176
Telîtu, 290
Tešub, 784
Tiʾāmat, 640, 1094
Tigris, 511
Tišpak, 987
ᵈTU, 1426
Tutu, 1236

Ug-Elamma, 1427
Ulmaššītum, 740, 1168
Ulsigga, 462
Ūmu, 1428
Ungal-Nibru, 110, 544, 1429
Uqur, 807, 997, 1430
Uraš, 172, 493, 1431–32
Urmaḫ, 1183
Urmašum, 247
Urnuntaea, 1344
Ušumgal, 223
Utaulu, 200, 423, 1212
Uttu, 263, 1425
Utu, 457, 915, 1433; *see also* Šamaš

Zababa, 37, 186, 200, 533, 633, 673, 785, 1075, 1151, 1434–36
Zannaru, 628
Zāriqu, 1437
Zarpanītum, 145, 243, 448, 461, 555
Zazaru, 1344

ᵈREC 290.KU.ra, 1438
ᵈx.si, 1439

## *Geographical Names*

References to places other than the location of each temple are selective.

## *Royal and Personal Names*

References to persons other than the builders, restorers, and patrons of each temple are selective.

## *Lexical Index*

References to the first element of each TN, of which the gazetteer is of course itself an index, are excluded.


a, 512
a.ra.al.li, 1153
a.ri.a, 108, 307
á, 1227–28
ab, 564, 1236
abzu, 134, 194, 264, 287, 559, 860, 955
ad, 255
áğ, 581–82, 818–19, 1079–80
aga, 583–84
ak, 416, 445, 458, 813
*akītu*, 207, 313, 414, 754, 940, 953, 993, 1266, 1280, 1431, 1435
akkil, 49, 618
alim, 433
am, 652
àm, 445
ama, 1201
amar, 91
amaš, 1116
an, 20, 91, 450, 672, 889, 955, 973, 1009
an.ki, 158, 218–19, 224, 240, 256, 268, 308, 329, 404, 409–12, 416, 440, 448–49, 475, 513, 755, 964, 1088, 1112, 1193, 1206, 1249, 1252
an.na, 124, 145, 159–65, 170, 220, 222–23, 251, 309, 349, 413, 459, 476, 503, 510, 599, 620, 747, 761, 763–65, 787, 789, 901–3, 909, 913–15, 926, 959–60, 964, 996, 1011, 1049, 1054, 1070, 1075, 1107, 1146, 1214–15
an.ta.ğál, 350
an.[zu?], 310
$anzu^{mušen}$, 898
$^{giš}$apin, 298
$aratta^{ki}$, 585

ba, 169, 895, 1233–35, 1240
ba.ad, 942
ba.la, 779
ba/ábbar, 10, 898, 931, 1250
bad, 943–46
bàd, 947
balağ, 4, 293, 708
bàn.da, 33–34, 123, 265–66, 408, 908
banû, 239
bar, 102, 104, 150, 256–61, 311, 526, 544–47, 682, 750, 1043
bára, 174, 664, 833
bil, 1053
bir, 751
bur, 190, 267, 294–95, 1054
búr, 190
$buru_{14}$, 190, 541–42

da, 20, 63–64, 741, 743–45
dab, 21
dağal, 285, 587, 748
dam, 262
dàra, 752
de, 121, 1145–48
dé, 22, 575, 1251
di, 88, 289, 731, 1262
$di_5$, 933, 1012
dib, 875
diğir, 421, 961
dil, 191, 515, 594, 841, 956–60
dili.bad, 648
dim, 243, 366, 494, 1140
dím, 330, 366, 548
dìm, 366
dìm.me.er, 962
diri, 278, 356, 460, 472, 861, 1178
du, 337, 516, 534, 699, 790, 835
dù, 125, 367, 517, 561, 749, 896, 1048–50, 1133, 1449
$du_6$, 53, 57, 122, 588
$du_6$.da, 296, 1173

# Index of Cuneiform Tablets

| *Museum Number* | *Text* | *Plate* |
|---|---|---|
| K 15262+Sm 289 | Canonical Temple List (no. 1) | 11-12 |
| K 19309 | Babylonian Temple List (no. 2)? | 13 |
| K 19495 | Canonical Temple List (no. 1) | 10 |
| K 20537 | Canonical Temple List (no. 1) | 9 |
| K 21429 | see K 4407+ | |
| Rm II 417 | Canonical Temple List (no. 1) | 9 |
| Sm 277 | Canonical Temple List (no. 1) | 10 |
| Sm 278 | Canonical Temple List (no. 1) | 7 |
| Sm 289 | see K 15262+ | |
| Sm 522 | Canonical Temple List (no. 1) | 7 |
| Th 1929-10-12, 718 | see BM 128062 | |
| Th 1932-12-10, 326 | see BM 123383 | |
| VAT 10755 A | Fragmentary List (no. 7) | |
| VAT 10755 B | Fragmentary List (no. 7) | |
| 82-3-23, 2120+3674 | see BM 51124+ | |
| 82-7-4, 49 | see BM 55476 | |



# Index of Previous Publication

Texts are cited under their place of first publication only.



| *Bibliographical Reference* | *Text* |
|---|---|
| *AJSL* 13, p. 220 | no. 1 |
| *CT* 51 178 | no. 7 |
| *CT* 51 179 | no. 7 |
| *KAV* 84 | no. 7 |
| *Kramer AV*, pl. 11 | no. 1 |
| *PSBA* 22, pp. 370-71 | no. 1 |
| II *R* 50, col. i | no. 4 |
| II *R* 61, no. 1 | no. 1 |
| II *R* 61, no. 2 | no. 1 |
| II *R* 61, no. 3 | no. 1 |
| II *R* 61, no. 5 | no. 2 |
| II *R* 61, no. 6 | no. 1 |
| II *R* 61, no. 7 | no. 1 |
| *RA* 17, p. 186 | no. 1 |
| *Topog. Texts* no. 39 | no. 9 |
| *Topog. Texts* no. 54 | no. 8 |

# Plates

The cuneiform texts are reproduced at $1\frac{1}{3}$ actual size, except where a scale indicates otherwise.

Text no. 1: (top) Ms A obverse, outline sketch
(bottom) Ms $A_4$

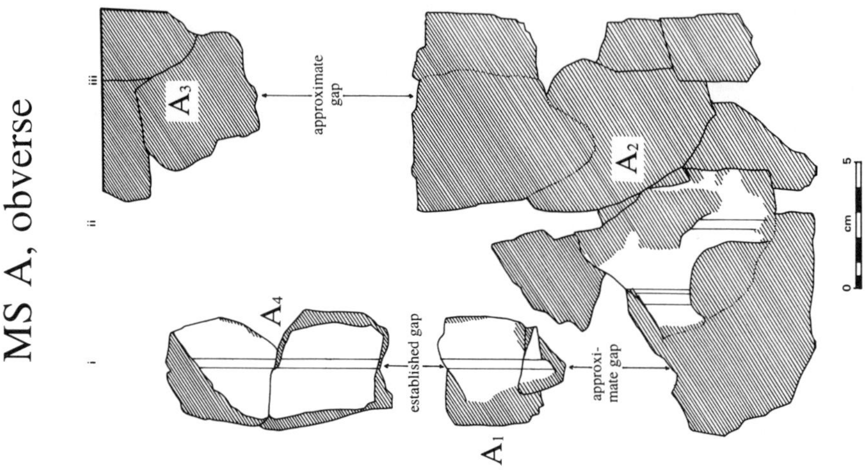


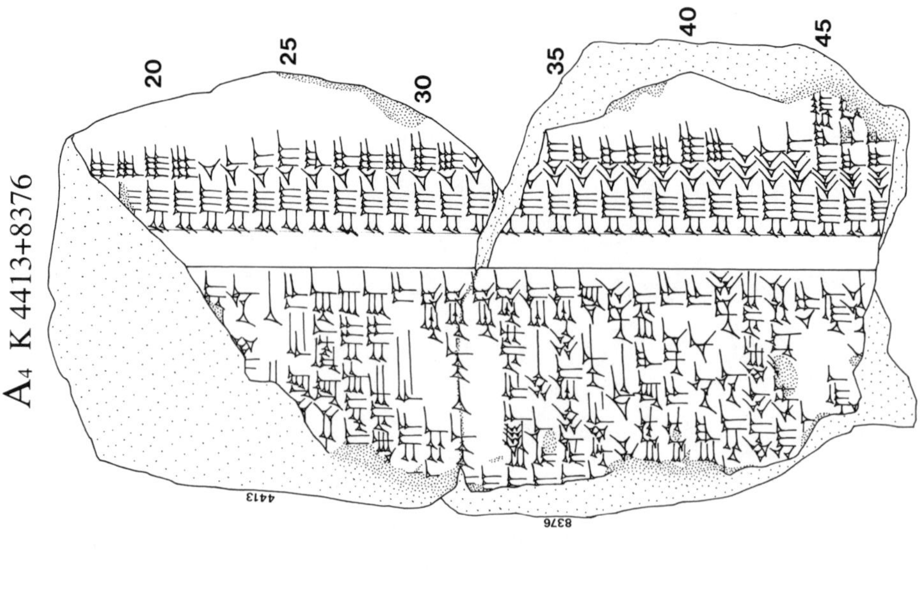

Text no. 1: Ms $A_1$ obverse (+) Ms $A_2$ obverse

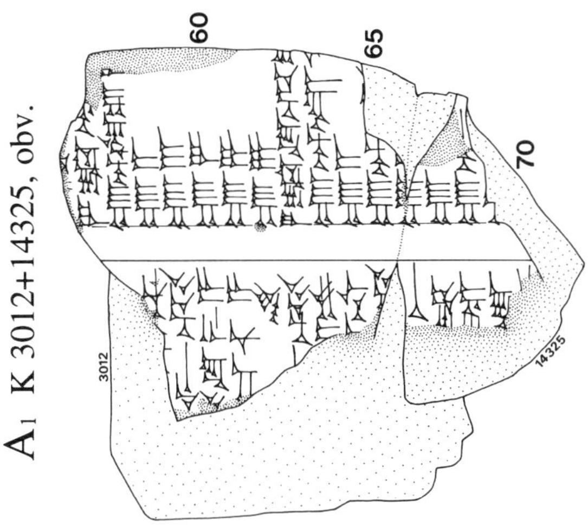

Text no. 1: Ms $A_2$ reverse, col. iv, upper part

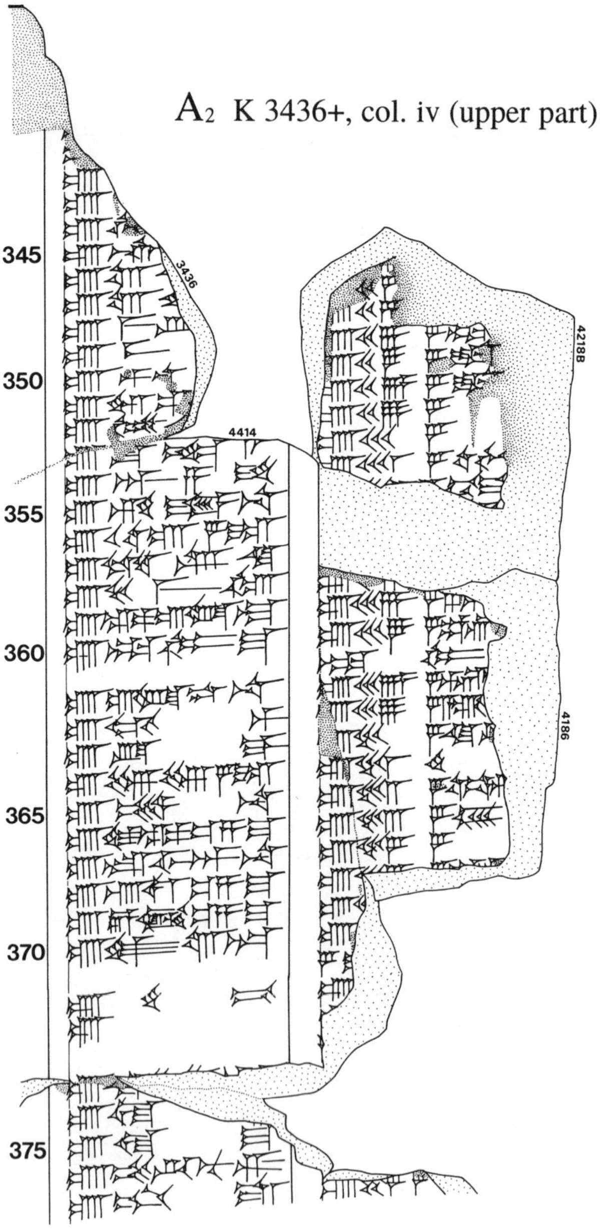

Text no. 1: Ms $A_2$ reverse, col. iv, continuation (+) Ms $A_3$

$A_2$ K 3436+, col. iv (continuation)

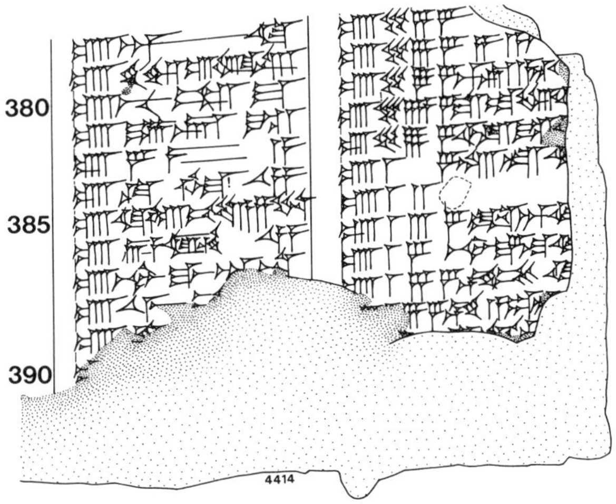


$A_3$ K 4224+10092+ 11188

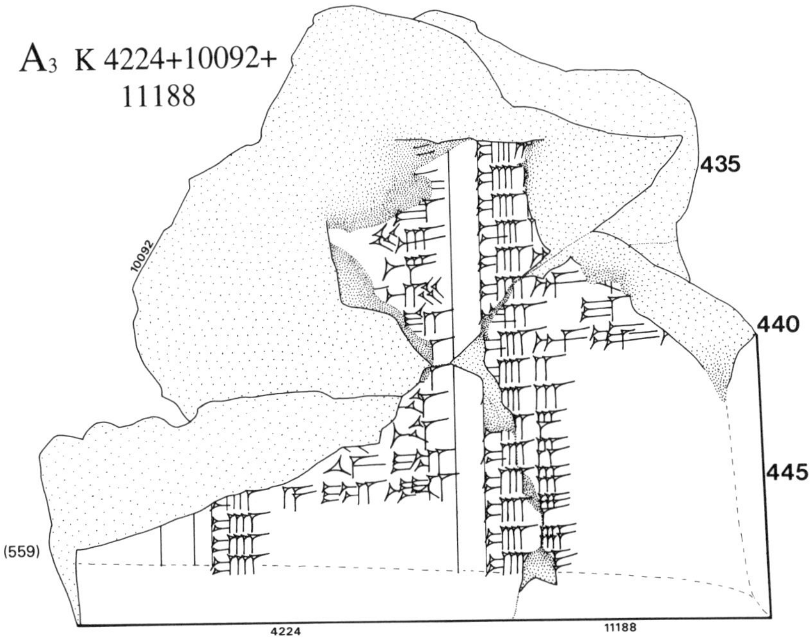

Text no. 1: Ms $A_2$ reverse, col. vi (+) Ms $A_1$ reverse

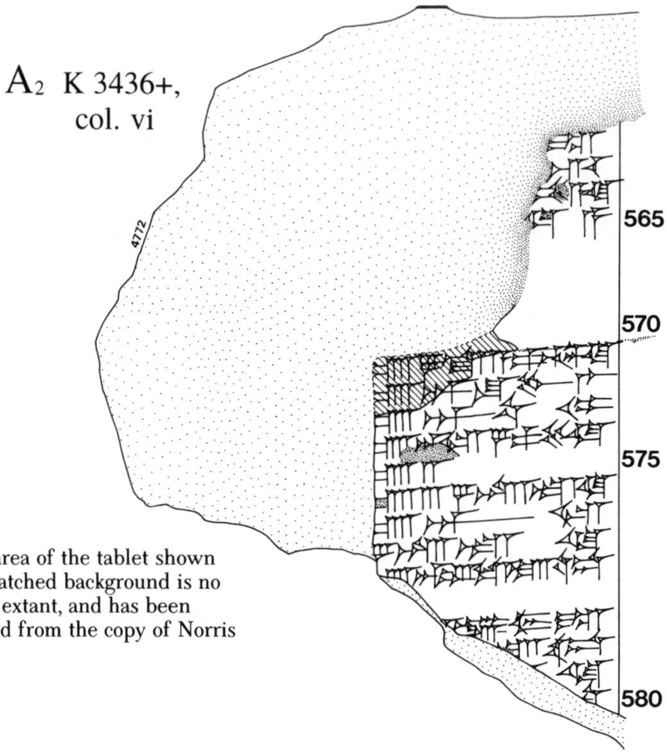


* The area of the tablet shown with hatched background is no longer extant, and has been restored from the copy of Norris

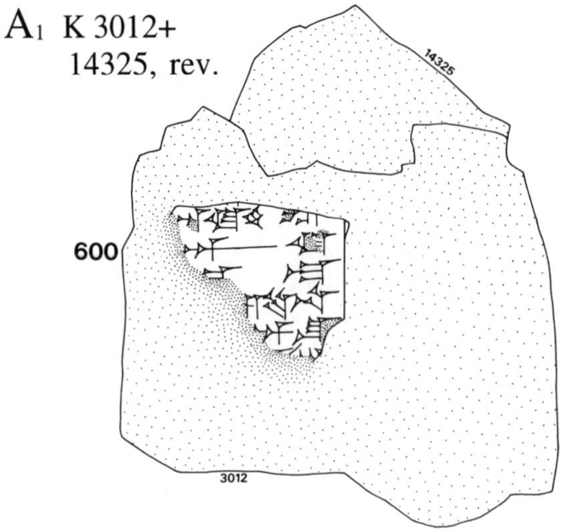

Text no. 1: Ms $A_2$ reverse, col. v

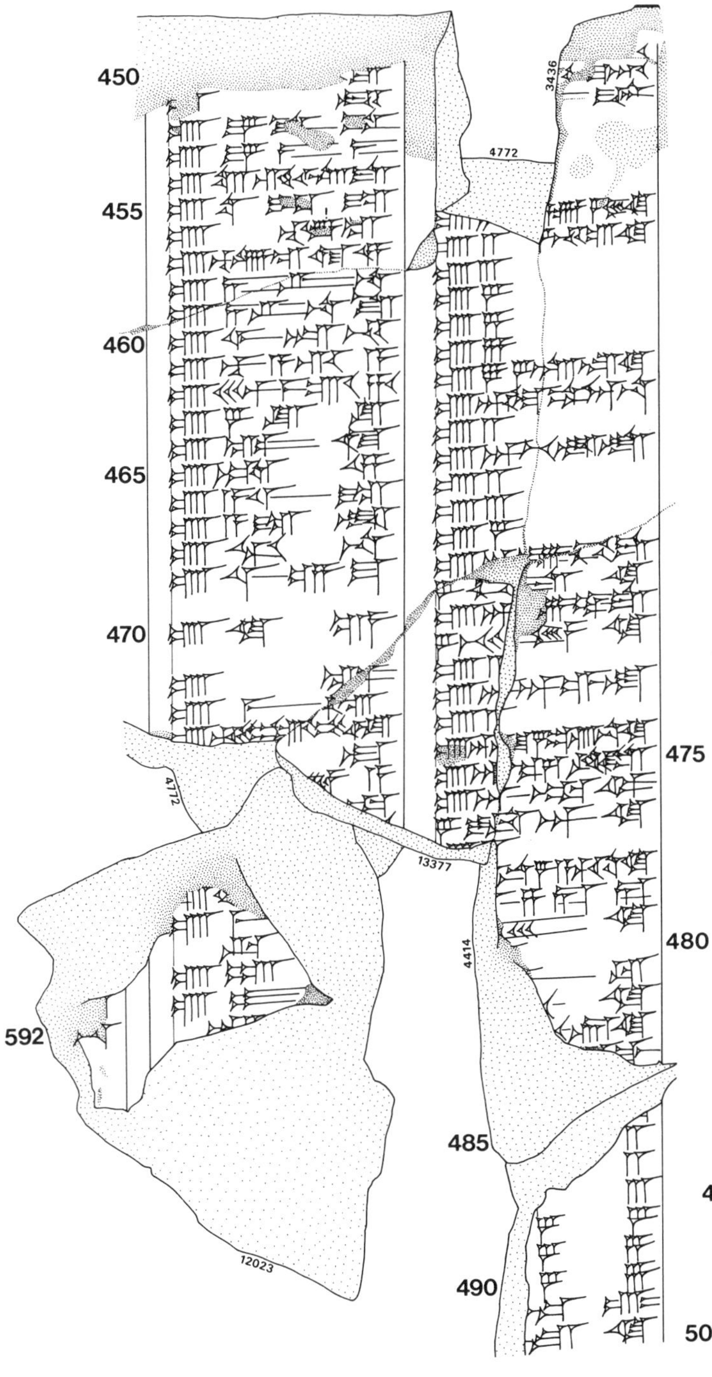


collation of l. 450

A2 K 3436+,
col. v

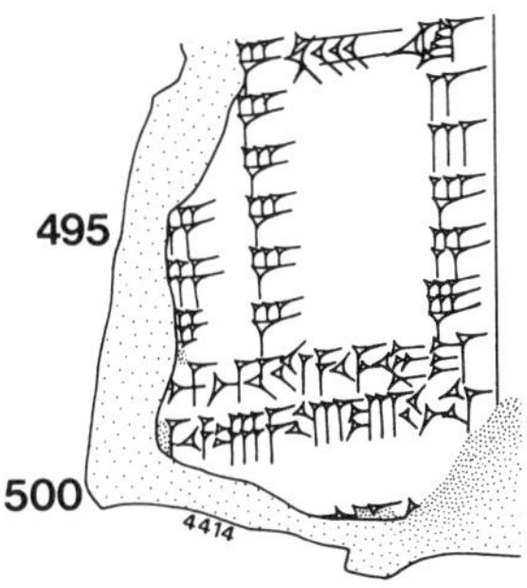

Text no. 1: Ms $B_4$ (+) Ms $B_5$

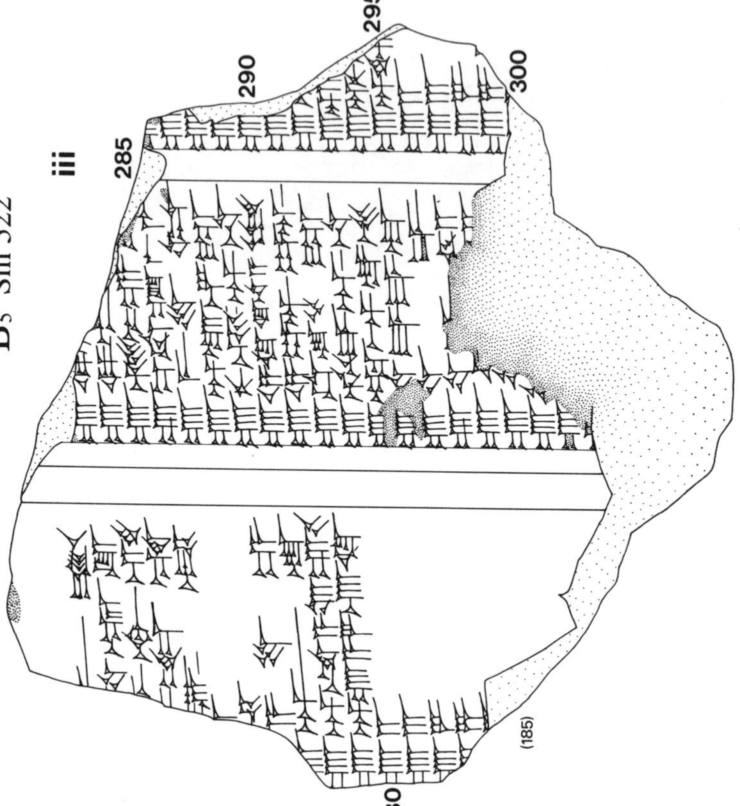


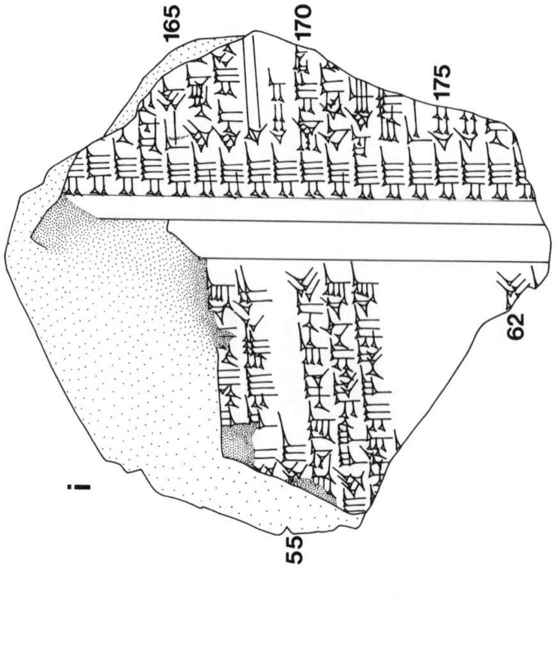

Text no. 1: Ms $B_1$

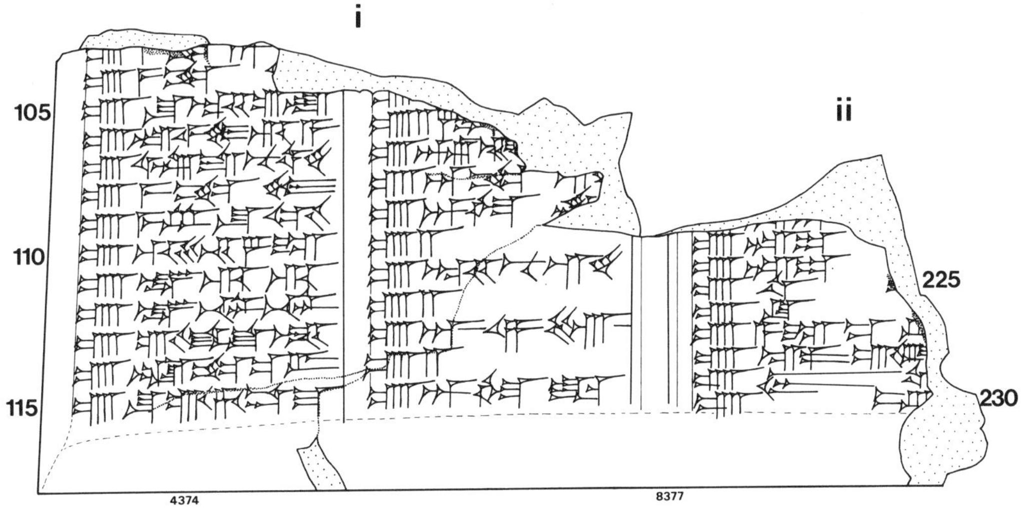


$B_1$ K 4374+8377

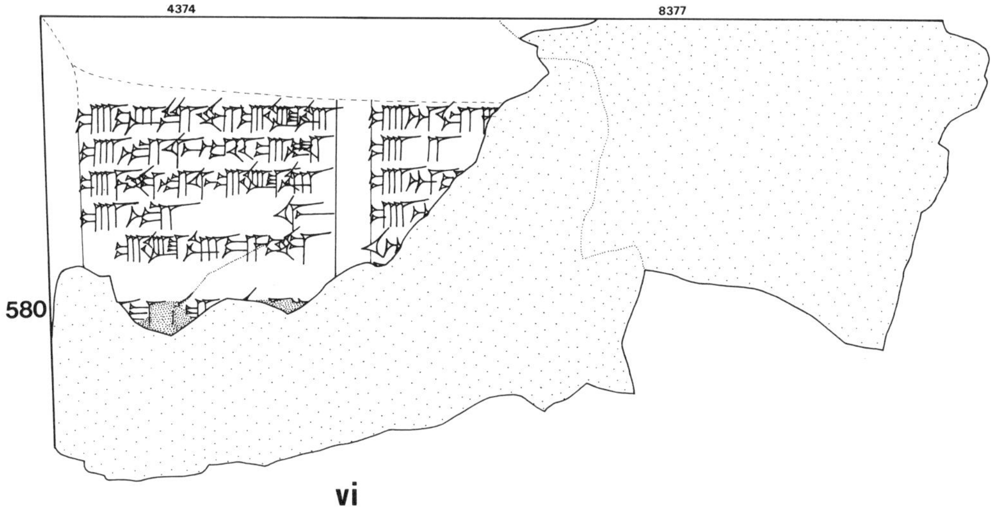

Text no. 1: Ms $B_2$ (+) Ms $B_3$ (+) Ms $B_6$

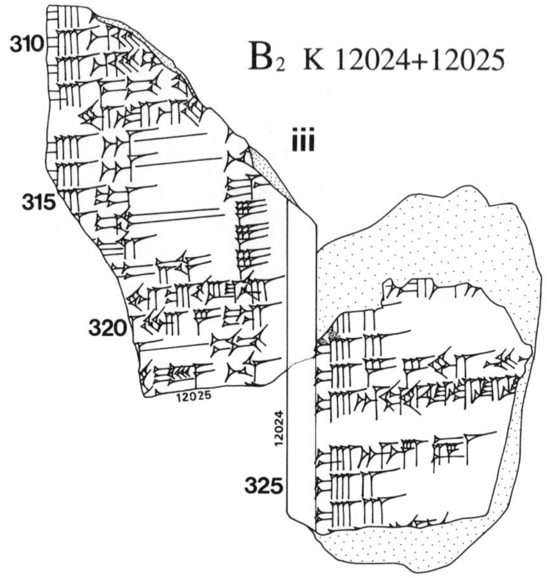


$B_2$ K 12024+12025

$B_3$ K 20537

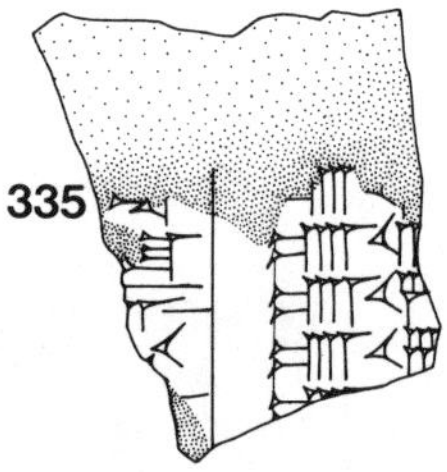


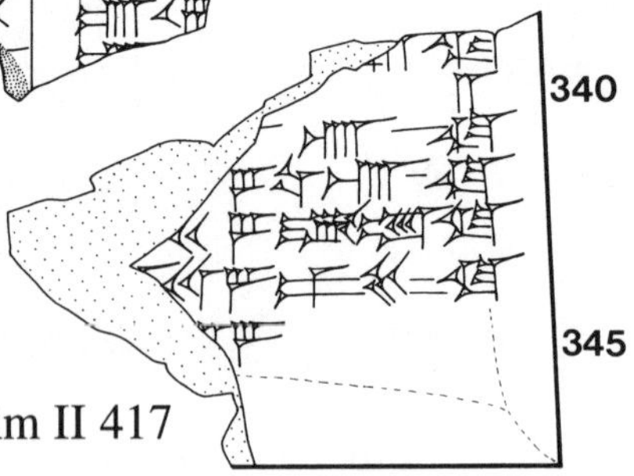


$B_6$ Rm II 417

Text no. 1: Ms $C_2$; Ms $C_3$

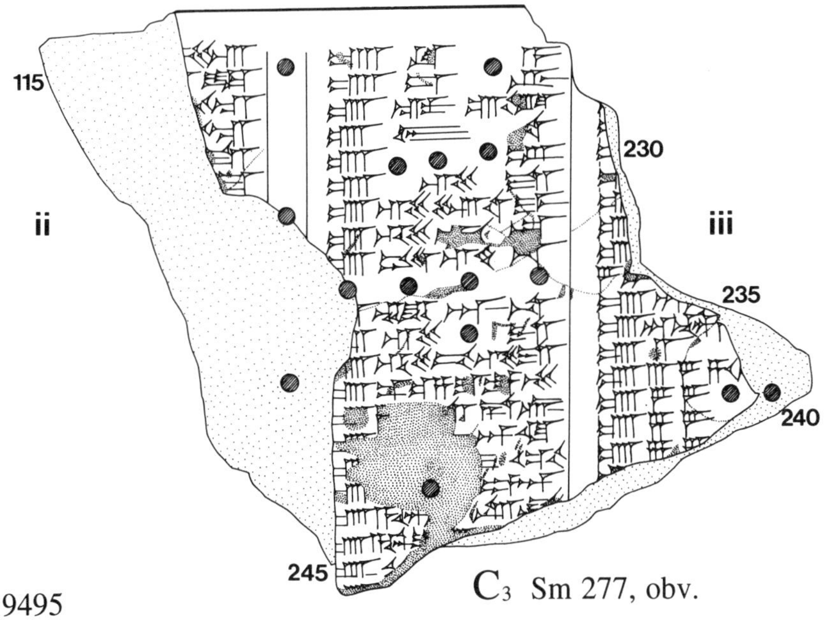


$C_3$ Sm 277, obv.

$C_2$ K 19495

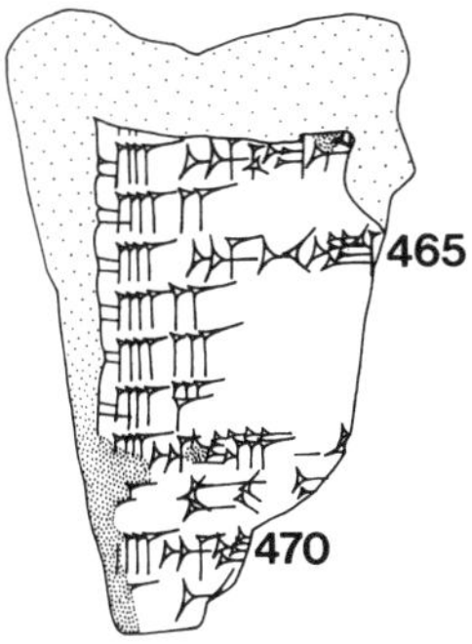


$C_3$ Sm 277, rev.

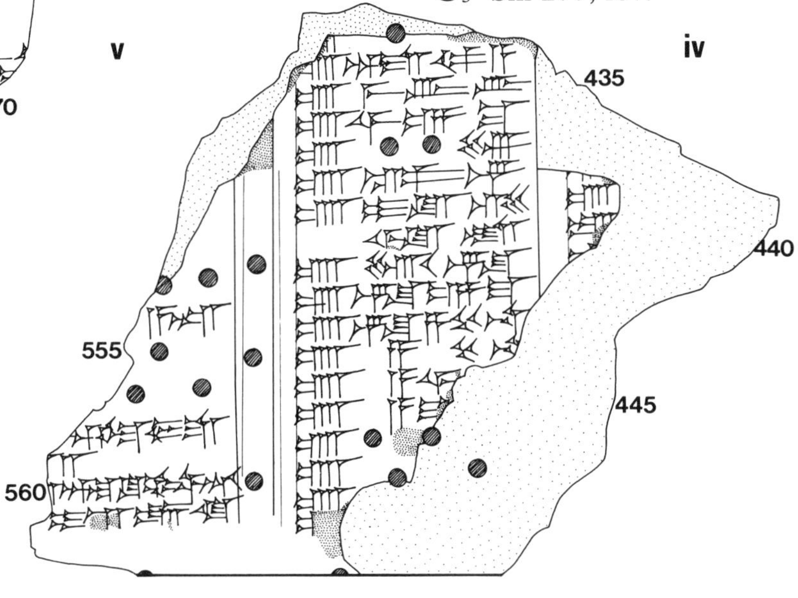

Text no. 1: Ms $C_1$ obverse

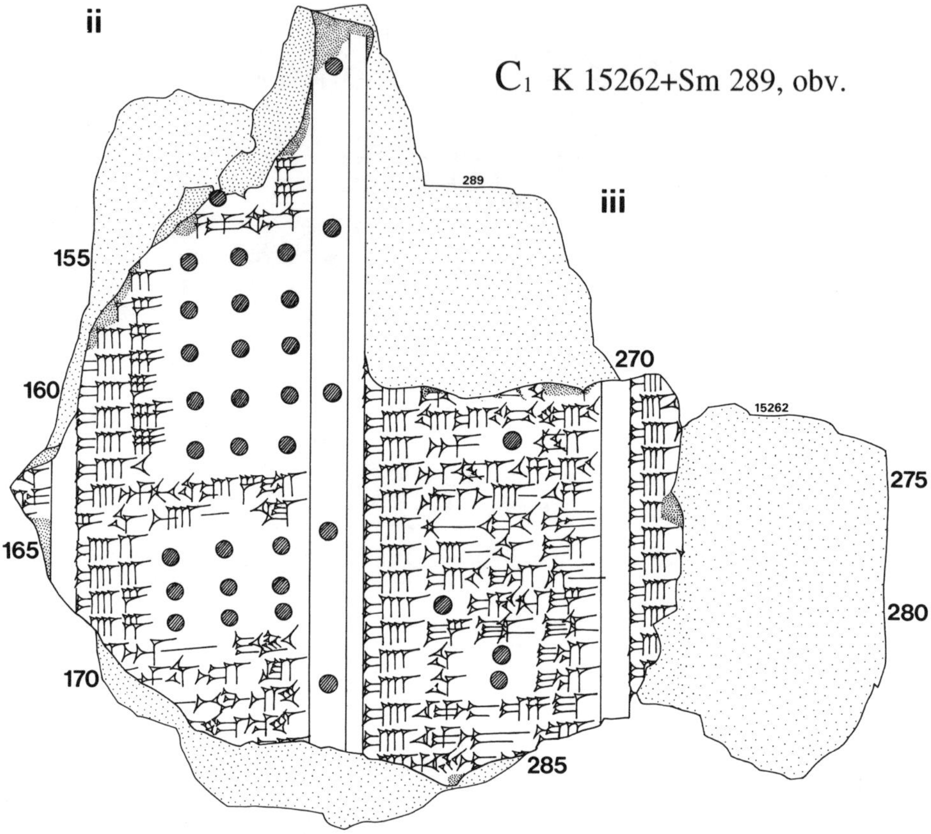

Text no. 1: Ms $C_1$ reverse

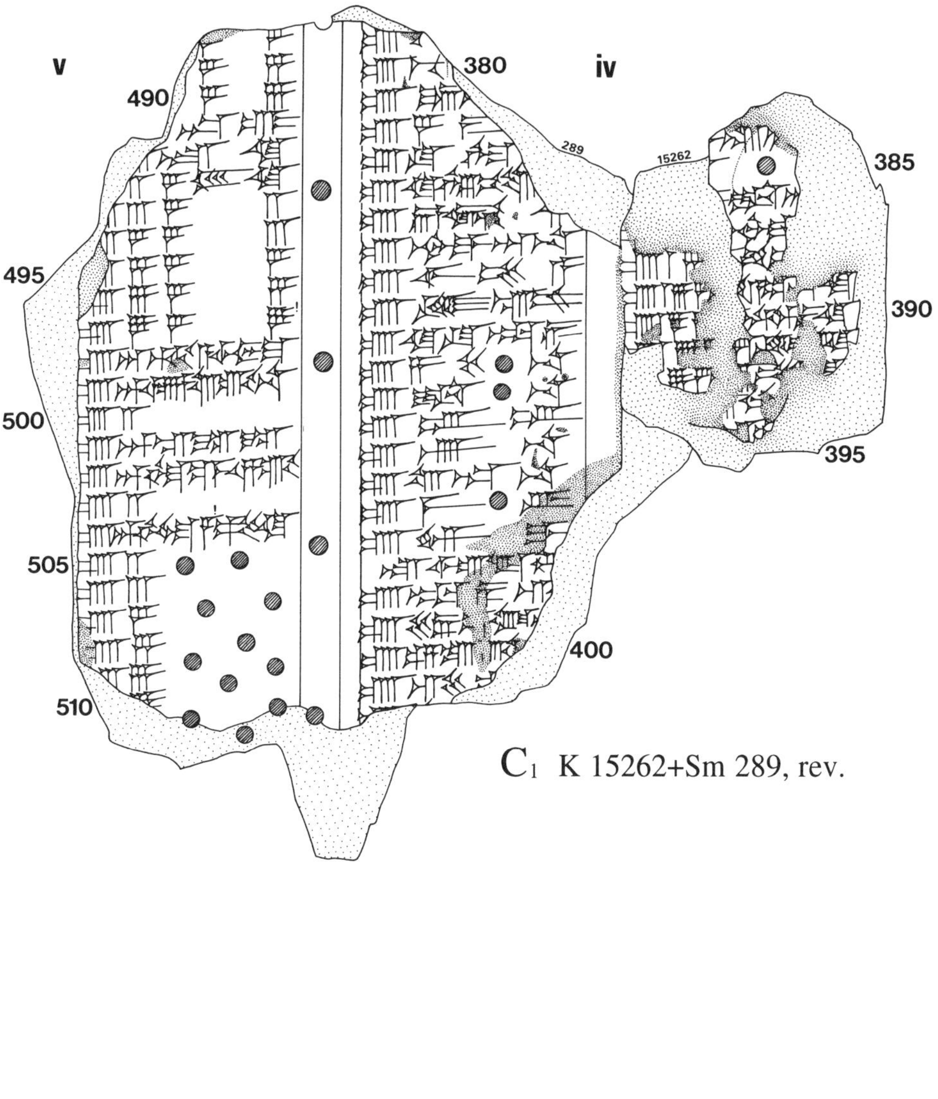


$C_1$ K 15262+Sm 289, rev.

Text no. 2

K 4407+21429

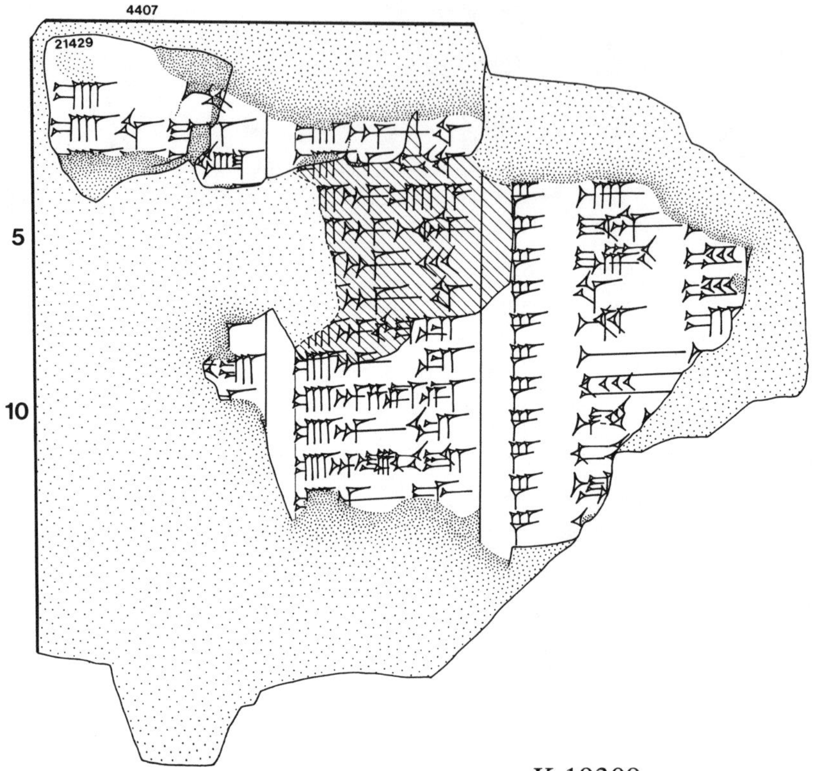


* The area of the tablet shown with hatched background is no longer extant, and has been restored from the copy of Norris

K 19309

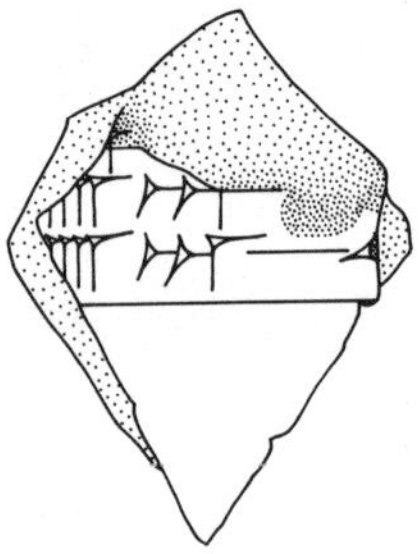

Text no. 5

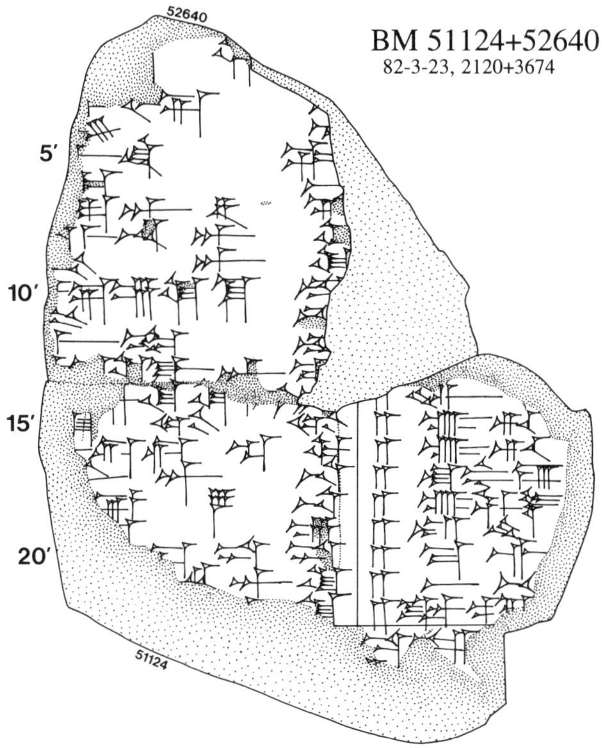

Text no. 6, obverse

BM 55476, obv.
82-7-4, 49

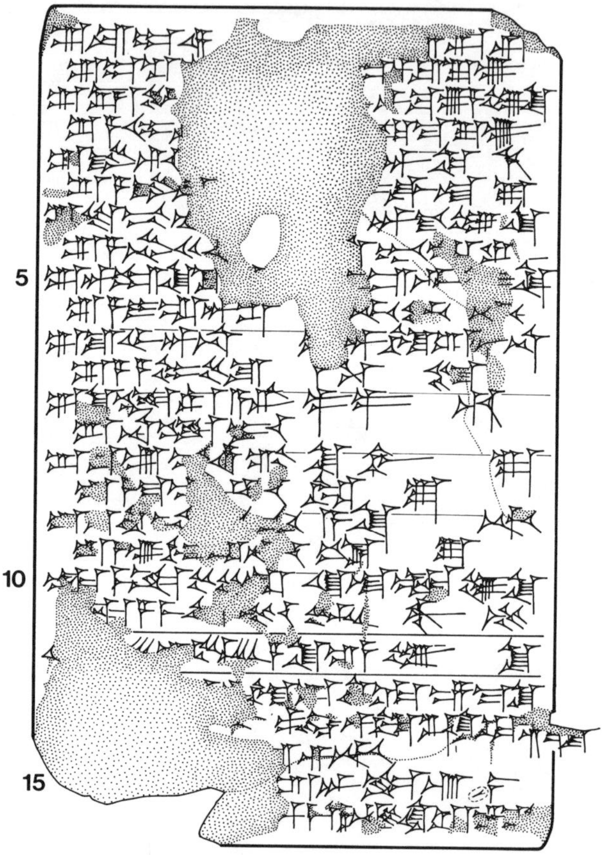

Text no. 6, reverse

BM 55476, rev.
82-7-4, 49

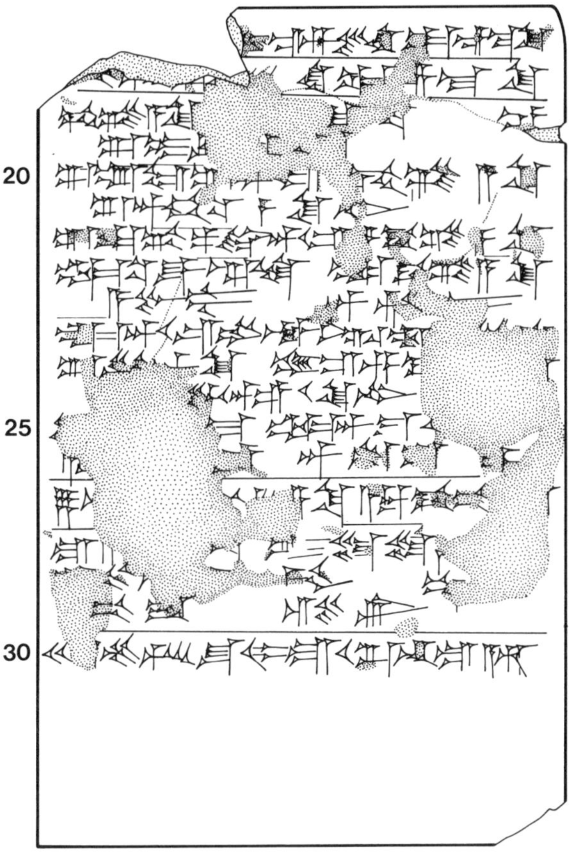